MALAN TO DE KLERK

Malan to De Klerk

Leadership in the Apartheid State

LAURENCE BOULLE
DEON GELDENHUYS
HERMANN GILIOMEE
NIC OLIVIER
LOUWRENS PRETORIUS
ROBERT SCHRIRE (*editor*)
ANNETTE SEEGERS
DAVID WELSH

ST. MARTIN'S PRESS, NEW YORK

All rights reserved. For information, write:
Scholarly and Reference Division,
St. Martin's Press, Inc., 175 Fifth Avenue.
New York, NY 10010

First published in the United States of America in 1994

Printed in Hong Kong

ISBN 0–312–10219–4

Library of Congress Cataloging-in-Publication Data

Malan to De Klerk : leadership in the apartheid state / edited
    by Robert Schrire.
        p.   cm.
    ISBN 0–312–10219–4
    1. Prime ministers—South Africa—History.   2. South Africa—
Politics and government.   3. Apartheid—South Africa.   4. South
Africa—Foreign Relations.   I. Schrire, Robert A.
JQ1941.M35   1994
354.6803'13–dc20   93–25824
                                                                          CIP

PREFACE

In this book the authors seek to examine the South African presidency from a distinctive perspective. The key question posed by the contributors is 'How have the office and the challenges associated with it altered since 1948?'

South African politics changed dramatically in February 1990 when President F.W. de Klerk announced that his administration would seek to dismantle the apartheid system and develop a racially inclusive democracy. This volume is thus largely a history of how South Africans reached that point, although all the contributors have attempted to outline the influence of this legacy on future political developments.

All the contributors are South African, although one is presently based in Australia. Without exception, they have had extensive exposure to other societies and have either taught at universities abroad, been educated in Europe or America, and/or undertaken research outside South Africa.

It should be mentioned that the format for this book was conceived by Malcolm Shaw, of Exeter University in England, who used it for a study of the US presidency, published as *Roosevelt to Reagan* (1987). It was the decision of Christopher Hurst, the British publisher who originated that volume, to extend the same analytical framework to some other polities, including that of South Africa.

In producing the book many debts were incurred. The Institute for the Study of Public Policy generously provided the finances to enable most of the contributors to attend a workshop in Greyton where the draft chapters were discussed. The final manuscript benefited substantially from this gathering. My assistant, Mrs Janet Sandell, played a major role in handling the administration of the project. The editorial assistants, Mr Tim Ross-Thompson and Mrs Martha Bridgman, made a significant contribution to the style and readability of the finished manuscript. Elizabeth van Rijssen originated the 'camera-ready copy' from which the book was printed. My sincere appreciation goes to all of them.

University of Cape Town　　　　　　　　　　　　　　ROBERT SCHRIRE
January 1993

Note: This book uses the term 'black' to embrace collectively Africans, people of mixed descent known as 'coloureds', and Indians. The individual terms are used when referring to each group separately.

CONTENTS

Preface   *page* v

Notes on the Co-Authors   viii

Introduction   *Robert Schrire*   1

Chapter

1. The Head of Government and the Constitution
                                            Laurence Boulle   7

2. The Head of Government and the Executive
                                            Annette Seegers   37

3. The Head of Government and the Party   *Nic Olivier*   80

4. The Leader and the Citizenry   *Hermann Giliomee*   102

5. The Executive and the African Population –
   1948 to the Present   *David Welsh*   135

6. The Head of Government and Organised Business
                                        Louwrens Pretorius   209

7. The Head of Government and South Africa's
   Foreign Relations   *Deon Geldenhuys*   245

8. The Future of the Presidency
                           Robert Schrire and David Welsh   291

Appendix: A Chronology of Historical Developments
   under South Africa's Prime Ministers/Presidents
   since 1948   300

Index   306

NOTES ON THE CO-AUTHORS

LAURENCE BOULLE is Professor of Law at Bond University, Queensland, Australia, where he teaches Constitutional Law, Administrative Law and Alternative Dispute Resolution. He is Director of the Dispute Resolution Centre in the university's School of Law, practises as a mediator, and conducts mediation and conflict resolution training workshops.

DEON GELDENHUYS is Professor of Political Science at the Rand Afrikaans University. He formerly taught at Stellenbosch University and holds a Ph.D. from Cambridge University.

HERMANN GILIOMEE is Professor of Political Studies at the University of Cape Town and a former editor of the journal *Die Suid-Afrikaan*. He holds a D.Phil. from the University of Stellenbosch, where he lectured for many years.

NIC OLIVIER is Director of Research for the Democratic Party. He was educated at the University of Stellenbosch, where he later became Professor in the Department of Development Administration and Indigenous Law. He is a former Member of the South African Parliament.

LOUWRENS PRETORIUS is Associate Professor of Sociology at the University of South Africa and a Research Associate of the Centre for Policy Studies. He has lectured in Political Science at the Universities of Durban-Westville, Stellenbosch and South Africa and was a Senior Researcher with the Urban Foundation.

ROBERT SCHRIRE is Professor of Political Studies at the University of Cape Town, and Director of the Institute for the Study of Public Policy. He holds a Ph.D. from the University of California.

ANNETTE SEEGERS is Associate Professor and Head of the Department of Political Studies at the University of Cape Town. She holds a Ph.D. from Loyola University in Chicago. She was a Fellow of the Woodrow Wilson Center for International Scholars of the Smithsonian Institute in 1991.

DAVID WELSH is Professor of Southern African Studies at the University of Cape Town. He was educated at the University of Cape Town (where he obtained a Ph.D.) and Oxford University, and has held visiting appointments at several American universities.

INTRODUCTION

Robert Schrire

A large and growing literature exists on South African government and politics. However, the focus of all these studies tends to be on race policies and apartheid and thus on the unique. Few studies examine the political institutions and even fewer, if any, have adopted a comparative perspective.

This volume, although not explicitly comparative, seeks to examine the South African presidency in a broader context and is part of a series devoted to the executives of different countries. The approach is largely institutional, which will enable the interested reader to examine topics such as the party system and the constitutional framework from the perspective of international comparisons.

Although the dynamics of history do not have a beginning or an end, it is possible to delineate watersheds and historical epochs. In the United States, the emergence of Roosevelt's New Deal constitutes an historical landmark. Similarly, the victory of Dr D.F. Malan's National Party in the 1948 South African general election constitutes the beginning of a new phase in that country's history. The contributors to this book begin their analyses at this historical point, although they recognise that antecedent events and processes cannot be ignored.

The period under examination has a certain historical coherence. It begins with the victory of Afrikaner nationalism within white politics and concludes with the end of a united Afrikanerdom and the beginning of an uncertain but more pluralistic future. In historical terms, it covers the entire apartheid era from its inception in the 1940s to its final demise in the 1990s.

One of the features of this period was the stability of the leadership core and especially of the Prime Ministers/Presidents. While the United States had nine Chief Executives during these years, South Africa had only six. Both countries experienced one assassination. While three American Presidents were defeated at the polls, not a single South African leader suffered a similar fate. Two died in office, while three eventually retired as a result of age and ill-health.

Since 1948, South African politics, and with it the presidency, has changed dramatically. As in the United Kingdom, its Westminster-inspired executive framework has changed under the influence of factors such as modern technology, especially mass communications (including television), and changing interests, values and expectations of the general public.

Indeed, in many ways South African society of the 1990s is dramatically different from that of the 1940s. When Malan, the first of the Afrikaner leaders of the present ruling National Party, took office in 1948, South Africa was a small semi-modern society in a world which was still controlled largely by people of European descent. With only a few exceptions, the African continent was under European colonial control. South Africa, despite the eccentricities of its rigid apartheid policies, was thus not fundamentally out of step with the Africa of the early 1950s. A confident white community ruled over an apparently passive black majority with seeming ease.

Much was to change in the next 40 years. South African society became industrialised and urbanised, and this led increasingly to the destruction of traditional African communities and their incorporation into a Western-type capitalist order. However, blacks remained excluded from the polity. Indeed, it would not be an exaggeration to claim that the consuming task of all South African post-1948 political leaders until F.W. de Klerk was to maintain and protect white domination. Almost without exception, the men chosen to be the heads of government were victorious either because of their presumed toughness on racial matters (Strijdom, Verwoerd), or because they were strong men on order and repression (Vorster, Botha).

The structure of the state changed in response to new pressures too. Under first Vorster and later Botha, the state expanded in resources and power as elaborate strategies were devised to protect white rule. Ever more powerful Prime Ministers were succeeded by ever more powerful imperial Presidents. Underpinning this growth in executive and presidential power was an increase in the web of secrecy.

Ultimately, however, the executive state was to fail. The strengthening of the office of the chief executive under Botha coincided with a more generalised weakening of the power of the state. If power is defined as the ability of a leadership group to attain its objectives, then by that definition the power of the South African state began to decline. The imperial Botha, in command of a massive state structure, was no more able to achieve his goals than his predecessors, Malan or Strijdom, who controlled only limited state resources.

Several factors contributed to the paradox that as executive power increased, state power declined. First and perhaps most importantly, the economy began to weaken markedly. The inherent inefficiencies in the apartheid system which sought to exclude Africans from the 'White' economy were partly disguised throughout the 1960s and 1970s as a result of booming prices for gold and other commodities. By the late 1970s, however, the costs of apartheid began to become apparent and growth rates declined.

These structural economic problems were aggravated during the

1980s by South Africa's growing international isolation. Anti-South African sentiment, initially restricted to Third World states, became more widespread in the United States and Western Europe, culminating in economic sanctions and a significant disinvestment campaign. South Africa, a traditional capital importer, was forced to become a capital exporter in order to meet its international debts in the absence of new foreign investment or loans.

In addition, black South Africans became increasingly politicised and estranged from the polity. Whereas from 1948 to 1960 they were the 'objects' of politics rather than participants, from the 1960s on – especially from the mid-1970s – they became increasingly politically active, despite their exclusion from parliamentary and executive politics. The emergence of black trade unionism and community organisations, including the United Democratic Front, gave political muscle to black politics. The issue of black exclusion from South African politics became central to the new political debate.

The white community, under growing pressures from both the black majority at home and the international community abroad, began to fragment. Between 1948 and 1966, Afrikaner nationalism under the banner of apartheid became increasingly united to the point where about nine out of ten Afrikaner voters could be described as supporters of the National Party. As pressures against white rule increased, the government began to redefine the issue, claiming that it was not just a matter of Afrikaner interests but the broader question of white survival. 'Total onslaught' and a presumed communist campaign against South Africa became slogans used by the government, not entirely cynically, to increase and maintain white support for the National Party. Despite this strategy, the greater the pressures on the white community, the greater did their divisions become. In 1982, the 'great divide' within Afrikanerdom took place when the National Party (NP) split over the issue of political rights for the minority coloured population.

The response of the government to these challenges was to develop and expand the imperial presidency. Paradoxically, the power of the state expanded at precisely the period when the power of 'white politics' was in decline. During the 1980s the NP became considerably weaker in the white community as it lost some support to the Democratic Party on the left and even more support to the Conservative Party and the forces of the right. At the same time the balance between the forces of white domination and those representing black liberation began to shift away from traditional white hegemony.

Thus the massive state structure of repression and control, created largely by Vorster and Botha, began to rest increasingly on shifting and eroding foundations. When F.W. de Klerk became South Africa's second executive President in 1989, he did so with a minority of white votes in a general election – the worst electoral performance of the NP in more than 30 years. At the same time he faced growing dissent from the black communities and a declining economy.

The concluding chapter to this book examines the De Klerk presidency and explores the implications of these forces for the future of the presidency. Some of the constitutional options for a new South African leadership are then developed. Before we get to that point, chapters 1 to 7 explore the changes which have already taken place in the presidency and emphasise the dynamic factors, both within society and the state, which have shaped and continue to influence the evolution of South Africa's political institutions.

The analyses contained in these chapters confirm the insight that South African political history contains elements both of the unique and of the more general. For example, despite the obvious significance of unique factors such as Afrikaner nationalism and African exclusion, South African politics has often followed trends which have been at work in other societies as well. Thus politics has become increasingly personalised in response to the impact of television, and powerful personalities such as Botha and De Klerk have been able to dominate the political dialogue to an extent not possible under Malan or Strijdom. The institution of the cabinet has therefore declined correspondingly, and the 1984 constitution accelerated this trend. The dominant role of the supreme leader has also been furthered by the length of time that leaders have remained in office. De Klerk's two predecessors, Vorster and Botha, each served for more than a decade in the highest political post in the land, and in time were able to shape the cabinet, state administration and party leadership to reflect their own preferences and policy values. Indeed, the Thatcher phenomenon in the United Kingdom has been repeated several times in South Africa, most recently when the critical referendum in 1992 on constitutional change was personalised around the leadership of President De Klerk.

At the same time, the art of governing has become more complex. Paradoxically, just as leaders have become more prominent in the process of governing, so the problems they face have become more complex and intractable. To an increasing extent, government is overloaded and lacks the techniques to resolve societal problems unilaterally. This is especially true in the area of economic policy, which, to be effective, demands cooperation between the state, the global community and powerful trade unions and consumer groups. The simple world of Afrikaner politics in the 1940s and 1950s, revolving around symbolic issues such as the republican status of the country or social segregation, has been replaced by the complications of massive urbanisation and economic decline. These, then, are some of the themes which infuse the analyses in this book.

In chapter 1, Laurence Boulle places the presidency within the context of the constitution. Although he correctly notes that constitutions conceal as much as they reveal, the legal framework within which politics takes place is clearly important. Boulle's analysis confirms the arguments made above that South Africa has experienced processes that have also been at work in many other societies: executive aggrandisement, the growth of the bureaucracy, the failure of constitutional checks and balances, the partial demise of the legislature and judiciary as countervailing forces, and the abrogation of the normative principles of constitutionalism. The legal principle of parliamentary supremacy was to place vast powers in the hands of the party that controlled the legislature, a theme taken up by Nic Olivier in chapter 3.

In chapter 2, Annette Seegers places the study of leadership in a wider institutional context by examining the role of the presidency within the executive body of government. She concludes that the executive should be conceptualised broadly as the state, which would include the bureaucracy, public corporations and control bodies. The growth of the state is documented with an emphasis on both its scale and its complexity. Seegers explores the implications for executive management and control of the bureaucracy of the peculiar mix of state functions – such as health and education – with racial departments for whites, coloureds, Asians and a large number of ethnically defined African communities.

In chapter 3 Nic Olivier argues that in addition to the importance of the constitutional principle of parliamentary sovereignty in consolidating power, other important factors at work included the decline of a credible white opposition party, and the cultural attitudes of Afrikanerdom towards leaders, ideology and Afrikaner nationalism. An important difference between South African parliamentary politics and its British equivalent was the momentous importance of continuing National Party rule for Afrikanerdom. As Olivier explains, 'retaining political power was, or was seen to be, a matter of life and death for Afrikanerdom'.

Hermann Giliomee's analysis in chapter 4 explores the logic of this insight. He argues that between 1948 and 1968 successive Prime Ministers viewed themselves primarily as Afrikaner leaders and thus defined most of the rest of the population as opponents or enemies. This began to change between 1968 and 1988, with a new perspective which saw the broadening of political leadership to include first English-speaking whites and later the minority coloured people and Indians. Since 1989, under the leadership of F.W. de Klerk, an attempt has been made to broaden the appeal of the presidency by including as citizens all who live in South Africa.

David Welsh in his chapter examines one aspect of this process, i.e. policies towards the African majority, in greater detail. He maintains that, until very recently, the trend towards a more inclusive definition of citizenship, as described in chapter 4, largely excluded Africans. He traces the evolution of government policy from apartheid to separate development to more pragmatic attempts to accommodate African aspirations. He analyses in detail Botha's failed attempts both to make separation work and to reach an accommodation with Africans living outside their 'homelands'. He concludes with an overview of the De Klerk administration's new approach to negotiations and nation-building.

In the following chapter, Louwrens Pretorius examines the relationship between the presidency and organised business. His analysis indicates the peculiar relationships which have developed between the private sector and the state, caused in large part by both the dominance of racial issues in the polity and the ethnic fragmentation of business organisations into English, Afrikaner and black groupings. Traditionally, the government has viewed only Afrikaner business as a fully legitimate partner in economic policy issues, chiefly because non-Afrikaner concerns have defined their interests as including state policies of power and privilege which the government of the day regarded as non-negotiable. Under the leadership of Botha, the government began to become more receptive to business interests because it started to recognise the interdependence which increasingly existed between the state and the business community. This trend has accelerated under the leadership of F.W. de Klerk.

In chapter 7, Deon Geldenhuys analyses the growing importance of foreign policy in shaping both the domestic debate within South Africa and in influencing policy outcomes. For a medium-sized state such as South Africa, the global system is an important influence on economic welfare and in shaping the political dialogue. Global pressures on the white regime began to emerge after the Second World War and hit South Africa with full ferocity during Botha's leadership, when the idea of sovereignty increasingly lost its meaning. Geldenhuys concludes with an overview of the new global position of De Klerk's South Africa.

The final chapter of this book, by Schrire and Welsh, examines the past and future presidency. They trace the evolution of the office of the imperial presidency, stressing how strong government was initially viewed by whites as necessary to secure their interests in an increasingly hostile environment. They conclude by placing the contemporary constitutional debate in the context of claims by powerful black groups for political rights, and note that power considerations are the dominant influences on the black demand for a powerful state and the white demand for a state limited in authority and based upon 'power-sharing'. The South African presidency will be shaped for many years to come by the way this debate is finally resolved.

1

THE HEAD OF GOVERNMENT
AND THE CONSTITUTION

Laurence Boulle

This chapter deals with the chief executive officer of government and the South African Constitution from 1948 to 1990. It assumes that any specific treatment of prime ministerial and presidential power also involves the general treatment of executive authority. It provides essentially a constitutional analysis and focuses on formal, legal and institutional factors. In this respect it provides a one-dimensional view of the topic.

All modern constitutions conceal as much as they reveal. In some cases they also distort, disguise and distract. The South African Constitution is no exception, particularly as far as executive authority is concerned. Some of the most important developments in relation to executive authority, its exercise and control, have taken place *dehors* the written instrument. The sub-sections in this chapter reflect formal stages in constitutional development, but the dominant themes show little regard for such formality; in South Africa changes of form have not always involved any changes of practical substance. As in all political systems, the power and functions of the South African executive branch of government are dependent to only a small extent on legal – institutional arrangements. On the one hand, the constitution is fleshed out by conventions, which in British law are somewhat quaintly (and sanguinely) defined as the 'rules of the constitutional game' or 'political morality'. On the other hand, there is a wide range of political and administrative practices which cannot be contained even within pliable notions of conventions, but which determine and define the living constitution. Parliamentary practice, electoral politics, party and caucus dynamics, administrative procedures, bureaucratic interests, fiscal policies and economic realities combine to modify, amend, reshape and transfigure constitutional form. Nevertheless, the formal side constitutes a useful point of departure. Other chapters in this work provide more detailed analyses of many of the issues covered in this institutional overview.

There are several dominant themes in the four decades under review. They include executive aggrandisement, the growth of the bureaucracy, the failure of constitutional checks and balances, the partial demise of

the legislature and judiciary as countervailing forces, and the abrogation of the normative principles of constitutionalism. These themes are
the product of formal constitutional amendment, political expediency,
the changing nature of the state system, crisis politics and economic
imperatives. They are also a function of the personality and style of chief
executives, most of whom have been forceful figures and have dominated government and their ministries, in particular Verwoerd, Vorster
and Botha.[1] But there have also been some important, and contradictory,
sub-themes – such as the unexpected resistance to executive policy
provided by the tricameral parliament and the resurgence of the
judiciary as a constitutional force towards the end of the period under
review. These challenges have made executive authority somewhat
ambiguous at the margins.

The Union Constitution

Constitutional principles. A critical variable in modern political
constitutions is the relationship between the legislature and the executive.
The South Africa Act of 1909 located the South African constitutional
system within the Westminster tradition as far as this formal relationship
is concerned. The Westminster system is one in which the head of state
is not the effective head of government; the effective head of government
is a Prime Minister who presides over a cabinet of ministers whom, in
practice, he or she appoints and removes. The executive branch of
government is parliamentary in that ministers must be members of the
legislature, and those ministers are individually and collectively
responsible to the legislature.[2] It was the intimate link between legislature
and executive which gave the Westminster system of government its
distinctive features.

Over a period of several centuries the cabinet was transformed from
an instrument of the Crown into a committee of parliament. By the
nineteenth century the English cabinet was drawn from and accountable
to parliament, and it was around this arrangement that the theory of the
Westminster constitution was constructed. The theory has survived, but
the practice has not. The political party system, bolstered by a strict
caucus tradition, has allowed the cabinet to dominate parliament in the
Westminster model and to secure the legislative enactment of all its
major policy measures. In general terms government policy can only be

1. See Albert Venter, *South African Government and Politics* (Johannesburg:
   Southern Book Publishers, 1989), p. 43.
2. From the classic definition of Stanley de Smith, *The New Commonwealth and its
   Constitutions* (London: Stevens, 1964), p. 77.

thwarted by electoral defeat or party defections, in which case the legislature exercises an ultimate power of control over the executive. For the rest, the executive can use its presence in the legislature, its powers of patronage and discipline, and its control of information, agenda-setting and policy formulation to achieve its goals within the bounds of parliamentary tradition. Only in the last resort does the legislature have any real control over the executive in parliamentary systems of government.

This arrangement is traditionally contrasted with American-style presidentialism, in which the fixed-term chief executive has a separate political mandate from the legislature, is not part of the legislature nor accountable to it for everyday matters of government, and cannot control the legislature through the caucus and party systems. Judicial review and sometimes, though not necessarily, a bill of rights provide the mechanisms for enforcing the separation of powers, checks and balances, and executive limitations enjoined by the presidential system. Presidentialism postulates the sharing of policy-formulation among various institutions; parliamentarism postulates its domination by a single governmental instrumentality.

The Union Constitution of South Africa introduced two major variations on the Westminster theme. The franchise was restrictive and the legislature was unrepresentative; these factors contradicted all the normative assumptions of parliamentary cabinet government. In other respects it was true to the Westminster tradition. Executive power was formally vested in the British Crown, to be exercised by its local representatives, the governors-general. The 'constitutional monarchy' was a legacy of British colonialism, and the Union Constitution bore no traces of either of the two variants of presidentialism adopted in the pre-Union Afrikaner republics. Before the National Party came to power in 1948, its policy manifestos had referred to the attractions of a presidential system along the lines of those which operated in the nineteenth-century republics, but despite the advent of the South African Republic in 1961 there was no serious move towards presidential government. This was because Westminster-type parliamentary government constituted a handy arrangement for the implementation of government racial policy, with little resistance offered by parliament or the courts. The only pre-1961 deference to Afrikaner nationalist aspirations was found in the Royal Styles and Title Act of 1952 which distinguished between the monarch of Britain and the monarch of South Africa, but this had no practical implications for presidential power.

The constitutional monarchy incorporates a notional duality into the arrangement of executive authority. This is claimed to be a minor check and balance in the Westminster system in that the head of state retains certain residual or reserve powers which, in times of crisis, can be exercised personally and not in accordance with the directives of cabinet. The dualism is reflected in the distinction between the Executive Council, a constitutionally prescribed body with formal executive powers, and the cabinet, a politically constituted body with no legal standing.[3] During the time of Union the Executive Council never met formally and its functions were carried out by the cabinet, the main organ of policy-formulation and government. In the post-1948 operation of the Union Constitution there were no conflicts of authority between the head of state and the head of government. The 'diffusion' of authority provided by the dual executive system did not, in the real world of constitutional politics, constitute a check or balance at any stage of its existence in South Africa.

In constitutional practice, executive power was located within a responsible cabinet and the head of state held a purely titular and ceremonial position. The role of the cabinet was defined partly by statute and partly by convention. However the Union Constitution provided only 'a fragmentary basis for responsible government'[4] in stipulating that cabinet ministers should be, or become within a three-month period of grace, members of either house of parliament. Despite the Westminster system's remarkable reliance on conventions, very few were referred to explicitly in the Union Constitution Act. It was assumed that in practice they would supplement and augment the constitution, which in fact they did. Convention required the leader of the majority party in the lower house to be appointed as Prime Minister, and the other ministers to be appointed on the recommendation of the Prime Minister. So powerful was the gravitational attraction of the Westminster system that it was regarded as axiomatic by all political actors that the Governor-General would always act on the advice of the responsible ministers and that real executive power would vest in the Prime Minister. This was indeed the case, and in this respect the Union Constitution was an authentic Westminster transplant.

Removal from executive office was also regulated by the conventions of responsible government. The Governor-General could be dismissed by the Crown, acting on the advice of the Union cabinet. Convention required the Prime Minister to resign upon losing the leadership of the majority party, after defeat in a general election, or after a parliamentary vote of no confidence in the government. Cabinet ministers could be censured by parliament and dismissed by the Prime Minister, acting through the head of state. Neither of the first two exigencies arose during

---

3. See Donovan Marais, *South African Constitutional Development* (Johannesburg: Macmillan, 1990), p. 178.
4. H.R. Hahlo and Ellison Kahn, *The Union of South Africa – The Development of its Laws and Constitution* (Cape Town: Juta, 1960), p. 129.

the period under discussion. There was no cause for the dismissal of Governors-General, the rigid party system precluded parliament from being able to change the government through a vote of no confidence, and no cabinet ministers suffered 'impeachment'. The conventions relating to removal from executive office were assumed to be operable, but were never tested in the heat of constitutional fire.

Under the Union Constitution the Governor-General was the nominal vestee of the prerogative power. In the Westminster tradition the prerogative is the only inherent power of the executive. It derives from the common law powers of the Crown which survived parliamentary incursion and statutory repeal throughout the evolution of the British system of government. The prerogative is an essentially Westminster institution, though in South Africa there was also some common law foundation for the head of state's prerogatives in terms of Roman Dutch law.[5] The prerogative comprises various immunities, privileges and powers, of which the last-mentioned are the most important. These powers include the appointment and dismissal of ministers, declarations of war and peace, and the summoning and dissolution of parliament. The significance of the prerogative is that in constitutional law the relevant powers can be exercised at the personal discretion of the head of state. From the early days of the Union Constitution, the South African executive secured control over the prerogative, which was exercised through the Governor-General without reference to the British Crown. Throughout the life of the Constitution, however, prerogative powers were always exercised according to the wishes of the political executive and there were no cases of the residual or reserve powers of the head of state being used to check or override the executive, as has happened in the United Kingdom, Australia and other Westminster systems of government.

Many ancient prerogatives were replaced by constitutional provision or ordinary statute, for example those relating to the summoning and proroguing of parliament and the appointment of judges. Prerogatives thus codified lose their common law status and their exercise is subject to the same constraints which relate to other statutory powers. In some cases the statutory conferral of power is so broad that any constraints are illusory; here the prerogative is reincarnated as a 'statutory prerogative'. Others have retained their common law nature, for example the head of state's control over foreign affairs, the conferral of honours and the granting of pardons. A controversial feature of the true prerogative was that its exercise was immune from judicial interference, save only to the extent that the courts could determine whether an act fell properly

5. On this theme see *ibid.*, p. 172.

within the purview of the prerogative. This implied an unfettered discretion for the executive when exercising prerogative powers. Later it will be illustrated how the South African courts have recently reconstrued the prerogative to provide a basis for its judicial review.

The dominant legal principle of the Union Constitution was the supremacy of parliament.[6] The supremacy of parliament had two important implications for the constitutional system. The first was that no parliament was bound by the legislation of its predecessors, including the Constitution Act itself. Through the normal legislative process, any law could be enacted by parliament in disregard of previous enactments. The second was that no court of law could pronounce on the validity of an act of parliament properly enacted. There was only one exception to these principles: parliament could not tamper with the voting or language clauses of the constitution without securing an extraordinary majority in the legislature. For the rest, the legislative supremacy of parliament entailed that it was the final interpreter and arbiter of constitutional meaning, except in respect of the entrenched clauses over which the courts had guardianship. This again entailed constitutional dominance for the executive. The absence of any fundamental rights in the constitutional order reinforced the doctrine of parliamentary supremacy. Insofar as the constitution failed to limit the authority of parliament, it also refrained from limiting the power of the executive.

The legislative supremacy of the national parliament, together with the reality of executive domination of parliament, had long-term implications for regional and local government in South Africa. Over the broad sweep of institutional history it can be said that all forms of sub-national government have been subject to the control or potential control of the central executive. The original provincial system had some features of federalism, but they did not endure. From the inception of the Union, Pretoria controlled the public finance system and the provinces were largely dependent on central grants for their revenue. Pretoria also removed some important functions from provincial jurisdiction, such as black education, and narrowed provincial autonomy through pervasive legislation, such as that relating to the use and ownership of land. The central executive could also veto provincial legislation, appoint key provincial officials and formulate national policies, for example on transportation and education, which had to be implemented by provincial governments.

When the provincial system was restructured in 1986 it led to a further concentration of power in the central executive. The provinces were

---

6. See Boulle, Harris and Hoexter, *Constitutional and Administrative Law* (Cape Town: Juta, 1989), pp.117–19.

stripped of policy-making powers and became devolved instruments of the central government. Provincial executives came to be appointed by the State President, with the chief provincial executive – the Administrator – a presidential delegee. The State President, in some cases with parliamentary approval, assumed the power to amend provincial boundaries by proclamation, to repeal provincial ordinances, and to create new provinces. Constitutional centralisation, in practice, has always led to the aggrandisement of executive power, a central theme of this chapter.

The other systems of regional government, the black homelands, were also subject to central executive control. During their constitutional evolution a wide range of legal controls were vested in the office of the President. Even after 'independence' the South African executive's dominance persisted, but through less overt institutions such as financial grants, administrative supervision and political influence. At the local level the dominant theme was the same, though with some variations referred to below.

The South African constitution since Union also followed the Westminster tradition in affording the executive some influence over the judicial branch. The relationship between the courts and the executive is explored later.

Parliamentary government in practice. Prime Ministers Malan (1948–54), Strijdom (1954–8) and Verwoerd (1958–60) held office under the Union Constitution. After Malan's victory in 1948 there was a delicate balance of power in the Union parliament and the conventions of responsible government operated with some clarity and force. Gains by the parliamentary opposition in by-elections reinforced the legislature's potential control over the executive, and political actors still had memories of parliament's overthrow of the executive in 1939, the only occasion in South African history when this occurred. Succeeding general elections, however, greatly increased the parliamentary strength of the National Party, and its ascendancy was enhanced through a series of manipulations of the electoral system, in particular as far as coloured voters were concerned. The dominance of the National Party weakened the two-party assumptions of the system of responsible government, though it was not only the South African experience which contributed to the redefinition of the principles of this system. The absence of a strong two-party system meant that the electorate lost the controlling influence over the executive which the Westminster system is supposed to provide via the legislature.

From the late 1940s until the early 1960s, National Party governments were able to implement their policies through the instrumentality of parliament in matters of anti-miscegenation, race classification, segregation of amenities, residential and educational segregation, security and censorship. Without exception, these statutory measures increased the scope and intrusiveness of the administrative power that was at the disposal of the chief executive and ministers of government. Far from being matched by new institutions of executive limitation and control, they were reinforced by a weakening of the conventional, legal and judicial constraints assumed by the Westminster model of government. As early as the 1960s the claimed imperatives of national security were used as a basis for denying parliament the information its members requested of the executive. During the following three decades successive ministers developed this form of obstruction to a fine art. Physical geography also played a part in weakening parliament's ability to check and control. The separate locations of the administrative and legislative capitals, and the essentially part-time nature of parliamentary operations, provided additional sources of leverage and control for the executive and bureaucratic branches of government.[7]

The 'constitutional crisis' of the 1950s confirmed the extent of executive dominance within the constitutional system. The crisis can be seen as one of the most significant constitutional developments during the period under discussion, and it had a strong formative effect on the constitutional system. The formal legal dispute concerned the validity of parliamentary legislation which affected the entrenched clauses of the constitution. The legislation incorporated the government's ideological policy, and pragmatic strategy, of diluting the political power of coloured persons by removing them from the common voters' rolls. The highest appeal court at first rebuked the legislature for not complying with the entrenching procedure, but ultimately it sanctioned a series of laws which not only disenfranchised the coloured population but distorted the composition of parliament through the packing of the Senate. The real victor, however, was the executive, which through its strategic control of the party, caucus and parliament was able to implement its policies of expedience. In positing legislative supremacy as the dominant legal principle of the constitution, the court conferred effective constitutional dominance on the executive. When the appellate division ultimately ratified the government's strategy for removing coloured persons from the voters' rolls, it was legally sanctioning the supremacy of parliament as a law-making body, but politically vindicating the right of the executive to legitimise its policy objectives through the instrumentality of the legislature. The government also reinforced the constitutional subordination of the courts by changing the composition of the appellate division in constitutional matters and, in the view of some, packing the enlarged court with sympathetic appoint-

7. Cf . Marais, *South African Constitutional Development*, p. 12.

ees. This episode foreshadowed a long era of executive dominance and lawlessness in the 1970s and 1980s, the niceties of constitutional ordering notwithstanding. The normative principles of constitutionalism were severely damaged by the crisis, and were not fully repaired over the next three decades.

The delegation of power to the executive was a major feature of the governing process during this period; it was firmly established early on during the prime ministerships of Malan, Strijdom and Verwoerd. The absence of a separation of powers doctrine enabled the executive to use parliament to confer on itself wide discretionary powers, involving policy formulation, adjudication and administration. Once parliament had delegated authority, it retained little control over its exercise, other than some formal requirements such as the tabling of the titles of delegated legislation in the legislature. The extent of some delegated powers was breathtaking. Section 25 (1) of the Native Administration Act of 1927, which remained in force and was used throughout the 1950s, empowered the Governor-General to legislate for black areas by proclamation, and this empowerment included the competence to amend acts of the national parliament. It emulated the tactics of the Tudor and Stuart monarchs in wresting legislative competence for themselves from the English parliament, and was referred to by commentators as a 'Henry VIII clause'. Moreover, where vast discretionary powers were conferred on ministers, boards and administrative officials, the courts were reluctant to exercise the administrative law review powers which they undoubtedly did possess, and in their executive-minded zeal repeatedly endorsed the arbitrary exercise of governmental power. In legal theory the exercise of all delegated powers is subject to judicial review, but the courts of the 1950s and 1960s were accused of being more executive-minded than the executive in their deference to administrative regulations, decrees and orders. In later years there were some changes in attitude and practice; these are referred to below.

One element of the constitutional order which was scrupulously upheld during this period concerned parliament's control of public funds. Since the earliest stages of the Westminster system, successive parliaments had demanded the right and sole competence to control taxation and appropriation measures – some of the greatest crises in British constitutional history involved attempted executive deviations from this principle. While it is true that executive domination of the legislature detracts from the contemporary significance of this principle, its enforcement during the life of the Union Constitution did render the executive formally accountable in a public forum for taxation and expenditure. In the following era of constitutional development, these hallowed principles were followed less assiduously. During the 'Infor-

mation Affair' of the 1970s the executive played fast and loose with
public monies – and history repeated itself in a constitutional crisis. This
matter is referred to in more detail later.

The First Republican Constitution

Constitutional basics. The Republic of South Africa Constitution Act
of 1961 showed a remarkable continuity with the previous constitution.
It introduced changes of nomenclature and form, but few important
alterations to the conditions of executive power. Republicanism entailed
that the office of head of state should be repatriated to South Africa, but
this was achieved with no significant changes to the institution, even
where the constitution was obscure, unhelpful or misleading. The most
important powers of the Crown and Governor-General were vested in
a titular State President. The distinction between the Executive Council
and cabinet remained, with the latter being largely ignored in the
Constitution Act. The conventions of the constitutional system were
also specifically left intact by the new Republican Constitution. In other
words, the system of parliamentary government was retained in the
same measure as had been the case under the Union Constitution, with
the assumption that both Westminster and Union constitutional practices
could be invoked to assist in defining its proper functioning.

The break in continuity did entail some additional constitutional
features. In the first place, republicanism required a mechanism, other
than hereditary tenure, for appointing the head of state. Direct appointment by the executive was considered too 'political' and parliament was
designated an electoral college for this purpose. The question of tenure
also required attention. The presidential term of office was fixed at
seven years and, in keeping with the titular nature of the office, it was
not linked to the fate of parliament. Re-election for a further term was
possible, provided a special resolution to that effect was passed by the
college. There was also the question of removal during tenure. Under
the Union Constitution the Governor-General could be removed by the
Crown on the advice of the Union cabinet, whereas under the Republican Constitution it was necessary to introduce an 'impeachment'
process involving both houses of the legislature acting in concert.
Removal was permissible on grounds of incapacity and misbehaviour,
but not for political reasons. In practice former high-ranking cabinet
ministers were appointed to the state presidency,[8] and in one case
(Vorster) the Prime Minister himself was elevated. Despite the political

8. The following persons served as State President or Acting State President in terms
    of the 1961–83 constitution: C.R. Swart (1961–7), J.J. Fouché (1968–75), J.F.

nature of the appointments, the incumbents generally respected the impartial and apolitical nature of the office, though whether that would have been the case in the event of a constitutional crisis is a matter for speculation. In one instance, referred to below, the impeachment process was threatened but not pursued, and an incumbent (Vorster) resigned from office for political reasons relating to his previous office.

The head of government under the first Republican Constitution was the Prime Minister, but the office was not established or regulated by the Constitution Act. The only constitutional reference to the position was of an inconsequential nature. The same was true of the cabinet. It was clear that the traditions of British and South African parliamentary government were to define and determine the exercise of executive authority by the political head of government and cabinet ministers. Some constitutional reference was made to the administrative arm of government, which it was assumed would continue to be of the neutral, politically anonymous type associated with the Westminster system. Although the potential impact of the bureaucracy on policy formulation was already obvious, no additional forms of administrative control were introduced. As with other constitutions in this tradition, there was full reliance on ministerial responsibility and judicial review as the mechanisms for bringing government to account for its policies and actions.

The constitution in practice. Prime ministers Verwoerd (1960–66), Vorster (1966–78) and Botha (1978–83) held office under the first Republican Constitution. Verwoerd is depicted in terms of the granite metaphor – rigid on matters of policy, unswerving in his commitment to principles of race separatism, dogmatic on the identity of the party. He served his party constituency exclusively, but also controlled the party, caucus and parliament through domineering and powerful leadership. Vorster, in personality and style, represented a change from previous National Party leaders. Although ruthless on matters of security, he used the prime ministerial office to reach beyond the traditional National Party constituency for political support. He began the tortuous process of incorporating new managers into the constitutional system and significantly developed the institutions of indirect rule. Botha's style was imperious and enigmatic. He too imposed ruthless security measures, but was non-dogmatic on racial matters and pragmatic in terms of economic development. He attempted the ultimate constitutional sleight of hand by changing the constitutional order so as to satisfy political outsiders without losing overall control of the system.

Naude (1967–9), J. de Klerk (1975), N. Diedericks (1975–8), M. Viljoen (1978, 1979–85) and B.J. Vorster (1978–9).

Both Vorster and Botha lost the leadership initiative in respect of policy matters in their attempts to satisfy numerous competing interests.

During this period the successive governments' control of the legislature enabled them to pursue further the implementation of National Party racial policies. The arithmetic of parliamentary politics prevented any real resistance within the constitutional system; executive dominance of the legislature was reinforced by the weakened state of the parliamentary opposition. This era also witnessed a series of drastic security measures aimed at those excluded from parliament, and oppressive enactments in the areas of residence, censorship, education, political activity and personal liberty. A feature of these measures was the wide latitude conferred on officials of the state in regard to their implementation. Near-arbitrary powers, broad discretions, loose statutory language and sweeping legislative objectives (such as promoting national security) gave the executive branch *de facto* legislative and judicial powers. That the legislature should have condoned and been instrumental in the usurpation of its powers was paradoxical but not surprising; the legislature had the same political mandate as the executive, and the latter's powers of patronage ensured compliance from parliament, caucus and party. That the courts should have meekly accepted the usurpation of their authority was less justifiable. It was only in the late 1980s that a series of judicial pronouncements revealed the extent to which the supreme court could invoke its inherent common law powers to rebuke a rampant executive and invalidate the worst excesses of administrative lawlessness.

The early years of the Botha prime ministership witnessed a reorganisation of the state system, outside of the formal constitutional structure. There was a major 'rationalisation' of the Public Service, with the number of government departments reduced from 40 to 22. At the same time the number of cabinet committees was reduced to four permanent committees, one of which, the State Security Council, had statutory foundations. Senior officials were included in the cabinet committees, in contravention of the principle of public service neutrality. The maximum size of the cabinet was increased to 20 and a secretariat was established with the necessary infrastructure to service the cabinet. The Department of the Prime Minister was extensively reorganised and considerably enlarged. The rationalisation of government was designed to enhance leadership, coordinate policy, promote sound administration and make government more efficient. Government was to become more managerial, more specialised and more technocratic. But the Botha changes also involved greater control, or potential control, by the chief executive. Moreover, rationalisation did not mean less government, and in the ensuing years the size of the bureaucracy increased rapidly. The administrative state arrived late in South Africa, but it came with a vengeance.[9] Separate development was still the official policy and mammoth state departments were required to give effect to its dictates. Simultaneously, political activity and social instability necessitated the development of both the security departments and the service departments in areas such as education, health and welfare, in pursuit of the conflicting policies of suppression and placation. Intended in constitutional theory to be the implementer of policy and administrator of legislation, the bloated bureaucracy developed interests and agendas of its own, eventually coming to be an obstacle and hindrance to the carrying out of prime ministerial policy.

The 'Information Affair' of the late 1970s exposed the extent of executive power and the limitations of the conventions of responsible government. In all Westminster systems of government, ministerial responsibility affords enormous latitude to public servants as regards their accountability for policy formulation, administrative business and budgetary activity. Occasional judicial dicta in South Africa recognised the constitutional accountability of ministers for the acts of public servants in their departments, but this control becomes strained where ministerial responsibility itself is weak. In the Information Affair public servants, with varying degrees of complicity from responsible ministers, breached numerous laws of the land and conventions of parliamentary government. The most serious allegations involved breaches of budgeting and accounting procedures, and the use of vast amounts of state funds on secret projects, both within the country and abroad. These activities not only breached safeguards provided through parliamentary appropriation measures but they were, in some cases, designed to propagate government policy and consolidate the National Party's position in the political system. The relevant ministers were protected by the shield of cabinet solidarity, until it became politically expedient to jettison the main culprit, 'Connie' Mulder, who eventually 'resigned' from office because of maladministration and abuse of funds. However, it was not parliament which removed Mulder from office, but the cabinet and caucus. Other ministers denied any knowledge of wrongdoing in their departments, and were not similarly sacrificed.

When Vorster relinquished the prime ministership and was elevated to the state presidency, new conflicts of interest emerged. Vorster testified about his activities as Prime Minister before the same commission of inquiry which he had appointed as State President. While the Constitution Act protected the dignity and reputation of the presidential office, it was necessary to allow parliamentary discussion of the President's former activities. There was even an attempt in parliament

9. On the rapid development of the public sector, in all its facets, during this period see Lawrence Baxter, *Administrative Law* (Cape Town: Juta, 1984, pp. 94–116.

to set in motion the presidential impeachment process, which could be founded on misconduct or unfitness for office, although this was unsuccessful. These conflicts were only resolved when Vorster resigned from the presidential office.

The judicial commission of inquiry into the scandal did serve to salvage constitutional principle to some extent. It emphasised that in terms of constitutional principle cabinet ministers were both the political and administrative heads of their departments, but this restated constitutional theory was not matched by new institutional forms of control and accountability. On the contrary, the scandal led to a wave of laws which allowed for secret departmental funds and placed their use beyond public audit and parliamentary scrutiny. For the first time the executive acquired the legal means of playing with public funds with impunity, and it did not relinquish this facility easily.

The abolition of the Senate in 1980 and its 'replacement' by the President's Council involved a further tightening of executive control over policy-making and the legislative process. While the Senate had always operated along party lines, and became a discredited institution after the constitutional crisis, its demise as a chamber of review involved the removal of one of the few checks and balances in the constitutional system. The executive now had a more streamlined legislative process at its disposal, with less potential opposition in an upper chamber and less public debate of policy-making. The President's Council was really an extension of the prime ministerial office, but had important advisory and legislative powers. Other innovations further increased executive control. Greater latitude was afforded in ministerial appointments through the provision that appointed ministers could retain office for up to 12 months before securing a parliamentary seat. The provision for executive-nominated members of parliament gave the executive further leverage in the legislature. These devices were promoted ostensibly to bring specialists into parliament, but in practice were used to reward party faithfuls, including cabinet ministers who had suffered electoral defeats. By comparative standards, these changes provided the executive with unprecedented control over all parliamentary processes and functions.

What becomes apparent from this analysis is an inverted relationship between the executive and the constitution. Far from the constitution regulating executive power, the executive manipulated the constitution. It changed not only constitutional laws and principles, but also the very source of its authority. During the first republic the Constitution Act was continually subject to the whims of government policy and expediency. Its flexible nature invited regular formal amendment, in some cases up to five times a year, with other amendments effected informally. Executive dominance extended to the drafting and enactment of a new constitution during the late 1970s and early 1980s in which, despite the pretence of consultation, specialism and scholasticism, the final model was the product not of a dialectical process but of 'the immediate political objectives of the governing party'.[10]

In some contexts the tendency of the executive to dominate the constitutional order is mitigated by the role of the courts. In South Africa the ability of the courts to frustrate executive activity was limited by constitutional fundamentals, the culture of legalism and the inactivism of the judges. In one celebrated constitutional case the court did obstruct the government, but only through a process of technical legal reasoning. In 1982 the government issued a series of proclamations designed to effect the transfer of the KaNgwane homeland and the Ingwavuma district of KwaZulu to Swaziland. This was ostensibly motivated by the failings of the homeland system and the need, according to the internal logic of National Party policy, to remove citizenship from blacks in the Republic. The government attempted to achieve the same ends in homeland 'independence' through a different legal process. The KwaZulu government challenged the proposed alteration of its territorial boundaries and diminution of its powers. The supreme court of Natal found in favour of KwaZulu, and on appeal by the government the Appellate Division upheld this judgment.[11]

The basis of the decisions was that, in respect of certain matters, the 1927 presidential power to legislate on black affairs had been superseded by the constitutional legislation establishing the homelands. While the former power was wide and discretionary, the latter was narrow and required the executive, in certain circumstances, to consult with the homeland concerned before exercising authority within its (the homeland's) jurisdiction. In the Swaziland episode this consultation had not occurred, although it should have, and the proclamations were ruled invalid. These were technical decisions in that the courts were concerned only with enforcing statutorily required procedures, which were more formalistic than substantive, and were not concerned with the lack of popular support for the proposal or its effect on the inhabitants concerned. Nevertheless they did serve to terminate the government's plans. After the Appellate Division judgment in the KwaZulu matter, the government agreed in an out of court settlement to revoke the proclamation which sought to disestablish the KaNgwane legislature and to restore the *status quo ante*. The whole matter was referred to a commission of inquiry, but this was subsequently disbanded and the matter was put to rest.

10. Boulle, Harris and Hoexter, *Constitutional and Administrative Law*, pp. 152–3.
11. *Government of KwaZulu* v. *Government of the Republic of South Africa* 1982 (4) SA 387 N; *Government of the Republic of South Africa* v. *Government of KwaZulu* 1982 (4) SA 427 A.

Reference is made later to other issues in respect of which the courts were able and willing to frustrate the implementation of government policy. In overall terms, however, the executive was the dominant constitutional organ in a system lacking politically active courts.

The tendency towards executive dominance over the legislature, judiciary and constitution which developed during this period should not be seen as unique in the history of parliamentary systems of government. However, in the South African context it was the dominant and inexorable feature of the system, precipitated by a convergence of constitutional and extra-constitutional factors: the unitary system of government, the power and personalities of the prime ministers, executive patronage, the closed access to official information, the disciplined caucus and party systems, the complexity of government affairs, perpetual security crises, the growth of the security apparatus and bureaucracy, and the financial pre-eminence of the cabinet.[12] These factors, in combination, gradually changed the political role of the South African parliament from that of policy formulation to that of policy legitimation. In functional terms this system of government was direct, effective and relatively efficient. However, the system of executive control and coercion could not cope with its own legitimacy crisis and the increasing demands of political outsiders. New forms of symbolic interaction were required, and this led to a new constitution.

The Second Republican Constitution

The Tricameral System. The Republic of South Africa Constitution Act of 1983 introduced changes of both terminology and substance into the system of government. Its institutions were ingeniously constructed to allow new black groups to participate in the political process while remaining politically excluded from 'white' politics and thus from the heart of governmental power. The main features of the new system that are of relevance to the present topic include the following:

– The position of a titular head of state was abolished and ceremonial and governmental functions were fused in one executive body, the State Presidency.[13]
– The tenure of the President was tied to that of parliament and an electoral college was constituted to appoint the chief executive.
– Executive power was distributed among four bodies, a national

12. See Venter, *South African Government and Politics*, pp. 43–4.
13. In a 1977 draft constitution bill, provision was made for a nominal head of state, in terms similar to that of the 1961 constitution.

cabinet and three ministerial councils, each responsible to different components of a tricameral parliament.
– The executive bodies were parliamentary in that, apart from the President, their members had to be drawn from one of the parliamentary houses, subject to the extended grace period.
– The President's Council was retained as a partly nominated instrument of the executive, with advisory powers in the executive domain and arbitral powers in the legislative domain;
– The composition of parliament allowed the executive to appoint, directly and indirectly, a specified number of members to each house;
– The cabinet and ministerial councils each acquired their own administrative resources in the form of state departments for general and for racially delineated ('own') affairs respectively.

It was significant, in the context of much rhetoric and posturing about 'power-sharing', that a collegial executive, similar to that in Switzerland, was not established by the 1983 constitution. This institution would have been irreconcilable with continued National Party dominance and would have increased the power of parliament, of which a collegial executive would have constituted a committee. Instead, two different levels of executive authority were established, with most power focused in the national cabinet and executive State President. The shift from a Prime Ministerial to a presidential executive was depicted as a major innovation in the 1983 Constitution. But not everything hangs on a name, and there was initial uncertainty as to the extent of the power which the new constitution was vesting in the presidency.

In the legislative sphere presidential authority appeared to be extensive despite the fact that, for the first time, the chief executive was not included in the constitutional definition of parliament. Sovereign legislative authority was vested in parliament and the State President together. A high degree of legislative flexibility afforded the President considerable potential influence in the legislative process. At the State President's discretion a Bill could be designated as an 'own affair' for disposal by a single house of parliament, thereby removing the other houses from the legislative process. In the case of boycott tactics or delays, the State President could refer bills to the President's Council, which could act as a surrogate legislator. The constitution provided several other ways in which presidential power could be used to influence and shape legislation. While there was some dispute over the extent to which these discretions were qualified,[14] the constitution

14. See Dion A. Basson and Henning P. Viljoen, *South African Constitutional Law* (Cape Town: Juta, 1988), pp. 143–6.

purported to oust any potential control by the courts.[15] Presidential assent was required for legislation to become effective; the assent power was not made subject to convention, but the constitution did stipulate the circumstances in which it could be withheld. The State President retained the power to dissolve parliament or its constituent parts and to control the sessions of parliament. The President could also appoint members to each house, nominate a majority of members to the quasi-legislative President's Council, and grant approval to all legislation passed by one or other of the variable legislative procedures. State revenues vested nominally in the State President and appropriation from the state coffers could only be effected through an act of parliament on the initiation of the President or an authorised minister.

In practical terms, the vesting of these vast legislative powers in the office of the presidency did not, in comparison with the previous constitution, amount to a substantial increase in the legislative influence of the executive. All executives in modern consitutions have a range of political, administrative, financial and populist devices through which they can influence legislatures. However, these features in combination provided the potential for the executive not only to influence but also to dominate the legislature in all its operations. Moreover, the use of presidential power could distort the symmetry and internal logic of the tricameral system. Thus it was not long before the State President used the President's Council as a special task force to legitimate legislation which was not proceeding smoothly through the tricameral parliament. This 1985 legislation, ironically, made provision for secret official funds for the police force. Parliament as a whole refused to comply in the derogation of its own functions, but ultimately it could only delay and not defeat executive policy.

In the executive sphere the head of state became the chair of the cabinet and, after a constitutional amendment passed in 1984, could administer a 'general affairs' government department. The system also assumed that the head of state would remain active in the majority white party. It has been suggested that in relation to the Ministers' Councils, the State President would play a similar role to the titular head of state under the 1961 Constitution, but that in relation to the cabinet he or she would wield real executive power, similar to that exercised by the Prime Minister in the previous system.[16] By and large this picture is accurate, but the generally conventional underpinning of the system invited problems. In 1988 the State President refused to dismiss a controversial

---

15. In *Savvas* v. *Government of the Republic of South Africa* 1988 (2) SA 327 T, the Supreme Court held that a determination by the State President that a legislative matter was an 'own affair' was judicially unassailable.
16. See Boulle, Harris and Hoexter, *Constitutional and Administrative Law*, pp. 156.

minister in the House of Representatives, despite being requested to do so by the minister's party and caucus, whose support he had lost. It appeared that the convention of responsible government was being breached, but the issue was resolved when the minister in question resigned.

The executive prerogatives were retained by the 1983 constitution, but with some modifications effected by the courts. While the constitution prescribed that general affairs were exercisable in consultation with the cabinet and own affairs powers on the advice of a Ministers' Council, the Supreme Court[17] held that the prerogative powers of the head of state were not subject to these prescriptions. They were *sui generis* powers which could be exercised by the State President personally. Established conventions suggested that only a few of the prerogatives, such as cabinet appointments, would not be exercised through a government minister. In fact all formal presidential acts, of whatever nature, required the counter-signature of a minister of state, an anomalous arrangement in the context of the new system. In another development affecting the prerogative, its established immunity from judicial review was called into question. In a case involving the withholding of a passport, the Supreme Court,[18] following British precedent, held that the prerogative is subject to judicial review in the same way as any statutory-based administrative power. The only exception to this new principle is that there can be no review of the 'political' prerogatives, which by their nature ought not to be reviewable – for example the appointment of ministers and the conduct of foreign affairs.

There was considerable uncertainty over the scope and application of the conventions relating to the executive. The new constitution purported to retain the existing conventions of responsible government, despite the shift to a semi-presidential system. However, as one commentary points out, there were few cases where conventions that were valid before the 1983 Constitution could be applied to the new dispensation.[19] Some conventions were codified in the Constitution Act. Thus it was stipulated that chairpersons of the three Ministers' Councils should enjoy the support of the relevant house of parliament, that ministers with own affairs portfolios should have the support of the majority in the appropriate house, that the head of state must assent to bills passed in accordance with the ordained procedures, and that parliament should be summoned at least once a year. These are all principles of responsible parliamentary government and they were given the explicit force of law.

17. In *Boesak* v. *Minister of Home Affairs* 1987 (3) SA 665 (C).
18. *Ibid.*
19. Basson and Viljoen, *South African Constitutional Law*, p. 41.

However, the scope of other conventions remained vague. There was, for example, no stipulation that members of the national cabinet should have the support of the parliamentary majority, which implied the possibility of minority party representation in cabinet. In 1988, moreover, an unsuccessful attempt was made to allow for the appointment of black ministers and deputy ministers within the context of the tricameral constitution. There was also a major problem with collective ministerial responsibility, as this clearly could not operate in respect of two bodies where the same individuals were members of both. Thus when MP Allan Hendrickse was dismissed from the national cabinet in 1987, it was quite feasible for him to remain as Chair of the coloured Ministers' Council. The principle of individual ministerial responsibility was placed under further strain by a 1987 constitutional amendment which provided for the appointment of ministerial representatives to replace provincial officials and to smooth over conflicts in the administration of own affairs. In practice these representatives were not all members of parliament. The government, apparently sensitive to the principle that executive authority should be accountable to the legislature, stressed that the appointees would be vicariously responsible through the relevant ministers.[20] This was an attempt to build responsibility on shaky foundations.

The new constitution was not generous in relation to controls over presidential power. While the President could appear in all three houses of parliament, he or she could not be called to account in the same way as cabinet ministers because he or she was not a member of any one house. Paradoxically, however, it was presumed that the President would enjoy the privileges of parliament, including immunity from any statements made in the legislature; this was probably the intention of the drafters, though the relevant provisions can be interpreted as excluding the President from the privileges. It is, of course, incongruous that an individual should enjoy the privileges of a body which could not call him or her to account. The parliamentary tradition of a vote of no confidence in the executive at the commencement of each session was abandoned in favour of a more benign debate on the presidential speech. The electoral college was empowered to remove an incumbent on the grounds of misconduct or inability to perform the duties of office, yet a motion of political no confidence from all three houses would not lead automatically to a presidential resignation but would allow, at the presidential discretion, for the dissolution of parliament. Moreover, the State President was not subject to the previous convention that the Prime Minister should resign on losing the leadership of the majority party,[21]

20. See *House of Assembly Debates*, 11 February 1987, col. 648.
21. Boulle, Harris and Hoexter, *Constitutional and Administrative Law*, pp. 154–5.

despite the fact that the party could control presidential appointments through the electoral college. This discrepancy caused problems in the last months of Botha's reign.

The new executive system was thus a hybrid of parliamentary, presidential and *sui generis* arrangements. While it was styled a semi-presidential system, its centre of gravity was in the parliamentary tradition. In the final resort the President had no separate electoral mandate of his or her own, and both President and cabinet were constitutionally dependent on the support of parliament. In political reality the Constitution rendered this form of accountability tentative and remote.

Tricameralism in Practice. Presidents Botha (1983–89) and De Klerk (since 1989) have held office under the second Republican Constitution. Of Botha it has been said that the new constitution was constructed around him, and he became its axis.[22] On his appointment as State President, Botha resigned from parliament, although the constitution allowed him to sit and speak, but not vote, in any of the three houses. In the first Botha cabinet of 18 ministers there were no fewer than 15 who had served with him under the 1961 Constitution. An Indian minister and a coloured minister, both without portfolio, were also included in the cabinet but after the dismissal of the former in 1987 and the resignation of the latter in 1988 the central executive was once again monopolised by members of the National Party.

Despite the preponderance of National Party members in the first tricameral cabinet, tensions soon mounted around the principle of collective responsibility. In 1987 Hendrickse resigned as Minister without Portfolio because of continuing conflict with the State President. In the wake of this episode the State President redefined the convention of collective responsibility. He indicated that, in cases of differences of principle on matters discussed by cabinet, the practice would be for a joint statement to be issued by himself and the ministers concerned. Apart from this, there should be no public disagreements among cabinet colleagues.

At the head of the political agenda during the early years of the Botha administration was reform, a concept susceptible to widely differing interpretations. Whatever the interpretations placed upon it, it was clear that the era of reform was characterised by an enormous increase in presidential power in all facets of government. This involved a continuation of trends evident in earlier periods of constitutional development, with several additional sources of impetus. In 1984 the Committee on

22. Venter, *South African Government and Politics*, p. 180.

National Priorities Act made provision for a standing commission to advise the cabinet on a range of matters, linked only by the requirement that they would involve the promotion of the 'public interest'. The abolition of the provincial system of government in 1986 also led to increased presidential power in respect of the appointment of provincial Administrators, the appointment of members of the Executive Committee and the administrative amendment of provincial ordinances. The last-mentioned power was later made subject to parliamentary ratification. Extensive use was made of the constitutionally countenanced delegation of power to support and maintain the instruments of indirect rule, including black local authorities and controversial regional services councils.

Presidential power was also increased through the chief political executive's access to the symbols and ceremonial accompaniments of the head of state. For the first time the head of government could also be presented as the personification of the state. Botha, more than any other head of government, made his influence felt outside the cabinet through his domination of the political agenda, control of information and manipulation of the media. The favoured legal instrument of presidential power was the proclamation, used for all matters of regulation, administration and even adjudication. Its public expression was made in the *Government Gazette*, produced with efficient regularity by the Government Printer, and occasionally appearing in Extraordinary versions in the early hours of Pretoria mornings. Even the borders of the country could be, and were, amended by presidential proclamation in terms of the Borders of Particular States Extension Act 2 of 1980.[23]

A countervailing initiative of the Botha presidency, which was continued by F.W. de Klerk, involved the partial disaggregation of the state system. Not only were the vast apartheid bureaucracies dismantled and reassigned to other portfolios in the Public Service, but the state attempted to shift responsibilities in matters of housing, education, welfare, planning and development away from itself towards the private sector. There was a blurring of the public sector/private sector divide; for example, private participation was facilitated in the formerly public sector Department of Transport Services. New ideologies of privatisation and deregulation were imported from Europe and North America to justify these measures. In reality there was more rhetoric than activity in this area. However, some developments were politically significant, and ultimately counter-productive as regards presidential power. The decision of the state to establish a relatively progressive statutory

---

23. The Act allowed the State President to transfer to the homeland states land designated in a schedule to the Act.

framework for collective bargaining in industrial relations involved a loss of state control over an important facet of modernisation and provided a countervailing political force to the presidency. It had significant implications for social and political developments in the late 1980s.

The Imperial Presidency. The 'imperial presidency'[24] of Botha straddled the two constitutional systems under which he headed the executive government. It commenced with the 'rationalisation' of the Public Service, which began soon after Botha's accession to office, and culminated in a protracted national state of emergency, which was still in existence at the time of his political demise. It involved the streamlining of the cabinet committee system, the expansion of the bureaucracy, the bolstering of the security apparatus, executive lawlessness and the destabilisation of the region. The South African Defence Force became a major political force, both internally and externally, and a network of information and surveillance authorities came to constitute a shadowy bureaucracy. Accompanying the emergency powers of detention, censorship and surveillance was an immense propaganda exercise, both covert and overt, which used vast state resources and added to the phenomenon of the presidential cult.[25]

Presidential power was most obvious in relation to security matters. The security regime introduced by the Internal Security Act of 1982 was described as a 'triumph for executive power'.[26] Moreover, for the first time even the cabinet came to be eclipsed as the prime policy-making organ. The State Security Council had been established by statute in 1972 and during the 1980s it assumed an important influence in some aspects of policy formulation. The empowering Act defined the function of the council as advising the government with regard to the formulation of policies in the field of national security and intelligence. It comprised senior ministers, bureaucrats and members of the military, intelligence and security establishments, and during Botha's reign it met regularly and developed a vast permanent secretariat. Many commentators suggested that it was a powerful, if not dominant, force in policy-making to the extent that it constituted an 'inner cabinet' which took decisions that were ratified by the national cabinet.[27] Not

24. The term is attributed to Arthur Schlesinger, *The Imperial Presidency* (London: Deutsch, 1974) and was the title of a book on Botha: Brian Pottinger, *The Imperial Presidency* (Johannesburg: Southern Book Publishers, 1988).
25. See Pottinger, *The Imperial Presidency*, pp. 449.
26. By C.J.R. Dugard, 'A Triumph for Executive Power – An Examination of the Rabie Report and the Internal Security Act 72 of 1982', *South African Law Journal,* vol. 99 (1982), p. 589.
27. See Basson and Viljoen, *South African Constitutional Law*, pp. 70–5.

only would such an arrangement flout its parliamentary-prescribed functions, but it would undermine any pretence of checks and balances in the constitutional system. As it was an 'extra-constitutional' body, there were necessarily few grounds on which to hold the council responsible and accountable. In 1986 the government publicly admitted to the existence of a system of Joint Management Centres which coordinated governmental activity at the regional and local levels. The centres reported ultimately to the State Security Council and constituted part of the 'shadow bureaucracy', of which constitutional form and principle took no account.

While the imperial presidency was most evident in matters of security, it was also apparent in some matters of reform. In 1986 broad discretionary authority was conferred on the State President to remove bureaucratic red tape in order to enhance the development of a free enterprise economic order. Whereas previously the executive had frequently ignored common law principles in its legislative and administrative extravagances, more recently it has ignored its own statutory prescriptions, for example in failing to enforce group areas laws (later repealed) and other legislation. While the former was condemned for its association with racist and exploitative policies, the latter has been largely overlooked by reason of its association with progressive reform. In reality, executive lawlessness is as much a feature of the latter as it is of the former. Ironically, convincing reform, even on government terms, required even more extensive use of presidential power, but this was not in evidence. The often-quoted 'Huntington option' demanded well-timed reform changes, a continuous and dynamic series of reforms and high-quality political leadership.[28] The constitutional order countenanced such initiatives, but Botha's personality and style did not.

Tricameral Resistance to the President. Although the tricameral arrangement was patently designed to allow for National Party dominance of the constitutional system, its incorporation of coloureds and Indians as junior partners in parliament created a new dynamic in the legislative process. Non-compliance by the houses of parliament controlled by these groups could be overridden by the executive, but only at a political cost. Within a few years of the system's inception, the tricameral parliament came to provide some resistance to the imperial presidency that had not been anticipated. The resistance was neither fatal nor destabilising, but it was significant in the constitutional politics of the day. The strategy chosen was to disrupt the legislative process, as a form of protest at executive action or at the content of proposed bills. Among the important institutions in the new system were the parlia-

28. Pottinger, *The Imperial Presidency*, p. 228.

mentary standing committees which, before joint debates for all three houses were instituted, provided the only forums in which there could be consultation among all political parties on the content of proposed legislation. The committees constituted a minor constitutional laby- rinth through which a bill had to find its way before emerging as a valid statute. In 1988 the State President refused to dismiss from the coloured Ministers' Council a minister who appeared to have lost the support of his party and caucus. The party retaliated against this refusal by walking out of the Standing Committee on Constitutional Affairs, thereby disrupting its consideration of constitutional legislation. Although this disruption could have been counteracted, in fact it posed a political embarrassment for the government and was only resolved when the minister concerned resigned from office.

Later that year both the coloured and Indian houses of parliament refused to pass a series of bills dealing with land affairs, including a proposed amendment to the Group Areas Act. The House of Delegates voted to defer consideration of the bills until the 1989 session of parliament, while the House of Representatives suspended all its activities until the following year. The government's response was to have the offending laws categorised as 'own affairs' legislation so that they could be passed by the white house of parliament alone, but this produced a strong reaction within the House of Assembly itself and the government desisted. When the bills were produced again later, the House of Representatives and the House of Delegates repeated their refusal to vote on them. Some bills were then submitted directly to the President's Council, whose inevitable approval allowed the State President to sign them into effect, but others were abandoned altogether.

The tricameral parliament even asserted itself outside the legislative process. In 1987 the State President announced that the Constitution Act would be amended to prolong the life of the current parliament, but the resistance to this measure which was foreshadowed by the coloured and Indian houses led to its quiet abandonment. These episodes illustrate the extent to which executive control of policy formulation and implemen- tation could be politically disrupted, even by circumscribed opposition parties. The cosy Westminster relationship among executive, caucus and legislature could not be reproduced within the complexity of tricameral politics.

These developments further reinforced the reality that the national cabinet was no longer the dominant and sole policy-maker, as had been the case before 1983. One commentator suggests that the role of parliament had changed from mere 'political acquiescence to that of active participation in policy-making',[29] though this may be overstating

29. Marais, *South African Constitutional Development*, p. 261.

the case. Nevertheless, the imperfectly democratic parliamentary system did allow for the occasional frustration of presidential policy. This reflected, in a minor way, the American constitutional system in which Congress is a countervailing source of policy-making to the president, as opposed to the smooth control of policy-making evident in orthodox Westminster systems.

Judicial Resistance to the President. In the story thus far the judiciary has been a consistently subordinate institution in the constitutional scheme of things. The various Constitution Acts devoted little attention to the judiciary and denied judges any meaningful power of constitutional review. Successive heads of government depicted the courts as paragons of judicial virtue, but did their best to keep them at arm's length from executive government and deny them any influence over policy or administration. As we have seen, judges did not rebel against this state of affairs. Two studies of the Appellate Division found that the highest court had served to preserve the existing orders of social formation and adopted pro-executive interpretations of statutes with little protest.[30]

In the 1980s and early 1990s, however, there were indications that the courts were moving away from these patterns of acquiescence and inertia. One illustration concerns black residence rights, where the courts in a series of decisions invalidated prior interpretations of the prevailing legislation and countermanded current administrative practice. This brought them into direct conflict with executive policy. While changes to that policy were in fact imminent, the judicial decisions may have precipitated them and in any event had significant consequences for thousands of black urban dwellers. A second example involves the many laws which purported to exclude the courts from exercising their common law powers of review of administrative action, the so-called ouster clauses. In another set of cases the Supreme Court held that these clauses could not exclude the courts' jurisdiction where the executive had acted beyond the confines of statutory authority. A third instance concerns the separation of powers doctrine. In a celebrated decision, the Supreme Court revived the constitutional relevance of this principle in holding that there were some functions, in this case decisions over bail,[31] which the executive could not exercise because they were intimately connected to the traditional judicial role.

One view is that judicial activism of this nature was motivated mainly by imperatives of self-preservation. Another is that it demonstrates the

---

30. Hugh Corder, *Judges at Work* (Cape Town: Juta, 1984) and C.F. Forsyth, *In Danger for their Talents* (Cape Town: Juta, 1985). Other commentators came to the defence of the Appellate Division on these matters.
31. *S* v. *Ramgobin* 1985 (3) SA 587 N.

paradox of executive sovereignty in a constitutional system in which there is a strong ideology of judicial independence. Thus while the constitution, in deference to parliamentary supremacy, explicitly excluded judicial reviews of legislation, it did not do so in respect of the judicial review of administrative action. While successive states of emergency allowed the executive to usurp most of the normal functions of government, they did not put an end to the courts or to all administrative law remedies. Under the influence of comparative legal developments elsewhere, as well as pressure from legal academics and more principled arguments from counsel, the courts found the means to confine the worst excesses of executive sovereignty to the margins.

This also occurred in a context less hostile to judicial involvement in affairs of state than had been the case in earlier decades. The 1983 Constitution incrementally increased the scope for constitutional review by the courts. The government itself provided more political space for the courts in appointing judicial commissions of inquiry on matters highly sensitive to executive policy and practice: the activities of the police in dealing with crowds, future directions on matters of basic human rights, and the role of the security forces in alleged assassinations of government opponents. In some cases the inquiries had little impact. However, in relation to police activities there was some trenchant criticism of standard practices, while in relation to human rights the official orthodoxy on group rights was demolished. There were no signs that presidential power could not accommodate this new dimension to the constitution.

Executive dualism revisited. During the later years of the Botha presidency there was speculation that a dual executive system might be reintroduced. It was becoming apparent that the fused executive was an onerous office for a single incumbent and that there was a need to lessen the burdens of presidential office. The demands of protocol attached to the head of state were combined with the executive and legislative demands attached to the head of government. In 1980 the position of Vice-State President had been introduced to relieve the head of state of some burdens and also to chair the President's Council. However, this did not diffuse executive power, partly because of the limited authority vested in the position and partly because the incumbent (Schlebusch) was a loyal party supporter and personally close to Botha. After the abolition of this office in 1984 there was speculation that the position of Prime Minister might be introduced, along the lines of the French semi-presidential system of government. In his 1988 budget speech Botha suggested that the position of Prime Minister be reinstated, with the incumbent being involved in day-to-day matters of administrative government while the President would be involved with policy formulation. Only tentative steps were taken to implement these proposals.

In January 1989 a *de facto* dualism developed when the State President, suffering from ill-health, relinquished the position of leader of the governing party while remaining in presidential office. The senior minister in the national cabinet was appointed as Acting State President during his ill-health and De Klerk was elected leader of the National Party. This appeared at first as a staged departure of Botha from the political scene, but in February he announced that he would resume his position as State President and might even seek a further term in office. Despite the idiosyncrasies of the tricameral system, it was obvious that this arrangement would involve intolerable strains on the constitution. A major problem arose from the uncertainty as to where the final policy-making power would lie. The National Party resolved that the presidency could not be separated from the leadership of the party, which was indeed the assumption of the tricameral system. Within a short time major differences of policy between Botha and De Klerk became evident and the former was obliged to resign from the presidency. The party nominated De Klerk as Acting State President and after the 1989 general election he became President, thus ending the uncertainty caused by this temporary dualism.

The Presidency and Constitutional Change

From the mid-1970s it was clear that constitutional change would be debated, negotiated and planned under the control of the National Party and the government. Several forums were mooted by the government, including a cabinet committee (1977), a national statutory council (1986) and state council or 'great indaba' (1988). All were to be extensions of cabinet and presidential power. In some cases a statutory foundation was provided; for example, the Promotion of Constitutional Development Act of 1988 allowed for the establishment of a negotiating forum which could consider a new constitution for the country. In the tradition of a series of such failed institutions, the council's composition would be dominated by presidential nominees. It never saw the light of day. Another failed attempt during the Botha era related to the appointment of ministers from outside parliament. In 1989 the Constitution Second Amendment Bill was drafted with the object of enabling the State President to draw cabinet ministers, including blacks, from outside parliament. The President's Council was the only institution which was actually established in this connection, but with its carefully contrived composition it too was seen as a legitimising agency for government policy. Its constitutional committee produced several reports of dubious distinction. Even this exercise was not altogether successful from the executive's point of view, as the committee's reports were not always compatible with government policy. There was a major difference of opinion on a recurrent theme in this chapter, namely the relationship between the President and the legislature. It has been suggested above that the resultant constitution in 1983 was not only an implementation of executive policy but was constructed, in part, around the chief executive.

In the 1990s a different strategy was adopted towards constitutional negotiation (see chapter 8 below). De Klerk was clearly more open than any previous head of government to advice from external sources of influence and less receptive to the traditional sources such as the security establishment, the party and caucus. Initial negotiations with the African National Congress were conducted with the loosest possible mandate from the President's traditional constituency. To distance the process even more from those quarters, a number of cabinet ministers relinquished office in early 1991 to devote time to the negotiation process, freed from the constraints of executive office or party discipline. The legitimising role of process came to be recognised as a crucial ingredient of a new constitution. It foreshadowed a different constitutional context for presidential power in the future.

Constitutionalism and the Presidency

Constitutionalism denotes a system of government in which state authority is controlled, divided, limited and shared and in which the wielders of state power are legally responsible and politically accountable for their actions. A major predicament for modern constitutionalism is the control and accountability of the executive, in particular the chief executive, whether presidential or parliamentary. The phenomena of the 'imperial presidency' in the United States and the 'elected dictatorship' in the United Kingdom have demonstrated the extent to which executive power can undermine the normative principles of constitutionalism, even in established constitutional systems in democratic settings.

The South African constitutional experience has reinforced this general thesis. Over the past four decades there has been a great deal of constitutional law, but very little constitutional principle. The constitution has always enabled more than it has restrained. The last 40 years have seen successive rampant executives cast aside rule of law imperatives as they have made their powers more intrusive and more discretionary, and less responsible and less accountable. It has been shown that this phenomenon is apparent in relation to reformist measures as well. The President has also been the ultimate repository of the meaning of the constitution in relation to matters such as the scope and extent of the conventions and the categorisation of legislation as own or general affairs. Constitutionalism cannot survive where the main functions of government are dominated by a single organ.

The most recent past has brought some important changes, including a new assertiveness from the judiciary. It has been demonstrated that the courts have refused to be excluded completely in relation to the review of administrative action, suggesting that they have themselves established a new fundamental principle in the constitutional system. The discussions on bills of rights suggest new scope for the enforcement of constitutionalist principles. The constitutional debate itself is informed by ideals inconceivable a few years ago. And the negative experiences of the past could yet have a positive effect on the constitutional order of the future.

2

THE HEAD OF GOVERNMENT
AND THE EXECUTIVE

Annette Seegers

This chapter concerns the relationship of the President (formerly Prime Minister) and the executive. It approaches the subject on an institutional basis, focusing on the size of the executive, its structure, governing political interests, relations between the Prime Minister and members of the cabinet, and leadership and management. Most attention is devoted to the post-1948 era but, since an institutional approach necessitates a long-term perspective, bureaucratic trends before this date are included.

One initial problem is definitional: who is the executive? Cabinet (or the executive council) and its leader should obviously be the starting point here, but does execution stop at the edges of the central state, or should homeland governments, for example, be included? Moreover, what of bodies only partly owned by the state? The view taken here is that the executive is interchangeable with the term 'state', which consists of the President and cabinet, plus nine other categories of bureaucracy:

- the central authorities (mainly first-tier departments under the authority of the Public Service Commission);
- provincial authorities (second-tier responsibilities for white education, medical and health services, roads and works, nature conservation and pleasure resorts);
- local authorities (responsible for some functions in urban and peri-urban areas);
- homeland governments (independent and non-selfgoverning);
- the South African transport services (SATS);
- the post office;
- control boards (mostly agricultural boards, but there are others, such as the Publications Appeal Board);
- statutory boards (like the Hotel Board or Council for Scientific and Industrial Research); and
- public corporations of products (such as ISCOR, ESKOM and SASOL), services (like the SABC and South African Tourist Corporation), financing (for example, the SA Reserve Bank), and development (the Industrial Development Corporation, for instance).

Another problem is information. Typically, reliable accounts of cabinets' deliberations are difficult to obtain because rules of confidentiality apply. Likewise, bureaucrats' actions are protected by secrecy laws. The researcher simply has to wait for the aggrieved politician eager to tell all, for the diaries and memoirs, and for statutes of limitation to expire. Before 1948, South Africa was by these standards not unusual; it subsequently and increasingly became a secretive state. Harsh legislation had something to do with this, but it is perhaps surprising that no former cabinet ministers, however scarred, wanted their experiences put into print. Biographies were shamelessly hagiographic.[1] Important officials retired and destroyed their records. Large gaps in information exist and simply cannot be filled.

In the existing literature, assessments of the state have moved along different avenues:

The path traditionally selected by students of public administration in South Africa explores the state in formal and/or managerial terms. Since law organises relationships into a three-part hierarchy of central, provincial and local tiers, inquiries are directed at how the parts relate to each other. A common theme is the imperial tendencies of the first or central tier, which simultaneously centralised decision-making and decentralised the administrative burden.[2] Regardless of the tier involved, studies try to help bureaucrats understand and improve their work. The best-known author here is J.J.N. Cloete, whose technocratic inclinations are evident in the identification of six generic bureaucratic functions: policy-making, financing, organising, staffing, work-procedures, and control.[3]

Other scholars reject a formal interpretation of state structure. Their perspective does not contest the existence of a formal hierarchy but argues that as such it is not constantly in play. A dynamic interpretation shows structure is specific to function (or purpose): to different degrees, according to the issue involved, only parts of the bureaucracy mobilise to execute goals. Thus the state has many policy structures. Hierarchy has its place but ought not be overstressed. One or another function draws together bodies with considerable political independence (municipalities, for example), personnel of equal status, and bodies unconnected by a chain of command.[4] All is not chaos, however, because the functions critical to the state rank structures in order of

---

1. Even the supposedly hard-hitting journalist Schalk Pienaar produced a mild book, *Getuienis van Groot Tye* (Cape Town: Tafelberg, 1979).
2. See the essays in Chris Heymans and Gerhard Tötemeyer (eds.), *Government by the People?* (Cape Town: Juta, 1987).
3. J.J.N. Cloete, *Introduction to Public Administration* (Pretoria: Van Schaik, 1981).
4. See, for example, Susan Booysen, 'Patterns of Political Influence in South Africa', *Politikon* vol. 13, no. 2 (1986); Hennie Kotze, 'Aspects of the Public Policy

importance. Race-related functions were traditionally considered to be the heart of the state; therefore the institutions of Bantu education, labour control and counter-urbanisation (to name but a few) constituted the dominant structure. Recently, however, the race focus has made way for strategic function, including military and regional affairs but also encompassing other more general concerns.[5]

A handful of scholars discuss the state in theoretical terms. Original efforts saw the state depicted as an instrument of class--race domination, but more recently scholars have tried to bring Marxist theory, or a variant of it, to bear on the South African case[6] and have searched for comparisons in the literature on bureaucratic-authoritarianism, corporatism and Latin politics.[7] The inevitable compromise between empirical depth and theoretical significance has not always produced happy results. In a few instances,[8] we get to know a portion of the state but, for the most part, the discussions often overrefine theory on the basis of patently flimsy factual information.

Technocratic, policy-oriented and theoretical interpretations of the state are informative and useful. However, the views grounded in law, management and universalities fail to explain the most obvious attributes of the state: its size and highly fragmented condition. It is here that an understanding of the executive must start.

Process in South Africa' in Albert Venter (ed.), *South African Government and Politics* (Johannesburg: Southern Book Publishers, 1979), pp. 170–200; Robert Schrire (ed.), *South Africa: Public Policy Perspectives* (Cape Town: Juta, 1982); and Garth Sheldon, 'Theoretical Perspectives on South African Foreign Policy-making', *Politikon* vol. 13, no. 1 (1986).

5. For example: Phillip Frankel, Noam Pines and Mark Swilling (eds.), *State, Resistance and Change in South Africa* (London: Croom Helm, 1988).

6. For example: Rob Davies et al., 'Class Struggle and the Periodisation of the State in South Africa', *Review of Africal Political Economy* vol. 7 (September–December 1976), pp. 4–30 and Harold Wolpe, 'Towards an Analysis of the South African State', *International Journal of the Sociology of Law* vol. 8, no. 4 (November 1980), pp. 399–421.

7. See the contributions to Wilmot G. James (ed.), *The State of Apartheid* (Boulder, CO: Lynne Rienner, 1987).

8. Such as Stanley Greenberg, *Legitimating the Illegitimate* (Berkeley: University of California Press, 1987).

The Size of the State, 1910–1980

The data presented here are taken from Barry Standish's excellent 'State Employment in South Africa',[9] which measures the size of the state by its employment after 1910.[10] Table 2.1 provides an estimation of all state employees across the nine categories, excluding only partly state-per annum. The fastest period of real growth was between 1950 and 1955 (6 per cent). The slowest was between 1930 and 1935 (1 per cent).

Table 2.1 TOTAL STATE EMPLOYMENT,
1910–1980

Year	Employment	Departments	Semi-government bodies
1910	N/A	13	2
1920	150,718	22	106
1930	227,408	25	226
1940	321,403	26	382
1950	481,518	27	430
1960	798,545	32	551
1970	1,105,295	38	683
1980	1,601,158	39*	952*

* In 1979

Sources: Ben Roux, 'The Central Administration, Provincial and Local Authorities, and the Judiciary' in Denis Worrall (ed.), *South Africa: Government and Politics* (Pretoria: Van Schaik, 1971), p. 82; Standish, 'State Employment in South Africa', part II, pp. 129–206; and C. Thornhill, 'Administrative Arrangements for Change' in D.J. van Vuuren *et al.* (eds), *Change in South Africa* (Durban/Pretoria: Butterworths, 1983), pp. 78–9.

9. Unpubl. MA thesis, University of Cape Town, August 1984.
10. Standish's measurement requires some explanation. First, there exists no single source of state employment. In each of the nine categories, different official sources are involved. Secondly, since not all authorised positions are filled and temporary workers used, actual employment is calculated where possible by the formula: authorised positions minus vacant positions plus temporary personnel. Thirdly, statistical devices make the data comparable over time. Fourthly, estimates are likely to be conservative, as the data exclude partly owned subsidiaries of state corporations. Finally, unless otherwise indicated, 'black' includes those classified as coloured and Indian. For more detail, see Joseph Barry Standish, 'State Employment in South Africa', Unpubl. MA thesis, University of Cape Town, August 1984, part II.

Table 2.2   TOTAL STATE EMPLOYMENT, 1920–1980:
PROPORTION OF WHITES

Year	% of total population	% of white population	% of black population
1920	2.20	4.47	1.57
1930	2.81	6.55	1.75
1940	3.10	7.45	1.97
1950	3.69	9.35	2.27
1960	4.66	10.79	3.32
1970	4.92	10.99	3.67
1980	5.56	13.20	4.03

Source: Standish, 'State Employment in South Africa', p. 140.

Table 2.3   TOTAL STATE EMPLOYMENT, SELECT YEARS:
PROPORTION OF ECONOMICALLY ACTIVE POPULATION

Year	Total E-A population	White E-A population	Black E-A population
1946	8.84	22.86	5.47
1951	10.71	24.93	6.84
1960	13.96	28.76	10.23
1970	13.62	27.94	10.35
1980	14.15	30.69	10.55*

* Excludes Bophuthatswana, Transkei and Venda.

Source: Standish, 'State Employment in South Africa', p. 137.

Central authorities employment (see Table 2.4) is most difficult to calculate, as areas have at different times been removed from the authority of the Public Service Commission. The numbers given in Table 2.4 include employment in the areas of coloured and Indian education, post office, the SADF, the SAP and the SATS except where indicated otherwise. SADF numbers, which are treated as white only, exclude national servicemen.

A large number of people were employed by the central authorities on a temporary basis. The numbers vary from year to year, reaching as high as 113,000 in 1966. Blacks form the largest but by no means the dominant group. Estimates for temporary workers given (in brackets) in Table 2.4 are extremely conservative.

Central authorities' share of state employment in 1980 was by far the largest for overall black and white state employment. In 1920, the SATS alone had accounted for 51 per cent of black and 61 per cent of all white state-employment, but its share subsequently declined to 16 per cent of black and 18 per cent of white state-employment in 1980. Provincial authorities are now the second largest employers of white state employees (see Table 2.5), while homeland authorities account for the second largest portion of black state employees (see Table 2.7).

Table 2.4   CENTRAL AUTHORITIES EMPLOYMENT,
1960–1980

Year	Total	(temporary)	White	Black
1930	140,042	(unavailable)	88,452	51,690
1940	177,392	(unavailable)	112,865	64,527
1950	280,310	(unavailable)	171,564	108,744
1960	454,692	(72,246)	182,257*	228,108*
1965	504,096	(71,274)	206,777*	249,872
1970	549,865	(74,917)	247,216	302,649
1975	509,424	(42,599)	261,277	329,147
1980	665,965	(42,282)	288,719	377,146

* Excludes post office employees

Source: Adapted from Standish, 'State Employment in South Africa', pp. 73, 80, 107, 129, 157, 163.

Table 2.5   PROVINCIAL AUTHORITIES EMPLOYMENT,
1961–1980

Year	Total	White	Black
1961	130,477	65,098	65,381
1965	149,174	73,131	76,043
1970	185,361	92,081	93,280
1975	220,248	108,441	111,897
1980	248,703	121,374	125,241

Source: Standish, 'State Employment in South Africa', p. 129

Table 2.6   LOCAL AUTHORITIES EMPLOYMENT,
1960–1980

Year	Total	White	Black
1960	151,459	38,361	113,098
1965	167,225	41,917	125,308
1970	191,294	47,364	143,930
1975	232,000	57,500	174,500
1980	244,600	56,600	168,000

Source: Standish, 'State Employment in South Africa', p. 129.

Table 2.7   HOMELAND GOVERNMENT EMPLOYMENT,
1975–1980

Year	Total	White	Black
1975	132,926	2,739	130,787
1980	191,309	2,481	188,808

Source: Standish, 'State Employment in South Africa', p. 129.

Table 2.8   CONTROL BOARDS EMPLOYMENT,
1960–1980

Year	Total	White	Black
1960	1,631	1,206	425
1965	1,833	1,292	541
1970	2,096	1,574	522
1975	2,339	1,600	739
1980	2,819	1,913	906

Source: Standish, 'State Employment in South Africa', p. 129.

The racial breakdown of employment for each year before 1960 is hard to assess, though the estimate for the 150,000 state employees in 1920 is 67,000 white and 83,000 black. Even after 1960 important information is unavailable. Table 2.11 is constructed by adding the number of employees, where available, in the nine categories of Tables 2.4 to 2.10. Because of missing information, estimates are conservative and totals differ slightly from those provided in Table 2.1.

Table 2.9   STATUTORY BODIES EMPLOYMENT,
1975–1980

Year	Total	White	Black
1975	21,349	11,313	10,036
1980	25,616	13,172	12,444

Source: Standish, 'State Employment in South Africa', p. 129.

Table 2.10   PUBLIC CORPORATIONS EMPLOYMENT,
1960–1980

Year	Total	White	Black
1960	42,598	Unavailable	Unavailable
1965	48,743	Unavailable	Unavailable
1970	60,355	Unavailable	Unavailable
1975	88,135	Unavailable	Unavailable
1980	117,389	Unavailable	Unavailable

Source: Standish, 'State Employment in South Africa', p. 129.

Table 2.11   TOTAL STATE EMPLOYMENT, 1960–1980:
RACIAL BREAKDOWN

Year	Total	White	Black
1960	780,857	286,922	407,012
1965	871,071	323,117	451,764
1970	988,871	388,235	540,381
1975	1,206,421	442,870	757,106
1980	1,496,401	484,359	872,545

Source: Standish, 'State Employment in South Africa', part II and page 129.

State-structure, 1910–1980

A glance at post-1910 history shows that the size of the state bureau-cracy expanded at a rate faster than population growth. Whereas state employment in 1920 comprised 2.2 per cent of the population, this figure had grown to 5.56 percent in 1980 (Table 2.2). The proportion of the economically active population employed by the state increased from 8.84 per cent in 1946 to 14.15 per cent in 1980 (Table 1.3).[11] Discounting the employment lag produced by the depression of the early 1930s, the fastest period of growth was in the early 1950s (Table 2.1). The 'semi-state' grew from two bodies in 1910 to 952 by 1980 (Table 2.1). 'Employment in public corporations alone grew from 42,598 in 1960 to 117,389 in 1980 (Table 2.10). The depression years aside, the most rapid growth of the semi-state was seen in the 1950s and 1960s.

The state fragmented in six ways: The first occurred in the general acceptance of the idea of a large number of small departments. At the first tier, proliferation is evident in the growth of departments from 13 in 1910 to 39 in 1980 (Table 2.1), an increase exceeding those of states with bigger populations and state employment (such as France and the United States). Given a relatively fixed number of ministers, depart-ments had to be grouped together under the authority of one minister. With only a few exceptions, local authorities were also organised into a large number of separate departments. Generally, the result was that senior officials (from the first to the third tiers) spent considerable time in coordinating activities.[12]

The second fragmentation happened at the third tier, where, by the 1970s, between 455 and 500 local authorities[13] had developed. The constitution did not recognise the third tier as fully independent. In general, local by-laws could be overruled by provincial authorities and national legislation applied. But the chain of command was weakened by local authorities' relative financial independence[14] and white local

---

11. Using different figures, Roux similarly concludes: 'Between 1937 and 1966 the *permanent* establishment of the public service (including the post office) increased by 276% while the white population and the total population (all races) increased by only 70% and 87% respectively. Between 1946 and 1966 the corresponding three percentages were 128%, 47% and 88%.' Roux, 'The Central Administration, Provincial and Local Authorities, and the Judiciary', p. 82.
12. *Ibid.*, pp. 81–2, 116–17.
13. J.J.N. Cloete, 'The Bureaucracy', in Anthony de Crespigny and Robert Schrire (eds.), *The Government and Politics of South Africa* (Cape Town: Juta, 1978), p. 55.
14. *Ibid.*, p. 124. By Roux's calculations, the trend in the 1960s and 1970s (for example) was for only about 4 per cent of local authorities' revenues to derive from central and provincial sources.

authorities' power over blacks living within their borders. Pressure from
the central state after the 1950s eroded this relative autonomy and the
1970s saw bitter battles over Bantu administration boards and community councils, intended (among other aims) to make black administration more uniform.[15] In the 1980s, however, there were signs of
municipal resurgence.[16]

The third was the growth of the semi-state. The giants ESKOM and
ISCOR today tend to dominate our image of the semi-state and
categorisation into control boards, statutory bodies and public corporations suggests some patterns of conformity. In fact, however, at least
952 bodies developed with differing forms and functions, size and
importance, connections to society, and sources of funding and ownership, thus complicating the chain of command. For instance, leaving
aside complications caused by the fact that many of these corporations
had subsidiaries, some bodies were run as a portion of a department or
departments themselves of the first tier. Annual reports to parliament
were required of some but not others. In several areas, bodies reported
to another in the semi-state, with only the loosest exercise of ministerial
control.[17]

The fourth fragmentation happened inside the state, as some institutions – specifically, the railways, the harbours and the post office – were
excluded from ordinary public service legislation, their personnel did
not come under the authority of the Public Service Commission, and
their budgets were separately approved by parliament. The railways and
harbours body, in particular, was unusual because of the strong unioni-
sation of its white employees. Three other areas were also often treated
separately by virtue of the classification of employees, legislation and
budgeting practices, namely defence, police and prisons.

The fifth fragmentation also occurred within the state, as institutions
based on services like education and health gave way to institutions
servicing on the basis of racial classification. The Population Registra-

15. See Simon Bekker and Richard Humphries, *From Control to Confusion*
    (Johannesburg: Shuter and Shooter, 1985); Greenberg, *Legitimating the Illegitimate*,
    pp. 29–55; and W.B. Vosloo, D.A. Kotze and W.J. Jeppe, *Local Government in
    South Africa* (Pretoria: Academica, 1974).
16. Doreen Atkinson, *Local Government Restructuring: White Municipal Initiatives
    1985–1988*, (Grahamstown: ISER, Rhodes University, 1989).
17. The position in agriculture, for example, was that there were several Departments
    of Agriculture of the first tier along with (by 1971) 21 produce control boards. The
    members of these boards were appointed by the State President or relevant
    minister. Revenue came mainly from levies. Budgets were not submitted to
    parliament or the treasury department but to the National Marketing Board, which
    was a statutory body. Roux, 'The Central Administration, Provincial and Local
    Authorities, and the Judiciary', p. 103.

tion Act was the foundation of, for instance, separate education departments for coloureds, Indians and Africans. In other words, the existence of some departments was primarily justified by race and not function.

Finally, the state fragmented by dividing the category of black employees among the institutions created for each of the homelands. Although the vast majority of the employees of homeland authorities were black (Table 2.7), the place of the homelands in the chain of command has always been a controversial subject. But it is safe to say that, in an administrative sense, they enjoyed some measure of autonomy.

To be sure, state bureaucracies' expansion and fragmentation are global phenomena. The growing preference is for rationalistic rather than discretionary service, and as populations increase and develop, so do demands for services. Once a bureaucracy appears, it never voluntarily shrinks. The habit of protecting existing budgets and employees, as well as the appearance of an interventionist posture in the twentieth century, translates directly into bureaucratic expansion. Typically, bureaucracies fragment for two reasons. One reason is simply historical, as organising principles reflect historical biases towards central or local control. The other reason is technocratic. Increasing specialisation, for example, encourages the growth of the semi-state, which tends to weaken prevailing hierarchies.

Although obviously affected by universal trends, the South African state's structure as described above far exceeded expectations about expansion and fragmentation. Size expands at a rate much faster than the population or economically active population – black, white, and overall – grows, and it grew fastest after the National Party came to power in 1948. Similarly, fragmentation not only increased rapidly from the 1950s onwards but involved a new reason. Originally, the vertical divisions were predominantly the products of pre-1910 traditions featuring strong provincial ties and the special consideration given to non-provincial entities, like railways, in the creation of Union in 1910.[18] Later the state inevitably acquired a semi-state. But then, with the National Party victory in 1948, administrative leadership was turned over to those governed by the twin ideas of promoting Afrikaner interests and social engineering along ethnic lines. The semi-state became the vehicle intended to vault Afrikaners into the middle class.[19]

18. One author describes the situation as a 'unitary state which contained traces of federalism'. The central government's design imitated the British unitary system, but the independence of provincial and local authorities suggested federal influence. F. Venter, 'South African Constitutional Law in Flux' in D.J. van Vuuren *et al.* (eds.), *Change in South Africa* (Durban/Pretoria: Butterworths, 1983), p. 2.
19. Hermann Giliomee, 'The Growth of Afrikaner Identity', in Heribert Adam and

With ethnicity as an organising principle, the state not only created more departments than one would expect but also divided horizontally:[20] each racial category was given a set of institutions. The category black was further divided and connected with the homelands.[21] Thus further sets of institutions come into being.

By 1980, the state had thus acquired features comparable to other state bureaucracies. Yet at the same time the local context left an often deeply ironic mark. The bureaucracy increasingly was led by Afrikaners and served their interests, but black state employment substantially outnumbered white employment in almost all sections of the state and semi-state. The structure of the state constitutes another irony. As the assault on the independence of municipal authorities showed, the state after 1948 displayed a strong centralising dynamic along a vertical axis. But racial policy also dictated fragmentation along a horizontal axis. One department divided into many – and one state produced homeland states.

Employees and Conditions of Employment, 1910–1980

The attributes of state employees and the conditions affecting them surfaced soon after Union, when the findings of the Campbell Commission of Inquiry led in 1912 to the *Staatsdienst en Pensioenwet* (covering state employment and pensions). Subsequently other inquiries, such as the Graham Commission (1921) and the Centlivres Commission (1944–7), recommended adjustments to this law. Although most descriptions of trends between 1960 and 1980 are anchored in the Public Service Act of 1957, this Act did not cover employees of provincial and local authorities, railways and harbours, the post office, and many semi-state bodies. Homeland authorities' employees came under the authority of separate public service commissions. Even when defining the Act as encompassing all central authorities' employees, discrepancies appear – as the two Government Pensions Acts (1965 and 1973) refer to a larger number of employees.

As regards a narrowly defined central state, the Public Service Commission exercised wide powers over matters relating to personnel.

Hermann Giliomee, *The Rise and Crisis of Afrikaner Power* (Cape Town: David Philip, 1979), p. 5 and David Welsh, 'The Political Economy of Afrikaner Nationalism' in Adrian Leftwich (ed.), *South Africa: Economic Growth and Political Change* (London: Allison and Busby, 1974), p. 261.

20. The term horizontal division is used by J.A. Lombard, 'Fiskale Beleid in Suid-Afrika', *The South African Journal of Economics*, vol. 47, no. 4, 1979, pp. 359–66.

21. According to the Promotion of Black Self-Government Act of 1959.

Aspiring employees were not required to sit an entrance examination.[22] Most central state employees were classified as holding either 'posts' or 'services' positions. The latter are easier to describe, as most SADF and SAP positions were regarded as services and organised into hierarchies typical of such institutions. Positions classified as posts were organised into divisions forming a hierarchy: (from the top down) administrative, clerical, professional, technical, general A, general B, and unclassified.[23] Administrative posts referred to the most senior positions, like the secretary or deputy secretary of a department. Assistants, clerks and typists or those supporting line officers constituted the clerical division. Employees with professional, university or technical qualifications were classified into, respectively, the professional and technical divisions. The general A division contained a variety of more senior employees, such as inspectors and foremen. Those without qualification were placed in the general B division.[24]

Most central state employees occupied service positions, with unclassified workers comprising the second largest and clerical workers the third largest categories. For these positions, matriculation was usually the highest qualification. Administrative personnel were the most influential, but only in the highest positions were incumbents likely to have university degrees. Most other administrative positions were normally filled by promoted clerical workers – and promotions did not necessarily favour the academically qualified, as experience was taken into account. Salaries also did not attract qualified employees. Although salaries could be negotiated through a system of joint consultation, conditions of service rather than remuneration usually dominated the agenda.[25] Thus the bulk of the central state's workforce consisted of relatively low-paid people with limited professional or technical qualifications.[26]

It is impossible to generalise about state employees not covered directly by the Public Service Act. In some areas, for example provincial authorities, the Act applied indirectly, as most employees worked in the fields of health and white education. In other areas, like local and homeland authorities, the Act was imitated in by-laws and other

22. Some training courses were gradually developed, but usually focused on junior ranks.
23. The Public Service Act of 1957, sections 3 (1) and 3 (2).
24. Roux, 'The Central Administration, Provincial and Local Authorities, and the Judiciary', pp. 87–8.
25. *Ibid.*, pp. 89–90.
26. J.J.N. Cloete, 'The Bureaucracy', pp. 60, 65. The mix of positions, of course, varied among the central state departments; some, like the Department of Foreign Affairs typically employed a large proportion of professionally qualified people.

legislation. Similarly, salaries varied quite dramatically, depending on
the wealth of the area.

What of the large number of blacks in state employment (Tables 2.4
to 2.10)? Of all blacks employed by 1980, the largest numbers worked
in: central authorities (20 per cent;), homelands (18 per cent), local
authorities (17 per cent), the SATS (16 per cent), and provincial
authorities (12 per cent).[27] Thus only a minority of black employees
were directly and formally covered by the provisions of the Public
Service Act. Although not specified in the Act itself, whites' salaries
were higher than those of blacks and top positions were occupied by
whites.[28] The Act also did not specify racial quotas; yet there is evidence
of racial bias. Labour shortages in the central state, for instance, would
at times be filled by temporary rather than permanent black labour.
Provincial authorities' black:white employment ratios remained stable
while overall black state employment increased substantially. Cutbacks
in black employment in the railways during the 1950s were obviously
the result of white unions' pressure. The semi-state presents a more
ambiguous picture. Here control boards reduced black employment
more regularly than white, but in large public corporations (ESKOM,
for example) both black and white employment grew at a stable rate.[29]

Although the growing size of state employment had economic
significance it was, almost from the start, certain that employees would
not come together as a social class, group or stratum. The racial divide
loomed large in every corner – rank and status, salaries, and qualifications – of the state. Even if this were not the case, collectivisation was
unlikely: employees were divided by qualifications; work was likely to
be in separated departmental environments; temporary employees
lacked incentive to transfer loyalties; and the tiers were based on and
perpetuated differences. The top leadership was no exception to this
rule. An Afrikaans background did effect some commonality but could
not wholly counteract the differences between a lifetime of state
employment and the possession of a professional degree.

Executive Leadership and Management, 1910–1980

Parliament's oversight of the bureaucracy followed the Westminster
model. The executive was formally headed by the State President
(formerly the Governor-General), but by custom it was led by the
cabinet whose members were determined by the leader of the majority

27. Standish, 'State Employment in South Africa', pp. 152–7.
28. J.J.N. Cloete, 'The Bureaucracy', p. 66.
29. Standish, 'State Employment in South Africa', pp. 162–84.

party in parliament. The Prime Minister and cabinet ministers were thus the active leaders.[30] This leadership is here assessed in the light of how it addressed three interrelated administrative issues: coherence, discretion and economy.

Until the late 1970s, political leaders found little electoral reward in the issue of administrative reform. In the two decades after 1910, the dominating political issues were labour relations, the poor-white problem, and Afrikaans–English relations intersecting with nationalist–imperial tensions. Later, the Pact Alliance (1924–33), Fusion (1933–9) and the United Party (1939–48) came to power on the basis of their response to the economic depression and the Second World War. None of these issues encouraged administrative economy; indeed, as Table 2.1 shows, state employment almost doubled between 1920 and 1940, while the number of semi-state bodies increased from 106 to 382. Electoral criticism of the state was either constitutional (that is, links with Great Britain served imperial interests) or functional (it was insufficiently interventionist or promoted the wrong kind of domestic interests). Once in power, political leaders also encountered several traditions not conducive to administrative reform.

The first of these was the widely shared view that the bureaucracy was apolitical. This meant that the ideal was supposedly a career-oriented, professionalised bureaucracy. In practice a series of formal and informal restraints applied. Patronage on a partisan white basis was discouraged. Officials could hold party membership but not lead parties or chair public party meetings. The cabinet made important political decisions. If officials were present in decision-making bodies, the rule was that they provided information and advised on that basis. Hiring, firing and other personnel matters were handled by a permanent Public Service Commission, which published annual reports. Established in 1910, this three-man commission came under the authority of the Minister of the Interior, a cabinet member. Yet the commission was protected from pressure by the seniority of its members (who were on a par with departmental secretaries) and by the stipulation that they could only be dismissed with the consent of parliament's two houses.

The second tradition derived from the old colonial approach of addressing important political issues through commissions and/or committees of inquiry. The Union adopted this approach generally, including at times when administrative problems reached a critical point. Commissions of inquiry excised problems from the political process. The intention was to gather impartial and specialist knowledge, through appointments (officials and non-officials on non-partisan

---

30. Deputy ministers were appointed after 1961 but did not participate in cabinet meetings.

grounds) and through hearings and submissions by a variety of interest groups and individuals. If (prime) ministers wanted to engage in reform, in other words, they had to do so through a laborious process which they themselves could not completely control. What eventually became administrative policy thus did not emanate principally from powerful politicians, from the caucuses of parties they led, or even from parliament.

The third tradition involved officials' discretionary powers over bureaucratic regulations and procedures. The example of the Public Service Commission here is instructive. It recommended to the cabinet and the Minister of the Interior regulations which then, via acts of parliament, became or had the power of law. Some of these public service regulations shielded bureaucrats from inspection by legal authorities, as well as from other political authorities. Procedures collected in the Public Service Staff Code did not have the power of law. Bureaucrats were simply empowered by parliament to determine procedures or 'the manner in which transactions are to be carried out'.[31]

Before 1948, therefore, political interests effectively abolished the notion of administrative economy. Expansion in part naturally dwarfed thoughts about how the elements of the state should cohere or how work should be organised. But in other areas, the state's traditional views and habits discouraged political executives from administrative reform. The prevailing ideal was that the bureaucracy ought to be subject to the least possible political influence. Problem-solving was a laborious yet electorally unrewarded process. It was left to officials to sort many matters out.

After 1948 political interests quickened the pace of state expansion. Initially, the National Party's alliance with the Afrikaner Party softened its agenda but, as the 1950s wore on, Nationalist goals were pursued with enormous determination and original aims became more radical. The aim of uplifting Afrikaners shifted from helping the poorest to assisting Afrikaner businesses. Republican aspirations were driven to a conclusion in 1961. Most importantly, segregationist notions were transformed under the leadership of H.F. Verwoerd. The old way (the era of 'simple apartheid') had been a not-always-consistent mix of enforced separation and paternalism in a single political order. The new apartheid ('separate development') was a uniformly applied policy connecting ethnicity with territory. Ethnic groups were entitled to determine their own political development, but in areas or 'homelands' separated to the maximum possible extent from the white political order. Until the 1980s, the National Party was not seriously challenged over this policy in elections; when the challenge came later, it was over their loss of faith in this type of apartheid.

31. J.J.N. Cloete, 'The Bureaucracy', p. 70.

Same-party rule and the force of the Nationalists' political interests shredded the remnants of administrative economy. By 1980, the Nationalists commanded a state which in 30 years had expanded the number of its employees from 481,518 to 1,601,158 (Table 2.1), and its share of the economically active population from 10.71 per cent to 14.15 per cent (Table 2.3). The form of expansion is as important as the overall growth of employment. The semi-state's growth – from 430 to 952 bodies (Table 2.1) – further complicated the chain of command. In addition came an ever-increasing number of new institutions created by dividing existing bodies into those servicing different races and ethnic groups. Within one institution, too, the impulse was to departmentalise – that is, to divide into smaller, more specialised units.[32]

An expanding but increasingly fragmented state produced a series of administrative problems. The demand for employment always exceeded its supply, either because the demand was excessive or because the wages offered could not attract or retain suitable employees. Shortages of suitable workers meant the state constantly battled with its training programmes. Fragmentation negatively affected procedural uniformity of work within the state. By 1979, central authorities alone enforced 2,080 legal acts and more than 16,000 regulations and proclamations, as well as over 1,100 provincial ordinances. Since departmental divisions were caused by racial, not economic considerations, state employees' work was duplicated or overlapped. This created a constant demand for coordination.[33]

Prime Ministers remained indifferent to the administrative consequences of their policies. At this highest level, coordination problems were most conspicuous. The cabinet was formally entrusted to deal with this issue, but it consistently rejected proposed mechanisms for enhanced coordination. Instead, the evolving practice was for Prime Ministers to rely on advisors and councils in specific fields (like economic development). In addition, a Department of Planning was created in 1964; however, its status and functioning failed to establish the practice of executive coordination. As before, solving the problems of training and uniformity was left mainly to officials. When the Nationalists came to power, officials' discretionary powers were already so extensive that two parliamentary investigations were undertaken (in 1948 and 1949), but their recommendations were shelved. The

---

32. Roux, 'The Central Administration, Provincial and Local Authorities, and the Judiciary', p. 122.
33. Annual Report of the Commission for Administration, 1980, cited by P.F.A. de Villiers, 'Governmental Institutions in the Republic of South Africa', in S.X. Hanekom, R.W. Rowland and E.G. Bain (eds.), *Key Aspects of Public Administration* (Johannesburg: Macmillan, 1986), p. 100.

Minister of the Interior continued as the head of all those covered by the
Public Service Act, and this minister delegated powers to the Public
Service Commission and heads of departments.[34]

Although administrative reform was omitted from the political
leaders' agenda until 1976, it would be wrong to think that successive
Prime Ministers and cabinets shaped the state only through unchecked
expansion and fragmentation. At least two influences deserve mention.
The first is that key positions in the state were by 1980 likely to be held
by Afrikaners. Outright patronage was impossible but, in the 1950s
English-speakers, those opposed to republicanism and people who had
volunteered for service during the Second World War were pressured
to leave state service through, for example, being overlooked for
promotion and being offered early retirement. Some institutions, like
the Active Citizen Force, were neglected during this time because they
were seen as attracting English-speakers. As the state became more
closely identified with the radicalising interests of the National Party
and as Afrikaners moved into top positions, the central state environment was less and less hospitable to English-speakers.[35]

The political leadership after 1948 favoured a balance within the state
which was tilted towards the executive branch and, within it, the central
authorities. There were many reasons for this trend. One was that, once
republicanism achieved its goal, the populist focus of Afrikaner politics
on strong parties and legislative control lost its force. Under conditions
of effective same-party rule, the executive was in any case more
powerful than the legislature. Another important reason for centralising
authority was the political leadership's refusal to tolerate opposition to
its racial policies. In the 1950s, it defeated the judicial branch's
opposition to the removal of coloured voters from the common voting
roll by the extraordinary means of enlarging the Senate. Opposition
from local authorities over black affairs was similarly neutralised by the
introduction of Bantu Administration Boards. Whatever the reason, by
1980 the judicial and legislative branches' ability to challenge, together
with the administrative powers of provincial and local authorities, were
eroded by pressure from the executive and central authorities.

---

34. Ben Roux, 'Parliament and the Executive', in Worrall (ed.), *South Africa:
    Government and Politics*, p. 72.
35. Cynthia Enloe, *Police, Military and Ethnicity: Foundations of State Power*
    (London: Transaction Books, 1980); Stanley Trapido, 'Political Institutions and
    Afrikaner Social Structures in the Republic of South Africa', *American Political
    Science Review* vol. 57 (1963), pp. 75–87.

Life at the Top: The Prime Minister and Cabinet, 1948–1978

Little has been said so far about the cabinet. In broad terms, after 1910 it resembled the cabinet of Great Britain. Based on a mixture of convention and law, a maximum of 18 ministers were appointed by the leader of the majority party in parliament. The Prime Minister and other ministers had to be members of parliament and thus played a dual role as legislators and overseers of the executive. The cabinet on average met once every fortnight, and its deliberations were not disclosed to the public.

All the Prime Ministers before 1948 – Louis Botha (1910–19), J.C. Smuts (1919–24 and 1939–48) and J.B.M. Hertzog (1924–39) – were revered military leaders during the second Anglo-Boer War and exceptional men in their own right. They were in various ways linked to Afrikanerdom but not wholly submissive to its imperatives; the ebb and flow of their careers indeed stemmed from their assertive, independent styles as much as from electoral/party shifts. Prime Ministers in the aptly described 'age of Generals' did not require their ministers to follow them blindly. Cabinet unanimity and collective responsibility were in fact at times strikingly absent. J.B.M. Hertzog, for example, took an openly independent line about Afrikaner interests when he was a member of the first cabinet. Potential dissent over racial policy was a constant factor – witness the actions of Tielman Roos in the Hertzog cabinet in 1925 and J.H. Hofmeyr in the Fusion cabinet in 1936.[36]

With one exception – B.J. Vorster (1966–78) – a Prime Minister's tenure after 1948 was ended only by death or illness. The relative certainty about who the leader would be and the 'unbroken line' of their tenure have led scholars to identify a strong ministerial tradition.[37] The radicalising agendas and homely but unbending public faces of D.F. Malan (1948–54), J.G. Strijdom (1954–8), H.F. Verwoerd (1958–66) and Vorster may well contribute to this interpretation. But from the perspective of relations with cabinet ministers, can it really be said that a strong prime ministerial tradition developed? To be sure, security of tenure existed. Its causes may well include some force of personality, but it can be more accurately said to be a product of the absence of challenges from party cohorts.

First, a major cause of challenge – electoral failure – was nullified by effective same-party rule. No matter how tactically maladroit the leader, the National Party would still prevail at the polls. Secondly, the cabinet was an unlikely scene for a fight. The Prime Minister was leader

36. Alexander Brady, *Democracy in the Dominions* (University of Toronto Press, 1947), pp. 330–1.
37. Leonard Thompson and Andrew Prior, *South African Politics* (New Haven/London: Yale University Press, 1982), p. 74.

of the National Party because he either led or enjoyed the support of its Transvaal caucus. Those who wanted to challenge could best do so when the Transvaal leader was first elected. Trying to dislodge him afterwards risked a life in the political wilderness. Thirdly, the republican goal required unity. At the very least, public disagreements among Afrikaners had to be avoided. Those fights which could not be avoided were driven deep into the recesses of Afrikanerdom. Fourthly, the political schooling of Prime Ministers was important. Unlike the leaders of the age of Generals, whose formative years came before the second Anglo-Boer War, the apartheid Prime Ministers spent years in the ranks of organised Afrikanerdom. Here committees and organisations stressed the risks of personal assertiveness and the virtues of unity, deference to authority and cultural conformity. Ministers of religion (like Malan) had long held leadership positions in the Afrikaans community and set an enormously influential example. A leader did not set himself – it was always *him*self – apart by rhetoric, political skill or the ability to command but, once in power, he was divinely ordained. Like a *dominee*, he was *gesalfde van die Here* (anointed by God).

The critical tradition which developed after 1948 was cabinet solidarity rather than prime ministerial assertiveness. The personal histories of almost all prime and cabinet ministers did not encourage them to set themselves apart or to try to 'bend others to their will'.[38] This is not to say the Prime Ministers were weak men, but they were not strong in the sense of possessing an ability to command or the freedom to strike out in new directions. A Prime Minister went as far as he thought Afrikaners would tolerate. Not until the rise of right-wing opposition in the late 1960s would a minister resign over matters of policy. Even when some ministers were later implicated in the Information Scandal, the defence of collective responsibility was invoked.

Political Interests and the State, 1980–1990

The 1970s was the first decade when political leaders' interest in administrative reform acquired demonstrable public force. These interests countered some of the state's institutional habits. Simultaneously, however, political interests contributing to state growth and bureaucratic proliferation continued to exist.

What were the dominant political interests of political leadership in the 1980s? One view is that white minority rule was still the ultimate interest, but an alternative interpretation is the modernising of apartheid

38. The phrase is from Robert A. Caro, *The Years of Lyndon Johnson: The Path to Power* and *The Years of Lyndon Johnson: Means of Ascent* (New York: Knopf, 1982 and 1990).

or counter-revolutionary thesis. A third view holds that, while the mass of Afrikaners and other whites may not have shifted their political views, the 1980s witnessed the emergence of a layer of political leaders ready to accept a post-apartheid world. This layer's political visibility and effect was delayed by the defenders of white minority rule but burst into public view with the ascent of F.W. de Klerk.[39]

The first interpretation is that separate development required new means of implementation. The government's reaction to the Theron Commission of Inquiry about the coloured population, for example, recognised the unworkability of existing arrangements. Other commissions led to alterations in influx control, industrialisation and labour practices, thereby softening the socio-economic aspects of separate development. Because reforms did not touch the pillars of separate development (the homelands, the key laws, or the principle of inequality), interpreters saw the governing political interest as the modernisation of apartheid.[40]

Adapting basic old goals to changing circumstances could be accomplished on an *ad hoc* basis, but many officials believed it required a new constitutional framework. In July 1979, a commission of inquiry (the Schlebusch Commission) was indeed appointed and its 1980 report recommended alterations to the Westminster parliamentary style. In 1981, when the Senate was abolished, parliament became a one-chamber body. A President's Council, incorporating coloureds and Indians as well as whites, was created to advise the cabinet and the State President mainly about constitutional matters. The President's Council issued influential reports and in 1983 its proposals culminated in a new Republic of South Africa Constitution Act. The Act was approved and came into effect in September 1984.

The 1984 constitution is more fully discussed elsewhere in this book, but for our purposes it is important to note here that it did not transcend the notion that institutionalisation should proceed on the basis of racial and ethnic categories. On the contrary, the constitution elevated this thinking to unknown heights by, for example, creating three chambers of parliament on an ethnic/racial basis, with each chamber debating issues on the basis of a distinction between 'own' (that is, exclusive to a classified group) and 'general' affairs. Homeland institutions were not disestablished. It is small wonder that the white referendum on and other elections held around the 1984 constitution introduced a spiral of violence and, later, successive states of emergency.

39. This interpretation is discussed below, pp. 71–3.
40. Originally the title of Heribert Adam's influential book, *Modernising Racial Domination: South Africa's Political Dynamics* (Berkeley: University of California Press, 1971).

The second interpretation of political leadership in the 1980s is that the years of international isolation, regional pressure in the aftermath of the Portuguese coup of 1974, and a variety of other conditions hostile to minority rule radicalised the white political leadership's view of the world. Already prone to a *laager*-mentality, key Afrikaner leaders of the state during the 1970s began to say that South Africa was caught in a *de facto* war with little outside support available. The assault was directed by the Soviet Union – leading other communist forces – with regional allies like the frontline states and domestic puppets such as (but not only) the African National Congress (ANC). No area of life was exempt from this assault: culture, human psychology and education were as much in the firing line as politics and economics. It was a 'total onslaught'.[41]

In the face of increasing domestic violence, total onslaught evolved into 'revolutionary onslaught'. A developmentalist line of thinking, which spoke of South Africa as a third world country beset by problems and 'bottlenecks' under conditions of scarcity, took hold. Past rulers too were held to have made 'mistakes'. Local activists of the left and right were busy exploiting these problems, and they were supported by the forces of communism and its regional allies. Under these conditions a counter-revolutionary strategy was necessary. This strategy had many components but its essential aim was to manage events; if this failed, it was believed, a revolution was around the corner.[42]

The 1980s stretched white political interests to breaking point. As regards modernising apartheid, it actually led to political opposition as, for some, reforms went too far and for others, not far enough. Total and revolutionary onslaught failed to mobilise the electorate, despite an awesome barrage of publicity. Until the political demise of P.W. Botha it was unclear what would replace these interests, but certainly its administrative executive difficulties were demonstrated daily.

Movement towards administrative reform was originally stimulated by the Information Scandal's revelations of bureaucratic arrogance, financial irregularities and poor management. Although the Department of Information was the main culprit, other senior officials were implicated and the scandal left the impression that the public would henceforth take an interest in bureaucratic behaviour. The succeeding Prime Minister, P.W. Botha, justified his political ascent by criticising the management of the discredited B.J. Vorster and announcing that he

---

41. One of the best treatments of this view is in Kenneth W. Grundy, *The Rise of the South African Security Establishment: An Essay in the Changing Locus of State Power* (Johannesburg: South African Institute of International Affairs, 1983).

42. See my 'The Government's Perception and Handling of South Africa's Security Needs', in Daan J. van Vuuren *et al.* (eds.), *South Africa: The Challenge of Reform* (Pinetown: Owen Burgess Publishers, 1988).

particularly valued clean and efficient administration.[43] Botha's ideas about good administration clearly emanated from his authoritarian personality and his record as a politician who had long been in charge of the South African Defence Force (SADF). In addition, Botha's reading of political circumstances in the 1970s led him to conclude that political reform was necessary but, since the economic boom of the 1960s was over, it had to be a cost-effective exercise. Consequently, to him, the ingredients of efficiency were management in the military style – using fear in order to motivate, hierarchical organisation, obedience to command and enthusiasm (to name a few) – together with the drawing on private sources of funding for state enterprises.[44]

The beginning of Botha's tenure roughly coincided with criticism, by officials and the political leadership, that all was not right with the state administration. Some of the perceived problems were purely administrative, with criticism focusing on the practice of too many bodies performing the same functions or on bodies being too large to be efficient. The reports of the Commission for Administration after 1976, for example, make repeated reference to a smaller, better organised and more efficient public service. That these criticisms were not simply annual *pro forma* items, was shown in 1976 in the shifting of the public services (or central authorities) from the jurisdiction of the Minister of Internal Affairs to that of the Prime Minister. At provincial level, too, there were similar suggestions to amalgamate units.[45]

Along with the general sense that state growth had become excessive came more specific negative assessments. One was of the security intelligence supplied to the cabinet. The State Security Council (SSC), which was supposed to coordinate information in the manner of a national security agency, had not managed since its creation in 1972 to overcome the rivalries among subordinate intelligence agencies. It was not that the SSC was inept; rather, reports found that it lacked the administrative means to fulfil its functions.[46] Another related criticism was of the department of foreign afffairs' inability to predict and manage the regional political events that followed the Portuguese

43. Deon J. Geldenhuys, *The Diplomacy of Isolation* (Johannesburg: Macmillan, 1984), pp. 84–9.
44. His emphasis on private support of public enterprises was made obvious in the Carlton and Good Hope Conferences of 1979. A critical biography does not exist, but see *ibid*.
45. For example, the Cape Province's Saaiman Commission of Inquiry about, among other things, divisional councils. P.F.A. de Villiers, 'Government Institutions in the Republic of South Africa', p. 100.
46. The Commission for Administration (then the Public Service Commission) conducted the investigations. The first report was delivered in 1975 and remains classified. It is known as the Venter Report.

withdrawal from Southern Africa in 1975/6. For instance, this department had produced a spectacularly inaccurate evaluation of Zimbabwean developments.[47]

While scandal, the arrival of a reform-minded Prime Minister, and the fact that problems were reaching a critical pitch encouraged administrative reform, powerful and more deeply political interests continued to encourage the state's growth. These interests sought to keep separate development in place while simply reforming some of its dimensions and/or managing opposition to it.

Life at the Top: The President and Cabinet, 1980–1990

P.W. Botha departed from the collegial style of cabinet leadership. His personality and history made him confrontational, a rough man of action who wanted to prevail through command. Subordinates spoke in fear of bruising encounters, gothic displays of bad temper, impatience and limited powers of contemplation. It was not so much that P.W. Botha was a militarist – although his association with the military suggested it – but that his was an authoritarian personality decidedly not given to egalitarian and collegial responses to problems. For political advice he tended not to rely on the advice of senior ministers, going instead to the ideas of three associates: the head of the Office of the State President (Jannie Roux), his press secretary (Jack Viviers) and a personal friend (Boet Troskie).[48]

The cabinet in the 1980s was affected by constitutional–bureaucratic changes as well as P.W.Botha's personal style. Superficially these changes appeared to strengthen the cabinet; after all, it became a statutory body and no limits were placed on its size. But in fact cabinets were weakened in four respects.

First, the 1984 constitution combined the powers of the Prime Minister and State President into one new office, the State President. Although the State President was elected by an electoral college, whose members were drawn from the three chambers of parliament, a closer look at the stipulations revealed that the (white) House of Assembly still controlled the nomination and election of candidates. Thus the State President simply acquired the powers of an executive President (as in the United States, for example) but his political base was still founded on his position as leader of the majority party in parliament.[49] The old

47. Deon J. Geldenhuys, *The Diplomacy of Isolation*, pp. 118–19.
48. See, for example, Brian Pottinger, *The Imperial Presidency* (Johannesburg: Southern Book Publishers, 1988).
49. L.J. Boulle, *Constitutional Reform and the Apartheid State* (New York: St Martin's Press, 1984), pp. 204–5. See also Dion A. Basson and Henning P.

Prime Minister had, in other words, acquired new powers of a symbolic and personalised nature not deriving from his role as leader of his party. While the political base of the State President broadened beyond the majority party, the remainder of the cabinet did not now have to come from this party because ministers, could be drawn from three different chambers, each with its own political parties. Thus this system weakened the collective capacities of the cabinet to pressure the State President over matters of policy. The cabinet became more obviously an expression of the presidential political will.

Secondly, all existing central state departments were classified in terms of general or own functions, and then allocated to either the cabinet or the three Ministers' Councils. Own affairs typically consisted of community development, education, health, recreation, social welfare and other matters relating to the identity and promotion of one population group.[50] The cabinet was responsible for general affairs. Thus 21 departments were entrusted to it; 5 to the Ministers' Council of the House of Assembly; 4 to the Ministers' Council of the House of Representatives; and 4 to the Ministers' Council of the House of Delegates.

Ministers' Councils imitated the cabinet's functions on a smaller scale and racially exclusive basis. Each council acquired its own administration or collection of state departments. The cabinet treated each 'own administration' as one separate department. The four departments of the Ministers' Council in the House of Delegates, for example, were designated as Administration: House of Delegates and came under the authority of the Minister for Indian Affairs. The Public Service Act continued to apply. But, since Ministers' Councils also took charge of the personnel administration of their departments, administrative oversight in fact became a two-tier process. The immediate overseers were the Ministers' Councils. Cabinet ministers were still the final executive directors but, where own affairs were concerned, they were at one remove from the scene of action.

Thirdly, during the 1980s people with powerful policy-making influence who were outside the cabinet appeared in the central state. Of course the advisory councils of the State President still existed.[51] One new voice emerged, however, in the development of the old office of the Prime Minister into an enlarged Office of the State President (OSP). The head of the OSP held high rank (director-general) and the position was

Viljoen, *South African Constitutional Law* (Cape Town: Juta, 1988), pp. 46–59.
50. Sections 14 to 18 of Act no. 110 of 1983.
51. The economic, planning, and scientific councils.

filled by a powerful Botha confidant, Jannie Roux. The authorised
establishment of the OSP was 200 employees, who through planning
branches influenced policy-making.[52] But perhaps the most important
voices were the committees created for cabinet,[53] with the State Security
Council (SSC) soon dominating others.

Although the cabinet's right to make final decisions was not challenged, observers quickly detected a *de facto* pattern of decision-
making which undercut the real influence of the cabinet. Because the
SSC was a statutory body, it was first among equals as regards other
cabinet committees.[54] Belief in an onslaught against South Africa
encouraged reliance on militaristic measures, about which the military
personnel of the SSC had the best advice and plans.[55] Even if this belief
were not shared by top politicians, the State President was an ardent
believer and he chaired the meetings of the SSC, which preceded cabinet
meetings. Under his leadership, deliberations of the SSC generated a
decision-making momentum that was hard for the cabinet to stop.

Finally, as previously noted, the SSC originated in poor security
intelligence advice given to cabinets during the 1960s. The SSC's initial
form and functions were to advise in the manner of a national security
agency, but later inquiries showed it lacked the administrative means to
perform its tasks. By the late 1970s, the SSC became caught up with the
larger cause of improving administrative efficiency, which was directed
by the then Prime Minister; it became the pinnacle of a National
Security Management System (NSMS), in effect from August 1979,
which was designed to co-ordinate government's executive functions
better. The NSMS took powers of presidential executive discretion to
previously unknown heights.

At the upper levels of the NSMS, the SSC was strengthened by adding
a staff and secretariat. In addition, 15 interdepartmental committees
(IDCs) and a working committee were created to pool efforts. The
number of IDCs was related to the most important functions of the state
– civil defence, culture, manpower and so on. The working committee
consisted of all heads of central state departments. Below the national
level, a hierarchy of coordinating bodies was created: 12 joint management centres (JMCs) at regional level; about 60 sub-joint management

52. See Mark Swilling and Mark Phillips, 'The Powers of the Thunderbird', in Centre
    for Policy Studies, *South Africa at the End of the Eighties* (Johannesburg: Centre
    for Policy Studies, University of the Witwatersrand, 1989), pp. 43–73; Fanie
    Cloete, 'Die Bedryf van Staatkundige Hervorming', *Politeia* vol. 7, no. 1 (1988).
53. A total of four were created, each with its own working group. The cabinet also
    acquired a secretariat.
54. Deon Geldenhuys and Hennie Kotze, 'Aspects of Political Decision-making in
    South Africa', *Politikon* vol. 10, no. 1 (1983).
55. Kenneth W. Grundy, *The Rise of the South African Security Establishment.*

centres (sub-JMCs) at sub-regional level; about 448 mini-joint management centres (mini-JMCs) within regions; and a host of local management centres (LMCs) for cities and towns. The administrative headquarters of the NSMS was located in Pretoria and, during 1986, it also acquired an operational headquarters in the national JMC (NJMC), chaired by the Deputy Minister of Law and Order.

The NSMS was intended to shorten and simplify the bureaucratic chain of command. LMCs reported to mini-JMCs, who reported to sub-JMCs, and so on up the line to the NJMC and SSC. Each NSMS entity had four committees. A committee for security (known by its Afrikaans acronym *Veikom*) required participation by the Department of Defence, the national intelligence service, the SADF, the South African Police, and the chief civil defence officer of the region.[56] A committee for constitutional, economic and social affairs (Afrikaans acronym *Semkom*) in practice drew most civilian bureaucrats together. A committee for communication (Afrikaans acronym *Komkom*), whose function was to manage information, required the compulsory participation of the Bureau for Information, the combined operations section of the SADF and other departments' public relations officers. Finally, the chairs of the *Komkom*, *Semkom* and *Veikom* met in an executive committee (*Uitvoerende Komitee*), elected an overall chair, and made use of a secretary. A four-part division of labour thus prevailed, with the *Veikom* dominating security issues, the *Semkom* developmental progress, the *Komkom* in charge of public relations and the *Uitvoerende Komitee* linking into the overall chain of command.[57]

Every government institution had to participate in one or other committee of the NSMS on national, regional, sub-regional, mini-regional and municipal levels. The individuals on the committees varied, but official representation by the most senior bureaucrat or her/his delegate was required. NSMS entities liaised with developmental associations.

In functional terms, the *Veikom* headed the security goals, the *Semkom* the 'welvaart' (progress/welfare) aims and the *Komkom* the public relations goals of the state.

56. This committee divided its activity between a joint intelligence committee (Afrikaans acronym *GIK*) and a joint operational committee (Afrikaans acronym *GOS*). The latter functioned when a security operation was in progress.
57. Annette Seegers, 'Extending the Security Network to the Local Level: A Clarification and Some Further Comments', *Politeia* vol. 7, no. 2 (1988); James Selfe, 'The Total Onslaught and the Total Strategy: Adaptations to the Security Intelligence Decision-making Structures under P.W. Botha's Administration', unpubl. MA thesis, University of Cape Town, 1987; Swilling and Phillips, 'The Powers of the Thunderbird', pp. 29–73.

Table 2.12   THE NSMS IN OUTLINE

CABINET

National level	SSC	National Regional Development Advisory Council	Parliament
	NJMC*		
Regional level	JMC*	Regional Development Advisory Committees	Provincial Administration
Sub-regional level	Sub-JMC*	Sub-regional Development Associations	Regional Services Councils
	Mini-JMC*		
Local level	Local Management Centres*	Local Organisation for Community Development	Local Authorities

* JMCs, sub-JMCs, mini-JMCs and Local Management Centres each divided into four committees: the executive committee, *Komkom*, *Semkom* and *Veikom*. At the NJMC level, the nomenclature of these committees varied.

Interpretations of the NSMS have understandably varied. Some argued that it represented a creeping military coup because it involved military ideas and men.[58] Similarly, others were concerned about the decision-making powers of the NSMS, which usurped those of parliament and other elected bodies.[59] But for our purposes it is important to note here that the NSMS wanted to make the bureaucracy more efficient and effect better coordination. This previously had been the task of the cabinet and bodies like the Commission for Administration.

Action on the perceived failure of the cabinet's leadership and bureaucrats' efficiency showed just how far presidential executive

58. E.g. Anton Harber, 'The Uniformed Web that Sprawls Across the Country', *Weekly Mail*, 3 October 1986; Peter Gastrow, 'The Real Message is: The Military's Ruling the Country', *Weekly Mail*, 7 November 1986.

59. Neill Ross, 'JMCs Usurping Role of Public Representatives', *Cape Times*, 28 November 1986, and the remarks of the Leader of the Opposition during the no confidence debate of 1984 in Republic of South Africa, *Debates of the House of Assembly*, 27 January–9 March 1984, cols. 29–106.

discretion could go. The NSMS' design emanated from the President's office in the late 1970s. A vast array of bodies were subsequently created to act as special overseers of administration, simply through a generous interpretation of the law which had created the SSC and by the President (then Prime Minister) taking over the portfolio dealing with the public service. And, although the chain of command led to the cabinet, it passed first through the SSC, which was chaired by the President.

The Size of the State, 1981–1989

Tables 2.13 to 2.18 are based on the Central Statistical Service's data cited in the South African Institute of Race Relations' (SAIRR), *Survey of Race Relations* for 1987/8, 1988/9 and 1989/90 (Johannesburg: SAIRR, relevant years). 'Employees' in this context refers to the average number of people employed per year, and is thus not strictly comparable to the figures given earlier. Figures here are likely to be conservative.

Table 2.13   TOTAL STATE EMPLOYMENT

Year	Employment		EAP*		White	Black
1987	1,679,051	(4.6%)	10,449,000		632,416	1,046,635
1988	1,757,994	(4.7%)	10,652,000	(1.9%)	659,295	1,068,377
1989	1,681,525	(-4.3%)	10,856,000	(1.8%)	609,188	1,072,337

* Economically active population, excluding Bophuthatswana, Ciskei, Transkei and Venda.

Note : Growth rates are given in brackets. The average growth rate of state employment between 1980 and 1987 was 4%.

Table 2.14   CENTRAL AUTHORITIES' EMPLOYMENT

Year	Employment	Change	White	Black
1987	519,031	30.7%	238,995	280,036
1988	511,051	-1.5%	232,815	278,236
1989	521,263	2.0%	233,673	387,590

Table 2.15   PROVINCIAL AUTHORITIES' EMPLOYMENT

Year	Employment	Change	White	Black
1987	194,469	-26.7%	68,716	125,753
1988	227,246	16.9%	74,973	152,273
1989	227,306	0.5%	73,549	153,757

Table 2.16   LOCAL AUTHORITIES' EMPLOYMENT

Year	Employment	Change	White	Black
1987	255,202	5.4%	61,982	193,220
1988	247,548	1.6%	62,292	185,256
1989	252,239	1.8%	63,533	188,706

Table 2.17   HOMELAND AUTHORITIES' EMPLOYMENT

Year	Employment	Increase (%)
1987	154,556	20.1%
1988	182,490	18.1%
1989	196,290	9.5%

Table 2.18 SEMI-STATE EMPLOYMENT

Year	Employment	Change (%)	White	Black
1987	557,793	n.a	262,723	295,070
1988	591,226	6.0%	289,215	302,011
1989	484,427	-18.1%	238,433	245,994

Note: The semi-state refers to: posts and telecommunications, transport services, public corporations, parastatal institutions, and the staff of universities and technikons. For 1989, agricultural marketing board-employment is excluded.

Until 1988/9 the state thus continued to expand, at a level well over the growth of the economically active population. A major cause of this growth – separate development – persists in the expansion of homeland authorities' employment. The growth in central authorities' employment is proportionally the largest, primarily because they were absorbing personnel from the provincial authorities in 1986/7. After 1987, however, growth slowed down and in some areas a negative growth is indeed detectable.

The Structure of the State, 1980–1990

As argued above, until well into the 1980s political interests deepened the expansionist and fragmenting habits of the state. The forerunners of the 1984 constitution and later legislation, as well as the mounting financial problems of the state, nevertheless introduced two sets of changes. These changes affected the horizontal and vertical dimensions of the state's structure.

The first series of changes refers to policies of privatisation. Although often explained as a necessary component of the government's capitalist/pro-Western bias, the embrace of the cause of privatisation was in larger part driven by government's need for money and efficiency. Revenue from taxation of the white population had reached an economic and political limit. Comparisons of public and private bureaucracies revealed gross differences in the quality of management and efficiency. Even state bodies run by management drawn from the private sector, like ARMSCOR, were held to be more efficient than ordinary state entities. The result was a general policy aimed at contracting the state's functions. The most visible example of this was the privatisation of the SATS. It remains to be seen what the final outcome of privatisation will be but, for the moment, it has expanded the size of the semi-state. A growing number of enterprises in which the state has a stake, but which it does not itself finance or manage, seems to be the prevailing trend.

The second set of changes concerns centralisation. It was previously noted that local authorities traditionally enjoyed some political autonomy, evidenced in (for example) resistance to post-1948 racial policy. The position of the provincial authorities was more ambiguous. About 85 per cent of their revenue came from the central state, but provincial councils were elected independently and, as such, were not merely leftovers of the circumstances of Union in 1910. What became of these second and third tiers in the 1980s?

The answer came in new legislation in 1986. Provincial elections were abolished. The State President henceforth nominated an Administrator and an executive committee for each province, an action justified on the grounds that blacks, coloureds and Indians needed to be brought into governance at this level. The provincial authorities were responsible for both general and own affairs. As the political base of provinces shifted to the central state, so important functions were lost to central authorities. Duties relating to education, hospitals and local government, among others, were transferred to the three Ministers' Councils and their Administrators.[60] The powers added to provincial authorities came at the expense of local authorities; after 1 October 1986 some black municipal affairs were transferred to the provinces.

Although some kind of second tier is likely to be retained in the future, it is unlikely to consist of four provinces. The Provincial Government Act of 1986 indeed makes sub-division possible. Indications about the direction of events also came in, for instance, several commissions of inquiry, the division of the country into developmental regions, reports of the National Manpower Commission, existing military districts and the format of the NSMS.[61] There also is evidence that, in at least one region (Natal), political interests favour regional/local arrangements, especially about race-related matters, over directives imposed by the central state.[62]

Local authorities felt the full impact of the distinction between general and own affairs. Most local matters were classified as own affairs and thus people living in the same area found their administration channelled into the three Ministers' Councils on the grounds of race. The remaining portion of local matters classified as general affairs was administered by a central state department, the Department of Constitutional Development and Planning. Legislation further eroded municipal autonomy, in financial affairs in particular; a 1985 Act provided for Regional Services Councils, which at the prompting of central and provincial authorities were able to transfer funds from wealthy municipalities to those judged to be more needy.[63]

Not all municipalities acquiesced to the centralising thrust of racial policy. Interestingly, cities and towns hit hardest by the violence, boycotts and other unrest of the 1980s developed 'local initiatives'. These continuing initiatives have included insistence on a colour-blind municipality, the incorporation of formerly excluded groups into local decision-making bodies, and even mobilising-populist approaches.[64]

60. See the Provincial Government Act, no. 69 of 1986.
61. A good account can be found in W. Cobbett *et al.*, 'South Africa's Regional Political Economy: A Critical Analysis of Reform Strategy in the 1980s', *South African Review*, vol. 3 (1986).
62. In the KwaZulu–Natal Indaba.
63. See the Promotion of Local Government Affairs Act (no. 91 of 1983) and the Regional Services Council Act (no. 109 of 1985).
64. Atkinson, *Local Government Restructuring*.

Managing the State, 1980–1990

Frequent use of the words 'rationalisation' and 'privatisation' created the impression that the state in the 1980s had discovered the principles of administrative coherence and economy. The figures for state growth indicate that these principles were, until 1987, overruled by political interests. The number of people employed by the state grew by an average of 4 per cent a year between 1980 and 1987. Employment in central and homeland authorities accounted for the largest share in this expansion.

The widely publicised 1979 rationalisation programme, initiated on the basis of a Commission for Administration study, had little impact on the overall size of the state. But the rationalisation programme did oppose the trend of institutional proliferation by advocating a reduction in the number of state departments: from 39, the number was reduced to 22, under the control of 18 cabinet ministers.[65] Only in 1987 did a 'personnel standstill' recommended by the Commission for Administration come into effect: in terms of this measure, positions vacant for six months could be abolished and, for every new post created, an old one had to be abolished.[66] At last a brake was applied to state expansion.

The state's need for qualified personnel did not abate. The rationalisation programme of 1979 introduced a category of senior posts, Director-General and Deputy Director-General, to attract highly qualified personnel from the private sector and semi-state. But critical shortages continued in major urban centres, especially in the nursing sector, the police, the judiciary and the auditor-general's office. One consequence of these shortages was the advancement of blacks and women into central state positions previously held by whites males.[67] Many local authorities' services suffered as a result of staff shortages and were forced to act on low and unequal wages. In the latter half of the 1980s, salaries and benefits for central state employees improved. Here increases and parity were also major issues, multiplying by 151 per cent the amount spent on state employees. In 1983, money spent on state-employees under the authority of the Commission for Administra-

65. Paul S. Botes, 'Public Service Reform: The South African Experience', *Politikon* vol. 7, no. 2 (1980); Republic of South Africa, *White Paper on the Rationalisation of the Public Service and Related Institutions* (Pretoria: Government Printer, 1980).
66. Commission for Administration, *Annual Report* (Pretoria: Government Printer, 1990), pp. 25–6.
67. In the railways during 1981 and 1982, for example, 23,000 blacks were employed in positions formerly held by whites. As regards gender, 67.6 per cent of new appointees to the central and provincial state were women. South African Institute of Race Relations (SAIRR), *Survey of Race Relations in South Africa 1981* (Johannesburg: SAIRR, 1982), pp. 165–6, 173.

tion alone required R5.3 billion, rising to R12 billion by 1986 and to R13.4 billion by 1988.[68]

Promotions remained racially biased, however, especially as regards top positions in the central state: by 1988, about 96 per cent of positions were occupied by whites. Put another way, although blacks vastly outnumbered whites, of 2,827 senior officials in 1988, only 5 were coloured, 16 Asian and 17 African.[69]

But that these officials were white is only half the story. The management of the state also reflected a peculiarly Afrikaner style of doing things. A culturally tinged style of management does not mean the South African state is indifferent to modern methods and models of bureaucratic management. It has increasingly become attuned to technocratic ideas, but the way it implements these has been influenced by the cultural characteristics shared by its top leadership after 1948. This manner of doing things has many manifestations; in recent years, for example, it has appeared in the justification of organisation and work within the state (or bureaucratic ideology).

The features of this ideology are, among others:

– An hierarchical view of institutions de-emphasises institutional autonomy and encourages deference to authority. Officials' explanations of their actions invoke the fear of those above far more than the fear of being criticised or even cast out by their peers.

– Small groups are preferred and their existence is institutionalised. The permanence of small groups is striking.

– Members of small groups are ideally not innovators or too robust. Ideally they are enthusiastic/tireless but resign themselves to collective decisions. A good bureaucrat is a team-player.

– A good manager thinks first of the group's preservation, and cultivates loyalty by being stern and sticking to rules. If disagreement over a decision threatens the group, the decision ought to be postponed or diluted. In circumstances where a decision must be reached and unity cannot be secured, the recalcitrants are cast out and crushed.

– Very rarely is work just work. It is a commitment to something larger than the individual, and one can routinely expect employees not to be motivated purely by money. The commitment cuts both ways, however, because loyal employees will gain institutional protection.[70]

68. South African Institute of Race Relations (SAIRR), *Race Relations Survey 1987/ 88* (Johannesburg: SAIRR, 1988), pp. 326–7.

69. *Ibid.*

70. See my 'Institutionalising a Cultural Style of Management? Afrikaners, the National Security Management System, and State Power', paper presented at the Association of Sociologists of South Africa (ASSA) Conference, University of the Witwatersrand, 2–5 July 1989.

The origins of this ideology and style of management lie far in the past. The evolution of an Afrikaner political thought, its ideological variants in the twentieth century, religious life, the organisational mechanisms developed to overcome Afrikaner disunity, as well as the perpetuation of these in the contemporary educational system and national service – all are ingredients of a 'manner of doing things'. Although it best suits Afrikaners, this manner of doing things creates patterns of exclusion and inclusion which often defy expectation. Black people and women are as such not consistently excluded: mastery of the Afrikaans language in state offices in the countryside, a firm but non-assertive personal style, explaining yourself as someone who is basically persuadable, finding a patron, and acceptance of group authority can lead to respect and inclusion.

The State in a Transitional Era

President De Klerk's speech of 2 February 1990, together with many subsequent government actions and the referendum early in 1992, created a belief that a post-apartheid era was at last beginning. The driving forces of this transitional era are many, but at its heart stands a political generation of whites who find apartheid morally unacceptable and unworkable in practice.

The roots of this generation probably lie in events in the mid-1970s – the Portuguese withdrawal from Africa, the Soweto riots, and the obvious failure of the counter-urbanisation policies, (to name but a few) – which forced upon some aspiring Afrikaner leaders the recognition that the *status quo* was both fundamentally flawed and eroding fast. Just as the parents of this generation, Afrikaners economically empowered by their service in the semi-state in the 1950s and 1960s, could envision a world beyond *their* parents' devotion to radical nationalist mobilisation in the 1930s and 1940s, so the emerging elite of the 1980s could see a world beyond apartheid and counter-revolution.[71] As this post-apartheid generation moved into positions of power in, for example, church organisations and the National Party, meetings and statements reflected steadfast post-apartheid views.[72]

Life at the top certainly has changed. Within weeks of President De Klerk presiding over his first cabinet meeting, it was announced that the NSMS had been replaced by a National Co-ordinating Mechanism (NCM). Coordinating state functions would henceforth mainly be the

71. I wish to thank André du Toit for pointing this out to me.
72. Some bitter infighting was of course part of this shift, resulting in the strengthening of right-wing organisations and eroding the political independence of the government's liberal opponents.

province of regional and local officials.[73] In state administration generally, more conventional Westminister style management returned in the stress on the responsibilities of cabinet, ministers and heads of departments.[74]

Although protected by statutory status, the SSC was divested of its national decision-making role. President De Klerk, never a member of the SSC, does not chair its meetings. A new stipulation that its members be political figures was an attempt to purge the SSC of civilian and military bureaucrats' influence. The SSC secretariat's administrative strength has been slashed.[75] The cabinet now also has a second security agency, as a Cabinet Committee for Security Affairs (CCSA) was created. These alterations stem from two kinds of criticisms, within the state, of the SSC. The first made a case for maintaining the 'apolitical' nature of the bureaucracy and criticised the SSC for pulling bureaucrats and the military into uncomfortable collaborations with policy-making figures. The second criticism came from military men who argued that although the SADF was an instrument of the state, it should stick to military matters and not prop up a failing civil service. A 'purification' of the SADF agenda was necessary.[76]

For those outside the state, contracting military influence at the higher levels of the state has been an ambiguous affair. The main reason for the mixed reactions to this is the escalating violence. Although some would so argue, the contention here is not that government is the sole cause of violence. Various political and societal processes – apartheid, uneven and poor economic growth, homeland development and decay, the struggle against apartheid, the transition itself, and a host of others – would cause violence according to most analytical criteria. Yet it is hard to escape the conclusion that, on the part of the government, the behaviour of members of the military and police during some incidents and episodes of violence have not been consistent with changes at the top of the state.[77]

The most common interpretation of the inconsistency between state behaviour at the top and elsewhere is that the cabinet, including

73. The Secretary of the Cabinet, *Handleiding: Nasionale Koordineringsmeganisme*, 22 March 1990, pp. 1–3 ff.
74. See Commission for Administration, *Annual Report* (Pretoria: Government Printer, 1990), pp. 15–17; Hennie Kotze and Deon Geldenhuys, 'Damascus Road', *Leadership*, vol. 9 no. 5 (1990), pp. 12–28.
75. Overall, 50 per cent of the posts were scheduled to be phased out by the end of 1990. Information supplied by Mr A.P. Stemmet on 5 March 1990.
76. Information supplied by Mr A.P. Stemmet on 11 November 1989 and 5 March 1990, and by Mr P. du Preez of MILISTAN, a private firm specialising in military contracts, on 20 December 1989.
77. See the various reports of the Goldstone Commission.

President De Klerk, knows of such inconsistency but finds it politically useful. Hence the cabinet follows a dual agenda. On the one hand, there is the politics of negotiation and demilitarisation but, on the other, the SAP (for example) is allowed or by indifference encouraged to be passive during attacks on the ANC. Given regulations about bureaucrats' security of tenure, it is of course difficult for any incoming President quickly to assemble a team loyal to him and his political goals. But to my knowledge no senior state executive has been fired by President De Klerk, not even on the grounds of evidence produced by two recent commissions of inquiry about corruption and a libel trial.[78] Other than at the top of the state, the pre-2 February 1990 pattern continues as long as it directly hurts the ANC and indirectly strengthens government.

Another more ominous interpretation is that the cabinet, regardless of whether it knows of such misconduct, is powerless to stop it. This may be because it fears offending powerful members of the security establishment. The cabinet's relative powerlessness may also result from the very fragmentation and dispersal of coercive agencies. Vested interests in one or other part of the state are thus free to pursue their own agendas. In contrast to processes of centralisation, the means of coercive power under years of ethnic separatism became 'overdecentralised' among homeland authorities, local authorities and various other official bodies. Indeed, one of the paradoxical legacies of the past is that the state is both over- and under-centralised as regards one centre monopolising the means of coercion. Our second interpretation suggests that we may well overestimate the prevailing degree of governmental control over government as well as society.

The largest and most unambiguous change underway, however, is the regionalisation of the state's structure. This new trend emerged in the late 1970s, with the *de facto* recognition that the economic independence of the homelands was impossible, leading to economic, decentralisation and industrial planning on a regional basis. Instead of the older ethnically inspired divisions, the practice became to devise units on regional-territorial grounds.[79] The NSMS, too, brought this non-ethnic framework to the security establishment. In policing, for example, the SAP structure was traditionally top heavy. All ranking generals served

---

78. The Commission of Inquiry into Certain Alleged Murders (the Harms Comission set up in 1990) and the Commission of Inquiry into Alleged Irregularities in the Johannesburg City Council (the Hiemstra Commission also appointed in 1990), as well as the subsequent libel trial presided over by Justice Kriegler in 1991.
79. Fur further discussion, see W. Cobbett *et al.* 'South Africa's Regional Political Economy: A Critical Analysis of Reform Strategy in the 1980s', *South African Review* 3 (Johannesburg: Ravan Press, 1986).

in headquarters located in Pretoria, and from here line and staff directives were sent to the 19 magisterial districts. Beginning in January 1990, the structure was regionalised by dividing the country into 12 policing regions. In 11 of these, a regional commissioner can finalise matters without higher intervention. Although the twelfth region is still the voice of the central state, the reorganisation aims for policing to be tied to communities and territory.[80]

Since administrative regionalisation has come about by way of bureaucratic discretion while a constitutional conference – Convention for a Democratic South Africa (CODESA) and its successor – is in progress, it is no surprise that it has been criticised as a unilateral and politically inopportune exercise of power. If the reasoning of regionalisation is based on efficiency and rationalisation, it begs the question whether a new government might not soon decide to re-rationalise the administration into new units. If regionalisation is politically motivated', it entrenches local political forces (ranging from homeland leaders and organisations to the political parties of the three-chamber parliament) against a central government. Thus it ensures that the logic of separatism continues, albeit in a non-racial form.

That the racial composition of the state reflects apartheid has been recognised, however, by the state itself as well as others. One calculation[81] of the central and provincial administration employment in terms of the old Population Registration Act reads as follows: at the level of deputy director and more senior posts in 1990, 96.6 per cent were white, 2.1 per cent Indian, 0.8 per cent coloured, and 0.5 percent African. Another calculation holds that, of the top five income brackets in the public service in 1990, 95.9 per cent of posts were held by whites.[82] As suggested earlier, simply to characterise these senior employees as 'white' fails to tell the whole story, as they are also 'male, generally Afrikaans-speaking, conservative, Calvinist and until recently NP-supporting . . . [a world closed to] Catholics, Jews and even English-speakers'.[83] Although it is not the only factor, this composition contributes to views that the state is a vehicle of minority interests, an enforcer of apartheid, illegitimate and unrepresentative. Even if transitional change were to bypass this state, it would still not be accepted.

What has been done? One avenue of change is the removal of racial barriers to promotions. Here the promotion of three policemen other

80. Republic of South Africa, 'White Paper on the Organization and Functions of the South African Police', (Pretoria: Government Printer, 1991); Republic of South Africa, *Annual Report of the Commissioner of the South African Police 1989* (Pretoria: Government Printer, 1990), p. 2.
81. *Hansard*, 14 March 1990.
82. *Ibid.*, 12 March 1990.
83. Patrick Fitzgerald, quoted in *Business Day*, 6 November 1991.

than white to the rank of general, as well as the promotion of a woman to a general's rank in the Department of Correctional Services late in 1992 have been hailed as breakthroughs in key areas of the state. The state has no affirmative-action-type policy, preferring to declare only that racial barriers have been removed. Another avenue is the training of suitable alternatives, either locally or abroad. As regards the latter, the Commonwealth Expert Group (CEG), notes that, of the top 3,000 positions in the state, 600 must be targeted for urgent replacement. The cost of training these people would be R18 million; the overall cost would be in the region of R300 million.[84] Of these, a scant ten people, drawn from various political parties, have thus far received a six-week training course at the Civil Service College in London.[85] The number of trainees in local government in Britain comes to 50.[86] Other training has been offered by the European Community, but this is on a far longer time-scale. Locally, several business schools and universities have rapidly developed management and training programmes. The business school of the Witwatersrand University, for example, aims to train 4,000 students from 1992 to 1997.[87]

Two constraints affect changes to the composition of the state. The first of these is cost. Training itself is costly, particularly for those designated to replace bureaucrats with 25 or more years of service. Further, if these senior positions become open by means of early retirement (with full benefits) and are then filled, the state effectively carries a double financial load. The second constraint is that any large-scale replacements will be viewed in a political light by both the employees affected and those who claim to speak for them. Given inflation, early retirement logically entails a slide towards economic distress for those involved. The government indeed has responded to fears about tenure by saying it will seek to entrench such tenure constitutionally.[88] Responding to the same fears, Dr Nelson Mandela has similarly argued for security of tenure.[89]

Regardless of their impact on changing its racial composition, cost and size have become the ruling themes of actions by and discussions about the state. As regards size, there is no political agreement on

84. CEG, *Beyond Apartheid: Human Resources in a New South Africa* (Cape Town: David Philip, 1992). The ANC targets 1,500 positions: ANC Director of Manpower, quoted in the *Weekly Mail*, 22 May 1992.
85. *Business Day*, 14 January 1992.
86. *The Sunday Times*, Johannesburg, 26 October 1991.
87. *Ibid.*, 26 October 1991.
88. Minister Gerrit Viljoen, quoted in the *Cape Times*, 25 October 1991. Reassurance about job tenure was a conspicuous feature during the Referendum. See *Die Burger*, 4 March 1992.
89. *Business Day*, 10 March 1992.

whether South Africa is over- or under-bureaucratised. The incumbent chairman of the Commission of Administration, for example, believes the bureaucracy is relatively small.[90] The Commission itself has indicated shortages in skilled personnel, as well as vacancies in non-skilled categories in certain areas.[91] The official view runs slightly differently, as it relates size to various factors. In these terms, the state has officially been described in various ministerial speeches as not cost-efficient, its role in the economy as too large and its structure not rational.

Between 1990 and 1992, figures on total state employment support the conclusion that size has remained fairly constant. Although employment figures fell in one sector, principally the semi-state, numbers rose in other sectors, mainly the central government (as in the rise in the SAP), some agricultural boards and the TBVC states (Transkei, Bophuthatswana, Venda and Ciskei).[92]

Cost has increased in leaps and bounds, particularly with announcements of wage increases. One official estimate of the state's total wage bill in 1992 is R48 billion.[93] Since wages constitute the major portion of state expenditure, savings have had to be attempted by other means. Initially, government was patently cautious about cost-cutting. It used private consultants to devise plans to make savings.[94] Smaller schemes involved cutting services provided by one part of government to another; selling assets, like the transport service, and privatising catering, cleaning, gardening and the maintenance of buildings.[95] Discussion about rationalising services duplicated under apartheid and the tricameral system was carefully avoided. Hence, for example, the 19 education departments of the three own affairs departments (with 192,762 employees in 1990) continued life as before.[96]

During 1992 bolder cost-cutting plans emerged. The target, according to Finance Minister Keys, was to reduce state spending by an 'ideal' of 3 per cent and the Public Service (defined by its Act) by 5 per cent. The brunt of cuts, estimated to affect 30,000 workers, was to be borne

---

90. His comparison, however, is with well-developed states, like Germany and Japan. One official figure estimates the current state employment as a percentage of the economically active population at 11.2 per cent. Figures deemed comparable were 25.5 per cent (Australia), 21.6 per cent (Britain), 23.2 per cent (France), 16.1 per cent (Germany), and 16.1 per cent (the USA). *Cape Times*, 17 July 1990; *Business Day*, 8 October 1991.
91. *Die Burger*, 6 January 1990.
92. Figures are drawn from the annual data of the Central Statistical Service.
93. Central Statistical Service figures for 1992.
94. The Minister for Administration and Economic Coordination in 1990. *Cape Times*, 31 August 1990.
95. *Business Day*, 26 January 1990.
96. Public discussion of such rationalisation was described as 'speculative and untimely'. *Weekly Mail*, 22 February 1991.

by early retirements and retrenchments in the security establishment. Elsewhere, vacant posts (as in provincial administrations) would be frozen and the contracts of temporary personnel not renewed.[97] Once a forbidden topic, the scrapping of the own affairs departments is regarded as the next phase, but of rationalisation rather than cost-cutting. Personnel would simply shift to general affairs departments.

Cost-cutting politicises workers. Indeed, a noteworthy feature of the transitional era is the expanding role of unions. These include organisations affiliated to the Congress of South African Trade Unions (COSATU), such as the Public Service League (PSL), the Posts and Telecommunications Workers Association (POTWA), the Railways and Harbours Workers Union (SARHWU), the National Education and Allied Health Workers Union (NEHAWU) and the Municipal Workers Union (SAMWU). Perhaps the greatest achievements of these unions were the strike of hospital workers during 1992, and successful wage negotiations. The Public Servants Association indeed was so impressed by the PSL's wage negotiations that it, too, sought recognition as a trade union.

At the start of the transitional era, the most frequently voiced fear was that white state employees were politically conservative and would block or try to derail the implementation of change. The Conservative Party especially would often designate the state as a last resort of resistance. Inconsistent state behaviour indicates that such fears may not have been exaggerated. But, given the geopolitical results of the referendum, the numbers of those resisting was inflated.

Yet ideologically inspired resistance is not the only attitude worth noting. Equally important is the bitterness of employees, regardless of their race, about poor salaries, the broken promises about wage increases and looming retrenchment. Surveys have already indicated that negative job-expecations, mainly financial in inspiration, have produced a cynical, fearful attitude about the future among the majority of state employees.[98]

Concluding Remarks

This discussion has taken note of the absence of a confessional tradition of writing about the executive, as it has of the availability of formal, policy and theoretical perspectives on the state. Taking an institutional approach, we know that the state sector expanded to employ well over

97. *The Argus*, 4 September 1992.
98. An Human Sciences Research Council survey, cited in the *Cape Times*, 29 July 1992.

1.5 million people, and that its form fragmented vertically and, especially, horizontally as well. This form clearly originated in the increasingly dominant political interest of minority rule: racial and ethnic separation. The South African state after 1948 simply became a product of Afrikaners' implementation of apartheid/separate development.

The flood of institionalisation was facilitated by a Westminster-style tradition regarding the public service, the oversight of the executive and the relationship between the Prime Minister and cabinet. These traditions were exaggerated – not eroded – by South African conditions, particularly the effective same-party rule by the National Party. The public service did not contain a high proportion of highly skilled personnel; rather, it included a large number of relatively unskilled employees who were nevertheless protected by typical Westminster-type regulations. Cabinet managers kept their hands off the bureaucracy to the point of indifference in administrative economy and coherence. The Prime Minister led by an apparently iron-clad consensus. Cabinet unanimity became solidarity. Although these habits may weaken, decades of rule by an Afrikaner bureaucratic elite bequeathed to the state a management style that will long outlive the end of Afrikaners' domination of the state.

What later came under the heading of reform in the 1980s in fact deepened post-1948 habits as far as the bureaucracy was concerned. At the same time as privatisation and rationalisation programmes were launched with much fanfare, the numbers in state employment grew by an average of 4 per cent a year. Ironically, the cure for the perceived illnesses of the state undermined the powers of the cabinet. As the underlying political interests, however, shifted from a belief in apartheid to a perception of the need for reform and then, by the beginning of the 1990s, as a post-apartheid order was initiated and a break with the past was attempted, new ideas and practices about the state have emerged.

The most visible indication of these emerging interests has been the declining influence of the security establishment at the pinnacle of the state. The diminishing influence of militaristic concerns and behaviour has not, however, been evident at other levels of the state. This may indicate duplicitous policies, but it may also point to one of the paradoxes of power in South Africa: that the state defined as a monopoliser of violence is, as a result of institutional separation, both too centralised and fragmented. The means of violence still 'belong' to too many entities who may find inspiration in any of the old ideas (like total onslaught) or new imperatives (mobilising against political opponents). The shaping of state administration on a non-ethnic regional basis may promote coherence in the interim, but its long-term acceptance and solution to the problem of violence remains unclear.

Measured in terms of its employees, the size of the state was affected by a freeze on new hiring as from 1987. This moratorium still holds, but not absolutely: figures between 1987 and 1992 still show an overall, albeit small, increase in state employees. The cost of maintaining the state has risen dramatically, however, and the wage bill alone has necessitated cutbacks. These have primarily affected the semi-state and the security establishment. Instead of politically inspired resistance, observers have subsequently identified a loss of morale and cynicism among state employees.

The racial character of state employment has remained fairly constant. In other words, although more than two-thirds of state employees are not white, the senior positions are held by whites. Change has been widely accepted as necessary, but the speed and cost of it are clearly controversial. Foreign programmes may assist in lowering the costs, but in the main these will have to be borne locally – with inescapable increases in the state's wage bill.

Finally, what state will any new rulers inherit? Reducing the size of the bureaucracy is an extremely difficult task. To remove bureaucrats on political grounds would violate regulations on which the entire public service is based. Retrenching larger numbers for reasons of economy would be just as difficult to achieve, as it would create a crisis for literally millions of current and former state employees. Much will depend on cost, and if inflation continues the state will come under increasing pressure.

3

THE HEAD OF GOVERNMENT AND THE PARTY

Nic Olivier

Between 1948 and 1991 important shifts occurred in the parliamentary and constitutional framework of South Africa which affected the powers, role and functions of the Prime Minister/State President and his relationship with the caucus and parliamentary party.

Between 1948 and 1983 there was a consistency in the functions and powers of the Governor-General and (after 1961) State President, and the relationship of these to the Prime Minister, reminiscent of the Westminster system. With the new constitutional dispensation of 1983, there was radical change (see chapter 1 above). The office of Prime Minister was abolished and the powers and functions of head of state and head of government came to reside in one office, that of State President. The much wider powers and functions of that office have since greatly influenced, both directly and indirectly, relations between the State President and the cabinet and caucus (in effect, the parliamentary party).

It is impossible, however, to divorce the office from the individual and his or her personality and personal style of government. Certainly, interpersonal relationships and attitudes play a major role in leading a country, as can be seen in a comparison between, for instance, Mrs Thatcher and her predecessors and successor in Britain. In South Africa, there have been tremendous differences in the style of government and in the nature and quality of leadership displayed by P.W. Botha and the current presidential incumbent, F.W. de Klerk, despite the fact that the constitutional framework remained the same during their terms of office. The widely divergent personalities, backgrounds and statures of Malan, Strijdom, Verwoerd, Vorster, Botha and De Klerk have likewise been key factors in determining the relationship between the leader of the nation and his party.[1]

Other related factors have quite important repercussions on this relationship too. These include the composition of the caucus and the age of caucus members; their exposure to other influences outside party associations; and the sense of unity within the party and the caucus – which seems to be a function of the absence or presence of dominant

---

1. See the section below on the personality of the leader.

controversial issues, of interpersonal and ideological conflicts and of debilitating personal rivalries which overshadow any shared convictions.

The following are some of the more important factors that influence the relationship between the Prime Minister/State President and the cabinet and caucus. At the same time they represent, I believe, some of the main factors that have helped maintain unity within the National Party (NP) and enabled it to remain in control of the government since 1948. These factors, to be discussed in this chapter, are:

- the electoral threat posed by the opposition;
- the need to retain power;
- the role of, and loyalty to, traditional leaders;
- the importance of a shared ideology;
- the principle of collective cabinet responsibility;
- the role of the caucus;
- the role of Afrikaner nationalism;
- control of the party machine;
- the role of political patronage;
- the role of the media; and
- the personality of the leader.

The Electoral Threat Posed by the Opposition

In parliamentary democracies one of the main concerns of a governing party is the threat posed by the main opposition party. The fear of being ousted at the next general election plays an extremely important role in government policies and actions. It places a strong compulsion upon the parliamentary leader of the party (Prime Minister/State President in the case of South Africa) not to estrange the parliamentary members of his or her party, as it is the parliamentary caucus which elects and can dismiss him or her. Thus he or she must ensure continued loyalty and support from cabinet colleagues and the party (caucus). As long as these members consider it likely that the party will win the next election under his or her leadership, they will continue to support their leader. But, as soon as they see the leader as an electoral liability, disintegrative forces emerge. As Rose states, '. . . the more portents of electoral defeat confront the governing party, the more the Prime Minister's authority is eroded.'[2]

This fear of losing an election is, of course, also influenced by the strength and the potential or real popular appeal of the opposition. Fear is more likely to arise in a two-party situation where each party has the

2. R. Rose and E.N. Suleiman, (eds.), *Presidents and Prime Ministers* (Washington DC: American Enterprise Institute for Public Policy Research, 2nd printing 1981), p. 11

potential to muster sufficient public support to win the election. In a deeply divided society, particularly when these divisions are compounded by great numerical differences in support, other factors may become dominant.

There is an impression that South Africa's political history has been characterised by this two-party phenomenon; in fact, at least before 1953, this is only partly true. After the death of Louis Botha, the first Prime Minister after Union, the Unionists and the South African Party joined forces to form the government. From 1924 to 1929 there was a pact government in office consisting of the National Party and the Labour Party; in 1933–34 the Fusion government comprising the National Party and the South African Party – later to become the United Party – was in power. After the declaration of war the United Party governed, assisted by the Dominion Party and the relics of the Labour Party. And in 1948 the general election was won by the combined forces of D.F. Malan's Herenigde Nasionale Party (the forerunner of the modern National Party) and Havenga's Afrikaner Party. Since then there has been an unbroken period (44 years) of National Party dominance, with the traditional opposition party or parties displaying increasing inability to pose an electoral threat to it.

However, the National Party–Havenga combination, (given the slight majority it had after the 1948 election, was deeply concerned about the outcome of the following election, due in 1953. The fear of losing was real, especially after the government had lost the Paarl Provincial by-election in 1949 (the parliamentary seat had been captured by the NP in the 1948 election). Bear in mind that losing a general election would have had, at that stage in South African history, far greater significance than merely changing the governmental office-bearers; what was at stake in the view of the NP was the future of the Afrikaner nation and of the whites.

The need to stay in power and the fear of losing the election had implications for relations within the cabinet, the caucus and the parliamentary party. On the one hand there was the section (basically under the leadership of Strijdom, later to succeed Malan as Prime Minister) which believed that the best way to win the election was to take an uncompromising stand on race policy, especially on the matter of the coloured vote, and on the republican issue. The other section, in which Havenga played a leading role, felt that precipitate action and policies might endanger the future of the government. Undoubtedly there were also deep philosophical and ideological differences under-lying these conflicts, and constant attempts had to be made to forestall a schism in the party.[3]

3. See, e.g. B.M. Schoeman, *Van Malan tot Verwoerd* (Cape Town: Human and Rousseau, 1973).

There is no doubt that the leadership of Malan and the respect in which he was held, plus the fear of losing the next election, created overriding loyalties that prevented these conflicts or any personal animosities from gaining the upper hand.

The perceptions about the outcome of an upcoming election, or of following elections, have an equally important impact on the main opposition party. If it is unlikely that the opposition will oust the ruling party, the loyalties within the former are put under severe strain. These tensions can easily lead to defections, challenges to the leadership and disintegration within the opposition. The United Party (the main opposition party in 1948) suffered from such tensions, to the point that the party eventually disbanded.

Fear of defeat is closely related to another factor, namely the need to retain power above everything else.

The Need to Retain Power

In parliamentary democracies the ruling party will do everything possible, within the framework of accepted democratic principles and the rules of the game, to stay in power.

Where the differences between the parties are relatively minor – and this will not be conceded easily by any of the parties, as it is the perception of the differences in policy which draws and maintains support from voters – any party can supplant another without much effect. Where the differences are truly fundamental, a change of government obviously has major consequences.

In the post-1948 South Africa the issues at stake for the National Party were momentous. The two driving forces which had catapulted the NP into power were Afrikaner nationalism and the policy of apartheid or separate development, which was presented as the only policy which could ensure white hegemony and racial purity in South Africa. NP supporters could imagine nothing more tragic than to be voted out of power, with all the incalculable implications and consequences of such a scenario. Retaining political power was, or was seen to be, a matter of life and death for Afrikanerdom. This perception was so powerful that it prevented potential conflicts and disintegrative forces within the NP from threatening party unity.

There were, indeed, important areas of difference within the party. There was little love lost between Havenga (co-leader with Malan) and Strijdom and some of his colleagues. These differences concerned not only personalities but important ideological issues too. For example, there was conflict over the procedure to be followed in order to remove the coloured people in the Cape from the voters' roll; over the entrench-ment of language rights, the sovereignty of parliament, the republican issue, and the relationship with the British Crown and the Common-wealth; over the policy to be followed regarding the Africans, and over the successor to Malan.[4]

Particularly virulent and threatening to the unity of the NP were the strong provincial loyalties; for a long time there was open antagonism between the Transvaal and the Cape branches of the NP. This came to the fore when new leaders for the provincial parties and a new national leader had to be chosen. After Malan, until 1978, all the leaders came from the Transvaal (Strijdom, Verwoerd, Vorster); had it not been for the Information Scandal it is unlikely that P.W. Botha of the Cape would have won the day against 'Connie' Mulder of the Transvaal in 1978.[5] Provincialism has remained a major factor in South African politics – as reflected in present-day Arikaner politics, in which the Transvaal and the Free State are the main power bases for the Conservative Party.

This provincialism was very evident in the Afrikaans press. For many years there was a bitter fight between the Cape-based NP newspapers and those in the Transvaal. Much of the acrimony centred on the decision of Nasionale Pers to publish its own Sunday newspaper in the Transvaal.[6]

Despite these differences and the heat they engendered, however, there was never a real possibility in those years of the NP breaking up. Such a break-up was precluded, I believe, by the implications it held for the Afrikaners and for their belief system and political future.

These concerns, which themselves prevented dissenters from forcing issues to the point of causing a rift in the party and thereby endangering the very fibre of the still tenuous Afrikaner unity, provided the leadership with a powerful tool. So equipped, they were able to enforce acquiescence and quell any incipient challenges, and to keep alive a sense of joint destiny within the caucus.

Loyalty and the Role of Traditional Leaders

The success of the National Party in maintaining political dominance for so many years is due in large part to the respect enjoyed by its leaders. This is especially true of the 1948–58 period and, to a lesser extent, of the years from 1966 to 1978.

Malan had led the NP out of a political wilderness into an election victory in 1948. Prior to that, he had built a reputation as an effective,

4. For a description of the role played by some of these issues in the caucus and parliamentary party see e.g. chapters I to VI of *ibid*.
5. For a graphic description of this fight, see chapter VI in *ibid*.
6. See in this connection John D'Oliveira, *Vorster – the Man* (Johannesburg: Ernest Stanton, 1977), pp. 128–76.

hard-hitting and clear-thinking opposition leader after 1934. He had made notable contributions while part of the Hertzog cabinet. For example, he had pressed successfully for the recognition of Afrikaans as an official language, which carved a special niche for him in the hearts and minds of many Afrikaans-speaking Nationalists. In that sense he wielded enormous influence in his cabinet and especially in the caucus – and consequently in the parliamentary party. As a result, even with the substantial degree of infighting noted in available records from his period, there was never any serious challenge to Malan's leadership.

The same is true, to a considerable extent, of the premiership of Strijdom, the 'lion of the north' who for so many years was the only representative of the party in the Transvaal. He had become known for his uncompromising attitude, especially on race relations, Afrikaans–English relations and dedication to the republican principle. After defeating Havenga in the premier stakes, Strijdom succeeded in consolidating the cabinet and caucus behind him. Although there were people in the party who disliked him personally, he succeeded in winning their nominal support and prevented a split. Despite his often voiced intransigence he was prepared to compromise, and he had a charming and endearing personality. (This could not be said of his predecessor, Malan, nor of his successor, Verwoerd.) I have often wondered whether South African history would not have taken a totally different direction had he not died after only four years as Prime Minister.

I do not include Verwoerd or P.W. Botha in my list of traditional leaders, for obvious reasons. I shall discuss their leadership roles later.

In the sense that Malan and Strijdom are described as traditional leaders, John Vorster is not. He succeeded Verwoerd after his assassination in 1966, in the midst of raging rumours outlining various plots to overthrow the government. His election is ascribed to his record as a tough Minister of Justice and as somebody who could deal with any possible threat to security.[7] Vorster had also previously been a member of the pro-Nazi Ossewa-Brandwag organisation, and his internment for anti-English sentiments during the Second World War enhanced his status. He had a powerful personality, was a good orator and had a sense of humour. In certain respects, however, he was the forerunner of change in South Africa and had serious problems within the caucus; this eventually led to the breakaway in 1968 of the Herstigte Nasionale Party (Reconstituted National Party) under the leadership of Jaap Marais and Albert Hertzog. It also marked the beginning of the ideological fight between Vorster and Botha on the one hand and the Transvaal right-wingers on the other.

7. See in this connection *ibid.*, pp. 44–104.

In this respect an interesting question arises. Do Afrikaners, who at least until fairly recently formed the bulk of the NP membership, have a particular reverence for their traditional leaders? It would appear that they do, although far less so now than a few decades ago. Apart from historical events which shaped this attitude, it is also likely that Biblical beliefs and precepts played an important role. Considering the close identity the older generation of Afrikaners felt with the history of the Jews in the Old Testament, it is not without significance that for the first 38 years after the Union the political leaders were all generals from Boer War days. And the fact that Malan was a Dutch Reformed minister of religion was an important element that enhanced his stature among his own people and prevented any serious challenge to his leadership.

The Importance of a Shared Ideology in Maintaining Unity

In the NP endeavours to achieve and retain political power, ideological factors played an important, if not dominant, role. There can be little doubt that for the Afrikaner, nationalism and racism (afterwards embodied in the doctrine of apartheid) were probably the two most powerful factors bringing them into the NP fold. The National Party was fully aware of the strength of appeal these two factors had for the white electorate and successfully exploited them for its own purposes. It must be borne in mind that NP members actually firmly believed in Afrikaner nationalism and in a racial policy which denied the concepts of racial equality and common political nationhood. Once it became clear that the white (Afrikaner) electorate was susceptible to this kind of exploitation, however, the NP's determination to stay in power led to increasing party-political use of these forces. And when a man like Verwoerd, with his outstanding intellectual capacity, presented these ideas with what appeared to be a logical, coherent and consistent policy in full accord with their own beliefs and prejudices, it is perhaps understandable – sad as it may be – that Afrikaners supported the policy without questioning its practicability, its moral content or its inevitable consequences.

The NP's repeated electoral successes – winning one after another general election with increasing majorities, resulting in the increasing powerlessness of the opposition – had the effect of reinforcing the potency of the ideology of apartheid and of Afrikaner nationalism. It also weakened the position of those NP supporters, inside and outside parliament, who had, or might have had, reservations about the racial policy of the NP. The hegemonic nature of Afrikanerdom, as reflected in and represented by the NP, rendered open dissension and criticism virtually impossible; those Afrikaners who dared to indulge in such activities were ostracised or had to pay the penalty in some other way.

Whatever judgment may be passed on the role of these two forces in securing for the National Party such a long period of uninterrupted rule, it is the effect these had in cementing the unity of the party, binding the caucus to its leaders and preventing major splits, that should be stressed. Even when there were serious disagreements about strategies to be followed (as happened on the issues of the majority required for a republic, the continued membership of the Commonwealth, and the removal of the coloureds from the common voters' roll), these did not fundamentally threaten party unity. This is amply illustrated by the nature of the two major breakaways from the National Party – in 1968 by Albert Hertzog, forming the Herstigte Nasionale Party (HNP), and in 1982 by Andries Treurnicht, forming the Conservative Party (CP). These splits came about because the leaders of the NP were perceived to have deviated from the path of Afrikaner nationalism and from the policy of apartheid.

The Role of Afrikaner Nationalism

As indicated above, Afrikaner nationalism and racism were the two main forces which wielded the NP into a single unit. After 1939, and especially during the late 1940s and 1950s, the Afrikaners were unified into a single entity which became almost organic in nature. This was the nature of the process which, although at times on the point of breakdown because of differences among the leading political figures and Afrikaner organisations, eventually led to the political embodiment and realisation of Malan's appeal: 'Bring together those who belong together.'

There was no room for non-Afrikaners, at least not as full participants and sharers. The Afrikaners outside the fold (in other words, those who still supported the opposition, the United Party) were excluded from any involvement in Afrikanerdom and from participating in its various semi-political, cultural and other organisational activities. The National Party served as the political arm of this organism; but as in any other organism there were also other functional organs which constituted this entity. The National Party did not, could not, operate otherwise than as an essential cog in the whole structure. Important other elements were the Afrikaans churches and cultural associations like the Afrikaner Broederbond, the FAK (Federasie van Afrikannse Kulturverenigings), the ATKV (Afrikannse Taal en Kultuurvereniging), the (white) Mineworkers Union, the Ruiterwag, the Rapportryers, the Economic Institute and Reddingsdaadbond, and the Voortrekkers and other youth movements. Most of the NP politicians (including most members of the cabinet) were members of one or more of these organisations; the cross-cutting and overlapping membership created a particular bond, a sense of unity and common destiny among Afrikaner nationalists. This was of immense significance in solidifying the unity within the parliamentary party (superceding possible personal conflicts and differences) and bringing about a sense of loyalty to the elected leader of the party.

It is fascinating to investigate the relationships between the leaders of the NP and some of these organisations, stormy though they sometimes were,[8] but this cannot be done in this chapter. Suffice it to say that a process of growing disintegration and separation took place, evidenced by, *inter alia*, the breakaway of the HNP and the CP. Today the NP is no longer the sole, and perhaps not even the dominant, political home of the Afrikaner. This disintegration, however, made it possible for the NP to rid itself of some of the shackles of political immobility and senseless ideology, and gain a much broader base of public support.

The Role of the Caucus

The relationship between the caucus (in effect the parliamentary party) and the Prime Minister/State President is of crucial importance. In the Westminster model, the caucus is the one place where discussions take place in an atmosphere of complete openness, where differences of opinion are expressed freely and all members have equal status. Age and seniority play a minor part in that everyone is entitled to express an opinion and be listened to by his or her colleagues – although in practice speakers are often subtly ranked and the opinions expressed by the leader, members of the cabinet and other party stalwarts would carry more weight than that of a newcomer.

Caucus decisions are binding upon the parliamentary party, including members in the cabinet. An important caucus function is to keep party members, especially ordinary members of parliament, in close touch with the leader and the cabinet.

In South African politics, attendance at the caucus is compulsory (the chief whip or the chair of caucus has to be advised of a member's absence). Discussions take place *in camera*, which means it is assumed that caucus members do not discuss caucus matters with outsiders. It is well known that elements of the media, particularly those opposed to the government, and the opposition parties will try very hard to discover the nature of caucus discussions and decisions, especially when there are suspicions that the governing party is undergoing a crisis.

On many occasions the relationship between the NP caucus and the

---

8. This happened at different times under all the NP leaders – see e.g. the discussion on Vorster's sport policy described by B.M. Schoeman, *Vorster se 1000 Dae* (Cape Town: Human and Rousseau, 1974), pp. 22–32; also pp. 195–207.

Prime Minister/State President has been quite stormy.[9] On issues of policy and strategy, successive leaders have made it clear that ultimately the decision is the leader's, and the caucus cannot prescribe to him.[10] At one stage Malan even ruled that there were to be no more caucus meetings to discuss a specific issue. But an unduly dictatorial attitude on the part of the leader has the effect of estranging the caucus, as happened in the last months of the Botha regime, and severely undermining the loyalty of party members.

An interesting phenomenon is that the caucus has its own administrative structure, that is, its own chair and other officials. The caucus, in addition to nominating the candidate for the premiership/presidency, also nominates its candidates for other important posts such as speaker and chief whip.

The Principle of Collective Cabinet Responsibility

The principle of collective cabinet responsibility has the effect of inducing and ensuring solidarity and preventing conflicts and differences from surfacing publicly. The cabinet normally allows free discussion of issues, without any formal voting. As chairman, the Prime Minister/State President expresses what he believes to be the consensus or majority feeling of the meeting and gives his decision on the point at issue. His colleagues are then committed to this decision; if a member does not agree he or she may either ask for the discussion to be reopened at a subsequent meeting, or refuse to accept the decision. Normally steps will be taken to resolve the impasse, usually by appointing a committee to negotiate some settlement, but if these attempts fail and the recalcitrant member feels strongly about this matter he or she has no option but to resign. Such a member may go so far as to attempt to get support for his or her stand from the caucus, but if the rest of the caucus supports the leader, it is extremely unlikely that this will succeed. (The caucus usually would also attempt to heal the rift.) Obviously this creates a

9. Vorster described his role and function *vis-à-vis* the caucus in the following terms: 'In the first place, you must do the very obvious: You must lead. You must lead in caucus, in parliament and outside parliament you must give a lead to your people. But, as I have so often said, no leader must ever get out of sight or out of earshot of his followers. And he must never try to lead from behind. Your followers expect that in all fields, but especially in the caucus where the most intimate matters are discussed, that you should give them a clear lead. A man who cannot give a lead in the caucus will find that his party slowly disintegrates. I would like to think that I am giving a lead and that I am keeping the correct distance between myself and my followers. And I like to think that I know where I am going . . .' Quoted in D'Oliveira, *Vorster – the Man*, p. 255.

10. See e.g. the episode described in Schoeman, *Van Malan tot Verwoerd*, p. 118–19.

crisis which could have serious repercussions for the member concerned, the leader himself and the parliamentary party.

The personal relationship between the Prime Minister/State President and his cabinet colleagues must be a positive one if the cabinet is to run smoothly. If the leader is unduly dictatorial or intrusive, he would in the long run undermine his own authority and the loyalty of his colleagues – which seems to have been the case with P.W. Botha.

It is equally important for cabinet colleagues not to embarrass the leader by taking a public position on an important issue that is contrary to his own, especially to the point that would provoke an open repudiation.[11] This happened, for example, when Foreign Minister 'Pik' Botha was repudiated by State President P.W. Botha for admitting the possibility of a black State President in South Africa. There is usually the understanding that the leader will not interfere in the public handling of a minister's portfolio. There is an equally important understanding that a minister will not encroach upon the terrain of a colleague or express public views on important political issues which rightfully fall within the domain of the leader – at least, not without prior consultation.

Control of the Party Machine

Control of the party machine, both inside and (especially) outside parliament, has been a decisively important element in securing the position of the national leader in South Africa's history.[12] The NP is federally constituted. There had always been a grave danger (from a political and ideological point of view) of a split within the NP, owing to competitive and disintegrative provincial loyalties. Throughout the NP's reign since 1948 these loyalties have played an extremely important role, more pronounced at some times than others. Provincialism was especially strong in the conflict between Malan and Strijdom, between Verwoerd and the so-called Cape liberals and Vorster, and between Botha and the Transvaal *verkramptes* (hardline nationalists). The NP Federal Council, which includes representatives of the four provinces, has played an important role in preventing splits and unifying the party behind the leader of the day and the policy advanced by him. Successive NP leaders have consistently had the support and coopera-

11. Consider in this light the events at the meeting of NP office-bearers in Pretoria in August 1968 (during Vorster's premiership), described in Schoeman, *Vorster se 1000 Dae*, pp. 170–6.
12. For examples, see Dirk and Johanna de Villiers, *P.W.* (Cape Town: Tafelberg, 1984), pp. 68–70; Alf Ries and Ebbe Dommisse, *Leierstryd* (Cape Town: Tafelberg, 1990), p. 186–7.

tion of the NP Federal Council and consequently of the party. Quite obviously this support has tended to strengthen the hand of the Prime Minister/State President in the cabinet and caucus.

The Role of Political Patronage.

There is no doubt that in South African politics, as in most political systems, patronage has played an extremely important role in securing the loyalty of party members towards the leader. Rose states, with reference to the British Prime Minister:

Patronage is the most immediate and tangible resource that a Prime Minister can use to ensure loyalty within the governing party...The constitution vests this power solely in the hands of the Prime Minister. From the exercise of patronage — or the anticipation of backbenchers of receiving favour — flows much of the Prime Minister's influence upon colleagues, both senior and junior . . .

In making appointments, a Prime Minister can use any of four criteria: personal loyalty (rewarding friends); personal disloyalty (bribing enemies); representatives (naming a woman or a Scot, for example); and departmental competence. Of these four criteria, three are meant to maintain the solidarity of the governing party in support of the Prime Minister; only one relates to skills instrumental in running the government . . .[13]

Patronage, which often leads to disproportionate representation in policy-making bodies, has been a particular problem in the area of provincial representation in the South African cabinet. Unequal provincial representation has long been a divisive factor in the country's politics – consider the dissatisfaction felt by Strijdom when Malan appointed only three members from the Transvaal in his first cabinet, as against seven from the Cape. And Strijdom himself was given the politically unimportant post of Minister of Lands and Irrigation.[14]

Likewise, there was extreme dissatisfaction when Strijdom appointed his brother-in-law, J. de Klerk, to the cabinet in preference to other contenders, and there was great competition for Senate seats after the Senate was enlarged in 1955.

That increasing patronage is characteristic of the South African political scene is evident from Table 3.1. The introduction of the tricameral system expanded the potential for patronage; apart from the general cabinet, there are ministers' councils in each of the three houses, with ministers (five from each house) and a number of deputy ministers.

13. Rose and Suleiman (eds.), *Presidents and Prime Ministers*, p. 5.
14. See, e.g., Schoeman, *Van Malan tot Verwoerd*, pp. 12–13.

Table 3.1 LEADERS AND MINISTERS, 1948–1984

Date	Leader	No. of Ministers (excluding leader)	Deputy Ministers
1948	Malan	11	None
1954	Malan	13	None
1960	Verwoerd	15	4
1966	Vorster	17	6
1972	Vorster	17	6
1978	Vorster	17	6
1984	Botha	18	9

The Role of the Media

Disclosure of caucus discussions to the press is viewed as an extremely serious offence. Attempts to discover the guilty member, however, usually end without success as most media representatives will not disclose the identity of a source.

A healthy relationship with the press is an important aspect of politics. Commensurate with that, political parties work to develop and maintain a cooperative and friendly relationship with the press, especially with the parliamentary press gallery. Understandably, newspapers supporting the governing party are usually the first to be informed about important plans that the government may have, and serve as front runners in the public presentation of the views and reactions of the government to the issues of the day.

The Afrikaans press has been a staunch ally and invaluable supporter of the NP, and has probably played an even more important role than the politicians themselves in consolidating support for the NP, its leaders and its policies. From its inception there was a close link between the NP and *Die Burger* (the Cape Town Afrikaans daily), for instance. At one stage Malan was its editor, and thereafter he maintained close relations with the paper. Strijdom and Verwoerd had a less friendly, even critical, relationship with the press. Verwoerd went out of his way to compel the editor of *Die Burger* to toe the party line. It appears that there was a good understanding between Vorster and the editor of *Die Burger*, as there undoubtedly was between P.W. Botha and the paper in the early days of his term as leader.

Because of these close links, *Die Burger* has often carried information about the cabinet's decisions and discussions long before these officially become public knowledge, and sometimes even before the caucus is informed. *Die Burger* has also played an important role in referring to critical issues within the NP and taking a line that paves the way for actions by the Prime Minister and the caucus.

The extension of the influence of Nasionale Pers, the publishing company which produces *Die Burger*, from the Cape to the rest of the country (particularly in the Eastern Cape, the Free State and the Transvaal) played an enormously important role in strengthening the position of the NP leadership and in spreading the NP gospel.[15] The influence of the NP papers was important in containing the first major defection from the NP, which led to the creation of the HNP.[16] I am convinced that if the larger and more important split which occurred in 1982 (the CP breakaway of Treurnicht and his colleagues) had had backing in the Afrikaans press it would have had far more traumatic implications for the NP. The dominant position of the NP leader, the maintenance of unity within the party, the consolidation of Afrikaner support for the NP and the party's electoral successes – all these have been largely due to the close bond existing between the NP and the Afrikaans newspapers.

The Personality of the Leader

The personality of the leadership figure, whether in politics, business or any other sphere of activity, plays an extremely important role in consolidating support and in preventing internal conflicts within an organisation. Except for the initial period after a leader has been chosen, when by unwritten agreement he or she is given a fair trial and sufficient time to prove leadership qualities, a poor personal performance can lead quickly to that leader's demise.

For a number of reasons, the leadership of men like Malan and Strijdom was never really critically questioned, despite possible differences of approach among members of caucus. Malan's leadership was unchallenged partly because, as detailed earlier. for many years he had earned his political credentials. He was the man who had led the Afrikaners to the electoral victory in 1948. In many respects Malan represented, in his personality, the patriarch in Afrikaans society whose leadership, as far as his followers were concerned, was not easily to be criticised.

Strijdom's short period of leadership also went unchallenged. He was the sole MP in the Transvaal who had refused to join the Hertzog–Smuts coalition and he was known for his deep convictions and principles. He

---

15. For a discussion on the strong rivalry (ideologically and otherwise) between the newspapers of the Nasionale Pers and the other NP-supporting papers in the Transvaal, see Schoeman, *Vorster se 1000 Dae*, pp. 164–8, 177–203.
16. See e.g. Dirk and Johanna de Villiers, *P. W.*, pp. 34–7.

was politically fearless. He also had the personality and talent for creating and sustaining a sense of comradeship and collegiality among the members of his party. While he was Prime Minister he apparently enjoyed the unstinting support of the caucus and his colleagues in parliament.

Verwoerd, because of his intellect and ideological commitment to a particular approach and vision; his ability to provide an intellectually acceptable and logical motivation for apartheid; the consistency he displayed in implementing the principles of that policy; his ability to render his opponents' arguments worthless or illogical; his ability to utilise the political forces at his disposal both within and outside the NP; and, some would say, his ability to exploit the innate prejudices of the white electorate, was able to squash effectively the opposition which existed or arose within the NP against his policies. The fact that he provided the NP with what appeared to be a logical and coherent racial policy; that he stood up to Harold Macmillan's 'winds of change' speech; that he stood firmly against the vendetta waged against South Africa in and by the United Nations; that he was the man who transformed South Africa into a republic (and won the referendum on this issue) – all these tended to promote him beyond reproach. The first attempt on his life served merely to increase his stature and the loyalty and support of his followers.

Vorster, with his academic background, his record in resisting the 'war effort', his legal career, his toughness as Minister of Police and the circumstances under which he became Prime Minister (to some extent a rebound after the assassination of Verwoerd), enjoyed a status which in certain respects was even more unassailable than that of his predecessor.[17] He had an imposing personality and an excellent sense of humour, he was a marvellous orator and he dominated the political scene to a greater extent than possibly anyone before him. At the same time he was prepared to take political risks, for example in changing some of the

17. D'Oliveira in *Vorster – the Man* refers to a speech made by Vorster in 1968 in which he said: '. . . every prime minister in any country, not only South Africa, has his own specific problems and in most cases, if not in all cases, the problems with which he must cope differ from the problems of his predecessors . . . and he has his own specific approach to these problems. All that he has in common with his predecessors is that all of them were members of the same political party and all of them were bound by the principles of that party. But . . . I have noticed that it is fashionable to make comparisons so let me say very clearly: Methods which may have been valid in Dr Malan's time or possibly in Mr Strijdom's time can no longer be valid in 1968 because circumstances have changed radically since those days – and it is a foolish prime minister who does not take changed circumstances into account. I must apply the National Party's policies and its principles in the light of the changed circumstances in which I find myself.' See also Dirk and Johanna de Villiers, *P.W.*, pp. 96–9.

patterns in race relations.[18] The first split in the NP since 1948 occurred during his term of office, basically because of accusations that he was departing from the ideological foundations of NP policy.[19] In fact, it would have been difficult for anybody to match the ideological dominance of his predeccessor Verwoerd and hold the NP party together.

That split illustrates the importance of a shared ideological commitment in maintaining the unity of the NP; once that commitment loses predominance, other mostly disintegrative forces come into play. Neither Vorster nor his successor P.W. Botha were ideologues in the mould of Verwoerd, in part because they were not intellectually capable of emulating him. But, more importantly, after the demise of Verwoerd there was a gradual realisation that apartheid, at least in its original form, was no longer feasible. By that time, however, the value system and principles underlying the policy had become so firmly entrenched in the minds and convictions of many white voters that departure from the ideology contained the real risk of serious defections and dissatisfaction. Indeed in 1982 the Conservative Party was formed and broke from the NP because its supporters could no longer acquiesce in the new approach of the NP leaders towards old-style apartheid.

Increasingly the NP, because of growing English-speaking support, became less and less a pure Afrikaner party. In this process both Vorster and Botha played an important role – the latter especially went out of his way to woo the South African business establishment.[20] The close relationship between Vorster and Afrikaner organisations like the Broederbond, however, was never in question, despite the serious attempts of the opposing Hertzog group to build a support base for themselves in these organisations.

P.W. Botha entered his period as Prime Minister (later State President) with the slogan 'adapt or die'. He, more than anybody else, was fundamentally responsible for the demise of Verwoerd's ideology as an ideology and for the move towards the creation of a more egalitarian society.[21] (The final steps in this process, however, came only with the advent of F.W. de Klerk). The effect of the Botha policy was to drive more and more Afrikaners away from the NP into the arms of the Conservative Party and other right-wing organisations,[22] to the point

---

18. For a detailed discussion of these events, see D'Oliveira, *Vorster – the Man*, pp. 225–44; Ries and Dommisse, *Leierstryd*, p. 51.
19. See e.g. Dirk and Johanna de Villiers, *P.W.*, 1984, pp. 156–64.
20. For a description of some of the changes, see Ries and Dommisse, *Leierstryd*, pp. 61–4; Dirk and Johanna de Villiers, *P.W.*, 1984.
21. See Ries and Dommisse, *Leierstryd*, pp. 18–26.
22. See e.g. Eschel Rhoodie, *P.W. Botha: The Last Betrayal* (Melville: SA Politics, 1989), pp. 89–98, Ries and Dommisse, *Leierstryd*, pp. 213–21, 228–39, 245–7; Dirk and Johanna de Villiers, *P.W.*, pp. 139–41.

where at the beginning of the 1990s the CP had the support of at least 35–40 per cent of Afrikaners. The 'reform' policy of F.W. de Klerk has obviously contributed extensively to the strengthening of these right-wing elements. Thus the NP movement away from apartheid ideology has split the Afrikaner nation asunder and weakened the unity of the NP considerably. In this context, the personality of the party leader takes on even greater significance.

This significance is very apparent when one compares the presidencies of P.W. Botha and F.W. de Klerk. Botha, so it appears, was inclined to dictate policy to his cabinet and the caucus; he did not take kindly to criticism. It would appear, in fact, that not many of his colleagues would have dared to disagree with him. The powers bestowed upon him under the 1983 Constitution, in terms of which the State President is head of state as well as head of government, made him an all-powerful figure whose path was not lightly to be crossed. A case in point is his altercation with Allan Hendrickse of the Labour Party, as a result of which Hendrickse left the cabinet.[23]

Botha also had no hesitation in manipulating the public media to serve his own purposes.[24] His office was often referred to as an 'imperial presidency'. He built up a strong security establishment – possibly influenced by his former role as Minister of Defence – and seemed to take guidance from that quarter much more than from the cabinet and his caucus. As a result he, more than any of his predecessors, was influenced in his administration and policy by a body of people outside the formal party structures. This style of leadership does not tend to develop party loyalties, except perhaps among those who are, or hope to be, the recipients of patronage and favours. Under the circumstances it was understandable that when the eventual crunch came and choices had to be made P.W. Botha was left largely without the support that he needed to stay in office.[25]

The De Klerk Era

At the time De Klerk became State President nobody suspected that South Africa was in fact entering a new political era, one which in all fundamental respects was totally different and distinguishable from

23. For a description of this conflict, see Ries and Dommisse, *Leierstryd*, pp. 29–34, 72.
24. See e.g. Rhoodie, *P.W. Botha: The Last Betrayal*, p. 25; Ries and Dommisse, *Leierstryd*, pp. 73–4.
25. See in this connection Ries and Dommisse, *Leierstryd*, pp. 2–9.

those that went before. That era began with the unexpected and revolutionary policy announcements by De Klerk at the opening of Parliament in February 1990. Like Verwoerd, he brought into being a completely new direction – the very antithesis of Verwoerd's – in South African political and social dynamics, and one that is likely to be far more durable than Verwoerd's apartheid ideology.

In the process which has unveiled itself in the three years since the announcements, it has become evident that many of the factors and influences which played a role in the relationship between the State President, the caucus and the parliamentary party, as discussed above in this chapter, have either lost their significance or have been replaced by others. Two of the most important developments responsible for these changes are: (a) the fundamental change in the composition, and consequently the nature and character, of the National Party and more specifically in the NP parliamentary caucus and party; and (b) the much wider political environment (to a considerable extent created by De Klerk himself) in which the State President and the NP Government now have to operate.

From being an exclusively Afrikaner and white party the NP has become a multi-racial party, with a major injection of coloured members of parliament into its caucus. At the same time it has become more attractive to many white voters who in the past shunned it for various reasons. Increasing white support can be ascribed not to an ideological support for or involvement in Afrikaner nationalism, but to the consequences of the uncertainties and fears created by the very process which De Klerk had started. The binding force of Afrikaner nationalism, already weakened by the breakaway of the Conservative Party, has been relegated, at least as an internal unifying factor and driving force within the NP, to a position of practical insignificance (which does not mean to say that it is not still a major element in the political equation). As will be discussed below, the NP is intent upon recruiting to its ranks large numbers of voters from the black groups; consequently it has to project an image which is far removed from its traditional exclusively Afrikaner and white character. Symptomatic of this change is the uncertainty prevalent among some NP supporters about the future of the Afrikaans language and culture and the traditional symbols of South African nationhood, like the anthem and the flag.

It is understandable that the newcomers to the NP ranks do not and cannot share the same idealistic dedication to the party and probably do not have the same sense of loyalty to their colleagues that was characteristic of the old NP, in which dedication to its ideals, involvement over many years in advancing the interests of the party, working together in the various structures of the party, and so on, created strong bonds of friendship and mutual respect. Under the new circumstances personal ambitions and patronage may play an even more important role. In any case, the nature of the new composition of the caucus undoubtedly brings about a greater degree of diversity in political opinion and priorities, and consequently also potentially greater volatility. In such a situation the leadership qualities of the State President and his unifying, intercessionary and conciliatory function become more pronounced.

When President De Klerk decided to unban the ANC, the Pan-Africanist Congress (PAC) and the South African Communist Party (SACP), embarked on the road of negotiation with the express purpose of creating a new constitution and started repealing all the remaining racially discriminatory laws, he effectively brought to an end the era of white political domination. The various agreements arrived at between the South African government and the ANC (e.g. the Pretoria Minute, the Groote Schuur Minute) and the subsequent multi-party negotiations at CODESA changed the whole political environment in South Africa: it is no longer possible for the South African government to govern the country, or follow policies, or take unilateral decisions, without taking into consideration how these will affect the negotiation process and what the reaction will be among its negotiation 'partners'. It accepted the necessity to level the political playing field by, *inter alia*, allowing free political activity, including mass marches and so on. Internally it has been a very bumpy process, with breakdowns and deadlocks, accusations and counter-accusations, and new political rivalries and alliances. As indicated above, this has created uncertainties and fears among many of the whites; among the blacks it has exacerbated ethnic hostilities, leading to a virtual breakdown of law and order and 'black-on-black' violence on an unprecedented scale. Attempts to promote peace and tolerance (such as the National Peace Accord and the appointment of the Goldstone Commission) have had only limited success.

Moreover, to an increasing extent the government has involved international agencies and experts in the unfolding political process – a radical departure from the traditional rejection of 'outside interference'. Internationally many of the sanctions imposed on South Africa during apartheid have been lifted; diplomatically South Africa has developed relations which would have been regarded as unthinkable a few years ago. South Africa is no longer regarded as an outcast among the nations of the world. Concomitantly, the status of the ANC among the Western nations in particular has been seriously dented, and it is no longer regarded as the 'sole and authentic' voice of all the blacks in South Africa. Its cosy relationship with the SACP and the very strong influence of the SACP in and on the ANC is partly responsible for these developments and also for an increasingly unsympathetic attitude by many whites *vis-à-vis* the ANC and blacks generally. The increase in violence and serious crimes – to a considerable extent a function of massive unemployment and bad state of the economy – has contributed strongly to this reaction.

The general consensus which has developed about certain elements of the new constitution has also been of major importance and significance. One of these elements is the principle of applying a proportional election system to the election of the central legislature and, probably, to the regional constitutional structures as well. The various participants in the election due in 1993 or 1994 have have already started electioneering and recruiting new members; this is also true of the National Party, which realises that its future political influence and status will be determined by the electoral support it receives. The fundamental consideration, however, is that that electoral support will have to come from a combination of white, coloured, Indian and African votes. The days when it was sufficient for the NP to win white majority support are irretrievably gone. Many of the considerations and factors which determined the NP political strategy in the past, and which have been referred to above, are no longer relevant. The conventional electoral threat which played such an important role in unifying the National Party has assumed a totally different character – the choice facing the NP today is to form an alliance either with the ANC or with some of the other players in the political scene. Of course, this has to be seen against the background of the type of constitution which will be operative: whether it will be a Westminster winner-takes-all system (in which case the NP and its allies will do everything possible to gain the majority of votes), or whether there will be a system of power-sharing (in which case the NP will try to ensure that it has enough support to guarantee either a dominant or at least a major say in a shared government).

In the new political situation in South Africa the unifying force of a shared ideology will probably still play an imporant role in determining the political fortunes of the NP and the other parties, but that ideology will be something totally different from that which held sway in the past 40 years, viz. a combination of nationalism and racism. The dividing lines and inspirational philosophy will probably reflect issues like 'democracy', power-sharing, the economy (nationalisation against the free market), socialism/Marxism against capitalism, 'centralism' as opposed to 'federalism', the language issue and the issue of national symbols.

A legitimate issue which arises in the context of the developments sketched above concerns the leadership position of De Klerk and his relationship with the caucus. There seems to be little doubt that De Klerk's style (especially compared with that of P.W. Botha) is more informal and he has frequently used the format of a *bosberaad*, where the NP caucus withdraws to a private venue out of the public eye for intensive and open discussions. It is to be expected that the very nature of the political debate, and of the political decisions which De Klerk had or has to take, could or might have the effect of creating dissatisfaction or unhappiness among his cabinet colleagues. It is, for instance, rumoured that his 'demotion' of General Magnus Malan (former Minister of Defence) and of Adrian Vlok (former Minister of Law and Order) undermined the unity of, and his standing within, the caucus. It is also rumoured that there is unhappiness with the Memorandum of Understanding reached between the Government and the ANC on 26 September 1992; with De Klerk's handling of the ANC; and with the fact that the negotiation process has been entrusted to Roelf Meyer (in whom, because of his relative youthfulness and inexperience, some members of the caucus do not have the required faith). These rumblings have not seriously undermined De Klerk's position, but there is little doubt that he is walking a tight-rope within his own caucus and within the party. Any potential dissatisfaction with his leadership is muted by the fact that there is nobody else, at this stage, who is acceptable as State President and as leader. Indeed, South Africa needs his clarity of vision, his dedication, his integrity and purposefulness more than ever.

SOURCES

Birch, A.H., *The British System of Government*, London: Unwin Hyman, 8th edn, 1990.

Blondel, J., *Government Ministers in the Contemporary World*, London: SAGE Publications, 1985.

Campbell, C., *Governments under Stress: Political Executives and Key Bureaucrats in Washington, London and Ottawa*, University of Toronto Press, 1983.

De Villiers, D. & J., *P. W.*, Cape Town: Tafelberg, 1984.

D'Oliveira, J., *Vorster – the Man*, Johannesburg: Ernest Stanton, 1977.

May Erskine, *Parliamentary Practice*, London: Butterworth, 21st edn, 1989.

Ries, A. & Dommisse, E., *Leierstryd*, Cape Town: Tafelberg, 1990.

Rhoodie, E., *P.W. Botha: The Last Betrayal*, Melville: SA Politics, 1989.

Rose, R. & E.N. Suleiman (eds.), *Presidents and Prime Ministers*, Washington, D.C.: American Enterprise Institute for Public Policy Research, 2nd imp., 1981.

Schoeman, B.M., *Die Broederbond in die Afrikaner-politiek*, Pretoria: Aktuele Publikasies, 1982.

—— , *Van Malan tot Verwoerd*, Cape Town: Human & Rousseau, 1973.
—— , *Vorster se 1000 Dae*, Cape Town: Human & Rousseau, 1974.
Van Jaarsveld, F.A., & G.D. Scholtz (eds.) *Die Republiek van Suid-Afrika: Agtergrond, Ontstaan en Toekoms*, Johannesburg: Voortrekkerpers, 1960.
Wessel, F.J., *Die Republikeinse Grondwet*, Cape Town: Nasionale Boekhandel, 1962.

4

THE LEADER AND THE CITIZENRY

Hermann Giliomee

This chapter focuses on how the National Party leadership treated members of the different racial groups as citizens and on its conception of the citizenry in general. The discussion takes the citizenry to be all the permanent inhabitants of South Africa and citizenship as comprising three components: a political component concerned with the franchise, formal participation in the decision-making process and the more informal influencing of policy through party membership and the mass media; a civil component dealing with rights such as the security of the individual and of property, freedom of speech and of association, and equality before the law; and a social component which involves the provision of education, health and other social services to enable citizens to derive the maximum benefits possible from the exercise of political and civil rights.[1]

This chapter will not present analysis as that advanced by legal scholars on the dismal record of the apartheid state on each aspect of citizenship,[2] but will instead describe how the leadership mediated the differential rights and claims of the different political groups in the citizenry. To do so, it is necessary to look beyond the ideological pronouncements of the NP leadership or its black opponents.

Apartheid with its utopian ideal of separate nations, each with its own separate citizenship, fell far short of its ideological ambitions. Despite the divisions in the country there remained a common political and economic order which made it impossible to treat blacks as non-citizens in all the diffent components of citizenship. For example, for all the apartheid state's rejection of *gelykstelling* (levelling) between races, the principle of legal equality was a fundamental part of legal procedures and practice. As a recent analysis remarks,

1. This distinction between the different components of citizenship is derived from the work of T.H. Marshall (*Class, Citizenship and Social Development*, Garden City: Doubleday, 1964) and Talcott Parsons (*The Social System*, New York: The Free Press, 1964). See S.P. Cilliers, 'Industrial Progress: Its Social, Political and Economic Implications', in A. Paul Hare, Gerd Wiendieck and Max H. von Broembsen (eds.), *South Africa: Sociological Analyses* (Cape Town: Oxford University Press, 1979), pp. 209–18.
2. See John Dugard, *Human Rights and the South African Legal Order* (Princeton University Press, 1978); J.P. Verloren van Themaat and Marinus Wiechers, *Staatsreg* (Durban: Butterworths, 1981), pp. 344–96.

That blacks had access to the courts, that in principle (though not, of course, often in practice) they had equal standing as legal subjects, that whites could be held accountable in law for misdemeanours towards blacks . . . these principles became progressively established as uncontroversial aspects of the legal system and of a public order.[3]

Just as there was tension between the formal legal position and the apartheid ideology, the NP leadership was constantly torn between a commitment to apartheid as a goal in itself and apartheid as a mere instrument to preserve the state and the capitalist order. In the period under discussion, the latter conception increasingly predominated. Whereas the dictates of Afrikaner nationalism earlier impelled government to deny the citizenship of blacks, the demand for stability called for the recognition of the common citizenship of all South Africans.

This chapter will discuss three main periods during NP rule. The first is 1948–68, when the different Prime Ministers were Afrikaner leaders above all else; the second is 1966–89, when B.J. Vorster and P.W. Botha tried to transform themselves from Afrikaner leaders into leaders of the whites in general and, as imperial Presidents, the leaders of the entire South African peoples; and the final period is the rule of F.W. de Klerk, with the NP leader projecting himself as the leader of all 'minorities'.

From 'Volksleier' to White Leader, 1948–1968

The NP, which won power in 1948, saw the Afrikaners as the core group of the citizenry. Afrikaners comprised its primary constituency and it was they who would become the main beneficiaries of state privilege and protection. For the Afrikaners the state was 'their' state and the ministers 'their' ministers. Although white English-speakers enjoyed full citizenship, their relationship to the government and the state under NP rule was much more formalistic. Under the Westminster system their party had little opportunity to influence the political decisions of the executive and they soon tended to eschew employment in the civil service in favour of the private sector.

During the period 1948–68 the NP leadership tried first to cement the movement of ethnic mobilisation; secondly, it sought to win English-speaking support for the socio-political order and in particular for a republican form of government, and finally it attempted to deprive blacks of the political component of citizenship. The second and third trends prompted Afrikaner *volksleiers* (ethnic leaders) also to assume

---

3. André du Toit, 'Understanding Rights, Discourses and Ideological Conflicts in South Africa', in Hugh Corder (ed.), *Essays on Law and Social Practice in South Africa* (Cape Town: Juta, 1988), p. 261,

the role of leadership of all whites, but for most of the 1950s the leadership was concerned with the task of consolidating the Afrikaner *volksbeweging* (ethnic movement) behind it.

Consolidating the ethnic movement. Close associates of D.F. Malan report that after he had led the NP to victory in 1948 he exclaimed: 'At last we can feel at home again in our own country.'[4] 'We' referred to the Afrikaner nationalists. Malan's party saw the Smuts government (1939–48) as being dominated by unilingual English-speakers, of whom most had a stronger commitment to the British Empire than to South Africa. It also claimed with some justification that Afrikaner nationalists were kept out of high civil service positions during the war years on account of their political affiliations.

In winning the election narrowly (by a majority of eight) the NP attracted only 38 per cent of the vote against the United Party's 48 per cent. For Malan as leader, the highest priority was to cement the relationship between government, the NP and other Afrikaner political and cultural associations. Almost as much as being Prime Minister, Malan wanted to be the unquestioned *volksleier* – the leader of a unified Afrikanerdom which accepted the authority of the NP as the vanguard of the *volksbeweging* or national movement. The constituent parts of the *volksbeweging* – the Broederbond, the Afrikaans press, the Reformed churches and organised Afrikaner business – all served the Afrikaner people but at times tended to pull in different ways. Now the challenge was to consolidate Afrikaner rule through securing common acceptance of the political leadership of the NP. Malan depicted the party as the 'mother' of Afrikaner national consciousness and of the Afrikaners' language rights, their press, the broadening of their freedom and their determination to preserve white civilisation.[5]

For many years Afrikaner political unity was more an ideal than a reality. However, during the war years the NP had crushed the two pro-Nazi organisations, the Ossewa-Brandwag and the Nuwe Orde, which had set themselves up in opposition to the NP. Through an election pact with the Afrikaner Party in 1948 and the subsequent absorption of that party into the NP, Malan drew General J.B.M. Hertzog's supporters into the NP fold. Still on the outside, until as late as 1960, stood between a quarter and a third of the Afrikaners who continued to support the United Party. They had to be won over through persistent appeals to Afrikaner interests and ideals. Ben Schoeman, a member of Malan's first cabinet, frankly states that he advised NP candidates at election time to

4. Personal communication by Piet Cillié, ex-editor of *Die Burger*, 30 January 1991.
5. D.F. Malan (compiled S.W. Pienaar), *Glo in u Volk: D.F. Malan as Redenaar* (Cape Town: Tafelberg, 1964).

concentrate on Afrikaner voters and not to rely on the vote of English-speaking whites. If English-speakers did vote for the party it was a bonus.[6]

During the first ten years of NP rule Malan and Strijdom had great difficulties in establishing Afrikaner political and ideological coherence under NP leadership. Contrary to the impression given in many accounts, apartheid by 1948 was far from a ready-made system which the NP could purposefully propagate and implement. Looking back in 1985 Piet Cillié, doyen of Afrikaner journalists, gave an apt description of how NP rule unfolded. 'A system? An ideology? A coherent blueprint? No, rather a pragmatic and tortuous process aimed at consolidating the leadership of a nationalist movement in order to safeguard the self-determination of the Afrikaner.'[7]

Mindful of the Afrikaner schisms of the early 1940s, the leadership guarded against anything which could undermine the authority of the *volksleier* and of the party. The Broederbond was a case in point. Malan was a leading member of the Bond but his closest confidant, Paul Sauer, was not and on occasion expressed his dislike of secret organisations. Rather than turning to another Broederbond member, Malan appointed Sauer in 1946 and 1947 to head up important party commissions to formulate the NP's apartheid policy. Malan's successor, Strijdom, was also determined to prevent the Broederbond encroaching on his or the party's political turf. In 1954 he rejected a request from the Broederbond executive council to establish a special division of the Bond during the parliamentary session for out-of-town members of parliament. Strijdom subsequently told an executive council delegation 'with great emphasis' that the Bond should stay out of the political terrain and refrain from interfering in political policy, which was the prerogative of the NP. In 1957 Strijdom even refused a Broederbond request to arrange a discussion about the form a future republic should take.[8]

In the light of this it is baffling that a recent author can write: 'It was the Broeders who were the real authors of apartheid', and 'No Nationalist prime minister would dream of taking a major policy step without first checking it out with the Broederbond.'[9] In fact, the Broederbond during the 1950s clearly lacked a sense of purpose and direction. An authorised study of the Bond states that the organisation during this period was gripped by indecisiveness. In 1956 the Potchefstroom divisions of the Bond told the executive council that the Bond no longer

---

6. Ben Schoeman, *My Lewe in die Politiek* (Johannesburg: Perskor, 1978), p. 225.
7. Piet Cillié, 'Bestek van Apartheid', *Die Suid-Afrikaan*, Spring 1988, p. 18.
8. B.M. Schoeman, *Van Malan tot Verwoerd* (Cape Town: Human and Rousseau, 1973), pp. 120–1. Schoeman's book is based on the diary kept by Albert Hertzog, who was on the Bond's executive council and became a cabinet minister in 1959.
9. Allister Sparks, *The Mind of South Africa* (London, Heinemann, 1990), p. 177.

had a task or a vision. They had formed the impression that the NP kept the organisation on a leash, with the result that interest was waning. It added that many brothers were troubled by the fact that the authorities could not be criticised.[10]

The Bond received a fresh lease of life in 1959 when the new Prime Minister, Hendrik Verwoerd, instructed it to accept co-responsibility with the party to prepare the electorate for a republic. Verwoerd's intellectual strength, his long association with the Bond and close personal ties with its leadership made it easy for him to turn the body into his staunchest support organisation. It was Verwoerd who finally developed apartheid into a fully fledged, rigid ideology which could be applied to virtually any contingency. In the early 1960s the Bond appointed 14 'expert task groups' (later expanded to 19) which covered virtually the entire field of political, economic and social policy.[11] Since Verwoerd was at this stage in unquestioned control of the *volksbeweging* it can be safely assumed that the task groups accepted the ideological leadership of Verwoerd on all vital issues.

An uneasy relationship also existed between the *volksleier* and the Afrikaans press. This was closely linked to the conflict over the issue of provincialism. The NP was in fact not one but a coalition of four (or five if South West Africa – later Namibia – is added) provincial parties, each with its own leader, separate party organisations and congresses. The Afrikaans newspapers in Cape Town, Johannesburg and Bloemfontein were allies of their respective provincial parties rather than the national NP. To prevent the conflict from getting out of hand the *hoofleier* (leader or chief) had to project himself as transcending the provincial rivalries. Malan, however, was closely aligned both to the Cape Town paper *Die Burger*, of which he was the founding editor, and the Cape party. As a result strong resentment built up in the Transvaal against the 'Keerom Street clique'. (The offices of Nasionale Pers, which publishes *Die Burger*, and of the Cape NP were both in Keerom Street at that time.)

With Strijdom and Verwoerd in power the Transvaal began to dominate Afrikaner politics. This shift threatened to isolate Nasionale Pers both politically and financially. To regain its predominant position it had to publish its own newspaper in Johannesburg, the powerhouse of South Africa. This was inimical to the political and financial interests of the Transvaal leadership, who had begun to build up their own stake in newspapers. To block Nasionale Pers, Strijdom even resorted to

10. A.N. Pelzer, *Die Afrikaner-Broederbond: Eerste 50 Jaar* (Cape Town: Tafelberg, 1979), p. 177.
11. J.H.P. Serfontein, *Brotherhood of Power* (London: Rex Collings, 1979), pp. 84–8.

rejecting the company's application for an increased import quota for paper.

Nasionale Pers found an even more formidable opponent in Verwoerd. On becoming Prime Minister, Verwoerd succeeded Strijdom as chairman of the company which published the Sunday paper *Dagbreek* and also became chairman of the board of Voortrekkers Pers, which published the daily *Die Transvaler*. Thwarted, Nasionale Pers delayed expansion into the Transvaal market until the mid-1960s, when it sprang a Sunday paper, *Die Beeld*, on a resentful Verwoerd. With Vorster in power (his wife was a daughter of a Nasionale Pers director), *Die Beeld* quickly served notice that it would ignore the unwritten rule not to publicise differences in NP ranks in the Transvaal. With relish *Die Beeld* exposed the right-wing attempts under the leadership of Albert Hertzog to undermine Vorster's adaptations of apartheid policy. This brought into the open serious tensions within the Transvaal party and between the Cape and Transvaal press groups.

Perhaps anticipating problems of a similar nature, Verwoerd in 1959 opposed the introduction of television in South Africa. In cabinet he argued that it would be 'to the detriment of the Afrikaners'.[12] He was more confident of controlling the radio service and in fact turned it into an NP instrument by appointing Piet Meyer, head of the Broederbond, as chairman of the South African Broadcasting Corporation.

The NP leadership's efforts to promote unity depended ultimately on whether it could raise the Afrikaners to the position of a secure middle class and a racially entrenched status group. When the NP won power in 1948 some 40 per cent of the economically active Afrikaners were still blue-collar workers, while another 20 per cent were financially insecure farmers or agricultural workers. The NP's policy in the first two decades pf power was designed to give whites and Afrikaners in particular a protected position in society. The concerns of the leadership were well expressed by Malan in his 'Ouo Vadis?' speech:

Through the urbanisation of our volk Afrikanerdom has largely lost its protected position spiritually as well as economically. White poverty, coupled with the advance of non-whites and taken together with manifold daily contacts in all fields and on virtually an equal footing, makes the struggle for racial purity ever more difficult...What hovers threateningly above us is nothing less than the modern and ostensibly civilised *heidendom* as well as the sliding down into semi-barbarism through bloodmixing and the disintegration of the white race.[13]

12. Dirk Richard, *Moedswillig die Uwe: Perspersoonlikhede van die Noorde* (Johannesburg: Perskor, 1985).
13. Malan, *Glo in u Volk*, p. 136.

During the first five years of NP rule this matter was addressed through legislation such as the Mixed Marriages Act (1949), the Immorality Act (1950), the Population Registration Act (1950) and the Reservation of Separate Amenities Act (1953). In the legislation two considerations were inextricably linked: without a privileged position the Afrikaners could not survive as a separate people; without safe-guarding the racial separateness of the people a privileged position could not be maintained. The following words of Strijdom illustrate the connection:

If the European loses his colour sense he cannot remain a white man . . . On the basis of unity you cannot retain your sense of colour if there is no apartheid in everyday social life, in the political sphere or whatever sphere it may be, and if there is no residential separation. South Africa can only remain a white country if we continue to see that the Europeans remain the dominant nation; and we can only remain the dominant nation if we have the power to govern the country and if the Europeans, by means of their efforts, remain the dominant section.[14]

Verwoerd elaborated on this theme but cast apartheid in a more modern idiom. He also persuaded an astonishingly large part of his followers that it was morally defensible. Realising just how important the latter element was, Verwoerd promptly secured the rejection by the Dutch Reformed Church (DRC) of the concluding statement of the Cottesloe Conference in 1960. Convened by the World Council of Churches in the aftermath of the Sharpeville shootings, the conference rejected all unjust discrimination (specifically migrant labour, job reservation and the ban on racially mixed marriages) and recognised all racial groups as part of the total population. Delegates from the Transvaal and Cape DRC had supported the Cottesloe statement, but as a result of Verwoerd's appeal and strong lobbying by the Broederbond the synods fell into line, repudiating their own elected representatives. Subsequently no NP leader had to fear any attack on apartheid from the DRC or other Afrikaner churches.

The leader's position was greatly strengthened by the economic advance of the Afrikaners, which in turn was facilitated by the 'affirma-tive action' policy applied by the government to the Afrikaners. After 1948 Afrikaners rose rapidly into the senior positions of the civil service and public corporations like ESKOM, ISCOR and SASOL. By the mid-1960s they completely dominated the upper and middle echelons of the central state and parastatal organisations. Through protective policies and subsidies the NP government made the position of farmers and

14. C.M. Tatz, *Shadow and Substance: A Study in Land and Franchise Policies Affecting Africans, 1910–1960* (Pietermaritzburg: University of Natal Press, 1962), p. 113.

workers much more secure. Afrikaner business also benefited from the close association with the NP government, seeing their share in the private sector rise from 9.6 per cent in 1949 to 20.8 per cent in 1975. This Afrikaner economic advance expressed itself in a general movement away from less skilled, poorly paid labour towards skilled, better paid, usually well-protected careers. This general trend was accelerated as the government, bodies like the Broederbond and institutions like the church assiduously promoted Afrikaner education.[15] The movement can be discerned in Table 4.1.

Table 4.1. PERCENTAGE OF AFRIKANERS
IN THE BROAD CATEGORIES OF OCCUPATION,
1936–77

Occupational Category	1936	1946	1960	1977
Agricultural occupations	41,2	30,3	16,0	8,1
'Blue Collar' and other manual	31,3	40,7	40,5	26,7
'White Collar'	27,5	29,0	43,5	65,2
	100,0	100,0	100,0	100,0

Source: J.L. Sadie, published originally in Adam and Giliomee, *Ethnic Power Mobilized*, p. 169.

The Afrikaner ethnic entrepreneurs always stressed that a people cannot (and must not) live by bread alone. Malan, Strijdom and Verwoerd all constantly promoted Afrikaner nationalist symbols and ideals. Under Strijdom the Union Jack and 'God Save the Queen' lost their official status, leaving the 'Stem van Suid-Afrika' (Call of South Africa) and the South African tricolour as the sole national anthem and flag. The NP leadership also decided to test support for a republic by way of a referendum. It recognised that imposing a change to the form of the state by way of a simple parliamentary majority would cause great tensions in the white citizenry. To achieve its ultimate goal, the *volksbeweging* was prepared to recognise its limits. Starting with the referendum over the republican issue, the NP leadership increasingly tried to secure English-speaking support for the state as the guarantor of the interests and political survival of whites as a whole.

Securing English-speaking support. After the 1948 election Malan thanked the 'thousands' of English-speaking supporters who had made

15. I deal with this extensively in Heribert Adam and Hermann Giliomee, *Ethnic Power Mobilized: Can South Africa Change?* (New Haven, Conn: Yale University Press, 1979), pp. 145–76. The calculations are by Professor J.L. Sadie.

the victory possible. However, in the first ten years of NP rule virtually no English-speakers from the business community, professions or universities were prepared to support the NP as an ethnically exclusive party with undercurrents of anti-semitism (it was only in 1950 that the Transvaal NP removed a clause barring Jews from party membership). Throughout the 1950s the English-speaking middle class was largely repelled by the NP's racial explicitness, which substituted legislation for convention. The business community feared declining stability and profitability. Just after the 1948 election Smuts had warned: 'South Africa has lost the confidence of the world, the flood of capital and people that had been coming in has suddenly stopped. They can no longer trust South Africa.'[16] In 1949 the United Party established the United South Africa Trust Fund under the chairmanship of Harry Oppenheimer with the goal of raising £1 million to fight the NP in the forthcoming election. Capping all this was the fear among English speakers that the NP would strip them of their language rights (which Verwoerd and others had proposed to do in the Republican Constitution of 1942), and that it would lead South Africa out of the British Commonwealth.

Verwoerd's decision in 1959 to hold a referendum on the republican issue was a bold gamble, given that the UP was confident of a 'no' vote
Afrikaners and more than 90 per cent of the
every vote counted, the only effective change
the Governor-General would be replaced by
ead of state. Verwoerd also promised to apply
ued membership of the Commonwealth.
e electorate Verwoerd presented a republic as
ity between the two white groups and so avoid
rate cultures being used to establish separate
y was also presented as essential for economic
explicitly that the republic would be organised
d. In effect this meant coloured or Indian or
ot be allowed a say in 'white politics'.[17] He
ured people or Africans to vote in elections for
parliament, the provincial councils or 'white' city councils would inflame the relationship between the two white groups and between whites and blacks. The coloured vote, so his argument ran, was used by the UP for the cynical purpose of 'ploughing the nationalist Afrikaners under'. This was the NP's main justification for removing the coloured

16. Schoeman, *My Lewe in die Politiek*, p. 158.
17. For some of Verwoerd's most prominent speeches see the *Cape Argus* , 8 August, 18 August and 1 October 1960.

people from the common voters' roll in 1956 and for abolishing the indirect representation of Africans in parliament.

In the 1960 republican referendum the government excluded all people who were not white from the vote. Illiterate whites, however, could participate. Commenting on this a UP parliamentarian declared: 'While we hold a referendum to alter our constitutional form to a republic and do not even consult the coloured people or the Natives, we cannot be said to aim at real national unity'.[18] To this Verwoerd replied that it was only because the anti-republicans were afraid of losing that blacks were being 'dragged into the struggle'. He added:

It had always been generally acknowledged that the white man must decide his own affairs but now that point of view was being contested. It had always been the white man who decided on the affairs of South Africa and there had never been any objection to that.[19]

After having led the NP to victory in the referendum on the republic and later, under pressure, removed South Africa from the Commonwealth, Verwoerd sought to heal the divisions in white ranks. However, ruling elites in divided societies often find it difficult to suppress the temptation to go ever further in their attempts to homogenise the citizenry. Elites in the Broederbond were concerned that the blurring of intra-white division would undermine Afrikaner exclusivity and power. They were particularly concerned that a wrong interpretation could be placed on Verwoerd's call to relegate to the past all the historical differences which could impede white cooperation. In 1962 the Broederbond head office sent a circular to all branches that the Prime Minister's call should not be misunderstood: cooperation had to come from the English-speakers, while Afrikaners would not deny them the opportunity to do so. The circular went on: 'It is not they who should absorb us in their circles but we in ours.'[20]

In 1966 Broederbond Chairman Piet Meyer, in a secret meeting with the highest organ of the body, spelled out his quest for undiluted Afrikaner hegemony. He pointed to the danger of a steady anglicisation of the Afrikaners while English influence was so pervasive in virtually all walks of life. In his view, the political realm was dominated by the specific contribution the English section had made. This included the parliamentary system and an emphasis on 'citizenship as a collectivity of all state subjects, irrespective of differences of origin or culture, everyone potentially equal'. In contrast to this nation-state approach the Afrikaner emphasis on an ethnically homogeneous state, which formed the basis of the homeland policy, had not yet received 'full develop-

18. *Ibid.*, 18 August 1960, speech by J. Hamilton Russell.
19. *Ibid.*, 8 August 1960.
20. Pelzer, *Die Afrikaner-Broederbond*, pp. 101–2.

ment'.[21] What Meyer now proposed was nothing less than the homogenisation of the white citizenry through 'the Afrikanerisation of the English-speaker'. He believed that this task would have to be achieved primarily through the educational system and would mean:

> . . . that the English-speaker has to make the Afrikaans world-view his own; that he will integrate his ideals and life style with those of the Afrikaner; that he will adopt Afrikaans history as his own; that he will accept Afrikaans as his national language, alongside English as the international community language . . . We shall then be able to speak of Afrikaans- and English-speaking Afrikaners.[22]

Meyer was such a close associate of Verwoerd that it is difficult to believe that he could develop these ideas without sounding his leader out. In public, however, Verwoerd tended to preach Afrikaner–English reconciliation while warning about the dangers of the *Engelse geldmag* (the English money power). After Sharpeville the executive committee of the Associated Chambers of Commerce (ASSOCOM) pleaded for Africans to be granted freehold in townships, greater freedom of movement and permission to bargain collectively. Verwoerd charged that this intervention was part of an organised campaign against the state. Verwoerd openly opposed the United States/South African Leadership Exchange Programme (USSALEP) in which prominent American and South African business leaders and academics worked towards peaceful change and a lessening of the racial conflict in South Africa. He was also deeply suspicious of the SA Foundation, established in 1961 by South African business leaders to improve South Africa's image abroad and act as an informal lobby for changes to the apartheid policy. In 1964 Verwoerd refused the Foundation permission to recruit black members.

Verwoerd also allowed cabinet ministers to depict Harry Oppenheimer and his Anglo American Corporation as no friend of the Afrikaner and a bitter enemy of Dr Verwoerd and apartheid. According to a right-wing extremist, Professor Piet Hoek, Verwoerd was greatly concerned about the stranglehold which Oppenheimer, through his conglomerate, had on the South African economy and was looking for ways to break it. In 1965 Verwoerd warned that the South African money power was becoming entangled with an international money power which was alien to South Africa. The Nationalists would have to guard against the developing money power coming into conflict with their ideals and security.[23]

The background to this speech was the increasing interpenetration

21. Serfontein, *Brotherhood of Power*, p. 323.
22. *Ibid.*, p. 238.
23. B.M. Schoeman, *Die Geldmag: Suid-Afrika se Onsigbare Regering* (Pretoria: Aktuele Publikasies, 1980), p. 10; see also pp. 23–45, 78–82.

since the early 1960s of Afrikaner and English capital, a development which was given great impetus by Harry Oppenheimer when he enabled Afrikaner capital in 1964 to take over the mining house General Mining. Verwoerd and his allies feared that Oppenheimer had changed tactics. Rather than continue with the ineffectual attempts of the 1950s to unseat the NP, he was now using his influence to forge a political alliance of all white moderates which could oust the intransigent Prime Minister.[24]

Nevertheless Verwoerd's position was bolstered by the fact that the English-speaking business elite no longer directly opposed him. In addition he benefited from the success that tough security measures had in restoring stability after Sharpeville. In the 1966 general election Verwoerd led the NP to a landslide victory. For the first time the party won a majority of all votes cast (57.8 per cent, as against 46.2 per cent in 1961). In the predominantly English-speaking province of Natal its share of the vote was 40.6 per cent, up from 16.7 per cent in 1961. This 1966 victory was won a mere six years after Douglas Mitchell, UP leader in Natal, had declared: 'We do not accept the Republic in Natal . . . We live under a hostile government and this is tyranny and rule by force . . . We will seek the first opportunity to make our own laws'.[25]

This growing unity among the white citizenry calls to mind the observation that 'nations are the creation not of their historians but of their enemies'.[26] The whites, who were the government's first-class citizens and the 'state nation', were united by the common threats and challenges to their position of power and privilege. For example, the South African Defence Force developed as an institution which was either overwhelmingly or exclusively white in its ethos and in the composition of its officer corps. While the Defence Force accepted blacks who volunteered, compulsory military service was restricted to medically fit young white men, under the terms of the Defence Amendment Act of 1967.[27] A sense of white nationhood was also fostered by prosperity. The change to a republic did not turn out to be as costly as English-speakers had feared. The economy entered a boom period which lasted ten years. Moreover, the attraction of being tied to the British Commonwealth steadily faded as that body became increasingly black and as Britain applied sanctions to Rhodesia after its white-ruled state had declared unilateral independence.

24. Ronald Segal claims to have had an interview with Oppenheimer in which he said as much. See R. Segal, 'Portrait of a Millionaire', *Africa/South*, vol. 4, no. 3 (1960).
25. Schoeman, *My Lewe in die Politiek*, p. 271.
26. Kenneth Boulding, *The Image* (Ann Arbor: Michigan University Press, 1956), p. 114.
27. Kenneth Grundy, *Soldiers without Politics: Blacks in the South African Armed Forces* (Berkeley: University of California Press, 1983), p. 106.

Although only two of the NP's 126 elected representatives in 1966 were English-speaking, Verwoerd and the NP had for the first time become acceptable to English-speakers. The Afrikaners had arrived and had mellowed in the process. Their rapid, often traumatic urbanisation was behind them. By 1970 some 90 per cent lived in the towns and cities, compared with 50 per cent in 1936. Nearly 60 per cent found themselves in white-collar occupations, as against fewer than 30 per cent in 1936. The republican ideal was achieved and the Afrikaner culture was secure. The NP leadership saw its great task now as to harness the support of all whites to make the republic invincible and prosperous.

The leadership and the black population. The NP policy towards the African population took as its point of departure the idea that the whites had an undeniable historic right to all the land except those concentrations of black settlement known as the reserves. This 'white' land had to be safeguarded for future generations in the face of a steady increase in the African population. Unlike General Smuts, who declared that white supremacy 'will last forever'[28] but refused to take any further measures to safeguard it, Malan and his followers believed that drastic steps were necessary to prevent black liberation some day in the future. Along with the mainstream of the UP, the NP was a racist party which believed in the social and biological superiority of whites. However, developments like the independence of India forcefully brought the point home that a belief in white supremacy was by itself not sufficient to guarantee continued white domination. As one contemporary writer put it: 'The European assumption that the mere biological inferiority of the non-Europeans is sufficient to prevent them from displacing the Europeans, particularly in a predominantly non-European country, is an assumption that is found wanting.'[29]

The NP leadership directly challenged the UP's attempts to improve conditions for blacks, which took place in a political vacuum. In particular it questioned the money spent on education for Africans in white areas. As J.G. Strijdom put it, this would inexorably lead to Africans becoming developed and civilised, a process which would erode the distinguishing line of colour and would step by step bring about equality.[30] To forestall this, Malan, Strijdom and their successors had little compunction about denying blacks political rights.

In this respect Malan and Strijdom were nothing but hard-core segregationists, like their counterparts in the American South. But

28. 'The Doctrine of Apartheid', *Round Table*, vol. XXXIX, December 1948, p. 32.
29. Eugene P. Dvorin, *Racial Separation in South Africa: An Analysis of Apartheid Theory* (University of Chicago Press, 1952), p. 193.
30. H.B. Thom, *D.F. Malan* (Cape Town: Tafelberg, 1980), p. 279.

apartheid was not the same as segregation. Its distinguishing feature was the combination of paternalism and a peculiar rationalisation of racial discrimination.

The specific character of apartheid in its earlier phase is particularly striking in the pronouncements of Malan, an ex-minister in the Dutch Reformed Church. When an African deputation presented him with an address in October 1948, Malan expressed himself in the following terms:

I regard the Bantu not as strangers and not as a menace to the white people, but as our children for whose welfare we are responsible, and as an asset to the country. My government has no intention of depriving you of your rights or oppressing you. Nothing will be taken from you without giving you something better in its place.[31]

In another speech, given two weeks after the NP's electoral victory, Malan spoke in similar terms about the coloured people:

The days when people . . . speak . . . of racialism are past. We will get the co-operation of the various races. There will be no discrimination against any section. We have a policy in regard to non-Europeans, but this involves no oppression or removal of any other rights. We shall protect them against oppression.[32]

Likewise Hendrik Verwoerd, in addressing the Natives' Representative Council in 1950, declared that apartheid meant exactly the opposite of oppression.[33]

These statements must be understood within the context of the constraints with which the NP leadership had to contend. It was impossible for it to deny blacks citizenship in all its components – political, civil and social. Indeed, the Act on South African Citizenship of 1949 reaffirmed the common citizenship of all South Africans. On the other hand the NP leadership believed the white voters in South Africa's *herrenvolk* democracy to be powerful enough to block any attempt to grant blacks equal civil rights in a common political and social system. Even a gradualist approach would be met by ever fiercer resistance.[34]

The way the NP leaders thought they could resolve this dilemma was by offering 'something better' than segregation, to use the words of Malan in his October 1948 speech. In Malan's thinking, segregation also discriminated but offered nothing in return. While segregation had for Malan the connotation of *afhok* (separation or isolation), the NP proposed in its place apartheid, 'which could mean equality but each on

31. Dvorin, *Racial Separation*, p. 95.
32. *Ibid.*, p. 64.
33. H.F. Verwoerd, *Verwoerd aan die Woord: Toesprake, 1948 –1962* (Johannesburg: Afrikaanse Persboekhandel, 1963), p. 121.
34. *Ibid.*, pp. 20–1.

its own terrain' according to Malan. It was he who used the word 'apartheid' for the first time in parliament when, in 1944, he called for a policy which would give to Africans and coloured people the opportunity to develop under white leadership 'according to their character and ability'.[35]

In the NP leadership's thinking, the discrimination which blacks suffered as citizens would be compensated by a policy promoting the national development of the different black ethnic groups as segregated political entities. In typical paternalistic fashion, the leadership decided that this policy was in the best interest of blacks and what they actually themselves wanted. In his October 1948 speech to an African delegation Malan stated: 'What you want is a rehabilitation of your own national life, and not competition and intermixture and equality with the white man in his particular part of the country.'[36]

For the coloured people, the 'something better' was an explicit policy of granting them a position of privilege over Africans in the white part of the country and more opportunities to serve their 'own people' in the civil administration of the country and in their own communities.[37] The apartheid policy would also promote the social upliftment of coloured people, of whom a large part were trapped in acute poverty, alcoholism and illiteracy.

The promise of black upliftment and human development was for the NP leadership the essence of what it called 'positive apartheid' and as such a commitment to the social component of citizenship. This developmental aspect was considered a sufficient counter-balance to negative apartheid, which denied blacks political citizenship in common political institutions. Hence the leadership's belief that apartheid did not really entail discrimination or racialism.

The problem was that the black leadership saw politics in starkly different terms. This was highlighted in the responses on two separate occasions by the leadership of the African National Congress (ANC) and by Dr Richard van der Ross, a prominent coloured educator.

Before embarking on its passive resistance campaign in 1952 the ANC declared that its action was not directed against any national group or race. It called attention to its efforts

. . . by every constitutional method to bring to the notice of the government the legitimate demands of the African people . . . in particular, their inherent right to be directly represented in parliament, the provincial and municipal councils and in all councils of state.

35. *House of Assembly Debates (HAD)* 25 January 1943, col. 75. For the first use of 'apartheid' by *Die Burger* see Louis Louw (compiler), *Dawie: 1946 –1964* (Cape Town: Tafelberg, 1965), pp. 48–50.
36. Dvorin, *Racial Separation*, p. 95.
37. Thom, *Malan*, pp. 250–1.

In reply Malan disputed the claim to inherent rights of Africans, who, he said differed from Europeans in ways which are 'permanent and not man-made'. He continued:

If this is a matter of indifference to you and if you do not value your racial characteristics, you cannot in any case dispute the Europeans' rights, which in this case is definitely an inherent right, to take the opposite view and to adopt the necessary measures to preserve their identity as a separate community. It should be understood clearly that the government will under no circumstances entertain the idea of giving administrative or executive or legislative powers over Europeans, or within an European community, to Bantu men and women, or to other smaller non-European groups.[38]

Responding, the ANC leadership observed that when it objected to differentiating laws it did not refer to biological differences but to

. . . citizenship rights which are granted in full measure to one section of the population and completely denied to the other by means of man-made laws artificially imposed, not to preserve the identity of Europeans as a separate community, but to perpetuate the systematic exploitation of African people.[39]

In 1960, when mobilising mass action against the advent of the republic, Nelson Mandela contrasted the exclusive 'Boer republic' with a 'democratic republic where all South Africans will enjoy human rights without the slightest discrimination'.[40] The banning of the ANC as the most important organ of black resistance silenced this voice for nearly two decades.

Also in 1960, Van der Ross expressed the profound alienation of those coloured people who once enjoyed political rights but were now excluded from the republican referendum. Writing just after Referendum Day, he remarked that 5 October 1960 was 'a double R-day: Referendum Day for whites, Rejection Day for non-whites'. White South Africa had a chance to interpret citizenship in a grand manner but chose not do do so. In fact it made quite clear to the non-white peoples of South Africa that they had no part in running the affairs of the country. Van der Ross concluded:

We were excluded from partaking in the referendum, and by this very exclusion we understand that the term citizen is reserved for whites only . . . It

---

38. The exchange of letters is published in Leo Kuper, *Passive Resistance in South Africa* (New Haven, Conn: Yale University Press, 1957), pp. 233–41.
39. *Ibid.*, p. 240. In a letter to an American clergyman, also published in this volume (pp. 217–26), Malan also refers to the fundamental difference between the two groups, white and black. Here he states: 'The difference in colour is merely the physical manifestation of the contrast between two irreconcilable ways of life, between barbarism and civilization, between overwhelming numerical odds on the one hand and insignificant numbers on the other.'
40. Mary Benson, *Nelson Mandela* (Harmondsworth: Penguin Books, 1986), p. 100.

is important for us, too, that this was an exclusion of all non-Whites, African, Coloured, Indian, Malay, Chinese.[41]

Van der Ross's statement was remarkably prescient. The growing white unity of the 1960s had as its corollary a widening of the gulf between whites and the black groups. Three months after the republic was established Verwoerd declared: 'Let me be very clear about this: When I talk of the nation, I talk of the white people of South Africa.'[42] In Verwoerd's eyes coloured people were destined to become a nation in their own right. Van der Ross commented: 'It means that in future no non-white South African need regard Die Stem as his national anthem, or the South African national flag as his flag.'[43] In effect this was Verwoerd's view as well. In 1965 he argued that as much as Ceylon was the land of the Sinhalese, regardless of the presence of the Tamils, South Africa was a white state despite the presence of other groups. After all, in Verwoerd's reasoning, the Africans were being eliminated from the political life of the state, and the coloured people and Indians were mere marginal minorities.[44]

From this line of thinking followed the denial of political citizenship for blacks. The government abolished the indirect coloured representation in parliament and prohibited racially mixed political parties. In the apartheid form of political compensation, a consultative body, the Union Coloured Advisory Council, was upgraded to the Coloured Persons Representative Council (CPRC), which was partly elected by universal franchise. Designed to be the 'mouthpiece of the coloured population', it was also given limited powers to administer coloured local government, education, communal welfare and rural areas. The government contended that the funds allocated to the council were roughly equal to the amount contributed by coloured taxpayers.

In the case of Africans the denial of citizenship went even further. All political representation had to be channelled through their respective homelands. The NP leadership insisted that there 'can be no permanent home or permanency for even a section of the Bantu in the area of white South Africa'.[45] The recognition of civil and social citizenship of Africans was reduced to a minimum. The state's contribution to funding for African education was pegged and money for other services was linked to the African capacity to pay. Africans were also denied the right to own property, form companies or establish African-controlled finan-

---

41. R.E. van der Ross, 'Coloured Viewpoint', 6 October 1960, republished in R.E. van der Ross, *Coloured Viewpoint* (Bellville: University of the Western Cape, 1984), p. 133.

42. *Ibid.*, p. 102.

43. *Ibid.*, p. 181.

44. *HAD*, 1965, cols. 4403–10.

45. *HAD*, 16 April 1964, col. 4337, speech by P.W. Botha.

cial institutions and wholesale concerns. Intensified influx control severely restricted their right of free movement. The pass-law regulations spun an Orwellian web of control, preventing the influx of rural people to the towns except in terms of rigidly defined procedures and expelling the non-productive 'surplus' people to the homelands.

The apartheid state, in paternalistic fashion, continued to insist that it was committed to the socio-economic upliftment of the people under its care. However, with vast funds committed to shoring up the position of the white citizenry, the state always lacked funds to spend sufficiently on this. In fact, the basic pattern of taxation and state expenditure did not change much. In 1949–50 whites paid 81.1 per cent of the taxes; this figure declined slowly to 76.9 per cent in 1975–6, while the African share of taxes rose from 11.4 per cent to 16.2 per cent in the same period. In 1949–50 whites received 61 per cent of the state expenditure directly allocated by racial group, while the coloured, Asian and African shares were 11 per cent, 3 per cent and 25 per cent respectively. The proportions stayed fairly constant for quite some time. By 1975–6 the white share had declined to 56 per cent, while that of Africans had risen to 28 per cent. The proportions for coloured persons and Asians stood at 12 per cent and 4 per cent respectively.[46]

In justifying the continuing racial disparities in state spending, the NP leadership was unwilling to state openly that the government discriminated against blacks because they were inferior. Instead it argued on the one hand that the state needed to spend on whites to preserve a white nation in a black continent, and on the other that since whites carried the lion's share of the taxes they could expect preferential treatment. Indeed, they also had the right to expect gratitude for what was spent on blacks out of their taxes. As Malan wrote to an American clergyman in 1954: 'It is computed that every European taxpayer in our country "carries" more than four non-whites in order to provide the latter with the essential services involving education, hospitalisation, housing etc.'[47]

Rationalisations such as these helped to fortify the NP leadership in its belief that apartheid was offering 'something better' than segregation and was even in the interests of all the peoples in the country. Confronted by widespread resistance to apartheid by the mid-1980s, the

---

46. Michael McGrath, 'The Racial Redistribution of Taxation and Government Expenditures', unpubl. paper, University of Natal, 1979; Norman Bromberger, 'Government Policies Affecting the Distribution of Income, 1940–1980', in Robert Schrire (ed.), *South Africa: Public Policy Perspectives* (Cape Town: Juta, 1982), pp. 172–86; Hermann Giliomee and Lawrence Schlemmer, *From Apartheid to Nation-building* (Cape Town: Oxford University Press), pp. 103–7.
47. Letter from Malan to the Rev. John Piersma, republished in Kuper, *Passive Resistance*, p. 222.

NP political leadership and the Nationalist press found it difficult to admit that the basic point of departure of apartheid was wrong or unjust. In a series of articles analysing the legacy of apartheid, a senior journalist of *Die Burger* wrote that apartheid was to a large extent 'a tale of frustrated idealism'. He went on to say that there were idealists who supported the NP who did not want to humiliate or oppress but wanted to create new opportunities for development.[48] P.W. Botha answered in the same mould when asked what was the greatest mistake the NP had made. In his view it was the failure to give expression to the positive content of apartheid. He added: 'There was a time when we could have done much more with respect to housing, social upliftment and development. I don't know but we delayed for one reason or another and time caught up with us.'[49] There is no recognition here that the apartheid state failed in its obligations to black citizens because it excluded blacks from political participation. John Stuart Mill observed in the mid-nineteenth century in his essay 'Representative Government' that in the absence of its natural defenders the interest of the excluded is always in danger of being overlooked and, when looked at, is seen with very different eyes from those of the persons whom it directly concerns. So it was with black and brown (coloured) citizens of South Africa, particularly in the first three decades of apartheid.

From White Leader to Imperial President, 1966–1989.

In the 20-odd years between the death of Verwoerd and the coming to power of F.W. de Klerk, the NP leadership set itself three goals. First, it wanted to consolidate the white citizens in a political community which would anchor the South African state. Secondly, it sought to narrow the gap between white and black citizens in the treatment they received from the state in order to win some black acquiesence for the political order. Thirdly, it attempted to coopt leadership strata in the three black groups to administer 'their own people' and also to discuss matters of general concern, though always within the apartheid framework. In the first of these objectives – cementing white unity – the leadership was relatively successful, but in the other two its efforts were largely frustrated by the swelling tide of black resistance.

Consolidating the white nation. John Vorster, unlike Verwoerd, was no intellectual. Nevertheless he was a formidable debater who asserted himself strongly in parliament. He shunned the ideological flights of

---

48. J.J.J. Scholtz, 'Apartheid: verhaal van verydelde idealisme', *Die Burger*, 18 November 1985.
49. Dirk and Johanna de Villiers, *P.W.* (Cape Town: Tafelberg, 1984), p. 91.

fancy of a Verwoerd or the Broederbond's Meyer. As a senior cabinet minister recounted, Verwoerd projected apartheid as a goal in itself. Even if the grand designs of apartheid were impractical they had to be held up to the white citizenry as an ideal. Vorster, by contrast, had come to the leadership position after having been Minister of Justice and Police, where he had fought the security threats to the state. He had developed a more pragmatic sense of what was essential for the political survival of a shrinking white minority. In private he expressed the view that apartheid was simply not a goal in itself but an instrument in service of stability and security.[50] In public he gradually began to curb the ideological overreach of apartheid.

Vorster came to power in a period of surging NP confidence, owing to the 1966 landslide electoral victory, the economic boom and black political quiescence in the wake of draconian security measures. He understood that the time had come to consolidate white unity rather than pursue Meyer's absurd plans for the Afrikanerisation of the white people. In a major speech at the secret Jubilee of the Broederbond, Vorster explicitly rejected the view that the support of the English-speakers could be dispensed with. He made it clear that he had no intention of 'cheating' the English-speakers.[51]

In public Vorster paid tribute to the contribution of the English-speaking section, declaring that he respected their traditions and monuments as much as his own. He repudiated a speech by Hertzog in which the latter argued that English-speakers could not be trusted in the battle for white survival in Africa because they were infused by liberalism. Vorster became the first leader since the NP had won power in 1948 to declare that white unity was thwarted as much by 'super Afrikaners' as by jingoes.[52]

Unlike Verwoerd, who in his own words was a conviction politican demanding that cooperation take place according to his principles, Vorster's pursuit of white unity was characterised by the politics of (white) reconciliation. He told all English newspaper editors (except Laurence Gandar of the *Rand Daily Mail*) that his door was open to them. He addressed gatherings of English-speaking businesspeople in exclusive clubs and, while a quintessential Afrikaner politician, he won many over with remarkable ease. As the *Rand Daily Mail* remarked, Vorster introduced a more humane and relaxed touch which took some

50. Compare Schoeman, *My Lewe in die Politiek*, pp. 224–34, and Richard, *Moedswillig die Uwe*, p. 135.
51. B.M. Schoeman, *Vorster se 1000 Dae* (Cape Town: Human and Rousseau, 1974), p. 41.
52. *Ibid.*, pp. 254–7; John D'Oliveira, *Vorster – the Man* (Johannesburg: Ernest Stanton, 1977), pp. 224–43.

of the steam out of the body politic.[53] As anxious as his predecessors to maintain his Afrikaner base, Vorster nevertheless projected himself more as Prime Minister than as leader of the ruling party.[54]

Under Vorster and his successor, P.W. Botha, the NP managed to win the electoral support of between a quarter and a third of the English-speakers. This put paid to any hope the United Party had of winning power. The UP self-destructed in the mid-1970s, as Vorster had anticipated.

More importantly, while English-speakers never displayed enthusiastic support for the NP, few joined the liberation struggle. Resistance within their ranks to military conscription remained limited. Most English-speakers supported the Progressive Federal Party, the official opposition from 1977 to 1987, and its successor, the Democratic Party. Both parties espoused majority rule, but the great bulk of English-speakers remained solidly opposed to the kind of majority rule the ANC envisaged. In a 1989 poll only 7 per cent (as against 5 per cent of Afrikaners) supported a unitary state with one Parliament and one person, one vote.[55] A 1991 poll found that only 8 per cent of Democratic Party supporters agreed with the statement that an ANC government was capable of running South Africa.[56] What English-speakers wanted was a pro-capitalist state which steadily absorbed blacks as political managers while safeguarding stability. To them the NP still seemed essential to help manage this process.

In the sphere of culture and public morality the ethos of the *volksbeweging* lingered for quite some time. A leading Afrikaner opinion-former, Schalk Pienaar, wrote in 1969 that the National Party government 'cannot, will not and does not want to rule South Africa as if only Afrikaners live in the country'.[57] Pienaar was only partly correct. The government, through its censorship machinery, continued to impose Afrikaner norms of public morality. The easing and eventual scrapping of apartheid in the fields of sport, entertainment and public facilities occurred only after a critical mass of Afrikaner support had been won. In the economic field, by contrast, the NP gave up on this quest for Afrikaner parity with the English-speaking section and shed its fears of the Anglo-American Corporation and 'international money power'. The Carlton meeting of 1979 between top government people and business leaders symbolised the end of the public antagonism which

---

53. Cited by D'Oliveira, *Vorster – the Man*, pp. 212–13.
54. J.H.P. Serfontein, *Die Verkrampte Aanslag* (Cape Town: Human and Rousseau, 1970), p. 72.
55. Giliomee and Schlemmer, *From Apartheid to Nation-building*, p. 157.
56. Rory Riordan, 'Consolidating Negative Attitudes', *Monitor*, December 1990, p. 61.
57. Cited by *The Star*, 17 February 1969.

had long characterised the relationship between government and the English-speaking business elite. This Afrikaner–English *rapprochement* inevitably produced great strains within the ranks of Afrikaner nationalists.

From the mid-1960s sharp differences arose in Afrikaner ranks on the strategies and methods by which the political survival of the Afrikaners and the larger white group could be realised. During the 1970s these differences began to manifest themselves in the Afrikaans press and in the party, church and Broederbond, which all struggled to maintain ideological coherence. Yet despite internal discord the leadership could count on a great deal of implicit support. During the 1970s upwards of 60 per cent of NP supporters declared that they would support the leadership even if things were done which they did not understand or approve of.[58]

However, as Afrikanerdom became more stratified the leadership found it ever more difficult to impose discipline on Afrikaner institutions and organisations. Just after he had come to power, Vorster had expressed the view that in Afrikaner life only the party and the church had an independent right to exist and that there was a place for the other organisations only if they were prepared to become support organisations.[59] Vorster soon ran up against resistance to this belief. Confronted with a major public squabble between the northern and southern Afrikaans newspapers, he failed to persuade the newspaper publishers to sign an undertaking not to try to formulate policy or to criticise the party's policies. Even a threat to resign as Prime Minister if the press war was not resolved failed to produce results.

In the 1970s the Afrikaans press, particularly the Sunday newspaper *Rapport*, struck out on a more independent line. As a result both Vorster's and Botha's relationship with the paper and its editors became strained. The trend towards a more independent stance was reversed when Botha became the leader. He had been a director of Nasionale Pers and used close personal ties to forestall any criticism of him by newspapers in this group until his very last year or two in office. His notorious temper was sufficient to moderate greatly any criticism of him as leader in the Afrikaans press.

The worsening security situation after 1976 greatly increased the tendency of leaders towards news manipulation for the sake of maintaining unity. This put the Afrikaans press in a particular dilemma, since it posed a conflict between defending the state and remaining autonomous. Botha, as the spokesman for the security establishment when he

58. Theodore Hanf *et al.*, *South Africa: The Prospects of Peaceful Change* (London: Rex Collings, 1981), pp. 400–2.
59. Schoeman, *Vorster se 1000 Dae*, p. 37. See also Schalk Pienaar, *Getuie van Groot Tye* (Cape Town: Tafelberg, 1979), pp. 95–106, 126–32.

was minister for defence and then Prime Minister/State President, demanded a range of curbs on reports of unrest, acts of sabotage and strikes. His argument that this was imperative for the defence of the state struck a responsive cord in Afrikaans press circles. Ton Vosloo, editor of the Nasionale Pers paper *Beeld* and later managing director of the group, remarked in the early 1980s that the political struggle had become a matter of a conflict between white and black nationalism in which the press was being employed by both parties. 'It is us or them,' he declared.[60]

Despite threats and intimidation by Botha, both the Afrikaans and the English press managed to avoid becoming too subservient to the state. As a result Botha increasingly instructed the television and radio service to broadcast news about the security situation within the context of his view of a 'total onslaught' against the state. Botha even intervened directly when the television news did not give his interpretation of his sacking of the first coloured minister in the cabinet, Allan Hendrickse.

Both Vorster and Botha continued to employ the Broederbond to broaden their own power base and to gain acceptance for the NP's tortuous move away from apartheid. Vorster used secret meetings of the Broederbond to isolate Hertzog and his followers in the party, before driving them from both the party and the Bond. Suspicious of 'experts' who were not also staunch nationalists, Vorster allowed the Bond to develop proposals for multiracial sport, changes in coloured policy and a new constitution. Under Botha the Bond's usefulness in this regard began to wane: it had now become necessary to negotiate reforms with black representatives instead of just handing down policy. The Bond nevertheless remained influential in educational policy. Botha appointed Gerrit Viljoen, ex-chairman of the Bond, to deal with educational reform, while prominent Bond members Pieter de Lange (also a former chairman) and Tjaart van der Walt headed investigations into the crisis in African and coloured schools.

The leadership recognised that the Afrikaans churches, and in particular the largest one, the Dutch Reformed Church (DRC), had an important role to play in legitimising both apartheid and reform. Both Vorster and Botha tried to use the church for this purpose. Vorster was in a particularly strong position since his brother served as Moderator of the DRC, as did a close friend, the Rev. J.S. Gericke. When right-wingers in the caucus objected to a proposal for a new policy for multiracial sport, Vorster told them that a respected church leader (probably Gericke) had underwritten this, as had the full cabinet.[61]

60. For a fuller discussion see Hermann Giliomee and Heribert Adam, *Afrikanermag: Opkoms en Toekoms* (Stellenbosch: UUB, 1981), pp. 214–15.
61. Schoeman, *Vorster se 1000 Dae*, p. 42.

Confronted by divisions in party ranks about contentious issues like the racial sex laws, Vorster and Botha tried to get the DRC family (the white together with three black DRC churches) to speak out with one voice. It was, after all, the DRC which in the 1940s had put pressure on government to prohibit sexual contact across racial lines and to adhere rigidly to the principle of racial apartheid.

The church leadership could not help the political leadership in its tentative moves towards reform. How closely the former remained aligned to apartheid became clear in 1979 when it was revealed that the church leadership had received secret funds to counteract the campaign of the World Council of Churches against apartheid. Vorster's brother was unrepentant, arguing that the church had acted honourably because it had accepted the money for use against the 'enemies of our *volk*' – thus blurring the distinction between church and *volk*. In 1982 an over-whelming majority in a DRC synod meeting rejected a motion that the Mixed Marriages Act and section 16 of the Immorality Act were scripturally unjustifiable and should be revoked.[62] While the DRC became more sophisticated in its terminology, its basic support for the principles of apartheid remained the same until mid-1986, by which time the government had already moved away from it.

In the end two developments fundamentally changed the ethos of the *volksbeweging* and the leader's relationship to it. On the one hand there were political splits within the party which cost it its position as the sole authentic representative of the *volk*. During the late 1960s Vorster's support for a white nation and the relaxation of apartheid in sport led to the founding of the Herstigte (Reconstituted) National Party under the leadership of Albert Hertzog. Although it failed to win a single parliamentary seat, it soon became clear that large numbers of Afrikaner workers, farmers and civil servants in the lower-income groups had become disaffected.

In 1982 Andries Treurnicht and 17 NP parliamentary representatives broke away on the issue of power-sharing under the proposed new constitution to form the Conservative Party (CP). In the general election of 1987 the CP won the support of more than a third of the Afrikaners. A full 43 per cent of votes for the NP came from English-speakers. By now it was clear that it was futile for the NP leadership to attempt to mobilise support in all the Afrikaner institutions as a precondition for reform. The demise of the *volksbeweging* style of politics in fact considerably increased the government's freedom of action.

The other development was the rise in the 1970s of the executive state, headed after 1983 by a President on whom the constitution conferred

---

62. For an account see F.E. O'Brien Geldenhuys, *In die Stroomversnellings: Vyftig Jaar van die Kerk* (Cape Town: Tafelberg, 1982).

vast powers. The route to power of the first President, P.W. Botha, passed through the ministry of Defence, which strengthened his personal inclination towards authoritarian leadership coupled with administrative teamwork. The severe challenges to the state in the mid-1980s, together with Botha's temperament and vast powers, conspired to bring about an imperial presidency.[63]

As in so many other countries, the executive state in South Africa has pushed the political parties and parliament into the background as institutions through which the support of the citizenry can be mobilised. In their place has come a large bureaucracy reared on the principles of non-accountability, secrecy and the use of technical knowledge to mystify the citizenry. Leaders now demand large discretionary powers to deal with pressing political and economic crises. If legitimation is required it occurs in the form of television addresses, sidelining the press, parties and parliament.

These trends had already manifested themselves under Vorster. The watershed event was South Africa's invasion of Angola in 1975, about which the public was kept in ignorance for several weeks. The Information Scandal of the latter half of the 1970s revealed a disturbing lack of accountability. These tendencies were still somewhat tempered by Vorster's leadership style, which resembled a chairman of a board rather than an executive director. He was unwilling to act unilaterally and on most major policy decisions waited for consensus to develop in the cabinet and caucus before he acted.[64]

Botha, by contrast, was a technocrat through and through. He became as domineering as Verwoerd in cabinet and used the State Security Council as a forum where vital decisions about security, regional destabilisation and a settlement in South West Africa were taken. These were later referred to cabinet for rubber-stamping, while the caucus was left largely in the cold. In the final years of his period in office Botha was a remote figure, feared by office-holders in the party and largely out of touch with a citizenry who themselves remained ignorant of much that was happening in the struggle between the state and the ANC.

The leader and the black citizenry: insiders and outsiders. In the 20 years after Verwoerd's death apartheid was steadily broken down by the inexorable drift of blacks to the cities, the economy's demand for better

63. Brian Pottinger, *The Imperial Presidency. P.W. Botha – The First Ten Years* (Johannesburg: Southern Book Publishers, 1988), esp. pp. 34–44. For a discussion from a more sympathetic perspective, see Dirk and Johanna de Villiers, *P.W.* (Cape Town: Tafelberg, 1984).
64. R.A. Schrire, 'The Formulation of Public Policy', in Anthony de Crespigny and Robert Schrire (eds.), *The Government and Politics* (Cape Town: Juta, 1978), pp. 176–94.

skilled and stabilised black labour and the black quest for human dignity and freedom. Verwoerd wanted, in his own words, 'to be a rock of granite'[65] in resisting any concessions to his policy of maximum separation between race groups in all spheres of life. His successors, by contrast, had to go ever further in adjusting to the exigencies of the situation. All of them agonised before ultimately saying their farewell to a particular aspect of apartheid. Often they attempted to replace apartheid with policies which still bore the stamp of apartheid thinking.

The homelands are a case in point. For Verwoerd it was an open question whether blacks had the capacity to develop the homelands to the point where they could become politically autonomous. Vorster, by contrast, declared that the government would grant independence to any African homeland which demanded this right under the apartheid policy. But independence had an ominous catch as far as citizenship was concerned. The Bantu Homelands Citizenship Act of 1970 stipulated that every African person in the Republic of South Africa had to be a citizen of a homeland but that they and their children remained citizens of the republic. However, citizens of homelands which took independence, as the Transkei did in 1976, lost their South African citizenship. They became aliens who could be deported. Children of these citizens born after the granting of independence would be denied the opportunity to build up a claim to section 10 exemptions which allowed for permanent residence in the 'white' areas. In 1978 'Connie' Mulder, who was narrowly beaten by Botha in the same year's leadership contest, formulated the goal as follows:

If our policy is taken to its logical conclusion as far as black people are concerned, there will not be one black [meaning African] man with South African citizenship . . . Every black man in South Africa will eventually be accommodated in some independent new state in this honourable way and there will no longer be a moral obligation on this parliament to accommodate those people politically.[66]

Even the labour reforms which were first introduced in 1979 did not represent a bold break with the past. They were passed only with reluctance. The government's original idea had been to deny the industrial rights which the legislation gave to migrant workers and citizens of independent states. When the government accepted that influx control had broken down, it tried to limit freedom of movement to those who had jobs and houses. And when the government finally came to write a new constitution in the early 1980s it sought to erect a firm barrier between Africans, who were left out, and the coloured and

65. G.D. Scholtz, *Dr Hendrik Frensch Verwoerd, 1900 –1966* (Johannesburg: Perskor, 1966), vol. II, p. 162.
66. *HAD*, 7 February 1978, col. 579.

Indian peoples, who were now seen as members of the same nation as whites.

In general the government pursued a double-edged policy between the mid-1960s and the mid-1980s. On the one hand it pushed the 'outsiders' away and tried to limit their claims on the state and their access to the cities. On the other hand it tried to draw nearer the 'insiders' – the urban Africans, coloureds and Indians – by slowly turning the state into something which was racially neutral.

It was the coloured people, the group most intimately interwoven with the whites, who shattered Verwoerd's policy of separate nations developing in perpetuity parallel to each other.[67] Both Vorster and Botha assumed that improved education and training would inevitably yield irresistible demands for integration. Vorster conceded in a private conversation with Van der Ross that an injustice was being done to his group. He suggested that they mobilise themselves as the Afrikaners had done with respect to the English-speakers to win recognition as *volle mense* (full human beings).[68] Vorster was clearly using as an analogy the two-stream policy articulated by General Hertzog between 1910 and 1940. He had envisaged the merger of the Afrikaner and English streams after the former had the opportunity to develop to the full. Botha declared that unlike in the 1950s, the coloured people of the 1980s had to be accommodated; the consequences of the policy of social upliftment had to be accepted.[69]

Yet the NP policy remained ambiguous throughout the 1970s and 1980s. The leadership rejected appeals by Afrikaner academics in 1971 for full citizenship for coloured people because it would lead to political integration, which it rejected, and because the state lacked the means to provide for parity in welfare spending. The state slowly eliminated discriminatory salaries, but in general the coloured people were denied the means to mobilise in the way that the two-stream analogy presupposed.

In general, the crude racism which characterised apartheid's public discourse in the 1950s was replaced by the less offensive rhetoric of good neighbourliness and separate development. Verwoerd was a transitional figure who straddled the two strands of apartheid. Although he spoke of a potential nation of separate but co-equal racial groups, he

---

67. Verwoerd did make the 'concession' that once full separation had been achieved contact could again be allowed. See Scholtz, *Verwoerd*, vol. II, p. 173.
68. Van der Ross remembers Vorster as saying: '*Hy wou my sê dat die Afrikaners deur 'n era gegaan het waarin hulle maar so goed kon wees as hulle wou, maar nie as volle mense erken is nie omdat hulle Afrikaans was*'. (He wanted to say that the Afrikaners passed through a phase in which they could be as good as they wanted to be, but were nevertheless denied recognition as full human beings because they were Afrikaners.) *Rapport*, 17 February 1991, p. 10.
69. De Villiers and De Villiers, *P. W.*, pp. 89–90.

still nourished racist views. When he clashed with *Die Burger* about coloured policy he told his wife that he was not the man who would lead the Afrikaners to 'bastardisation'.[70] Vorster, by contrast, from the beginning stated explicitly that there were no inferior people in South Africa and that the government had to treat black diplomats and political representatives of black states (including homelands) in exactly the same way as their white counterparts.

It was, of course, Vorster more than anyone else who was associated with the remorseless suppression of radical opposition to apartheid. It was also he who allowed a cabinet minister to stay on in office after he had uttered the infamous words that Steve Biko's death left him cold. It is difficult to avoid the impression that a black enemy of the apartheid state was much more vulnerable than a white one. It was, however, also Vorster, first as Minister of Justice and Police and then as Prime Minister, who signalled clearly that the days were over when white citizens could take the law in their own hands against black citizens. In 1965 Vorster was asked by a delegate at the Orange Free State NP congress to reconsider the law of assault because farm labourers had become too easily inclined to lay a charge if their employers had given them 'a little slap'. Vorster replied as follows:

I issue many licences but one licence I cannot issue and that is for one man to assault another. I cannot do what the resolution asks me by implication to do. One general principle we must always maintain in all circumstances: nobody has the right to assault anybody else. Congress has my assurance that, if such assaults take place, I and the police will act accordingly.[71]

Given the racial character of the state it was unlikely that more than a small proportion of blacks who had been assaulted would lay charges. And in the courts equal justice remained a distant ideal. A study undertaken in the late 1960s of the perceptions of practising advocates found that half felt that a black tried on a capital charge stood a better chance of being sentenced to death than a white. Of those holding this opinion 41 per cent believed that such differentiation was conscious and deliberate.[72] Nevertheless the overall trend, however weak and incoherent at times, was in the direction of equality before the law of all citizens.

The leader and the apartheid institutions for blacks. Within Vorster's first five years in power all black representation in parliament, the provincial legislatures and local government had been removed. The NP now saw the task at hand as making the apartheid institutions which

70. Scholtz, *Verwoerd*, vol. II, p. 171.
71. D'Oliveira, *Vorster – the Man*, p. 169.
72. B.D. van Niekerk, 'Hanged by the Neck until You Are Dead', *South African Law Journal*, vol. 86 (1969), p. 467.

were created as substitutes work. It was here that its policies failed most abysmally.

A steadily deteriorating relationship characterised the association between the leadership and the Coloured Person's Representative Council (CPRC) which operated between 1969 and 1980. The Labour Party's declared objective was to participate in the council only to destroy it. In response the government packed the council with nominated members to prevent Labour becoming the dominant party. In 1975 Labour succeeded in this objective, but its rejection of the council's budget was an impotent gesture of despair, for the government had the power to override it.

In the mid-1970s Vorster made a half-hearted effort to establish a consultative cabinet council which would be composed of the CPRC executive and an equal number of white cabinet ministers under the Prime Minister's chairmanship. The Labour Party rejected this and pressed for full representation in parliament. Constitutionally the council would have created an impossible situation. As a recent study remarks:

Cabinet council decisions would automatically be imposed on the CPRC. This raised the question, that if the coloured members of the cabinet council had the final say in what laws would be made and what laws done away with, what was the purpose of debating the issues in the CPRC?[73]

The tricameral parliament was an effort to transcend the substantive and symbolic weaknesses of the CPRC and the Indian Council. Although the houses sat separately to discuss their respective 'own affairs', the scope for coloured and Indian participation was considerably widened, especially in joint committees and by the representation in cabinet of the leaders of the Indian and the coloured houses. The tricameral parliament helped to break down the racially exclusive character of parliament. However, it failed to transcend apartheid. By temperament Botha was not the kind of leader who was prepared to turn the system into a genuine form of consociational government, and coloured power in the tricameral structure was too weak to force him to do so. Botha also wrongly assumed that coloured people would accept a segregated position in the political system as a trade-off for the sectional advantage they had over the African 'outsiders'.[74] During a stormy session in the House of Representatives Botha exclaimed: 'Let me tell non-members something now: If it were not for [the] very

73. Roy Howard du Preez, 'The Role and Policies of the Labour Party of South Africa, 1965–1978', unpubl. MA thesis, University of South Africa, 1987, p. 157.
74. For a full discussion see Gerd Behrens, 'The Other Two Houses: The First Five Years of the Houses of Representatives and Delegates', unpubl. Ph.D. thesis, University of Cape Town, 1989.

Afrikaner and the National Party, the coloured population would not be in the privileged position it is in today'.[75]

What Botha failed to realise was that the coloured people had increasingly rejected their definition as a distinct group under the apartheid system. A study based on two surveys undertaken in 1976 and 1983 in the Cape peninsula found a striking change in coloured self-perception. In 1976 some 81 per cent considered themselves primarily coloured; by 1983 this figure had dropped to 35 per cent. In 1976 fewer than 1 per cent thought of themselves as South Africans first of all, but by 1983 the proportion had risen to 49 per cent.[76] As South Africans they wanted a common citizenship in common institutions. Only once this was granted would they generate pressure as a communal group on the basis of self-association.

As far as Africans were concerned, both Vorster and Botha considered the homelands the keystone of apartheid. While Verwoerd put the emphasis on their separation from the white state, both Vorster and Botha tried to reincorporate them into some larger apartheid framework. In the first half of the 1970s Vorster convened a series of meetings with homeland leaders to discuss matters of common concern. These meetings were largely ineffectual and in 1976 the homeland leaders asked that full human rights be granted to blacks instead of mere concessions. It was the Soweto uprising of 1976 which greatly accelerated the disintegration of the apartheid system. Already in 1977 the process had gone so far that M.C. Botha, the minister responsible for the homelands, asked in a memorandum: 'Does the limitation of black numbers and a secondary status for blacks in white South Africa not remain our basic aim?'[77]

Under P.W. Botha the Verwoerdian goal of separate viable homeland economies was abandoned. In its place Botha announced a new regional economic strategy, transcending the borders of the republic and the homelands. Economic regions would be functionally defined to meet the requirements for economic development, and balancing growth points would be developed in the regions to counteract the powerful attraction of the large metropolitan areas. A development bank would play a key role in implementing the new plans for economic development.

However, this attempt to bring the segregated white and black institutions together failed to make much headway. No political dispensation could have a chance of even minimum acceptance by blacks

75. *Debates of the House of Representatives*, 1987, col. 2286.
76. J.P. Groenewald, 'Reaksies op Minderheidsgroepstatus by Kleurlinge', unpubl. Ph.D. thesis, University of Stellenbosch, 1987, p. 241.
77. J.A. du Pisani, 'Die Ontplooing van Afsonderlike Ontwikkeling tydens die B.J. Vorster-era: Die Tuislandbeleid, 1966–1978', unpubl. Ph.D. thesis, University of the Orange Free State, pp. 261–301; the quote is on p. 301.

before the issue of a common South African citizenship was resolved. Secondly, the fact that some homelands were independent, while others (particularly KwaZulu) were not, created conflict among the home-lands' leaders and made it all but impossible to bring them into a federation on an equal basis. Lastly, the fragile economies of the homelands demanded an increased commitment of resources to ensure that the building blocks of the government's projected confederation – the separate white and black homelands – did not disintegrate.[78]

De Klerk and the New South Africa: From Imperial Pretensions to Minority Group

De Klerk's normalisation of South African politics came as a great surprise to many outside observers, for he had been known as one of Botha's more conservative ministers. In NP deliberations over the constitution of 1983 he argued for diverting as many governmental functions as possible to the own affairs (racially based administrative) machinery. When the tricameral constitution came into operation De Klerk favoured retaining the racial sex laws for some time.

In retrospect there were indications from the early 1980s onwards that De Klerk displayed quite different characteristics from his predecessors. In the first place he was not subject to the personal delusions of power and grandeur that afflicted Botha in his last years in office. When he assumed the leadership of the NP in Transvaal in 1982, De Klerk stated:

I want to commit myself to frank and reticent [*beskeie*] leadership. I want to be a leader who serves – not only on platforms but as one man to another [*van mens tot mens*]. I want to be a leader of a team . . .[79]

Secondly, De Klerk recognised better than Botha that the time was running out for reaching an accommodation with the other groups. In 1982 he declared:

We do not want to live permanently in a state of siege in which hatred and blood reigns supreme. If he wishes to survive the white person will have to reveal the pioneering vision of his forefathers and create a future for himself which does not block the vision of the 25 million who are not white.[80]

Finally De Klerk's road was made easier by the fact that the NP decided in 1986 to accept the principle of a single citizenship and

78. Hermann Giliomee, 'The Political Function of Homelands', in Hermann Giliomee and Lawrence Schlemmer (eds.), *Up Against the Fences* (Cape Town: David Philip, 1985), pp. 52–6.
79. Alf Ries and Ebbe Dommisse, *Leierstryd* (Cape Town: Tafelberg, 1990), p. 101.
80. *Ibid.*, p. 106.

nationhood for all South Africans (except those living in the independent homelands). In the five years before his election as leader De Klerk carefully retained a balance in which he spoke of both own affairs and of a common destiny in shared political institutions. In 1986 he said: 'There is a new generation of educated black people, brown people and Indians. They want to be genuinely free.'[81]

Under Botha the government was still committed to race classification. The implication was that it wanted to construct the nation on the pillars of the four apartheid communities – Africans, whites, coloured people and Indians. Under De Klerk the NP government has moved away from group identities based on statutory classification. Minority rights as articulated by the NP leadership no longer have an explicitly racial dimension. There is no longer talk of white group rights but rather of rights which all minorities claim, regardless of colour.

These claims as articulated by the NP fall into several broad categories. First there are its political claims, which stress the need for multiparty competition, regular elections, power-sharing and representation of minorities at all levels of government. Secondly, there are economic claims. These range from a firm demand that property rights be inviolable to the insistence that the free-market system be retained and expanded. Thirdly, there are claims related to communal life and culture. For instance, the state should provide schools for each community on an equal basis, with parents having the option of sending their children to the school of their choice. Moreover, people should have the right to a separate community life, if they so wish, but without any statutory compulsion underpinning this. Fourthly, there are individual rights, such as freedom of speech and religion and of cultural expression, which would be protected by a bill of rights and an independent judiciary.

The NP is articulating these demands and claims in terms of the project of nation-building. After the historic Groote Schuur talks in May 1990 between the government and a delegation of the ANC, Gerrit Viljoen, Minister of Constitutional Development, remarked that while the NP did not question the principle of majority rule it demanded to know whether stability and nation-building would be served by a majority governing all by itself. The NP's own conviction is that a common South African nationhood would be best promoted by the recognition of diversity.[82]

The NP is not alone in its concern for the protection of minority rights. Inkatha leader Mangosuthu Buthelezi has warned that failure to provide minority group rights in a new South African constitution would 'invite

81. *Ibid.*, p. 106.
82. *Die Burger*, 15 May 1990.

a white backlash far worse than that inflicted by Unita and Renamo on Angola and Mozambique respectively'. This warning shows the very high stakes involved. What is at issue is not a set of small, vulnerable minority groups asking for protection to ensure an endangered culture and way of life. In fact, there are in South Africa powerful sub-national groups with the capacity to wreck the economy and destroy any sense of a common citizenship and nationhood if they should find themselves in the position of a beleagured minority.

Conclusion

In the 45 years since the NP's 1948 electoral victory, its leadership has presided over the rise and the demise of the apartheid system. The tentative and fumbling efforts to construct the system in the 1950s were followed by the years of political hubris in the 1960s and 1970s. When South Africa entered a period of prolonged economic stagnation in the mid-1970s, the leadership began to curb the overreach and excesses of the system. This tendency was accelerated by the rising tide of black economic integration and resistance.

Citizenship was the core issue in the entire project of apartheid. During much of the apartheid era the leadership believed it could deflect black citizenship claims upon the state by introducing a separate political citizenship in the separate 'autonomous' states and other and subordinate institutions. Yet for all the attempts to maintain a fiction of international relations with the homelands, the apartheid system was unable to deny the reality of black citizenship and the demand for equal treatment by the state regardless of race. What lies ahead is the struggle over compensation for those who were pushed to the back when citizenship claims were made and pressed.

5

THE EXECUTIVE AND
THE AFRICAN POPULATION:
1948 TO THE PRESENT*

David Welsh

Introduction: The Context of Power

The evolution of the apartheid system is, by now, one of the most frequently described topics in modern history. This essay avoids covering familiar ground by focusing almost exclusively on the ideological presuppositions, leadership capacities and personal qualities of the six incumbents who, since 1948, have held the highest political office in the South African system of government.

Control over the African population since Union in 1910 has been nominally vested in the Governor-General (until 1961) and thereafter in the State President. By means of a politico-legal fiction, whose roots lay deep in nineteenth-century administrative practice, each was deemed to be the supreme chief of the African population and, accordingly, was vested with vast powers, supposedly those wielded by a paramount chief in traditional African polities. In reality the supreme chief bore little relation to any kind of institution ever known in such polities, but white administrators assumed that Africans would more readily accept colonial control if it were clad in this pseudo-traditional garb. Moreover, it gave the administrators an instrument of rule that was both flexible and authoritarian.[1]

South Africa's political system has been variously described as a racial oligarchy, a *herrenvolk* democracy and even a pigmentocracy. All of these designations denote a racially structured system of inequal-

---

* The writer wishes to thank Virginia van der Vliet, Michael Savage, James Selfe, Ebbe Dommisse and a former cabinet minister who wishes to remain anonymous for valuable criticisms of this chapter. It must be emphasised that none is to be blamed for errors of fact or interpretation, for which the writer is solely responsible.

All translations from Afrikaans publications quoted in the text have been made by the writer.

1. David Welsh, 'The State President's Powers under the Bantu Administration Act', University of Cape Town, *Acta Juridica*, 1968.

ity, functioning as a parliamentary democracy within the oligarchy; at best paternalistically in relation to Africans, at worst coercively.

The political institutions have been fundamentally shaped by the legacy of Westminster traditions. South Africa has always had a cabinet system of government. Even after the major changes introduced by the Constitution Act of 1983, which created an executive State President with considerable powers, the system remains more parliamentary than presidential in its operation.

As in all cabinet systems, each Prime Minister has brought his own style to the office. But formidable constraints have operated on each. Since 1948 South Africa has been governed by the National Party, a situation of *de facto* single-party dominance that meant, increasingly, a symbiotic relationship between party and state. Nowhere was this symbiosis more clearly to be seen than in the giant bureaucratic *imperium in imperio* that was charged with the administration of what was originally called Native Affairs, and thereafter underwent several changes of title.

After 1948 key positions in the ministry of Native Affairs went to officials sympathetic to the apartheid policy. In 1949 W.W.M. Eiselen, an important architect of the policy, was made secretary of the depart-ment, over the objections of the Public Service Commission. After H.F. Verwoerd became minister in 1950 the process of appointing and promoting ideologically sympathetic officials proceeded apace. In time, the department became a powerful ideological hot-house of apartheid and a strong defender of the system with a stake in its perpetuation.

A further peculiarity shaping the capacity of each Nationalist leader derives from the character of the National Party (NP). Historically the NP was more the political arm of an ethnic movement than a party in the conventional Western sense. The *hoofleier* (leader-in-chief), who was *ipso facto* Prime Minister, headed a coalition of ethnically based institutional and class forces that has conventionally been termed Afrikanerdom. The mobilisation of these forces in 1948 gave the NP (in alliance with the far smaller Afrikaner Party) electoral victory that was consolidated in subsequent elections.

As D.F. Malan (Prime Minister, 1948–54) well recognised, Afrikaner ethnic unity was the necessary condition of the NP's ascendancy. Unity, however, was not automatic, and even when it had been attained it had to be carefully nurtured. The point is that while ethnic unity was the condition of power, maintaining this unity required balancing the various constituencies that made up the support base of the NP. This was relatively easy when the support base was largely in agreement on the major issues confronting the NP, and when a powerful leader like Verwoerd (Prime Minister, 1958–66) could impose his will on the entire movement. From the late 1960s onwards, however, neither of these conditions applied, and maintaining the political unity of a socially and ideologically diversifying support base became increasingly difficult.

As far as apartheid is concerned, this essay will seek to demonstrate that the relative unity of purpose of 1948 had largely broken down 30 years on. Both B.J. Vorster (Prime Minister, 1966–78) and P.W. Botha (Prime Minister, 1978–84, State President, 1984–9) felt the tension between maintaining unity and making policy changes. Each reacted in different ways.

Another major variable determining the individual leader's capacity for action is the strength of the opposition, both parliamentary and extra-parliamentary, faced by the NP. For example, during the 1950s and 1960s the NP was able to ride roughshod over the African National Congress (ANC) and other organisations in ways that became impossible by the 1980s. While each of their predecessors could speak dismissively, even contemptuously, of the ANC, P.W. Botha and F.W. de Klerk had to come to terms with its strength.

The Coming of Apartheid: D.F. Malan (1948–1954)

The creation of a racially segregated social order did not, of course, begin in 1948. Since 1910 successive governments had been committed to segregation as the basis of racial policy. The more liberal Cape tradition, with its non-racial, qualified franchise, was in retreat. In 1936 a major display of bipartisan white consensus terminated Cape Africans' common-roll voting rights, while provision for the augmentation of the 'native reserves' in the same year signified the continued commitment to segregation.

During the 1940s Smuts' United Party government slowly and cautiously began to accept that the integration of African labour was inevitable, necessary and irreversible. As Minister of Native Affairs, Piet van der Byl said in 1947, in response to a stinging NP attack, that the government's policy remained one of keeping Africans away from the towns and preventing residential mixing, but

. . . seeing that industries and other enterprises in South Africa need native labour, and seeing that these large industries cannot develop if they have not got that labour, we must allow native labour to go to these areas, or we shall arrest that development.[2]

The old doctrine that urban Africans were temporary migrants from the reserves was becoming even more out of kilter with sociological

2. *House of Assembly Debates*, 61, 1947, col. 5009.

reality; even official estimates reckoned that there were over a million urban Africans who had never lived in the reserves.

In previous elections, notably in 1929, the exploitation of racial fears had provided rich electoral gains for the NP. After their heavy defeat in the 1943 'khaki' election, the Nationalists cast around for a strategy that would reunify the bitterly divided ranks of Afrikaner nationalists. By 1945 it was clear that the colour question would be a prominent issue in this process of mobilisation.

There has been some debate about whether the 1948 election was fought on the apartheid issue or that of Afrikaner nationalism. The answer is surely that it was fought on both, since they are inextricably interlinked. Implicit in Afrikaner nationalism's self-definition was a particular view of colour. Moreover, what has been called Afrikaner nationalism's historical paranoia was the belief that the minority English-speaking whites would seek to negate Afrikaner numerical superiority by importing a limited amount of African and coloured voting power into 'white' politics. The Cape's non-racial franchise was regarded as a piece of imperial chicanery, as D.F. Malan's comments make clear:

How did the non-European come by his vote? There is only one answer. Overseas imperialist authorities, when it came to granting self-government, were afraid because Afrikanerdom was in the majority and would strive for freedom. So non-Europeans were not only enfranchised, but were set against the Afrikaners.[3]

As Prime Minister during the period when apartheid was first implemented, Malan's views require analysis. He was 74 years old in 1948; his long political career had been dominated by issues of Afrikaner rights, English-Afrikaans relations and South Africa's status in relation to Britain. Colour issues were always important, but they were not Malan's priorities. His autobiographical book, *Afrikaner Volkseenheid* (published posthumously), contains not a single reference to racial issues; and there are only the sparsest of references to them in the edited collection of his major speeches *Glo in u Volk*.[4]

Malan had no pretensions to being a theorist in matters of colour. He had always believed in segregation, which he regarded as the traditional and therefore correct policy. Despite his *gravitas* he was no slouch when it came to political opportunism. Smuts' preoccupations with the war,

3. Quoted in G.H. Calpin, *There Are No South Africans* (London: Nelson, 1941), p. 197.
4. D.F. Malan, *Afrikaner Volkseenheid en my Ervarings op die Pad Daarheen* (Cape Town: Nasionale Boekhandel, 1959); S.W. Pienaar (compiler), *Glo in u Volk – D.F. Malan as Redenaar* (Cape Town: Tafelberg, 1964).

his deputy J.H. Hofmeyr's liberal proclivities and the palpable divisions within the United Party over colour issues presented Malan with an irresistible opportunity. Rapidly increasing African urbanisation, alleged growing urban crime rates, increased mixing (as in some of the universities) and the beginnings after 1943 of a new wave of African political and economic assertiveness all created a context in which Malan could, quite plausibly, argue that the old order of segregation was breaking down. Moreover, the NP's attacks on African urbanisation were the obverse of one of the critical issues for the farming community, then the NP's major constituency: the shortage of farm labour. Higher wages in the towns were drawing Africans away from the white-owned agricultural areas and from the mining industry. School-feeding schemes could also be attacked as magnets that drew African schoolchildren away from the farms.

How was the new concept of apartheid supposed to differ from the traditional policy of segregation? In Malan's view there was no real difference: 'These are two names for one and the same thing.' He went on to argue that there was apartheid inside the Dutch Reformed Church because white and black worshipped separately; there was apartheid in schooling and in the residential sphere. In all of these cases, said Malan, 'you have separation [apartheid] when there is no territorial partition.'[5]

In making the latter point Malan was attempting to refute United Party allegations that the new and as yet undefined policy of apartheid contemplated total racial separation, which would obviously have cataclysmic consequences for industry and white farming. This was not what Malan had in mind. His policies envisaged local segregation in which inequality would be firmly maintained in all interracial dealings. Some of his colleagues were more blunt; J.G. Strijdom, leader of the NP in the Transvaal, declared that in his view, 'in every sphere the European must be master, the European must retain the right to rule the country and to keep it a white man's country.' In Strijdom's view apartheid meant that 'in a bus I will not sit alongside a native.'[6]

In a now-famous essay written in 1985 Piet Cillié, former editor of *Die Burger*, the principal mouthpiece of the Cape NP, has dismissed any notion that apartheid was a carefully worked out programme:

A system? An ideology? A coherent blueprint? No, rather a pragmatic, tortuous [*slingerende*] process of consolidating a nationalist movement's leadership, of establishing the Afrikaner's right to self-determination, not primarily against a coloured force, but by preventing the return of the United Party. In its turn it [the United Party] would have tried to ensure that the

5. *House of Assembly Debates*, 59, 1947, col. 11, 301–3.
6. *Ibid.*, 62, 1948, cols 361–3.

Nationalists never again got a chance. Uprising and grabs for power would have been the only means left for them.[7]

On this hypothesis apartheid is reduced to being little more than an election gimmick. Undoubtedly there is much truth in this, but it should not blind one to the earnest efforts made by various Afrikaner nationalist intellectuals to provide a coherent and morally defensible base for apartheid. The writings of the Pretoria University sociologist Geoff Cronjé and, after its founding in 1948, the work of the South African Bureau of Racial Affairs (SABRA) sought to achieve this. The NP, however, wanted power, and the lucubrations of intellectuals were of less significance in that quest than cruder, more emotive political appeals. The role of intellectuals, thinkers and writers, however, has been of considerable importance in Afrikaner nationalism, and their relationship with successive political leaders has been a significant factor in determining policy outcomes. This (controversial) proposition will be examined in the conclusion to this chapter.

Faced with an election in 1948, Malan could not rely solely on a bundle of loose, vague propositions. Policy had to have some degree of coherence, and it was with this end in view that Malan appointed an internal party commission under the chairmanship of his friend Paul Sauer, a leading Cape Nationalist (and son of J.W. Sauer, who, ironically, had been one of the stalwarts of the mild liberalism of the old Cape Colony).

The Commission reported in 1947, and its recommendations were closely adhered to by Nationalist leaders in the 1940s and 1950s.[8] The document is too long to summarise but some of its main theoretical premises and recommendations need to be mentioned. Apartheid, it claimed, derives from the experience of the established white groups, Afrikaans- and English-speaking. It is based on the Christian principles of justice and fairness, and is opposed to any form of oppression. In answer to the critical question that opponents had put to the NP concerning the extent of separation envisaged, the Commission phrased its recommendation so that neither the idealistic thinker nor the labour-seeking farmer could take umbrage:

As an eventual ideal and goal total apartheid between whites and natives is proposed, which will be gradually implemented so far as practicable, always with consideration of the country's needs and interests, and with the necessary precaution against disruption of the country's agriculture, industries and general interests.

7. P.J. Cillié, *Baanbrekers vir Vryheid: Gedagtes oor Afrikaners se Rol in Suid-Afrika* (Cape Town: Tafelberg, 1990), p. 67.
8. *Verslag van die Kleurvraagstuk – Kommissie van die Herenigde Nasionale Party*, Sauer Commission, 1947.

According to the Commission, Africans had to be anchored in their ethnic uniqueness (*volkseiendomlike*) and the reserves had to become their fatherland:

For each native [the reserve] must be a spiritual home. It must be the seat of his system of government. It must be the centre of his churches. His most notable educational institutions must be located there. In short it must be made the cradle of his personal and national ideals.

Conditions had to be created in the reserves so that self-interest would draw even 'talented and progressive' Africans away from the towns to these territories.

The converse of this was a further set of recommendations dealing with urban Africans: they were to be regarded as visitors who came to offer their services for the benefit of whites and of themselves. The number of detribalised Africans in the towns must be frozen, and preference should be given to them in respect of rights and job opportunities while they were there and until the ideal of total apartheid could be attained. Every possible effort was to be made to limit the townward movement, and 'the native was to be informed about the disadvantages of urbanisation and the advantages of having one's own national home.'

The ideal was the gradual removal of Africans from industries in the 'white' areas, but the Commission acknowledged that this could be achieved only after many years. The same principle of separation, however, was not to apply to farm labourers: on the contrary 'every effort must be made to curb the outflow of natives from the [white-owned] farms.' In the meantime white workers must be vigorously protected, it being understood that 'it would be impermissible for whites to work under a native or on an equal footing with him.'

The historian F.A. Van Jaarsveld says of the Sauer Report that it reflects 'crude racism and discrimination'.[9] Two academic apologists for apartheid, however, insist that the adoption of apartheid marked a new phase: 'For the first time it was generally accepted that a successful and ethically just policy had to take into account the natural aspirations of the Bantu in all spheres of life.'[10] Much later on the pressing question of who was to be the arbiter of those aspirations would come to the fore.

There is no evidence to suggest that Malan or any other rising Nationalists who were to become his successors demurred at or dissented from the Sauer Commission. In his speeches Malan avoided the

9. F.A. van Jaarsveld, *Die Evolusie van Apartheid* (Cape Town: Tafelberg, 1979), p. 10.
10. N.J. Rhoodie and H.J. Venter, *Apartheid: A Socio-historical Exposition of the Origin and Development of the Apartheid Idea* (Cape Town: HAUM, 1959), p. 176.

cruder language of his successor, Strijdom, and invariably emphasised that apartheid was not repression. Malan's admiring biographer, H.B. Thom, stresses the differences between the two men and also Malan's insistence that apartheid was 'time-bound'. He quotes Malan as declaring in 1948 that the colour issue did not stand still, since it was always becoming more and more difficult. 'There is no question that calls so hard for a solution as this one, and if necessary to find a good solution, it may be necessary to review your earlier decisions.'[11] Apartheid, in other words, was not an immutable doctrine.

On becoming Prime Minister in 1948 Malan appointed E.G. Jansen Minister of Native Affairs. Jansen had occupied this portfolio during the Nationalist government of 1929–33; he had also been a member of the Sauer Commission. Because of his seniority in the party hierarchy and because he was leader of the NP in Natal, Malan could not afford to exclude him from the cabinet. Jansen was a gentle soul, representing the moderate wing of the NP. His appointment, however, was not welcomed by the zealots, who doubted his dynamism.[12]

Malan gave his ministers plenty of latitude. One of them, Ben Schoeman, avers that there was 'absolutely no discipline in the cabinet at all', Malan believing in 'leadership-in-council'. Jansen, accordingly, was not under pressure from his colleagues or the Prime Minister to initiate far-reaching new legislation. Rather he dithered, evidently being unsure of what to do and perhaps being intimidated by the daunting task of translating the rhetoric of the hustings into concrete plans. His inactivity led, in 1949, to pressure from the NP's native affairs group in the caucus, who demanded the implementation of apartheid measures.[13]

Laughter was evoked in parliament when Jansen artlessly observed, in his first major speech as minister after the 1948 election, that 'the precise manner in which apartheid or separation is to be applied to [Africans] in industries, and in the urban areas, has still to be worked out.'[14]

The issue was indeed a problem because shortly before the election an authoritative commission under the chairmanship of Judge H.A. Fagan had poured cold water on the view that urban Africans were in any sense temporary visitors. The Fagan Commission accepted that the townward flow 'has a background of economic necessity – that it may,

11. H.B. Thom, *D.F. Malan* (Cape Town: Tafelberg, 1980), p. 284.
12. B.M. Schoeman, *Van Malan tot Verwoerd* (Cape Town: Human and Rousseau, 1973), p. 40.
13. *Ibid.*, p. 42.
14. *House of Assembly Debates*, 64, 1948, col. 609.

so one hopes, be guided and regulated, and may perhaps also be limited, but that it cannot be stopped or turned in the opposite direction.'[15]

The NP had scorned the Fagan Report, but Jansen's cautious response to it suggested an awareness of the difficulties which lay in store for apartheid theorists:

On the whole I think we are prepared to accept the findings of fact, but we are not prepared to accept all the conclusions and the remedies recommended in that report . . . I am not satisfied that the move to the urban areas is entirely natural.[16]

According to Beaumont Schoeman's account (which is admittedly tendentious, but which has not so far been refuted), Jansen's main problem was that his officials were mostly United Party sympathisers who were said to be taking advantage of his gentle nature and his inability to offer policy innovations. The hardliners in the caucus were scandalised when it emerged that he was seriously considering giving property rights to urban Africans, in total violation of NP policy.[17]

In his two-year tenure as minister Jansen achieved nothing substantial by way of legislation, but he was responsible for setting up two commissions of considerable importance. The first, under the chairmanship of Eiselen, was to investigate African education; the second, under F.R. Tomlinson, was to investigate the possibilities of socio-economic development of the reserves. The latter Commission reported in 1955 and its recommendations were to cause Jansen's successor, H.F. Verwoerd, some displeasure.

By late 1949 unhappiness in the caucus with Jansen's performance was growing, and Malan was made aware of this development. So far as is known Malan did nothing except to appoint a cabinet committee to assist Jansen. Nor did he take steps against another moderate, Dr A.J. Stals, minister of social welfare, who had offended the hardliners by dragging his feet on the issue of abolishing African school-feeding.[18]

The resignation in 1950 of the Governor-General and Jansen's elevation to this ceremonial office gave Malan the opportunity of appointing a new Minister of Native Affairs. The circumstances of the (momentous) appointment of H.F. Verwoerd, then in the Senate, are curious. Malan thought first of his friend Paul Sauer, who, after all, had been chairman of the NP's commission on racial policy. But Sauer refused the appointment, declaring that he would rather resign than take on the native affairs portfolio. Sauer managed to persuade Malan that

15. *Report of the Native Laws Commission*, Fagan Commission, (Pretoria: Government Printer, 1948), para. 28.
16. *House of Assembly Debates* 64, 1948, col. 1654.
17. B.M. Schoeman, *Van Malan tot Verwoerd*, pp. 41–3.
18. *Ibid.*, pp. 45 and 47.

Verwoerd was the right man: 'I said to Dr Malan that we needed a very dynamic person for native affairs; more dynamic than I could see myself being. And then he asked me of whom I was thinking. I said Verwoerd.'[19]

Verwoerd knew little about Africans, but as a newspaper editor between 1937 and 1948 he had been an ardent advocate of apartheid.[20] He was also a close associate of Strijdom, whose extreme views on the racial question were well known. Equally well known was Malan's coolness towards Strijdom. Why then did he appoint Verwoerd to so crucial a portfolio? Even Mrs Malan was reported to have wondered why her husband was including so difficult a man in his cabinet. But Malan was insistent, retorting that he could not forgo so brilliant a work-horse for a trifling personal reason.[21]

Strong provincial rivalries within the NP and, in particular, the cool relationship between Strijdom, the Transvaal leader, and Malan, who was also the Cape leader, threatened the unity of the party. Strijdom believed that the Transvaal had been under-represented in the original 1948 cabinet.[22] Now, with the centre of political gravity within the NP having passed to the Transvaal, Verwoerd's claims to a cabinet portfolio could hardly be overlooked. With Sauer's refusing native affairs, Verwoerd became a logical choice. Perhaps Malan did not appreciate what he was letting himself and his government in for. Around the time of his retirement in November, 1954, he is reported (though it has not been conclusively confirmed) to have said to intimates that 'apartheid has got out of hand' (*apartheid het handuit geruk*).

Neither of two insider accounts of Malan's cabinet reports any clashes of principle between Malan and Verwoerd. Beaumont Schoeman (whose tendentiousness has been noted) explicitly denies that there was tension between them and suggests, plausibly, that there is no evidence that such disagreements over principle occurred.[23] Ben Schoeman, who was Minister of Labour, describes his first cabinet clash with Verwoerd in explicit terms: Verwoerd informed the cabinet that he proposed to introduce legislation that imposed a total prohibition on the entry of Africans to the Witwatersrand, particularly the municipal area of Johannesburg. Schoeman registered vehement objections, maintaining that this would make it impossible to establish new industries in the area, that it would limit the expansion of existing industries and, because there was already a shortage of white workers, that the effect on the

19. Dirk and Johanna de Villiers, *Paul Sauer* (Cape Town: Tafelberg, 1977), p. 10.
20. G.D. Scholtz, *Dr Hendrik Frensch Verwoerd: 1901 –1966* (Johannesburg: Perskor, 1974), 2 vols, vol. 1, pp. 109–15.
21. Piet Meiring, *Ons Eerste Ses Premiers: 'n Persoonlike Terugblik* (Cape Town: Tafelberg, 1972), p. 82.
22. Ben Schoeman, *My Lewe in die Politiek* (Johannesburg: Perskor, 1978), p. 147.
23. B.M. Schoeman, *Van Malan tot Verwoerd*, p. 41.

country's economic growth could be deadly. Verwoerd reacted strongly and hard words were exchanged. Malan, writes Schoeman, 'had to bring about peace'. Other ministers, however, supported Schoeman's view, and Verwoerd had to back down.[24]

The episode is revealing in two respects: first, it illustrates the extreme lengths to which Verwoerd was prepared to go; secondly, it suggests that Malan either had no very strong views on the issue at hand, or that his cabinet was chaotic. Ben Schoeman's account does not suggest a Prime Minister who was prepared to give a decisive lead, at least in this area of policy: he did not seem willing either to spur Jansen into action or to cool Verwoerd's ideological ardours.

So far as is known, Malan had no direct contact with the African National Congress during his tenure of office. No doubt he shared the view of many of his colleagues that the ANC was 'communistic'. Even the moderate Natives' Representative Council (a powerless advisory body on which several leading ANC figures sat) he deemed to be a 'hot-bed for agitators' bent on creating 'a unified native nation' when no such thing existed.[25] Malan had little comprehension of the political forces stirring in the African population or of the ferment inside the ANC, which was moving to more militant strategies. His successors Strijdom, Verwoerd, Vorster and Botha were similarly purblind. Apartheid created its own system of cognitive dissonance.

At its annual conference in December 1951 the ANC decided to write to the Prime Minister informing him of their decision to hold protest demonstrations in April 1952 as a prelude to the implementation of a plan of passive resistance against unjust laws. The ANC called on the government to repeal a number of discriminatory laws not later than 29 February, failing which the defiance campaign would be commenced.[26]

Malan replied through his private secretary, noting pedantically that previous communications from the ANC had been sent to the minister of native affairs. His letter was inflexible in content and patronising in tone (it may have been drafted by Verwoerd) but its warning was clear: 'should you . . . incite the Bantu population to defy law and order, the government will make full use of the machinery at its disposal to quell any disturbances . . . ' The letter restated the government's views, claiming that Bantu and Europeans differed in ways that are 'permanent and not man-made', and insisting that apartheid laws which differentiated between people 'are largely of a protective nature'.[27]

24. Ben Schoeman, *My Lewe in die Politiek*, pp. 198–9.
25. *House of Assembly Debates*, 62, 1948, cols 71–2.
26. The letter is published in Leo Kuper, *Passive Resistance in South Africa* (London: Jonathan Cape, 1956), pp. 233–5.
27. The reply is published in *ibid.*, pp. 235–9.

The exchange revealed that there was no basis even for an exploratory dialogue between the government and the organisation that would, in time, become a formidable opponent. In the early 1950s, however, the ANC was still a comparatively weak organisation, although its capacity for mass mobilisation was increasing. Compared with the state, which did not hesitate to use vigorous methods of control, the ANC's political resources were puny. The defiance campaign of 1952–3, although it marked an important development in opposition strategy, was hardly a threat to the state. There is little doubt that the campaign actually helped the NP to fan racial fears and thereby increase its majority in the 1953 election.

In its essence apartheid was directed at precisely the class of urban-based ANC people whom Verwoerd used to dismiss as 'imitation Englishmen'. Their pretensions to leadership and their goal of African solidarity were wholly at variance with his thinking. Both as Minister of Native Affairs and as Prime Minister Verwoerd would lay heavy emphasis on the old tribal order and chiefs as the 'true' leaders of the various 'Bantu nations'. That Africans should 'develop along their own lines' became a principal *leitmotif* of policy.[28]

The underlying motivations were a complex blend of idealism and cynicism: idealistic to the extent that Afrikaner nationalists knew from their own experience just how alienating cultural domination could be; but cynical because cultural apartheid served the ends of racial domination. The preservation of 'tribalism' and 'tribal homelands' emphasised differences among Africans and between white and black, as well as providing some justification for the denial of citizenship rights to Africans in a common state. In one of his early major speeches as minister, Verwoerd with his customary frankness made clear the political rationale:

. . . it is clear that the key to the true progress of the Bantu community as a whole and to the avoidance of a struggle for equality in a joint territory or in common political living areas lies in the recognition of the tribal system as the springboard from which the Bantu in a natural way, by enlisting the help of the dynamic elements in it, can increasingly rise to a higher level of culture and self-government on a foundation suitable to his own inherent character.[29]

28. David Welsh, 'The Cultural Dimension of Apartheid', *African Affairs*, vol. 71, 1972.
29. A.N. Pelzer (ed.), *Verwoerd Speaks: Speeches 1948–1966* (Johannesburg: APB, 1966), p. 40.

J.G. Strijdom (1954–1958)

Malan's retirement and his replacement by Strijdom made little impact on the apartheid policy as far as Africans were concerned. Verwoerd continued his ruthless experiment in social engineering, though now with the backing of his long-time close ally from the Transvaal. Strijdom was frank and honest in his approach, but he was essentially a limited man whose views on racial issues embodied the harshest of white South African traditions. Strijdom represented the rural Transvaal constituency of Waterberg, then, as now, one of the most conservative constituencies in South Africa. (Until his death in April 1993, it was represented in Parliament by Dr A.P. Treurnicht, leader of the ultra-right Conservative Party.)

As early as 1930 Strijdom had concluded that total separation between white and black was impossible.[30] A more limited segregation, resting upon the *baasskap* (mastership) of whites, was, however, imperative. Strijdom, who had had a hand in formulating the recommendations of the Sauer Commission, subscribed emphatically to the view that urban Africans were temporary visitors and that their numbers could be reduced by replacing them in industry with poor whites and other whites coming in from the countryside.[31] His biographer, J.L. Basson, summarises his views thus:

He was also in favour of the native population in the cities being gradually reduced. The unemployed must be transferred either to the native areas or to the white farms where they would feel more at home. The natives were basically agriculturalists who experienced difficulties in adjusting to the town. On the farms, however, there were plenty of job opportunities for those who were prepared to work. Often farm labourers were presented with a falsely romantic view of the city, but after leaving the farms found themselves in miserable conditions. Strijdom repeatedly maintained that the native in the countryside represented no danger to white civilisation. The main reason for this is that he has maintained respect for his tribal membership there, and has not tried to become an 'imitation white man'.[32]

Strijdom's views contrasted with Malan's more in accent than in substance. Malan was from the Western Cape where, historically, comparatively few Africans lived or worked; whereas Strijdom's constituency was in many respects part of a frontier zone. Then, as now, whites perceived themselves as hugely outnumbered by nearby black multitudes. In comparison the Western Cape was settled and tranquil and, because of the presence of the large intermediate category of

30. J.L. Basson, *J.G. Strijdom: Sy Politieke Loopbaan van 1929 tot 1948* (Pretoria: Wonderboom, 1980), p. 581.
31. Thom, *D.F. Malan*, p. 280.
32. Basson, *J.G. Strijdom*, pp. 582–3.

coloured people, racial attitudes there tended to be less sharply polarised.

Strijdom even took the view that the whites would be threatened if undue efforts were devoted to African advancement. In a private letter to Malan in 1946 he warned:

When I listen to some of our MPs, clergy and others I think we are running a very great danger of accepting policies regarding school and university education for non-whites, the creation of large non-white, especially native colonies or towns or neighbourhoods in and near our white towns, which must eventually, if we have first civilised and developed those natives with schools and universities and other training, make the maintenance of the colour-bar impossible, and if, after we have developed and civilised the people, we want to withhold from them equal rights with the whiteman, bloody clashes and revolutions must follow. If we allow the natives in their millions to settle among us and in our towns, and they gradually develop and become civilised, as must and will necessarily happen, I am convinced that the existing colour line will slowly disappear and that equality will also slowly be established.[33]

Strijdom warned Malan about the danger of appointing a commission (he was referring to the future Sauer Commission) that would be too much under the influence of 'the Liberal School'. He feared that many of 'our' (i.e. Dutch Reformed) clergy, although theoretically in favour of the colour bar, were on the wrong track when it came to African education because 'they want to compete with other Church societies as to who could let the most Little Kaffers [*Klein Kaffertjies*] enjoy school education each year. The same, alas, is true of some of our Politicians.'[34] (Unfortunately, Strijdom did not name which NP politicians he had in mind. If there were closet liberals in the NP of those times they made an effective job of concealing their views. Perhaps Strijdom was making a veiled allusion to some of the Cape MPs, including possibly Sauer himself.)

Naturally Strijdom did not use such brutally frank language when he became Prime Minister. His views, however, remained rigid and inflexible, with the commitment to *baasskap* undiminished. There is no evidence to show that high office led to any significant softening of his basic attitudes. In a major speech on racial issues in 1956 Strijdom devoted much of his time to boasting about the government's achievements in implementing 'negative' apartheid: the segregating of trains and residential areas, the removal of so-called 'black spots' (African-owned freehold land situated away from homelands), and the extension of the prohibition of mixed marriages to include unions between white and coloured. He repeated also his view that total territorial apartheid was an unattainable ideal.[35] As Henry Kenney writes, Strijdom's term

33. Thom, *D.F. Malan*, p. 279.
34. *Ibid.*, p. 280.
35. *House of Assembly Debates*, 90, 1956, col. 43.

of office 'was marked by no noticeable policy advances, but rather by a still more uncompromising assertion of apartheid in South African life'.[36] Verwoerd and Strijdom remained close to each other, an alliance that had been strengthened by Verwoerd's major role in securing Strijdom's election as *hoofleier* of the NP and hence as Prime Minister, after Malan's retirement in 1954. No evidence of any significant ideological differences between the two men has emerged.

Ben Schoeman does, however, tell the interesting story of how in 1956 Verwoerd tried to persuade his cabinet colleagues that although total territorial separation was impracticable, it should nevertheless be proclaimed as an ideal to be striven for as this would encourage NP supporters to support policy even more strongly. Schoeman attacked this idea vigorously, declaring that it would be blatant fraud to propound what they knew to be incapable of realisation. Schoeman was not one to mince his words and Verwoerd did not like to be crossed on ideological matters. Strijdom, Schoeman records, had to intervene between the two to restore the peace.[37]

Schoeman also relates his refusal on behalf of his department (Transport) to abide by Verwoerd's policy (announced in 1955 by Eiselen) of treating the Western Cape as a coloured labour preference area from which African work-seekers would be debarred. Schoeman said bluntly that this was a stupid recommendation and that as far as the railways were concerned, 'I will continue to employ blacks.' Verwoerd was furious, accusing Schoeman of stabbing him in the back. Again, Strijdom had to make peace.[38]

Further angry words between the two occurred in 1957 when Verwoerd introduced highly controversial legislation without first circulating it in draft form among his cabinet colleagues. This was the so-called church clause, which gave the Minister of Native Affairs, in conjunction with the local authority, power to prohibit Africans from attending church services outside the African townships. Verwoerd, according to Schoeman's account, merely discussed the legislation, mentioning in passing the church clause, without referring to its controversial implications. These implications were immediately seized upon by the press, and a major church–state confrontation was underway. Even some of the Afrikaans churches expressed reservations.

The matter was raised at the next cabinet meeting. Schoeman writes:

As usual, when I had anything to do with Verwoerd, I expressed myself strongly. He defended the clause equally strongly. I said that it had been a

36. Henry Kenney, *Architect of Apartheid: H.F. Verwoerd – An Appraisal* (Johannesburg: Jonathan Ball, 1980), p. 143.
37. Ben Schoeman, *My Lewe in die Politiek*, p. 224.
38. *Ibid*.

mistake because the English churches would take no notice of the clause and that this would lead to confrontation with the government. The cabinet felt, however, that although the clause was undesirable it was at that stage too late to withdraw it.[39]

All three of the episodes described by Schoeman raise similar questions to that raised by the earlier clash between him and Verwoerd in Malan's cabinet: Strijdom seems to have been reluctant to take a decisive stand on either issue, neither supporting nor repudiating his protégé Verwoerd. In view of Strijdom's strength of will, the suggestion that the sickness which was to kill him in 1958 was already diminishing his capacity for decisive leadership is implausible. Schoeman was equally puzzled by Strijdom's deference to Verwoerd on colour issues. Strijdom, personally, was slightly more flexible than Verwoerd, but if Verwoerd had made up his mind about some issue Strijdom appeared reluctant to oppose him. 'I always had the feeling that Verwoerd was his conscience, which I could never understand since Strijdom was not a weak man.'[40]

Notwithstanding conflicts of the type mentioned by Schoeman, Verwoerd seems to have been given an extraordinary amount of latitude to shape policy in so critical an area. So far as is known, Verwoerd's rejection of the major recommendations of the Tomlinson Commission in 1956 went unchallenged in cabinet and caucus. His disastrous policies on Bantu education, which plunged African education into a crisis from which it is yet to recover, were similarly supported. Verwoerd, however, might legitimately have responded that criticisms of his policies from within the NP fold would have been both unlikely and improper since he was doing no more than implementing existing NP policy, most of which had been enshrined in the Sauer Commission's report. Verwoerd, contrary to the received view, was less the architect of apartheid than the indefatigable executor of apartheid policies.[41]

Verwoerd's attitude to the Tomlinson Commission provided revealing insights into the arrogance, ruthlessness and racism of the man who would in due course become Prime Minister. As has been said, the Tomlinson Commission was appointed by Verwoerd's predecessor in Native Affairs, E.G. Jansen. Verwoerd complained about the Commission after he had become minister, believing that his and his officials' knowledge of the problems of the reserves was sufficient to render the endeavours of the Commission superfluous.[42]

When the 16-volume report was finally completed in 1955 Verwoerd proceeded to reject some of its major recommendations, notably that

39. *Ibid.*, p. 228.
40. *Ibid.*, p. 237.
41. Cillié, *Baanbrekers vir Vryheid*, p. 61.
42. Scholtz, *Verwoerd*, vol. 1, p. 242.

white capital should be permitted in the reserves, that individual tenure should replace communal land tenure, and that an amount of £104 million should be spent on developing the reserves over the next ten years. Verwoerd is reported to have justified his refusal of white capital by saying, *inter alia*, that this 'would keep the Jews out'.[43]

Tomlinson was devastated. Relations with Verwoerd had deteriorated sharply during the Commission's life; at one stage Verwoerd is said to have accused the scrupulously honest Tomlinson of embezzling the Commission's funds. In a posthumous tribute to Tomlinson, his friend and colleague J.L. Sadie revealed further facts about the relationship: Verwoerd pressured two of his departmental officials who were serving on the Commission to retract their previous support for certain recommendations and instead to sign a minority report (which Tomlinson believed to have been formulated by Verwoerd himself); secondly, Tomlinson was required to refrain from any public comment on the report; and thirdly, Tomlinson's career advancement in the public service was blocked.[44]

Strijdom shared all the prevailing NP views about the ANC. Malan had at least replied to ANC representations, even if only through his private secretary. Strijdom, however, did not deign to reply to the letter sent to him in 1957 by the ANC's leader, Chief Albert Lutuli. Lutuli's letter recounted the impact discriminatory legislation was having on his people and entered a powerful plea for a common, democratic society. It was a firm and dignified statement of the ANC's position, which could hardly have been described as 'extreme'.[45] (Over 30 years later the ANC still mentioned Strijdom's failure to respond to their appeal: the snub had not been forgotten.)

With the unfurling of apartheid in the 1950s Verwoerd became the most prominent member of the cabinet, and it was this prominence that gave him the springboard to the premiership in 1958. By 1957, his private secretary has written, Verwoerd had begun to feel that he had served at Native Affairs for long enough – he had held the portfolio for longer than anyone else in South African parliamentary history. The criticism of apartheid was wearying him (not that he thought for a moment that the policy was wrong), but more importantly he believed that it was undesirable for an individual member of a government to be

43. Kenney, *Architect of Apartheid*, p. 110.
44. J.L. Sadie, 'Was Professor Tomlinson Verwoerd se Slagoffer?', *Rapport*, 3 March 1991.
45. The letter is published in Thomas Karis and Gwendolen M. Carter (eds.), *From Protest to Challenge: A Documentary History of African Politics in South Africa 1882–1964*, (Stanford, CA: Hoover Institution Press, 1977), 4 vols, vol. 3; Thomas Karis and Gail M. Gerhart, *Challenge & Violence 1953–1964*, pp. 396–403.

so closely associated with a policy for so long. Remarkably enough, criticism of him was coming even from NP supporters who accused him of 'doing too much for the Bantu'.[46] Verwoerd was deeply hurt by criticism of this kind. (Years later Vorster was to accuse Albert Hertzog, the *verkrampte* leader, of starting a group among ultra-rightists in the NP who believed, improbably enough, that Verwoerd was moving too far left.)[47]

H.F. Verwoerd (1958–1966)

Verwoerd's accession to the prime ministership did not lead to any sharp changes in the apartheid policy. He appointed ideological clones to the two portfolios into which Native Affairs had now been split. M.D.C. de Wet Nel, who became minister of Bantu Administration and Development, was supposed to be an expert on African life and custom (though a number of Nationalists doubted his competence), while another ideological acolyte, M.C. Botha, became Nel's deputy minister in 1960. W.A. Maree, the Natal leader of the NP and an ideological zealot, became minister of Bantu Education. With this trio the possibilities of ideological deviation were slim.

During Verwoerd's term as Prime Minister dissent within the ranks became equated with treason. The young NP backbencher Japie Basson who dissented from the legislation of 1959 that removed all African representation from parliament was drummed out of the party; SABRA intellectuals and NP-supporting newspapers were savaged for daring to demur at certain aspects of policy; Anton Rupert, the foremost Afrikaner entrepreneur, was cold-shouldered for venturing to suggest that Verwoerd had been mistaken in refusing to allow white capital into the homelands;[48] and some Dutch Reformed clergy, who had participated in a World Council of Churches deliberation on apartheid at Cottesloe, Johannesburg, were pilloried in a campaign of villification orchestrated by Verwoerd (see chapter 4 above).[49]

Verwoerd's zeal, dynamism and intellectual prominence within the government gave him a domination of the state that was not matched by his predecessors or his successors. He was determined, according to Nico Smith who heard him say it, to entrench apartheid so deeply in the society that whatever government came to power afterwards would find

46. Fred Barnard, *13 Jaar in die Skadu van Dr H.F. Verwoerd* (Johannesburg: Voortrekker Press, 1967), p. 49.
47. J.H.P. Serfontein, *Die Verkrampte Aanslag* (Cape Town: Human and Rousseau, 1970), p. 201.
48. W.P. Esterhuyse, *Anton Rupert: Advocate of Hope* (Cape Town: Tafelberg, 1986), pp. 46–9.
49. A.H. Lückhoff, *Cottesloe* (Cape Town: Tafelberg, 1978), pp. 163–7.

it impossible to undo what had been done.[50] Verwoerd was never wracked with self-doubt: once he had made up his mind that a particular course of action was the right one he was virtually unshakeable in his conviction. As minister he would go to endless lengths to get the information he wanted. His private secretary wrote: 'Hour after hour, until late in the night, they [Eiselen and Verwoerd] would ponder over a problem, debating and reasoning until a solution was found.'[51] In cabinet Verwoerd's style differed from that of Malan and Strijdom:

Each Minister had the fullest opportunity of putting his case. At the same time it became rapidly apparent that Verwoerd was not going to be simply the chairman of the Cabinet. We soon were made aware that he would not hesitate to give the lead. If a colleague differed from him, he was prepared to argue. Indeed, he liked nothing more than to argue, though he was not unamenable to persuasion. But he would have to be convinced, and if a colleague did not succeed in doing so, Verwoerd did not hesitate to overrule the Minister concerned.[52]

Naturally this oversight of all portfolios applied with especial force to African affairs, in which Verwoerd continued to take a deep interest. Sauer's biographers offer a similar picture of Verwoerd's domineering style as Prime Minister. Was he dictatorial? Yes, he was, replied Sauer, 'in so far as he could succeed in knocking down all opposition with logical argument – even when he started from a mistaken premiss.'[53]

Another insider from the Afrikaner nationalist establishment, Dirk Richard, makes the perceptive comment that for Verwoerd 'there was only one way, and that was the relentless road of no compromise. The slightest concession in matters of cardinal importance was for him corruption of commitment to principle.'[54] Verwoerd, in other words, was *konsekwent*: conventionally this word is translated as 'consistent' or 'logical', but the Afrikaans carries a moral connotation that is lacking in the English version. For Verwoerd the problem of 'petty' apartheid did not exist: all rules, large and small, providing for separation were necessary, and those deemed petty (separate entrances, separate lifts, prohibitions on mixed theatre audiences and the like) were actually necessary because even apparently small infractions of rules could cumulatively bring down the bigger apartheid structures. Moreover, the petty apartheid rules were apartheid's cutting edge; to the great mass of apartheid supporters these absurd rules were apartheid. As Piet Cillié

50. Interview with the Nederduitse Gereformeerde Kerk minister Nico Smith in Gerrit Olivier (ed.), *Praat met die ANC* (Johannesburg: Taurus, 1985), p. 26.
51. Barnard, *13 Jaar in die Skadu*, p. 49.
52. Ben Schoeman, *My Lewe in die Politiek*, p. 245.
53. Dirk and Johanna de Villiers, *Paul Sauer*, p. 124.
54. Dirk Richard, *Moedswillig die Uwe: Persoonlikhede in die Noorde* (Johannesburg: Perskor, 1985), p. 54.

ruefully noted, '"Petty apartheid" was popular, "grand apartheid" was the preoccupation of the intelligentsia . . .'[55]

In 1959 Verwoerd proclaimed what was regarded as a major break-through from 'negative' apartheid (intensifying colour barriers) to the adoption of 'positive' separate development, in terms of which new possibilities of unfettered development for the eight ethnic African nations were identified. In terms of traditional apartheid the reserves had been designated as the territorial base of each nation, but neither Malan nor Strijdom had ever contemplated that such embryonic nations could become formally independent sovereign states. In Strijdom's view the principal of *baasskap* might be somewhat attenuated in the reserves, but even so there was no doubt where ultimate control and legal sovereignty would lie.

Initially Verwoerd shared this view. Schalk Pienaar related how in the late 1950s a Dutch Reformed clergyman, Willem Landman, embarked on a speaking tour under the aegis of SABRA, of which he was chairman. Landman, a gentle, decent clergyman who took an optimistic view of the emancipatory possibilities in apartheid, stressed in his addresses that the status of the reserves could be raised, and he did not exclude the possibility of eventual independence. Verwoerd heard of these then-heretical thoughts and put a stop to Landman's trip. Pienaar remarks that those close to Landman knew what this episode cost him in body and spirit.[56]

However, in 1959 Verwoerd produced the idea of independent homelands as if it were his own, like a rabbit conjured out of a top-hat. Only a few months before this announcement no less a figure than Eiselen had expressed the view that homeland political evolution would stop short of full sovereignty.[57] Verwoerd dismissed any idea that there was a difference of opinion between him and Eiselen, saying that although Eiselen's article had appeared in March 1959 it had been written months before Verwoerd's statement in January that the home-lands might ultimately enjoy 'full authority'.[58]

In his speech on the Promotion of Bantu Self-Government Bill in May 1959 Verwoerd avoided delicate circumlocution and accepted that political evolution in the homelands could lead to 'full independence'.[59] In a long speech, probably his most significant statement on the racial issue, Verwoerd used his powers of remorseless logic to pulverise the

55. Cillié, *Baanbreker vir Vryheid*, p. 70.
56. Schalk Pienaar, *Getuie van Groot Tye* (Cape Town: Tafelberg, 1979), p. 60,
57. W.W.M. Eiselen, 'Harmonious Multi-Community Development', *Optima*, vol. 9, no. 1, 1959.
58. Pelzer, *Verwoerd Speaks*, p. 241.
59. *Ibid.*, p. 278.

ambivalent position of the opposition United Party, which offered the untenable alternative of 'white leadership with justice'.

Verwoerd was right in supposing that white South Africa was on the eve of making a crucial choice: either to integrate, which in Verwoerd's view must inevitably lead to 'Bantu control' (i.e. black majority rule), or to follow the separate nations route of separate development. Even before Harold Macmillan reminded him in 1960 in the 'wind of change' speech, Verwoerd was well aware of the decolonisation process in Africa and its implications for South Africa. Increasingly he would try to assimilate his own policies with those of the colonial power in its heyday.

The new vision of apartheid that Verwoerd was propounding suffered the same basic design fault as the earlier model: it was not separation in any real physical sense. Rather, it was political separation superimposed upon economic and social inequality in an integrated society. Africans could not share political power with whites in common political institutions; nor could they be granted equal status with whites in the white-controlled areas of South Africa. The white-controlled sector of the economy would continue to be dependent on African labour (bureaucratically canalised by the huge Native Affairs *imperium in imperio*); that labour would be migrant as far as possible so that the numbers of so-called 'detribalised' Africans would be held to a minimum.

The dependence of white farmers on African labour presented no theoretical problem to Verwoerd's scheme of things because this was not integration. The casuistry of his reasoning deserves critical attention because the propositions it supported were fundamental to the policy – and their untenability ultimately brought it crashing down. Economic integration, according to Verwoerd, occurred only when there was intermingling on the basis of equality:

We say that when a Native drives a tractor on a farm, he is not economically integrated . . . Merely because he helps the farmer to produce, is such a Native who operates a tractor integrated into the farmer's life and community? Of course he is not, because the concept of integration relates to people, and here we do not have people whose activities are becoming interwoven. They will only become interwoven in this way if the other forms of integration, namely equal social and political rights, result from these activities. I therefore repeat for the umpteenth time that we dare not succumb to this confusion . . . When a factory is reorganized, certain labour can be reduced or removed. If automation is introduced into a factory manual labour can in many instances be eliminated. But if the Native who was previously employed in that industry has been absorbed into one trade union with the Whites, and has acquired a share in the industrial and capital assets of the country, he cannot easily be removed at a later stage from the economic industrial entity. This is the difference between labour which we can remove and labour which

156 *David Welsh*

has become interwoven in so many other ways into the White community that it cannot be removed, even if we want to.[60]

This was an extraordinarily useful dogma – at least to those who believed it. It contained in it the germ of what Verwoerd's successor, John Vorster, would maintain; namely, that the actual numbers of people inside or outside of the homelands made no difference to the principle of separate development: what counted was their attachment to a nation. Verwoerd, however, was concerned with numbers. He recognised that if his policies were to have some credibility there must come a time when the flow of Africans to the white areas would turn around and their numbers begin to decrease. Verwoerd believed that 1978 would be the *annus mirabilis* in which this reversal would start.

The date 1978 had been arrived at in the mid-1950s in the debate surrounding the Tomlinson Report. Schalk Pienaar writes that sometime in the early 1960s (he does not give the exact year) the Minister of Bantu Administration and Development, De Wet Nel, clearly implied in a parliamentary speech that the 1978 target was unlikely to be achieved. Pienaar duly wrote in his newspaper that 'we had now taken leave of a good friend, the year 1978'. Pienaar recounts that two things occurred thereafter: Nel was given a dressing-down by Verwoerd and he, Pienaar, was heavily attacked by Verwoerd at an NP caucus meeting, without any mention being made of Nel's original speech. The mantra-like status of the magical year was thus retrieved, and it served as an ideological fiction for the rest of the Verwoerd era. It was finally abandoned by Vorster.[61]

Complementing Verwoerd's ideological contortions on the question of integration was an even more dubious analogy between South Africa and the European Community.[62] Black workers in the 'white' state, Verwoerd argued, resembled the *gastarbeiters* from Turkey, Algeria, Yugoslavia and other poorer countries who worked in Western Europe. They remained nationals of their countries of origin and did not obtain citizenship rights in the states in which they worked as migrants. Similarly, Verwoerd reasoned, the emerging European Community offered a possible model for South Africa to emulate. States retained their political sovereignty while becoming economically interdependent. Why should the emergent black states in South Africa not similarly enjoy political sovereignty while cooperating in a common market or commonwealth with the 'white' state? It irked Verwoerd that the High Commission Territories, which became independent Botswana, Lesotho

60. *Ibid.*, p. 183.
61. Schalk Pienaar, *10 Jaar Politieke Kommentaar* (Cape Town: Tafelberg, 1975), pp. 57–8.
62. Pelzer, *Verwoerd Speaks*, p. 279.

and Swaziland, were being groomed for independence by Britain and, while no one would question their status as sovereign political entities, their economic dependence on South Africa was as great as that of the homelands.[63]

Verwoerd's decision to concede the possibility of the homelands' becoming independent undoubtedly involved him in some political risk. His summary silencing of Landman a few years before suggested that he may have been sensitive about the issue. The opposition UP, although slowly declining as a political force, remained powerful and its opportunistic exploitation of the homelands independence issue as fragmenting South Africa might have been an effective weapon against the NP. It cost the NP few votes, but Kenney maintains that the new vision worried ultra-conservative Nationalists and thereby 'weakened Verwoerd's ability and inclinations to pursue a genuinely new course'.[64]

Kenney may be correct, but it is doubtful if Verwoerd was weakened for long. After his remarkable off-the-cuff response to Macmillan's 'wind of change' speech, his miraculous survival of an assassination attempt and his victory in the referendum over the republic issue – all of these events occurring in 1960 – Verwoerd was practically deified by his followers.

Verwoerd had not produced his 'new vision' in order to catch the UP between two stools (although it did exactly that). As has been suggested, he anticipated how much more isolated and exposed South Africa's racial policy would be when decolonisation of Africa gathered pace. He concluded that a policy based upon racial discrimination, as traditional apartheid undoubtedly was, could not be defensible in the long run. Verwoerd despised what he regarded as the spinelessness of the West. It was sick, he told parliament in 1964.[65] But, he recognised, it could not be ignored.

In a revealing speech in 1965 he explained why the old policy now had to be given a new justification:

We would rather have seen the old position maintained, but in the circumstances of the post-war world that was obviously not possible . . . Years ago the position prevailed where nobody doubted the White man's supremacy. The old British colonial policy itself was one of White supremacy over other states, and particularly the Black states. We had this policy in South Africa under Generals Botha [Prime Minister 1910–19] and Smuts [Prime Minister 1919–48], and even thereafter. The position was always that the White man ruled and expected the Bantu always to regard him as his guardian. For obvious reasons I said that we all wished that all these post-Second World War changes had not come about, because then surely the world would have been very comfortable

63. *Ibid.*, p. 246.
64. Kenney, *Architect of Apartheid*, p. 164.
65. *House of Assembly Debates*, 9, 1964, col. 53.

for us . . . But . . . in the light of the new spirit and the pressures exerted and the forces which arose after the Second World War it is clear that no country could continue as it did in past years. The old traditional policy of the White man as the ruler over the Bantu, who had no rights at all, could not continue.[66]

On 21 March 1960, 67 protesting Africans were shot dead by police at Sharpeville. On hearing the news in parliament Verwoerd leaned over to his bench-mate, Ben Schoeman, and said, 'Now we are going to have great problems.'[67] He was right. Sharpeville and the unrest around the country that ensued was in some sense the result of and a comment upon nearly a decade of policies for whose implementation Verwoerd had been largely responsible.

The immediate cause of Sharpeville had been a protest against the pass laws. In 1952 Verwoerd had drastically tightened their scope in an attempt to restrict urbanisation; in addition he had included women in the provisions of the legislation. More generally, urban Africans had been trussed in ever-tightening coils of restrictive legislation. In 1954, in his notorious speech on Bantu education, Verwoerd uttered words that were being flung back at the NP government even 30 years later. One of the most quoted of his remarks directly concerned the urban African: 'There is no place for him in the European community above the level of certain forms of labour.'[68]

Whatever Verwoerd's private emotions or the thoughts he may have exchanged with intimates, he showed no public sign of losing his nerve. He assured the party faithful at Meyerton, just five days after Sharpeville, that the troubles had not been caused by the black masses: 'The black masses of South Africa – and I know the Bantu in all parts of the country – are orderly. They are faithful to the government.'[69]

It was indeed true that Verwoerd had many meetings with Africans, almost certainly more than any of his predecessors, whether Ministers of Native Affairs or Prime Ministers. Invariably, however, his audiences were chiefs, headmen and their retinues who constituted the tribal ruling elite whom Verwoerd regarded as the authentic leaders. Apart, possibly, from a frosty occasion in 1950 when Verwoerd addressed the Natives' Representative Council (on which sat several ANC people), there is no evidence of Verwoerd's meeting with even moderate activists, whom he would have been disposed to describe as agitators. In none of his speeches during his entire parliamentary career does he once betray even the slightest recognition that his policies might be hurting people. He was the social engineer *par excellence*. Individuals or communities who were harmed in the implementation of the 'great

66. *Ibid.*, col. 627.
67. Ben Schoeman, *My Lewe in die Politiek*, p. 260.
68. Pelzer, *Verwoerd Speaks*, p. 83.
69. *Ibid.*, p. 375.

plan' had to be regarded as necessary sacrifices to the attainment of the 'higher good'. In a memorable description, Dawie (the pseudonym of the editor Piet Cillié) of *Die Burger* wrote:

Dr Verwoerd's spiritual make-up was overwhelmingly intellectual: ordered thoughts, clear doctrines, fixed future patterns. What was justified and correct in principle, had to be capable of implementation. Obstacles in human nature must give way to regulation and systematisation. The ideal must be imposed on the society.[70]

Not all of Verwoerd's cabinet shared the widespread belief in his omniscience. According to Beaumont Schoeman, soon after Sharpeville three senior ministers – Eben Dönges, Ben Schoeman and Paul Sauer – demanded far-reaching policy changes, notably that serious consideration ought to be given to abolishing the pass-book system. Verwoerd, however, reacted with impatient irritation and dismissed any such proposal as being out of the question.[71]

On 9 April 1960, with the tense country under a state of emergency, Verwoerd was shot by a would-be assassin. As senior minister, Sauer acted as Prime Minister while Verwoerd recuperated. Sauer had, cautiously, expressed misgivings about government policy on previous occasions. Faced with the Sharpeville crisis he did not share the *rotsvastheid* (literally 'being-as-firm-as-a-rock') that most of his other cabinet colleagues felt obliged to display. Instead, Sauer chose to deliver a major speech in his constituency, Humansdorp.

He began dramatically, saying that 'the old book of South African history was closed a few weeks ago at Sharpeville'. Now, he continued, the entire basis of the racial question would have to be reconsidered with seriousness and honesty. He called for a new spirit of trust between the races and major changes in how the government's policy was applied (he was careful to qualify this recommendation with the remark that no deviation from the declared policy would be involved). Black people, he said, must be given hope for a contented existence 'and not feel that they are continually being oppressed'.

In particular Sauer called for major changes in the enforcement of the pass laws, which, he noted, were one of the main causes of friction; the prohibition on the sale of liquor to Africans should be changed; contact between whites and peace-loving urban black leaders should be strengthened; serious attention should be given to raising black wages; and large-scale development of the homelands should be undertaken.[72]

70. Dawie (pseudonym of Piet Cillié), *John Vorster – 10 Jaar* (Cape Town: Tafelberg, 1976), p. 1.
71. B.M. Schoeman, *Van Malan tot Verwoerd*, p. 201.
72. Dirk and Johanna de Villiers, *Paul Sauer*, pp. 135–6.

In the light of subsequent developments Sauer's suggestions seem small beer, but with Verwoerd at the helm and in the circumstances prevailing in 1960 they were explosive. Before delivering his speech Sauer showed his notes to Dönges, who was Cape leader of the NP. Dönges responded: 'I agree with you, but I will not say so.'[73] Ben Schoeman, who also agreed in essence with what Sauer was going to say, cautioned him, saying 'You are going to cop it [*'Jy gaan bars'*] if you say this.'[74] That even such powerful and senior ministers, one of whom was a provincial leader, evinced such fear was a telling comment on the atmosphere in the Verwoerd cabinet.

Even from his hospital bed Verwoerd made his displeasure known. Sauer's biographers, unfortunately, do not describe in detail what actually transpired when Verwoerd and Sauer met four days after the Humansdorp speech, except to report Verwoerd's view that Sauer had gone too far. Major statements on policy were to remain his sole prerogative.[75] Predictably, relations between the two deteriorated. Sauer's comments on Verwoerd make clear his distaste for the man:

If you disagreed with Dr Malan, it never counted against you. With Verwoerd it did count against you. If you did not agree with Dr Malan over some specific issue, it was never anything personal for him. If you disagreed with Verwoerd he never forgot it.[76]

Sauer's speech and the flurry of concern over Sharpeville even within the white establishment led to the briefest of Prague Springs. Nationalists themselves were confused about whether Sauer's speech reflected new policy or not; some journalists, academics and clergy, though admittedly few, voiced carefully phrased disquiet. Dawie, of the most influential NP-supporting newspaper *Die Burger*, quickly perceived the real significance of Sharpeville:

It is clear to me that the future of our country and its whites is going to be made or broken by our future handling of the urban native. And I am not talking about five, ten or fifteen years from now. Our national timetables will have to be revised from top to bottom. It is what we do in the following weeks and months that will be decisive, otherwise we will totally lose the initiative that we still have.[77]

Dawie was correct: fundamental to the racial issue was the urban African population, those 'temporary sojourners' on whom the apartheid system bore hardest of all. Separate development, however, focused on homelands. Burgeoning freedoms in rural backwaters made

73. *Ibid.*, p. 137.
74. *Ibid.*
75. *Ibid.*, p. 138.
76. *Ibid.*, p. 140.
77. Louis Louw (ed.), Dawie — 1946–1964 (Cape Town: Tafelberg, 1965), p. 175.

no impression on urban dwellers, who wanted rights and security where they lived. To grant those rights would rip the heart out of separate development and, as he made clear, Verwoerd was not about to do that. In the course of a message read to parliament on 20 May he said:

The Government sees no reason to depart from its policy of separate development as a result of the disturbances. On the contrary, the events have now more than ever emphasised that peace and good order, and friendly relations between the races, can best be achieved through this policy.[78]

The basic principles would be adhered to: such political rights as might be enjoyed by urban Africans had to be exercised through the homelands, and there could be no relaxation of the pass laws – indeed, it was announced that as from 1 December 1960 it would be compulsory for African women also to carry reference books, the document that hooked individuals into the pass-law system.

While Sharpeville was undoubtedly a crisis, there was never any serious danger that the countrywide disturbances could escalate into a revolutionary uprising. Compared with what it was to acquire later, the state's instruments, both legal and physical, for coping with unrest were rudimentary. The ANC and the Pan Africanist Congress (PAC) were proscribed, over 11,000 people were detained under the state of emergency and public meetings were banned. By mid-April of 1960 protest had substantially petered out and the police felt confident enough to resume enforcement of the pass laws, which had been suspended shortly after 21 March.

Verwoerd had satisfied himself that the mailed fist was an effective way, indeed the only way, to deal with what his presuppositions made him believe was a small, unrepresentative bunch of agitators. In time Verwoerd introduced far tougher security laws and acquired an expanded and more efficient security police and, from August 1961, a Minister of Justice who had declared that 'you could not fight communism with the Queensberry Rules.' This was John Vorster's statement to Verwoerd on being offered the justice portfolio. Verwoerd agreed with this view and, according to Vorster, 'said that he would leave me free to do what I had to do – within reason.'[79]

The 1960s were a period of high growth in the economy. The country stabilised itself quickly after Sharpeville, and foreign investor confidence slowly returned. Both major banned organisations attempted to regroup underground and to mount guerrilla operations. By September 1966, however, when Verwoerd was assassinated on the floor of the House of Assembly, the state was congratulating itself on having smashed the underground organisations and extirpated the remnants of

78. *House of Assembly Debates*, 18, 1960, cols 8337–8343.
79, John D'Oliveira, *Vorster –the Man* (Johannesburg: Ernest Stanton, 1977), p. 125.

the ANC and the PAC. Several thousand people had been convicted of security offences, mostly involving the activities of banned organisations. Mopping up operations continued, but the authorities believed that with Angola, Mozambique and Rhodesia providing a *cordon sanitaire*, the wind of change could be neutralised or diverted into the harmless channels provided by the homelands.

Verwoerd had swiftly terminated the 'Prague Spring' and come down heavily on dissenters, waverers and others who showed tendencies towards independent thought. His narrow victory in the 1960 republic referendum gave his popularity inside the NP an immense boost, rendering him politically unassailable. In January 1961 he invoked the federal council of the NP – a body that is seldom convened – to put an end to the internal debate. His principal targets, according to Schalk Pienaar, were those Cape Nationalists who were becoming restive at the alienating effect of apartheid on the coloured people.[80] It had not gone unnoticed that no coloured people had joined the stay-aways in 1960, and none had participated in the protest march by 30,000 Africans in Cape Town shortly after Sharpeville.

Some senior Nationalists like Ben Schoeman were saying privately (though not, one may be sure, to Verwoerd) that a new and better relationship with the coloured people should be forged. Their cultural similarities made them 'a natural ally of the whites'.[81]

The federal council ended these public and private musings with a statement that bore the unmistakeable stamp of Verwoerd's arrogant sense of his own omniscience:

The Federal Council expresses its conviction that the Government is better placed than outsiders to judge on such matters as: who the leaders of the different racial groups are and how best consultation with them should take place; what need there is for legislation against mixed marriages; what forms of migrant labour were for various reasons unavoidable and even necessary.[82]

Only a few of the formidable number of matters cited by the federal council as off-limits have been quoted. As Pienaar wearily noted, 'lesser mortals had better keep quiet.'[83] The debate was killed off, and did not really resume until after Verwoerd's death.

Verwoerd's ascendancy remained unchallenged. At the time of his death in 1966 he was at a pinnacle, facing minimal opposition from the white electorate (indeed, the elections in March 1966 had seen unprecedented English-speaking support for the NP) and the extra-parliamentary forces. As Minister of Justice, Vorster was building up a fearsome

80. Pienaar, *Getuie van Groot Tye*, p. 60.
81. Ben Schoeman, *My Lewe in die Politiek*, p. 263.
82. Pienaar, *Getuie van Groot Tye*, p. 61.
83. *Ibid.*

reputation. If by the 'Queensberry Rules' he meant the rule of law, civil liberty and ancient principles like *habeas corpus*, they were indeed steadily eliminated. As Verwoerd's prominence at Native Affairs had propelled him into the premiership, so Vorster's prominence at Justice was his launch-pad in 1966.

B.J. Vorster (1966–1978)

Vorster was an entirely different kind of Prime Minister from Verwoerd. He possessed a certain native cunning and was a skilled political infighter but, unlike Verwoerd, he was no intellectual. Verwoerd could take a long view, however disastrously wrong his predictions (like that about 1978 being a turning point) might prove to be. Vorster was the political manager, the pragmatist and fixer. As a member of the pro-Nazi Ossewa-Brandwag organisation in the 1940s he had incurred Strijdom's and Verwoerd's displeasure, and he may have felt himself something of an outsider in the NP in the early days after winning the Transvaal constituency of Nigel in 1953.

His rise, however, was meteoric: he became a deputy minister in 1958 and a member of the cabinet in 1961. In 1966 he was still a relatively junior member of the cabinet. After Verwoerd's death the contest for the succession was vicious and acrimonious. Both of Vorster's rivals, Dönges and Schoeman, pulled out of the race, so Vorster was technically elected unopposed. But he was sensitive enough to know that he was not the first choice of a large number of his caucus, and that preservation of party unity was an issue that would have to receive his continual attention.

Verwoerd's complete domination of the cabinet, moreover, was not something that Vorster could hope to emulate, at least in the short run. His brief cabinet experience meant that he knew little about the workings of departments other than his own, as he openly acknowledged. Frank Waring, who was a member of both the Verwoerd and Vorster cabinets, says:

Soon after he [Vorster] took over he made it clear to the Cabinet that he was relying on his ministers. Each minister would have the responsibility for looking after his own portfolio. Vorster would not hand down decisions, he would listen to his ministers, question them, make suggestions . . . never give orders. While Verwoerd was largely a dictator, Vorster brought us back to true Cabinet rule and true Cabinet responsibility.[84]

Vorster himself knew little about the African population and the inner workings of the huge departments of state that governed their lives.

84. D'Oliveira, *Vorster – the Man*, p. 233.

M.C. Botha, already described as an ideological acolyte of Verwoerd, became minister of Bantu administration and development and of Bantu education in April 1966 (he was actually appointed by Verwoerd, which was testimony to his ideological reliability) and continued to hold these portfolios until early 1978. Botha will perhaps be remembered mainly for his appeal, before 1960, for white mothers 'to have a baby for the republic.'[85] This foolish statement did incalculable harm to the cause of family planning by politicising birth control. Like Verwoerd's speech on Bantu education in 1954, Botha's call was being flung back at the country's population development programme by African critics of birth control programmes decades later.

M.C. Botha was an unimaginative and wooden reactionary who, predictably, sought to keep his earlier patron's principles alive. Ben Schoeman confirms Botha's adulation of Verwoerd, commenting that his actions often coincided precisely with what Verwoerd would have done.[86] His claim to be Verwoerd's ideological heir also strengthened his position in the party hierarchy. There were from time to time murmurings that separate development was stagnating through insufficiently vigorous implementation, but Botha's reputation as the custodian of ideological orthodoxy largely neutralised whatever force such criticisms may have had.

By now Botha's ministries had become bureaucratic leviathans and strongholds of Verwoerdian orthodoxy. Such administrative reformism as crept into the system in the Vorster era seems to have been principally the work of reformist deputy ministers waging guerrilla war against bureaucrats.[87]

The horrifying circumstances of Verwoerd's death could not conceal another emotion that was widely felt even inside the NP's support base: relief.[88] Vorster's more relaxed style and the disappearance of the atmosphere of fear created by Verwoerd opened up some space for more internal debate. Verwoerd, the saying in the NP had it, 'thought for all of us'. This was an exaggeration, but the penalties that were visited upon innovative and independent thinkers were sufficient of a deterrent to what the Stellenbosch philosopher J.J. Degenaar called 'moral-critical' thought.

No one in the NP, and certainly not Vorster, possessed Verwoerd's unique blend of brilliance, zeal and omniscient dogmatism. No one could assume his mantle. In a shrewd assessment of Vorster's first full

85. Virginia van der Vliet, 'South Africa's Population Crisis', *Optima*, vol. 32, no. 4, 1984, p. 153.
86. Ben Schoeman, *My Lewe in die Politiek*, p. 414.
87. Matthew Chaskalson, 'Apartheid with a Human Face', *African Studies*, vol. 48, no. 2, 1989.
88. Pienaar, *Getuie van Groot Tye*, p. 65.

parliamentary session as Prime Minister, Gerald Shaw, political correspondent for the *Cape Times*, noted that Vorster was 'treading water': there was

not much sign of a distinctive Vorsterian framework. Here it has been the mixture-as-before. True, Mr Vorster's generally pragmatic approach and his obvious disinterest in ideology have injected a new flexibility in to the political atmosphere. But, so far, this has been mainly a question of atmosphere.[89]

Vorster reaffirmed all the basic tenets of separate development, and would continue to do so throughout his premiership. He assured the senate in 1967 that blacks would never be represented by blacks in parliament: 'it will never, under any circumstances, take place because it is wrong in principle.'[90] He defended separate development as a policy that 'can be tested against the requirements of Christianity and morality.' He declared it to be 'the nation's policy . . . it has become the policy of white and non-white in South Africa.'[91]

Vorster's pragmatism, nevertheless, entered his speeches as a distinctive sub-theme. He told an NP meeting in Koffiefontein in August 1967 that while the NP had always been conservative in outlook, to be conservative had never meant that the NP would stand still or stagnate. Privately he was telling scandalised ultra-right-wingers in the NP something with highly subversive potential: that separate development was a method, not a dogma. Dirk Richard quotes him as telling a group of NP MPs shortly after his election:

No, chaps, you have all got it wrong. The cardinal principle of the NP is the retention, maintenance and immortalisation of Afrikaner identity within a white sovereign state. Apartheid and separate development is merely a method of bringing this about and making it permanent. If there are other better methods of achieving this end, then we must find those methods and get on with it.[92]

A.M. van Schoor's account is similar, being derived from the same informant, Jaap Marais, who was to become one of the leading *verkrampte* dissidents.[93] Marais, no doubt with the benefit of historical hindsight, declared subsequently that his belief that Vorster was reneging on fundamental principles, or at least going soft on them, stemmed from this meeting. He claimed that this was the origin of the huge fight that

89. *Cape Times*, 17 June 1967.
90. *Senate Debates*, 1967, col. 3619.
91. O. Geyser (ed.), *B.J. Vorster: Select Speeches* (Bloemfontein: Institute for Contemporary History, University of the Orange Free State, 1977), pp. 78 and 83.
92. Richard, *Moedswillig die Uwe*, pp. 134–5.
93. J.A. du Pisani, *John Vorster en die Verlig/Verkrampstryd: 'n Studie van die Politieke Verdeeldheid in Afrikanergeledere, 1966 –1970* (Bloemfontein: Instituut vir Eietydse Geskiedenis, Universiteit van die Oranje-Vrystaat, 1988), p. 24.

developed inside the NP and led, in 1969, to the breakaway of four ultra-right MPs and the formation of the Herstigte Nasionale Party (HNP).[94]

This allegation became interwoven with others in the *verkramptes'* catalogue of complaints against Vorster: that diplomats from the African countries which Vorster was assiduously wooing in terms of his 'outward' policy would have to live on a basis of complete non-discrimination, which would be the thin end of the wedge; that Vorster's painful revision of Verwoerd's strict enforcement of the apartheid principle in sport (including a refusal to allow Maori players to tour with New Zealand rugby teams) was an unacceptable deviation from apartheid; that the policy of encouraging 'national unity' between Afrikaans-and English-speaking whites was unacceptable because it diluted Afrikaner exclusivity; that the immigration policy would lead ultimately to the swamping of Afrikaners; and that too much was already being spent on black development.[95] In time, the *verkramptes* would also accuse Vorster of 'selling the Rhodesian whites down the river'.

The first four years of Vorster's premiership were dominated by the internal dispute. In the end the breakaway was small, and the rough, crude style of the newly formed HNP proved to have minimal electoral appeal, as the 1970 election showed. Vorster, nevertheless, was emotionally drained by the intensity of the struggle. In August 1967 he was on the point of resigning, but was dissuaded from doing so.[96] Vorster recovered his nerve and went on to establish a towering ascendancy in the NP. In the third election he fought as Prime Minister, in 1977, Vorster's NP won 134 out of the 164 contested seats, the biggest victory in South African parliamentary history.

He seemed politically unassailable, and had he wished to do so he could have pushed through significant reforms to the apartheid order. Some of Vorster's critics have held this failure to use his authority against him. The criticism is to some extent misplaced since Vorster at no time in his premiership showed any sign of preparedness to do more than effect minor tinkerings with the system he had inherited. Vorster was the party manager *par excellence*. He was also aware that those who defected in 1969 were the merest tip of a substantial conservative iceberg. Many of these conservatives, like Andries Treurnicht, believed that to join the HNP was to go into the political wilderness.

That Vorster lacked vision is another criticism that has some validity. His temperament and style as a manager predisposed him to avoid thinking in long-term projections – as Verwoerd had never hesitated to do. It was for this reason that he declined to associate himself with the

94. *Ibid.*
95. *Ibid.*, pp. 33–55.
96. Ben Schoeman, *My Lewe in die Politiek*, pp. 334–5.

magical date of 1978, or to spell out what the political future of the coloured people might be: that, he said, was a problem for which 'our children after us will have to find a solution.'[97] Vorster's biographer John D'Oliveira wrote that in lengthy discussions with him 'he consistently evaded serious discussion of the future, like a chess player determined not to reveal his moves to anybody.'[98]

Notwithstanding Vorster's lack of vision and his refusal to tamper with the basic apartheid order, certain important processes began in the Vorster era, especially in the 1970s, which turned out to have major consequences for the fate of apartheid. These processes included ideological and material change, whose combined effect served to undermine the confidence that Verwoerd had inspired in his followers.

Vorster did not like *lojale verset* (loyal opposition, i.e. that which came from within his primary support base), but he did not persecute and hound it with the vindictiveness and viciousness shown by Verwoerd. Vorster's time was reminiscent of the post-Stalinist thaw under Khruschev. He tolerated more freedom of discussion in his cabinet, while the robustness of the *verligte–verkrampte* dispute, in which newspapers were centrally involved, significantly unfroze the debate within Afrikaner civil society. The extreme rigidity of the *verkramptes* and the crude racism of the HNP began to have subtle effects on a rising generation of Afrikaners, who were better educated, better off financially and more secure in their Afrikaner identity than their elders. Increasingly the parameters of traditional conceptions of Afrikaner nationalism would become restraints against which they chafed; simultaneously the stultified vision of the *verkramptes* repelled them absolutely. The *verligtes* were themselves symptomatic of the growing diversity of Afrikanerdom that encompassed far more than mere widening internal class differentiation.

Vorster's refusal to regard apartheid as anything more than a method must also have played a part in deconsecrating Verwoerdian orthodoxy. Vorster's view may have been heresy to the *verkramptes*, but it became commonplace in the 1970s. In 1972, for instance, C.P. Mulder, a rising star in the Transvaal NP hierarchy and the Minister of Information, could defend separate development as the only policy yet devised that could meet the requirements of the South African situation, but insist that 'the policy is not based on ideology but on pragmatism.'[99] Vorster's cautious, pragmatic moves in adjusting policy to meet changing realities and requirements set up, in turn, pressure for more moves. Methods,

97. *House of Assembly Debates*, 65, 1969, col. 369.
98. D'Oliveira, *Vorster – the Man*, p. 287.
99. C.P. Mulder, 'The Rationale of Separate Development', in N.J. Rhoodie (ed.), *South African Dialogue: Contrasts in South African Thinking on Basic Race Issues* (Johannesburg: McGraw-Hill, 1972), p. 49.

after all, are judged by their effectiveness, and if that became the test there was no reason why the whole range of institutions, administrative procedures and practices should not come under scrutiny.

Early on in Vorster's premiership critics targeted an obvious weak point: separate development was not working because the number of Africans in the 'white' areas was increasing. Vorster fended off this criticism with the tortuous argument that numbers were not the only issue:

Numbers are not the most important factor, nor can they ever be the most important factor, for the simple reason that one can have separate development with a million people in one's midst, whereas one can have integration with a hundred thousand people in one's midst. It simply depends on what one's approach is.[100]

In the same debate M.C. Botha had expressed a similar view, though emphasising that it was the prevention of racial equality within the 'white' areas that was crucial, since equality would mean that 'they can integrate with the whites into one entity.'[101] This was reminiscent of vintage Verwoerd. Botha had also claimed that numbers were not the only criterion, but he insisted that the numbers of Africans in the 'white' areas should be limited: 'According to our policy one should be in the majority in one's own homeland and in the minority in another person's land.'[102] The main instrument for limiting numbers, the pass laws, continued to be enforced with full rigour throughout the Vorster era. Increasingly, though, their effectiveness was declining, as the percentage of Africans whose presence in the white towns was technically illegal rose.

Vorster himself showed no sign of recognising that his administration was sinking more deeply into self-deception. His speeches emphasised its commitment to the main principles of separate development. Moreover, he took a hard line on the land issue: no more land could be added to the homelands other than the 13.7 per cent allocated in terms of the land legislation of 1913 and 1936.[103] Vorster subscribed fully to the historical myth that African land had not been alienated in the nineteenth century. Thank God, he said, that 'the black man retained his land in South Africa.'[104]

It was in Vorster's time that separate development first bore what was supposed to be its finest fruit – a sovereign homeland in the form of Transkei, which received independence in 1976. It was followed by

100. *House of Assembly Debates*, 65, 1969, col. 356.
101. *Ibid.*, col. 46.
102. *Ibid.*, col. 47.
103. *Ibid.*, col. 363.
104. *Ibid.*, col. 362.

Bophuthatswana in 1977 and, in P.W. Botha's time, Venda in 1979 and Ciskei in 1981. If Vorster had hoped that this mode of decolonisation would reap some benefits in the form of vindication of South Africa's policies in the West and in black Africa, which his outward policy had targeted, he was sadly disappointed. None of the independent states (referred to collectively as the TBVC states) received international recognition, except of course from South Africa and from one another. And whatever credibility the South African government might have achieved was substantially outweighed by the storm of criticism, both local and international, that was evoked by the compulsory deprivation of South African citizenship that citizens of the new states suffered, regardless of whether they lived inside or outside the homeland in question. Vorster stuck firmly to the traditional apartheid principle that Africans could exercise political rights only in 'their' homelands, regardless of where they actually lived. In an interview in 1976 he said:

The urban Black, when it comes to exercising his political rights, will exercise them in his own state. They have the vote and urban Blacks have made themselves eligible for election to the parliaments of the various Black states. Urban Blacks have served in the Cabinet of Black states and in one case the leader of a Black Homeland is an urban Black.[105]

The homeland led by an urban black was QwaQwa, which was hardly a persuasive example for the argument Vorster was trying to make. QwaQwa was minuscule: fewer than 10 per cent of its citizens actually lived within its boundaries, and over 80 per cent of its GNP was generated outside the homeland, by migrants and commuters.[106]

In another interview Vorster rehashed the same arguments to a sceptical American interviewer who thereupon put the following (largely rhetorical) question:

As I understand your parallel, Sir, it would be similar to saying that if a man came from the State of Louisiana and lived all his life and reared his family in New York, his children could only exercise their rights in Louisiana because that was their homeland. Is that the kind of state you really want for your country?

Vorster's lame response was that that had always been the position 'and nobody seemed to find fault with it'.[107]

Naturally, Vorster's assumptions about the nature of African politics were refracted through the apartheid prism. He denied the reality of African nationalism and scorned the pretensions of its modern political

105. Geyser, *B.J. Vorster*, p. 335.
106. South African Institute of Race Relations, *A Survey of Race Relations in South Africa*, Johannesburg, 1975, p. 140; *ibid.*, 1983, p. 364.
107. Geyser, *B.J. Vorster*, p. 343.

leadership in the urban-based organisations. His paranoid views on communism inclined him to view all domestic nationalist organisations as basically communist-inspired. His visceral hatred of the Namibian leader Sam Nujoma stemmed from this belief. With the exception of what sounds like a chilly and brief meeting with Duma Nokwe, a leading ANC activist, in the early 1950s, before he entered parliament, Vorster is not known to have met any non-homeland political leader of note in South Africa.[108] In 1975 President Tolbert of Liberia asked if the Pan Africanist Congress leader Robert Mangaliso Sobukwe (who had been confined to Kimberley after his release from prison) could visit Liberia for Tolbert's installation as President. Vorster refused to permit this, saying that Sobukwe was not the leader of the African people in South Africa: 'It would have been a slap in the face to the actual, the elected and natural leaders of the black people in South Africa if I had done so.'[109]

Vorster was no doubt pleased with the relative absence of large-scale urban protest after the presumed destruction of the ANC and PAC in the 1960s. No doubt, too, he placed considerable faith in the advice of the security police and, more especially, in that of his long-time associate General Hendrik van den Bergh, who headed the Bureau of State Security. Almost certainly neither the security police nor Van den Bergh would have advised any let-up in the vigilance that had characterised the post-Sharpeville era. After the mid-1960s homeland leaders like Chief Kaiser Matanzima of Transkei and Chief Mangosuthu Buthelezi of KwaZulu appeared to fill the vacuum in African politics that the banning of the two Congresses had created. However in the late 1960s a new phenomenon, black consciousness, arrived on the scene; it grew powerfully in the segregated schools and universities in both urban and rural areas. By the early 1970s protest, demonstrations and defiance of the authorities became frequent in several black university colleges, including the University of the Western Cape, which apartheid planners had designated specifically for the coloured people. In the emerging political context, however, 'black' embraced African, coloured and Indian, the category formerly known as 'non-white'.

In addition to the stirrings among the youth, large-scale strikes occurred during 1973, particularly in Natal. These were harbingers of the mobilisation of a powerful focus of African protest: the independent trade union. Vorster's reaction to the Natal strikes was moderate, even sensible. He did not wield the big stick, nor did he blame the strikes on communist manipulation. On the contrary, he declared that all involved, including the government, could learn from what had happened. Vorster

108. D'Oliveira, *Vorster – the Man*, pp. 260–1.
109. Geyser, *B.J. Vorster*, pp. 300–1.

had obviously been informed about the pitiful wages that the striking workers were receiving from largely English-speaking industrialists. He told parliament that

. . . there have been too many employers who saw only the mote in the Government's eye and failed completely to see the beam in their own. Now I am looking past all party affiliations and past all employers, and experience tells me this, that employers, whoever they may be, should not only see in their workers a unit producing for them so many hours of service a day; they should also see them as human beings with souls.[110]

Later on, in 1977, Vorster was to appoint a commission of inquiry into labour legislation under the chairmanship of Professor N.E. Wiehahn. This Commission's recommendations formed the basis of momentous legislation in 1979 that recognised African trade unions and brought them within the scope of the industrial conciliation machinery for the first time. The recognition was a milestone because the denial of legitimate or effective trade union rights to Africans was so deeply entrenched in South Africa that many observers could, with justice, consider it one of the props of the segregated order. Mobilised worker power represented leverage, both economic and political, and previous administrations had not tolerated that.

The *coup* in Portugal in 1974, and the subsequent independence of Angola and Mozambique, as well as the intensification of civil war in Rhodesia, all served to reinvigorate black protest in South Africa. The message of black consciousness spread like wild-fire, imbuing its young adherents with a more intense determination to end racial opposition than their elders had been able to summon up. Since its strongholds were in the schools and universities it is not surprising that Verwoerd's legacy, Bantu Education, became the flashpoint of the Soweto uprising in June 1976. The details of the ensuing period of turbulence have been widely described in several studies and need not be recounted here; what concerns us are Vorster's role in the events that led to the initial confrontation between police and protesters on 16 June, and his reactions to events.

As Prime Minister, Vorster, of course, had to bear overall responsibility for what happened, but the evidence thus far revealed does not directly implicate him in the remarkable sequence of official bungles and the complacent ineptitude of both the education officials in the Witwatersrand area and Vorster's appointed deputy minister, A.P. Treurnicht. But what happened was a far-reaching indictment of the whole separate development policy (as even the cautiously worded

110. South African Institute of Race Relations, *Survey of Race Relations 1973*, p. 283.

Cillié Commission implicitly acknowledged),[111] and for this Vorster must take a large part of the blame.

With the introduction of the new system of Bantu education in 1955, official policy insisted that the official languages of Afrikaans and English be used on a 50–50 basis as media of instruction in African secondary schools. (This insistence, incidentally, stemmed from a long-standing resentment among certain Afrikaner nationalists as well as the Broederbond that Afrikaans was being eclipsed in African schools, thereby jeopardising the longer-term security of Afrikaans in the country as a whole.)[112] A shortage of African teachers who were bilingual in both official languages, however, made it impossible fully to implement the policy.

In a meeting with homeland leaders in March 1974, representations were made to Vorster and other ministers that the official language used in secondary schools in the homelands should also be used in African schools in the 'white' areas. In practice this would mean that English would be used virtually universally. Overwhelmingly this is what Africans themselves wanted and Vorster, according to the record, voiced no fundamental objection. Indeed, he suggested that the possibility should be investigated.[113] So far as is known his suggestion was ignored, because the old policy was not only retained but began to be enforced with increased rigour.

On 26 January 1976 Treurnicht was appointed Deputy Minister of Bantu Administration and Education (M.C. Botha was still minister in this portfolio.) Treurnicht had entered parliament in 1971; as has been noted, even then he enjoyed the reputation as spiritual leader of the ultra-right forces within the NP fold. His rapid ascent in the hierarchy reflected the strength of his grassroots support in the Transvaal. Probably Vorster felt obliged for political reasons to make him a deputy minister. It was also a way of reining in any propensities that Treurnicht might have shown to strike out on an independent *verkrampte* line. Little, if anything, however, separated him ideologically from those who had broken away. Whatever Vorster's reasons may have been, the appointment of Treurnicht to so sensitive a post was a monumental blunder. Moreover, Vorster could not plead ignorance, because Treurnicht's hardline views were well-known.

All through the first half of 1976 the situation in Soweto schools

111. *Verslag van die Kommissie van Ondersoek oor die Oproer in Soweto en Elders van 16 Junie 1976 tot 28 Februarie 1977*, Cillié Commission (Pretoria: Government Printer, 1979).

112. B.F. Nel, *Naturelle – Opvoeding en Onderwys* (Bloemfontein: Nasionale Pers, 1942), 2 vols, vol. 1, p. 37.

113. South African Institute of Race Relations, *Survey of Race Relations 1976*, pp. 51–8.

deteriorated. Treurnicht was informed at least twice by non-official sources of the seriousness of the growing conflict, but he reacted with no sense of urgency. It is not known whether Vorster was kept abreast of developments, but in the light of Treurnicht's apparently casual attitude this seems unlikely. However, Vorster's ignorance and the fact that the government was taken by surprise does not exculpate him. Even a casual newspaper reader at the time would have been aware of the crisis that was building up, and in any case Vorster's government as a whole, on the principle of collective responsibility, should have had to take the blame for what happened.

Vorster, of course, did not see it that way, and nor did he apparently see the debacle as an indictment of his particular style of conducting government. Treurnicht was unrepentant. Willem de Klerk, then editor of *Die Transvaler*, has described how in November 1976 Vorster took umbrage at a cartoon of Treurnicht sitting back-to-front on a horse, pulling its tail, thus suggesting, none too subtly, Treurnicht's attempt to prevent necessary changes. That Vorster could indignantly demand proof that Treurnicht's views were anything but fully in line with NP policies demonstrated his continuing efforts to straddle the widening division in the NP, even to the extent of trying to protect Treurnicht – several months after the Soweto debacle – from hostile comment in the Afrikaans press. De Klerk notes that 'Vorster was furious, and enlightened [*verligte*] people repeatedly had to put up with humiliating insults, also from his ministers.'[114] Amazingly enough Treurnicht remained in his post until mid-1979, acquiring the equally sensitive post of Deputy Minister of Plural Relations in April 1978. (Plural relations was a new and euphemistic title for the former ministry of Bantu Administration and Development.) It was only after Treurnicht's breakaway and the formation of the Conservative Party (CP) in 1982 that NP members began openly to blame his negligence and his wilful adherence to the 50–50 policy for an uprising that could have been defused or prevented.

Apart from a few brief comments in parliament after 16 June and a tough statement on the need to maintain law and order, Vorster remained silent for nearly ten weeks after the rioting began. In August the *Cape Times* was commenting on the 'long silence of the Prime Minister and the apparent paralysis of his Government'.[115] Gerald Shaw wrote: 'Mr Vorster, as seems to be his custom in times like this, is waiting until he is sure of the drift of public opinion, particularly among Nationalists, before he shows his hand.'[116]

114. Willem de Klerk, *F.W. de Klerk: The Man in his Time* (Johannesburg: Jonathan Ball, 1991), pp. 111, 114.
115. *Cape Times*, 14 August 1976.
116. *Ibid.*, 28 August 1976.

Vorster was indeed paralysed. He was an intelligent and surprisingly sensitive man who could not fail to have understood the significance of the massive demonstrations of black anger, but neither could he see a way out of the mess. Eventually he seems to have decided that he would proceed with minor tinkerings while perpetuating the major pillars of the old policy. In November 1976 a Broederbond circular reported Vorster's thoughts at a secret meeting of its executive:

The Executive was riveted by the declaration of faith with which the Prime Minister recently concluded a frank discussion. He stressed with great determination that his profound analysis of the recent trying months and weeks had convinced him anew that there is no way to handle race relations but the way of separate development. He added that the greatest legacy of Dr Verwoerd was his vision of separate homelands which could be developed to full independence. Without the homeland policy, he said, we would now have been in the same position as Rhodesia. He called on the [Broederbond] to take stock and throw everything into the battle to maintain and promote this policy.[117]

The violence rumbled on into 1977. On 12 September Steve Biko, the black consciousness leader, died in horrifying circumstances while in police custody; in the following month 18 organisations, mostly black consciousness in their views, were banned. This was the traditional Vorster approach. It helped him to an overwhelming victory in the general election of November 1977, but the huge margin of electoral success could not conceal a bankruptcy of policy and, even more, evidence of heartlessness – as in the notorious comment by Jimmy Kruger, the Minister of Justice, that Steve Biko's death 'leaves me cold'; or in the disgraceful remark by an NP MP, Frank le Roux, that he 'would have killed Steve Biko'.[118]

To their credit some NP candidates repudiated le Roux, who is now a Conservative Party MP. Kruger, however, was not publicly repudiated, and even though he is said to have offered his resignation Vorster declined to accept it. To the immense chagrin of *verligtes*, Kruger remained in office until mid-1979, when he was dropped by P.W. Botha and despatched to the Senate. After 1982 he joined the CP.

Vorster's premiership ended in humiliating circumstances in September 1978. He was a victim of the Information Scandal, but in a significant sense the scandal arose out of circumstances that he himself had perpetuated. First, the unorthodox activities of the Bureau for Information stemmed directly from efforts to counter the growing international hostility to apartheid; secondly, the irregularities that

117. Ivor Wilkins and Hans Strydom, *The Super-Afrikaners: Inside the Afrikaner Broederbond* (Johannesburg: Jonathan Ball, 1978), p. 214.
118. *Cape Times*, 9 November 1977.

occurred stemmed from an abuse of ministerial power that might not have occured in a more tightly controlled cabinet (see chapter 3 above). The latitude that Vorster allowed his ministers led ultimately to his downfall.

Vorster's changes to the legal and administrative expression of apartheid were, to say the least, modest. By an extraordinary process of conceptual *legerdemain* Vorster's Minister of Sport and Recreation, Dr Piet Koornhof, managed to secure some limited desegregation of sport by invoking the fiction of multinationalism: each national group had to play sport separately, but they might play against one another in multinational events. At all events Vorster's reformulation was a repudiation of Verwoerd's crass statement of sports policy in 1965.

Similarly, higher class hotels and restaurants might acquire multinational status and thereby admit people of all races. An elaborate (and ultimately unworkable) system of permits for mixed gatherings, events and venues was initiated. Moreover, a start was made in weeding out 'unnecessary' discriminatory rules.

Opponents mocked these tortuous processes of change, but in fact each was a significant symbolic beachhead won against the serried ranks of entrenched *verkramptes*, who, rightly, saw that each concession, however trifling in itself, set up a precedent and created its own momentum for further change. For them *konsekwentheid* was not just obsessiveness for its own sake, but a necessary condition of maintaining the 'correct' level of colour-consciousness.

Concerning the crucial issue of urban Africans, Vorster disingenuously insisted that the main principles of policy were not being changed when he announced in 1977 that Africans could acquire their own homes in urban areas on a 99-year leasehold basis; they could inherit, sell or mortgage these homes, but they could not own them in freehold, for 'That is in conflict with the policy of the NP,' said Vorster.[119] In another change at the same time Vorster announced the rescinding of an earlier regulation that prevented urban Africans from owning more than one business.[120]

This section on Vorster has stressed that he tolerated a greater degree of internal debate than Verwoerd. Afrikaner civil society recovered its nerve and increasing numbers of individuals and organisations took advantage of the palpable stagnation of separate development to press for change. What might be called a *verligte* counter-orthodoxy took shape within the NP fold. It bemoaned the failure of homeland development, warned against delusions like the watershed year of 1978 or the temporariness of urban Africans as 'visitors', deplored petty apartheid

119. *House of Assembly Debates*, 1977, col. 390.
120. *Ibid.*

and pleaded for the expedited removal of discrimination. The *verligtes*, however, were in no sense a cohesive group and, in any case, they were a distinct minority within the NP. Vorster tolerated them, provided they did not stray too far out of line. R.F. 'Pik' Botha, for example, was permitted to make a maiden speech in parliament calling for a South African bill of human rights (although, in consequence, he was ostracised by many of his colleagues for two years),[121] and in 1977 he expressed his opposition to petty apartheid, declaring that he was not prepared to die for discriminatory signs on a lift.

The 1960s and most of the 1970s were years of substantial growth. The NP's support base steadily diversified and, with the emergence of new and thrusting Afrikaner business and professional elites, class divisions within Afrikaner society widened. For a younger generation that was better educated and upwardly mobile, the memories of poor-whiteism and the depression years of the 1930s were irrelevant. Even the rituals and *volksfeeste* (people's festivals) that an earlier generation of Nationalist leaders had used as instruments of mobilisation lost their ability to inspire. They were hardly needed, since the cultural hegemony of the English was no longer an issue that bruised Afrikaner psyches.

Vorster's presumed success in smashing African political resistance dissipated the earlier sense of urgency and purposefulness that Verwoerd had generated. Making the homelands economically more viable and consolidating them into more coherent entities required that white taxpayers would have to dig deeply into their pockets, and Vorster, a party manager who was concerned to preserve the delicate balance in the NP, was not the kind of visionary who was prepared to run the risk of upsetting the balance. Fundamentally, he kept treading water, rationalising each adjustment of policy as an emendation of traditional policy or as a means of strengthening it, but eschewing any dramatic policy innovation.

Meanwhile, the homelands continued to stagnate; consolidation remained a utopian ideal whose likelihood of implementation receded further each year; the myth of urban Africans as temporary sojourners degenerated into a bizarre fiction; and African population growth increased at a rate nearly double that projected by Verwoerd's planners in the 1950s. With good reason, Schalk Pienaar warned the Nationalists in 1970 'to stop bluffing themselves'.[122] In spite of such *verligte* warnings the apartheid juggernaut rolled on.

Increasingly Afrikanerdom and its political vehicle, the NP, found it difficult to hold the balance. Between the two wings sat a large grey mass of ordinary Nationalists, many of whom could shift either way,

121. *Debates of Parliament*, 1991, 265, col. 7837.
122. *Die Beeld*, 12 August 1970.

depending principally on the implications of such a shift for their personal careers. The differences between an M.C. Botha or a Treurnicht on the one hand, and a Koornhof or a Punt Janson on the other, illustrated the width of the gulf. Vorster might have given *verligtes* like Pik Botha their heads, but the NP as a whole was going to shift its ideological centre of gravity only at the pace of the great rump of the party. That would be a glacially slow process.

Writing in 1970, Gerald Shaw pointed to the government's dilemma:

It is subject to two different kinds of verligte pressures - the Nationalist big business lobby which wants more non-Whites to be available in the 'White' areas, and the intellectual lobby which is more concerned about massive development and consolidation of the reserves. And it knows that the intellectuals' demands cannot be even half-way met unless there is a buoyant, growing economy which would require capitulation to the business lobby. But this, in turn, would draw even more Africans into 'White' South Africa, making nonsense of the basic aims of the whole policy![123]

Vorster never resolved the sharpening contradictions within his party and bequeathed to his successor a situation of latent conflict that could be made manifest by leadership that was determined, one way or the other, to yank the NP out of its torpor. This was indeed what transpired.

Vorster's limitations and his innate cautiousness prevented him from being a daring, creative and innovative leader. In some respects this was no bad thing, since the country would have been even worse served by another zealot in the Verwoerd mould. Vorster, moreover, presided over a subtle shift in the basis of policy legitimation. He gave more emphasis than Verwoerd did to the links that would hold together the evolving state system in a future South Africa. He rejected federalism ('the most pernicious idea'), or the local application of the Swiss canton system with which some of his ministers (notably Koornhof) had flirted. He favoured an economic power bloc which would be 'a bloc of independent states, but politically and constitutionally no one state would in any respect be subordinate to another.'[124]

In 1974 he told an NP audience in his constituency that:

as the policy evolved and as the emphasis shifts to differentiation, discrimination will disappear. That was the prophetic vision of Dr Verwoerd in his day. What is happening now is that the *multiracial* policy of South Africa is increasingly coming to the foreground. Races that are distinguishable, between whom one can differentiate, but races who help and support one another, who honour and respect one another and who do not interfere with one another's domestic affairs — that is how I see South Africa's future. [Emphasis added][125]

---

123. *Cape Times*, 12 September 1970.
124. Geyser, *B.J. Vorster*, pp. 212–13.
125. *Ibid.*, p. 240.

Verwoerd's mania for ever-increasing separation was not easily compatible with any form of multiracialism. Moreover, the term 'multinationalism', which came into increasing use as a description of policy under Vorster, implied that there were distinct limits to the extent of separation envisaged. After all, the then USSR, Yugoslavia and other countries were multinational, but they were also single states in whose central legislatures all nations were nominally represented. Increasingly, the notion of pluralism was invoked, as when, for a brief period, the old portfolio of Native Affairs was reincarnated as Plural Relations and Development. This new designation (which caused some mirth among critics of the government) survived only for little more than a year and was replaced by the bland (and ethnically non-specific) title of Cooperation and Development.

The changes of name symbolised growing recognition that the separate nations/partition model of apartheid was of only limited usefulness in coping with the growing interdependence of South Africa's people. It was only a short ideological step to P.W. Botha's conceptualisation of South Africa as a country of minorities. Writing of Vorster's last years, F.A. van Jaarsveld says:

> The Afrikaner leaders had to become reconciled to the fact that they were a minority group, who, in the new circumstances, could no longer act as a white elite government and make laws for the whole population without their consent, or take unilateral decisions on behalf of 'all the people' of the country.[126]

P.W. Botha (1978–1989)

Botha was an unlikely reformer. He had grown up inside the political sub-culture of the NP as a party organiser in the 1930s and 1940s (his detractors in the party used to say that he always retained the mentality of an organiser). His service as a cabinet member from 1961 onwards spanned much of Verwoerd's and all of Vorster's premiership. When he became Prime Minister in September 1978 he had held the defence portfolio for over 12 years. His hawkish stance and his belief in the so-called total onslaught theory did not suggest strongly reformist tendencies. Botha, however, surprised his critics. Although his term as State President ended almost as ignominiously as Vorster's, he did a great deal, particularly in his earlier years, to eliminate apartheid's ideological pillars. In 1986 he finally killed off the separate nations thesis. Botha, in major respects, laid the foundations upon which F.W. de Klerk was able to build.

126. Van Jaarsveld, *Die Evolusie van Apartheid*, p. 18.

During his long years as a cabinet minister Botha gave no visible signs of dissent from the prevailing separate development orthodoxy. Between 1961 and 1966, when he held the portfolios of Coloured Affairs and Community Development, he does not appear to have demurred at enforcing one of apartheid's cruellest laws, the Group Areas Act. Nor are there references to reformist sentiments on his part in any of the insider accounts of the Verwoerd and Vorster cabinets. On the eve of his becoming Prime Minister Botha gave an interview to Anna Starcke (this was, in fact, published only after he became Prime Minister) in which he parroted some of apartheid's hoariest cliches, most notably: 'The moment I accept that the urban black is something different from his own people I'm being illogical . . . Surely a Zulu is a Zulu, whether he is in Johannesburg, Cape Town or Zululand.'[127]

By his own account, Botha disliked the word apartheid and avoided using it as far as possible. He maintained also that apartheid was 'never an end in itself; it was an instrument'.[128] Botha always favoured separation measures, on the principle that 'good fences make good neighbours, but, from the earliest days of the Nationalist government in 1948, he believed that the NP had gone too far with some of the apartheid regulations.[129] He did not mention which regulations he had in mind, but presumably he was referring to petty apartheid rules.

Botha's biographers quote him as saying that as a young politician he was often in conversation with Malan (who, in significant respects, was Botha's original political patron), to whom he would say, 'Doctor, our positive work is going too slowly.'[130] The implication here is that Botha believed that there was too much negative, and too little positive, apartheid. He lamented the failure to implement the development proposals suggested by the Tomlinson Commission in the 1950s, and he was critical of Verwoerd's refusal to allow white-owned capital to develop industry in the homelands.[131] Vorster had partially relaxed Verwoerd's ban; Botha abolished it altogether. He also reversed Vorster's earlier declaration that no more land could be added to the homelands on top of that provided for in terms of the 1936 legislation.

The extreme fragmentation of the homelands was a source of especial concern to Botha, who believed that it undermined the credibility of separate development. Soon after assuming office he instructed a commission to undertake an exhaustive investigation to ascertain

127. Anna Starcke, *Survival: Taped Interviews with South Africa's Power Elite* (Cape Town: Tafelberg, 1978), p. 59.
128. J.J.J. Scholtz (ed.), *Vegter en Hervormer: Grepe uit die Toesprake van P.W. Botha* (Cape Town: Tafelberg, 1988), p. 56.
129. *Ibid.*, p. 57.
130. Dirk and Johanna de Villiers, *P.W.* (Cape Town: Tafelberg, 1984), p. 183.
131. J.J.J. Scholtz, *Vegter en Hervormer*, p. 56.

whether consolidation could be accelerated, and to look critically at the question of whether 'the freedom that we and the peoples around us desire is compatible with the rounding off of the black states.'[132] Subsequently Botha ordered that consolidation be completed by 1987, but his hopes would be dashed.[133]

After the paralysis of the last years of Vorster, Botha was determined to breathe new life into NP policy. This spirit was encapsulated in the famous 'adapt or die' speech delivered at an NP meeting at Upington on 28 July 1979. It contained no concrete policy proposals, but it was a powerful plea for racial tolerance and for adaptability. A month later Botha did what no Prime Minister before him had ever done: he visited Soweto, to be swamped by a 'smallish, but enthusiastic crowd' and to have his hand shaken by a small township boy.[134] It seemed to symbolise the dawning of a new era.

Botha was consciously seeking to exemplify the NP's capacity for renewal and reform. Contrary to what its critics supposed, the NP was no political dinosaur destined for extinction. It had profound abilities to adapt to changed circumstances – and thereby to confound its opponents. At a time when ultra-right-wingers were still within the NP fold and there were murmurings of discontent about where Botha might take the party, his speeches stressed the need for adaptation: 'You cannot keep your policy the same year in and year out, because the world doesn't stay the same year in and year out.'[135] He was also fond of telling his audiences that it was not a sin to change one's mind or to acknowledge that one had made a mistake. There was nothing wrong with changing policies in the light of new facts brought to your attention.

As an example of this flexibility, Botha cited his decision to abandon the 30-year-old policy of trying to preserve the Western Cape as a coloured labour-preference area. Botha told parliament in 1986 that he had supported this policy because he had wanted to protect the Western Cape against social ills and the social and economic problems it was now facing. But:

I lost against reality, however. I lost because the economic interests of people made [the policy] impossible. Let us be honest. Let us not run away and chase after snowflakes. I do not ask to be excused for having tried to enforce the policy, but also I do not ask to be excused for recognising reality.[136]

Such frankness was rare among NP politicians (or indeed, among any

132. Dirk and Johanna de Villiers, *P.W.*, p. 214.
133. *Ibid.*
134. Brian Pottinger, *The Imperial Presidency: P.W. Botha – The First 10 Years* (Johannesburg: Southern Book Publishers, 1988), p. 65.
135. J.J.J. Scholtz, *Vegter en Hervormer*, p. 17.
136. *Ibid.*, p. 7.

politicians), whose inclinations were usually to maintain that changes were no more than the logical development of the original policy.

There were, however, definite limits to Botha's flexibility. His pragmatism was pragmatism only within the bounds of a strong ideological conviction that South Africa was a society of groups or minorities, each with its own traditions, ideals and interests, each one of which was entitled to protection against domination by others. In a careful study of the themes of P.W. Botha's speeches between 1978 and 1984, Koos van Wyk and Deon Geldenhuys have shown that this idea of groups was the dominant element in Botha's convictions. Indeed, they say that it was virtually an obsession with him.[137] His strong commitment to continuing with the homeland policy and his insistence that legislatively defined groups must be the building blocks of any constitutional development are testimony to this.

Botha's first major programme statement was the Twelve Point Plan, announced in October 1979.[138] This was based squarely on the conception of South Africa as a society of minority groups and the acceptance of 'vertical differentiation, with the built-in principle of self-determination on as many levels as possible' (point 2). It provided for the creation of constitutional structures for black peoples to achieve maximum possible self-government in those homelands whose fragmentation had been reduced as far as possible by means of consolidation. Regarding the political relationship between whites and the coloured and Indian people, the plan proposed both a division of power and co-responsibility that foreshadowed the distinction between own (group-specific) and general affairs in the future Tricameral Constitution of 1983.

Independence for those homelands who wanted it was retained as an option. The plan foresaw a peaceful constellation of Southern African states, based upon economic interdependence and the properly planned use of labour power. Any suggestion of a confederation or a federation was ruled out as premature.

Botha continued with the removal of 'irritating, unnecessary, discriminatory rules'. He even denounced the key enabling statute for petty apartheid, namely the Separate Amenities Act of 1953, saying that he had never thought that it was practicable.[139] The Act, however, was not repealed until 1990.

The statutory basis of job reservation was repealed in 1981, while statutory protection of white workers survived in its last redoubt, the

---

137. Koos van Wyk and Deon Geldenhuys, *Die Groepsgebod in P.W. Botha se Politieke Oortuigings* (Johannesburg: Rand Afrikaans University, 1987), p. 51.
138. J.J.J. Scholtz, *Vegter en Hervormer*, pp. 37–8.
139. *Ibid.*, p. 63.

mining industry, until 1987. African trade unions were granted statutory recognition in 1979. In view of the significant leverage that African workers acquired through the unions it is worth asking whether Botha realised this possibility when the legislation was enacted. The legislation was piloted through parliament by the *verligte* Minister of Labour, S.P. (Fanie) Botha. As Brian Pottinger notes, P.W. Botha had little time for the intricacies of reform in the industrial relations field and he seldom, if ever, mentioned the topic in speeches.[140] In the absence of insider accounts of the Botha cabinet, however, the question must remain unanswered for the time being.

Botha also repudiated the traditional dogma about the temporariness of urban Africans as 'visitors'. Freehold tenure was permitted. In 1986 the government struck down one of the most deeply entrenched apartheid measures, influx control. Pass laws, as they were commonly referred to, had a long history in South Africa. They were also a major source of anger for Africans, millions of whom were prosecuted for purely technical offences. Botha became convinced of what critics had long been saying: that the pass laws were not only expensive to administer, they were ineffective in doing what they were supposed to do, namely in keeping Africans out of towns.

The centre-piece of the Botha administration is undoubtedly the Tricameral Constitution of 1983. The exclusion of Africans from representation could not be explained away by repeated Nationalist assertions that Africans were constitutionally catered for through homeland legislatures. Nor did critics believe denials that the incorporation of the coloured and Indian categories represented a ganging-up (the quaint phrase of South African political parlance) against Africans. Their scepticism was heightened when it emerged that in the exchange of letters in 1982 between Treurnicht and Jan Grobler, chief information officer of the NP, Grobler had appealed to Treurnicht's sense of *realpolitik* to support the proposed constitution:

. . . Doctor, I would like to know your view on the idea that we have got to associate the coloureds as a bloc of 2,5 million with the whites in order to broaden our own power-base, and not surrender them up to the 'black-power' situation.[141]

This was not how the NP marketed the draft constitution in the campaign for the referendum in November 1983, but it certainly was an indication of the strategic thinking of many. Provided one had a firm power base in one's own group, alliance-building, even across colour lines, was an acceptable strategy.

140. Pottinger, *The Imperial Presidency*, p. 92.
141. Cited in Alf Ries and Ebbe Dommisse, *Broedertwis: Die Verhaal van die 1982–Skeuring in die Nasionale Party* (Cape Town: Tafelberg, 1982), 112.

The inauguration of the tricameral parliament and the rancorous referendum and election campaign that preceded it were an important cause of the violence that began in the Vaal Triangle in late 1984 and spread thereafter to much of the country. As its critics predicted, the tricameral parliament would destabilise the country because it was tantamount to the constitutionalisation of apartheid. Botha had won the referendum among whites on 2 November 1983 by a wide margin, but low polls among the coloured and Indian electorates and outright rejection by even the most moderate and pliable of African leaders indicated not just opposition but a sense of outrage. Botha, like most white political leaders, appeared to be incapable of grasping the symbolic injury inflicted by discriminatory measures such as the Tricameral Constitution. Before him, Vorster too had been quite insensitive to the symbolic affront felt by Africans when they were deprived of their South African citizenship and instead given citizenship of a now-independent homeland.

Botha had left the details of the constitutional draft to his Minister of Constitutional Development, Chris Heunis, but there is no doubt that the final product bore Botha's seal of approval. From the beginning Botha insisted that the constitution was merely the starting point of a process. He told parliament in 1988 that 'we in South Africa cannot afford to try to draw up a final constitution. This is not something which can be disposed of quickly in this country.'[142] No doubt it was true that Botha could not, politically, have gone much further than the provisions of the 1983 constitution. This was argued by many of those who, though critical of the constitution's provisions, supported its introduction. It passed a critical threshold, they argued, by admitting for the first time people of colour into the portals of parliament, albeit in separate chambers. After this, they reasoned, could the admission of Africans be far off?

In the light of hindsight it seems that the arguments of both the critics and the supporters of the tricameral system contained a measure of truth. There can be no doubt that the constitution exacerbated conflict and destabilised the society, but these consequences of its blatant exclusion of Africans forced the issue of African political incorporation to the top of South Africa's political agenda. The question 'and what about the black people?' was used as the title of an NP pamphlet written by Stoffel van der Merwe and released early in 1985 a few months after the inauguration of the new system.[143] The question was a timely one.

Another issue that was highlighted was the legitimacy of political

---

142. J.J.J. Scholtz, *Vegter en Hervormer*, p. 52.
143. Stoffel van der Merwe, MP, . . . *And What about the Black People?* (Cape Town: Federal Information Service of the National Party, 1985).

institutions and the representativeness of political leaderships. Critics had warned that the tricameral parliament had little or no chance of putting down roots of legitimacy, and that effective political institutions would have to be negotiated among leaders with substantial bases of support. A leader such as Verwoerd had no hesitation in claiming to know who the real leaders of any particular group were: the tribal chiefs were the natural and authentic leaders. Vorster, albeit less dogmatic, was of the same opinion. Although Botha did not elaborate on this theme in any great detail, his attitude was a slightly more agnostic one. His dogmatic belief in prescriptive groups automatically placed limits on his ability to envisage or accept a leadership that had arisen outside those group boundaries and, moreover, was explicitly committed to abolishing the very concept of the statutory group.

Pressed on these issues in 1986 by two persistent interviewers, Botha refused to budge from his earlier view (cited above) that 'the black man himself does not look at himself as being part of a big black majority.' There were different black communities, each with its own leader who could sit around a negotiating table. But, the interviewers pressed him, could these different communities be represented as one black mass if they chose to? To this Botha replied:

But they won't be, they *won't* prefer to have it that way. Bishop Tutu will tell you that they . . . wish to have it that way, but he is *not* a representative of *all* of the Black people in South Africa. Chief Buthelezi tells me that *he will not* recognise Bishop Tutu as a leader . . . [emphasis in original][144]

This was an unconvincing response, but Botha would not recognise any claims that the ANC might make to command majority support among Africans. In his view the ANC consisted of two groups, one communist and the other nationalist, mostly Xhosa. He acknowledged that it was very difficult to determine how much support the organisation had, but he did not believe that it was more than enjoyed by someone like Buthelezi.[145] And indeed opinion surveys conducted by an unnamed American polling company for the (South African) Bureau of Information showed in the late 1980s that support for the ANC came from no more than about 30 per cent of the African population. The data were never published but were revealed to selected audiences at off-the-record briefings. Ministers were certainly aware of the figures.

In 1980 a little-noticed new beach-head was made when an NP-dominated parliamentary commission of inquiry on the constitution submitted a brief interim report which contained the following recommendation:

144. Michel Abeldas and Alan Fischer (eds.), *A Question of Survival: Conversations with Key South Africans* (Johannesburg: Jonathan Ball, 1987), pp. 512–13.
145. *Ibid.*, p. 517.

that in the process of designing future constitutional structures there should be the widest possible consultation and deliberation with and among all population groups, in an attempt to raise the level of acceptability of any proposals in this regard.[146]

The significance of this was that it made legitimacy the test of any new constitution's viability. In another recommendation the commission said that 'persons recognised by their respective communities as leaders' should be a category represented on the proposed president's council. The test of leadership, in other words, was a popular support base, not recognition by the government as an 'approved' leader.

The implications of these recommendations did not immediately affect the NP's strategy, but they surely contributed to a growing perception inside the NP that one could not prescribe to groups who their real leaders were, and that negotiations (or, more accurately, consultations) with leaders whose support bases were small or non-existent were a waste of time. Botha's era would also make clearer to significant elements inside the NP (if not necessarily to Botha himself) that it would be impossible to negotiate a new constitution which could enjoy legitimacy while significant organisations like the ANC and the PAC remained banned and thousands of individuals were serving prison sentences for political offences. Moreover, to the extent that Botha's NP insisted upon the statutory population group as the essential building block in any new constitution, no black leader of credibility would come near the negotiating table through fear of being inveigled into the administration of apartheid and consequently being labelled a stooge by more radical elements.

In another crucial respect the Tricameral Constitution helped to clear the decks for more far-reaching reform later on. In 1982 Botha drove Treurnicht and his supporters out of the NP, thereby shedding the support of some 30 per cent of Afrikaners. It was an act of considerable political courage. At one level, Botha could now get on with his own version of reform without having to worry so much about watching his right flank or to fear that political troglodytes were undermining his position in the Transvaal NP. There would be a murderous struggle for the soul of Afrikanerdom, but the NP was at last free from an incubus that had long burdened it. At another level, the decisive breakdown of Afrikaner nationalist solidarity liberated outward-looking Afrikaners and prepared the way not only for coalitions but even for acceptance of the idea of a South African nation.

In 1986 Botha himself reversed previous policy and accepted the concept of one citizenship for all South Africans, saying that the

146. *Commission of Inquiry on the Constitution Interim Report* (Cape Town: Government Printer, 1980), para. 8(b).

'peoples of the Republic of South Africa make up one nation. But our nation is a nation of minorities.'[147] Even with this caveat, the central proposition of separate development had been negated.

As has been shown, Botha attempted in the earlier years to reinvigorate the homelands policy. He never disavowed it, but he came to recognise that it could by no means be the complete answer. By 1984 his government had accepted that no more than 40 per cent (and this was an optimistic view) of the African population could ultimately be accommodated in the homelands, independent or otherwise.[148] He promised that earnest efforts would be made, in consultation with homeland leaders and leaders in the urban African communities, to find a solution to the question of their political and citizenship rights. In a major speech to parliament early in 1985 Botha reluctantly accepted that African communities permanently domiciled outside the home-lands could not be expected to express their political aspirations through the political structures of the homelands. He said:

It has therefore been decided to regard such communities for constitutional purposes as entities entitled in their own right to political participation and a say [*inspraak*] in the higher levels, subject to the proviso that no population group might be put in a position in which it could dominate others. Consequently structures must be developed for black communities outside the national states [i.e. non-independent homelands] whereby they can enjoy self-determination over their own affairs up to the highest level.[149]

Again, this was significant, for what else could the phrase 'up to the highest level' mean other than representation in the central legislature of South Africa?

Botha now waged unsuccessful struggles on two fronts. Hard though he strove to make the homelands credible, the policy unravelled before his eyes: the consolidation project was effectively pronounced dead by the government's own central consolidation committee in 1981;[150] the homelands themselves were, with few exceptions, palpable economic failures, bottomless pits into which South African taxpayers poured money; and the banana republic character of the independent home-lands and the fact that they were prone to corruption and *coups* became an embarrassment to the South African government.

A critical factor in the unravelling of the homelands policy was the refusal by the KwaZulu government to accept 'independence', notwith-standing the mixture of threats and inducements offered by the South African government. Since the Zulu are the biggest single ethno-

---

147. J.J.J. Scholtz, *Vegter en Hervormer*, p. 53.
148. Van Der Merwe, . . . *And What about the Black People?*, p. 3.
149. J.J.J. Scholtz, *Vegter en Hervormer*, pp. 27–8.
150. South African Institute of Race Relations, *Survey of Race Relations 1981*, p. 289.

linguistic group in the country (22 per cent of the total population in 1990), their opting for independence and its concomitant loss of citizenship would have lent credibility to the policy, at least in the minds of its architects. Moreover, it would have meant that over 50 per cent of the African population had, nominally at any rate, 'accepted' independence, and in terms of the crazy logic of apartheid South African whites would have been well on the way to becoming a statistical, if not demographic, majority! KwaZulu's leader, Chief Mangosuthu Buthelezi, has incurred the wrath of more radical African leaders for working 'inside the system', but he is legitimately entitled to claim that his consistent opposition to independence protected the citizenship of the Zulu and millions of other Africans, as well as helping to abort apartheid.

Despite the best efforts of Botha's ministry to develop appropriate structures for Africans outside the homelands, successive models of local government foundered on the rocks of illegitimacy. Botha was also unsuccessful in a third area. He accepted that a new constitutional dispensation had to be negotiated and that the new constitution would have 'to offer all citizens of the state the opportunity meaningfully to participate in decision-making processes where their interests are at issue'.[151] But there were few credible takers for his proposed national council, a negotiating forum finally legislated into existence in 1988.

As Botha envisaged it, the council was to consist of representatives of South African government and the governments of the non-independent homelands as well as leaders of urban communities and other interest groups. Pending the adoption of a new South African constitution, this body would act in an advisory capacity on 'matters of common interest'.[152] Critics immediately pointed out that it resembled the Natives' Representative Council of the 1930s and 1940s, whose advisory (i.e. powerless) capacities achieved nothing, except to bring it into disrepute among its members.

The national council (or 'great indaba', as Botha thought it might be called) never got off the ground. As Pottinger wrote: 'The inevitable happened; a series of professional black committee men – some of whom chose to remain anonymous – pushed themselves forward and were gratefully embraced by Government. But they could contribute neither influence, constituencies nor solutions'.[153] The enabling statute remained a dead-letter.

Botha's failure to attract significant African leaders into negotiations did not happen through want of trying. Officials in Chris Heunis'

151. J.J.J. Scholtz, *Vegter en Hervormer*, p. 50.
152. *Ibid.*, p. 48.
153. Pottinger, *The Imperial Presidency*, p. 241.

department worked hard to allay the suspicions of some of the more radical political actors, but it was a hopeless task. The 'great indaba' was obviously conceived in an apartheid framework, and it was equally obvious that for Botha the own/general affairs distinction that was central to the tricameral parliament was non-negotiable.

The violence of the mid-1980s caused a further deterioration in Botha's opinions of the ANC. He had always displayed hostility; now, gauged by the tenor of some of his comments, that bordered on hatred. Botha and his military advisors blamed the ANC for the violence, asking how you could negotiate 'with a gun pointed at you, and the handing over of power to the revolutionaries as the only item on the agenda?'[154] Botha insisted that there could be no negotiation with the ANC until it forswore violence. Improbable as this may sound, Botha's statement was in itself a small advance since he did at least imply that there were circumstances in which the ANC could be a participant in a negotiating process. No previous NP leader had even bruited the possibility. Botha's words were, however, calculated and deliberate as always:

If the ANC forswears violence, ceases to live abroad at the expense of foreign governments and returns to their own country to participate in the constitutional process, naturally they can have a part in the negotiating processes. The ANC must cease being tools of the South African Communist Party in the service of a foreign government.[155]

The ANC favoured a negotiated solution but it had no intention of complying with Botha's requirements. The armed struggle and its increasing success in persuading foreign governments to impose sanctions on South Africa were, as far as the ANC was concerned, major bargaining chips. If the South African government had in the past held the lion's share of the chips, the imbalance was now changing.

Botha's final three years in office were sterile. After the last major reform in 1986, the abolition of influx control, he appeared to have run out of steam. South Africa grew more isolated, increasingly beleaguered, its currency nearly halved in value after Botha's disastrous Rubicon speech in 1985. The debacle of the Commonwealth Eminent Persons Group (EPG)'s visit to South Africa in 1986 and the continuing violence pushed the country more deeply into the mire and increased Botha's truculence.

The EPG's attempt to broker an accommodation seemed at first a promising initiative. Although deeply suspicious of the South African government, the ANC agreed to consider cooperating with the EPG. Several ministers on the government side also appeared to want to cooperate with the EPG, although Botha seemed to acquiesce in the

154. J.J.J. Scholtz, *Vegter en Hervormer*, p. 49.
155. *Ibid*.

EPG mission rather than enthusiastically welcome it. On 19 May 1986, however, the South African Defence Force launched raids on Harare, Gaborone and Lusaka, thereby extinguishing whatever (slight) chance the EPG might have had of succeeding in its mission. Ruefully the EPG observed: 'It was all too plain that, while talking to the Group about negotiations and peaceful solutions, the Government had been planning these armed attacks.'[156]

By the 1980s South Africa had become a deadlocked society. P.W. Botha's reforms were irreversible: no future government would be able to ban African trade unions, reimpose job reservation, reassert the idea that urban Africans were temporary sojourners or undo the principle that parliament was no longer an exclusively white preserve. But Botha's role as a reformer tended to be eclipsed by his uninhibited use of force and his reliance on states of emergency that gave extensive powers to the security forces.

The EPG's findings on the attitude of the government, which were based upon extensive talks with ministers, provide an interesting comment on the political *cul de sac* which the Botha administration had entered. The EPG confirmed what had become evident since roughly 1985, namely that Botha was embittered by the failure of his domestic opponents and much of the world community to give him credit for his reforms. The EPG noted:

The Government was deeply concerned that its reform programme had elicited no response from the black community and that violence was on the increase. There was no recognition that apartheid itself was sustained through violence and that the inequities and injustices it perpetrated fostered violence.[157]

The EPG was gloomy about the prospects for real negotiations unless 'the South African Government is prepared to deal with leaders of the people's choosing rather than with puppets of its own creation'. Moreover, the group was distressed by Botha's evident determination to break the ANC and by his government's belief 'that it can contain the situation indefinitely by use of force'.[158]

There seemed no good reason why the stalemate should not continue for a long while, seriously haemorrhaging the society at the same time. Sober analysts spoke in terms of a 20-year time-frame for what was nebulously called 'fundamental change'.

An end to the political logjam seemed to come about because of a partly fortuitous link of circumstances. Botha suffered a stroke on 18 January 1989. Shortly afterwards he announced that the post of leader-

---

156. The Commonwealth Group of Eminent Persons, *Mission to South Africa: The Commonwealth Report* (Harmondsworth: Penguin, 1986), p. 120.
157. *Ibid.*, p. 82.
158. *Ibid.*, pp, 133, 135.

in-chief of the NP was to be separated from that of leadership of an NP government (which was a clean break with past practice). On 2 February F.W. de Klerk, the Minister of National Education, won a narrow victory over Barend du Plessis, the Minister of Finance. Immediately after the election De Klerk is reputed to have told the caucus that a dramatic change was needed.

The separation of the party and governmental roles deprived Botha of his power base and spelled the end of his effectiveness as a political leader, but not before he had (perhaps unwittingly) struck one more symbolic blow for change: Nelson Mandela was brought from his prison residence on 5 July to have tea with Botha in his Cape Town office. Exactly how this remarkable meeting was engineered is not publicly known, nor is there detailed knowledge of what the two men spoke about, although it seems to have been mostly an exchange of courtesies. Prior to the meeting Mandela had sent Botha a powerful and dignified letter expressing his grave concern at the deepening political crisis, setting out the ANC's position on various issues, including violence, but concluding with a plea for compromise and reconciliation.[159]

It is not known what effect the letter had on Botha, but the meeting was almost certainly a formal response to it. In crucial respects the ice was broken; Mandela's release could not be delayed for much longer. Few, however, supposed that someone of Mandela's stature could be released into a political vacuum without potentially serious destabilising effects. Rather, he would have to be released into a process – and that could mean only a negotiating process that involved an unbanned ANC. De Klerk seems to have summed up the situation in the same way.

F.W. de Klerk (1989–)

De Klerk came to the leadership of the NP and to the state presidency with an ambiguous reputation. On the one hand, he was perceived as being on the conservative wing of the NP and a strong advocate of group rights and the own affairs concept. His responses to interviewers' questions in 1986 were entirely faithful to the prevailing orthodoxies about group rights, own power bases and own community life.[160] (No doubt De Klerk was well aware of the probable drubbing ministers would receive from Botha for heterodox utterances, although he was said to be one of the few members of the cabinet who were not afraid to take on *Die Groot Krokodil* (the Big Crocodile) – the unflattering

159. The text of the letter is reprinted in E.S. Reddy (ed.), *Nelson Mandela: Symbol of Resistance and Hope for a Free South Africa – Selected Speeches since his Release* (London: Kliptown Books, 1990), pp. 103–15.
160. Abeldas and Fischer, *A Question of Survival*, pp. 483–91.

nickname for Botha.[161] Willem de Klerk's explanation of his brother's apparent conservatism is that it was a deliberate strategy:

In Afrikaner politics, power is based on conservative thinking; in the long run it gains you confidence, and once you have that you can do magical things with the Afrikaner. That was FW's strategy, not rigid conservatism. He was pragmatic and ambitious enough to build his image on the middle course between enlightened and ultra-conservative, and he was astute enough to convert his basic reluctance to give offence into a personal style, a strategy that gained him acceptability and influence.[162]

On the other hand, De Klerk was known to be highly intelligent, with a lawyer's clinical approach to issues. None of his previous ministerial portfolios had directly involved security matters. He was sceptical of, if not opposed to, the securocratic approach of the Botha administration, and he believed that political solutions had to be found to political problems. This combination of qualities at least made it seem that De Klerk 'would be able to read the writing on the wall sooner than most', as some who knew him predicted.

Another factor was De Klerk's membership of the *Gereformeerde Kerk* (or *Dopper* Church), the smallest of the three Dutch Reformed churches. The *Doppers* tend to be high achievers with a strong, even fundamentalist, sense of moral principle. As leading *Doppers* had been saying for some time, what was morally wrong could not be politically condoned. De Klerk almost certainly owes much of his strong sense of *konsekwentheid* to his *Dopper* connection. Verwoerd had followed the principle of *konsekwentheid* in his obsessive drive towards ever greater separation; De Klerk was not obsessive, despite having strong convictions, but he would be *konsekwent* in giving effect to the NP's historic decision in 1986 to restore a common South African citizenship to all races; he would also be *konsekwent* in removing those obstacles that stood in the way of the realisation of the NP's commitment to a negotiated settlement of the constitutional problem.

As late as September 1989, when he was installed as State President, De Klerk was still voicing extreme hostility to the ANC, even rebuking his brother Willem for holding confidential discussions with its representatives in London. It was 'hobnobbing with terrorists,' he said.[163] Indeed, in the campaign leading up to the parliamentary elections on 6 September, the NP asked for a broad mandate for reform, but ANC-bashing was as much a feature of its rhetoric as usual. No hint was given of the momentous changes around the corner, as the CP has never stopped pointing out.

161. Willem de Klerk, *F. W. de Klerk*, p. 20.
162. *Ibid.*, p. 22.
163. *Ibid.*, pp. 54–5.

In a review of his achievements, delivered in parliament on 2 May 1991, De Klerk observed that South Africa was reaching 'an absolute impasse', 'a dead-end street of increasing unemployment and impoverishment that had begun in the early 1970s'. He continued:

The policy of separate development was visibly and tangibly failing. The realities of our society compelled us to the realisation that absolute self-determination in a heterogeneous country such as ours was not attainable. The fact that we were demographically and geographically interwined as well as socio-economic realities, made this impossible. The best efforts of outstanding leaders over a period of almost four decades proved irrefutably that policies of ethnic and territorial separation could not offer our country a viable solution. More than half of South Africa's Black population live and work permanently outside the TBVC countries [Transkei, Bophuthatswana, Venda and Ciskei] and the six self-governing territories. There is almost no magisterial district in the country . . . in which black people are not in the majority.[164]

Further factors helped to sway De Klerk. Several NP ministers had held meetings with ANC leaders, including, especially, Nelson Mandela, who was of course still in gaol. Little is known yet about these meetings or the activities of various intermediaries, mostly members of the Afrikaner establishment, who similarly engaged the ANC in exploratory dialogue. The message that came back was that the ANC leadership was more reasonable than 'total onslaught' thinking had suggested.

A crucial factor in these developments was the decline of the Soviet Union and the domino-like fall of successive Eastern European regimes. At one stroke the central theme of the total onslaught theory was knocked out and some of the ANC's principal patrons were weakened. Many in the NP and in the security agencies genuinely believed that the ANC was little more than a client of the Kremlin and that the South African Communist Party effectively controlled the ANC. The failure of Marxism–Leninism encouraged De Klerk and his colleagues to believe that few South Africans would now find the doctrine attractive. The other side of the coin was a heightened recognition of the power of the masses to destroy unpopular regimes. As the paradox of Vaclav Havel in former Czechoslovakia makes clear, 'the power of the powerless' is considerable. The South African government had had experience of massive popular demonstrations in the 1970s and 1980s. Although the state was not in danger of being overthrown, the possibility of even larger and more continuous mass protest in the 1990s was a real one.

It is an exaggeration to say that South Africa had become 'ungovernable', as the ANC-inspired campaign had sought to achieve, but

164. *Debates of Parliament*, 14, 1991, cols 7271–2.

endemic protest and violence in many parts of the country substantially prevented effective government. So great was the crisis of legitimacy and so imminent the possibility of civil war that no more tinkering with apartheid structures could ward off impending catastrophe. An already weakened economy would accelerate its downward spiral, as capital continued to flow out and sources of foreign loans dried up. In the absence of fundamental reform the sanctions noose would only grow tighter. De Klerk realised that only pre-emptive measures could avert the dangers. He also realised that it would be prudent to initiate negotiations sooner rather than later, before the strength of white rule was further eroded.

In the latter part of 1989 the Namibian issue was settled, and an orderly and fair election was held there on 2 November. From the South African government's point of view its extrication from this imbroglio was a success, bringing limited foreign policy gains and ridding itself of a millstone. Indirectly the Namibian experience helped pave the way for a prospective negotiated settlement in South Africa. It demonstrated, moreover, that in this kind of situation the once-reviled United Nations would function fairly and helpfully.

A further consideration that weighed with De Klerk was the possible outcome of the general election to be held on 6 September 1989. Siren voices warned of major Conservative Party gains, perhaps giving them a total of between 50 and 60 seats and resulting in a hung parliament. The predictions proved wrong: the Conservatives won only 39 seats while the liberal Democratic Party won 34, thus enabling De Klerk to claim that 70 per cent of the white electorate had voted for reform. The 93 seats won by the NP assured it of a comfortable majority.

Developments inside the NP caucus and within the wider support base of the party strengthened the reformist drive. A younger generation of NP MPs was also growing restive at the lack of progress in negotiations. Many wondered whether the Botha administration, with its heavy-handed emphasis on coercive methods and its insistence on statutory race groups as the building blocks of a new constitution, would be able to steer the country away from the impending crisis. Botha's volcanic temper (said to be capable of reducing ministers to tears) and his authoritarian style further alienated caucus members. Barend du Plessis, although a more junior minister than De Klerk, was representative of this broad grouping, and the fact that he received 61 votes (compared with 69 for De Klerk) in the NP caucus' election of the *hoofleier* was an indication of gathering *verligte* strength inside the party.

While there is no doubt that De Klerk underwent a conversion of sorts, it is also clear that it was no Damascene conversion that led him to make his historic announcement on 2 February 1990 that the ANC, PAC, South African Communist Party and other banned organisations would be unbanned, and that Nelson Mandela and other long-serving prisoners would be released. Rather, it was a long process of recognising that there was no alternative to abandoning all the old apartheid nostrums and striking out on the uncharted course of democracy. His comment on the ANC, quoted by his astonished brother, makes clear that he had come by new insights:

The ANC is a fairly important element with a solid power base among the people. Negotiations with others, without the ANC, would be incomplete, and their legitimacy questionable. I do not doubt for a moment that the ANC is prepared to compromise on the major issues. We must get away from the situation where the government is perceived to be abusing its powers for party-political purposes, by suppressing the ANC's political views. [165]

De Klerk has repeatedly insisted that he has done no more than carry the reforms initiated by his predecessor to their logical conclusion. He has denied CP allegations that the election of 6 September 1989 did not give him a mandate for the far-reaching steps he has taken, asserting instead that he had received a broad mandate for negotiated reform, which implicitly included a mandate to remove obstacles to negotiation. Since the banned status of the ANC and other organisations was the major obstacle to reform, unbanning them and releasing imprisoned leaders was, accordingly, necessary. While De Klerk's logic was impeccable, his claim to have received a mandate for these measures was, to say the least, dubious. It would not be until the referendum among white voters on 17 March 1992, when the negotiation process was well underway, that he would get a mandate – and a convincing one at that – to continue.

An awkward issue in the liberalisation process was P.W. Botha's insistence that the ANC forswear violence before being permitted to participate in negotiations. Since the ANC regarded the armed struggle and the international sanctions campaign as major bargaining chips in the conflict, there was no chance that it would comply with Botha's demand. In his speech of 2 February 1990 De Klerk made clear his refusal to tolerate violence and pointed out that the justification for it no longer existed, but Botha's condition was replaced with the requirement that parties to the negotiating process commit themselves to a search for peace. Nelson Mandela had made such a commitment while still in gaol, thus enabling De Klerk to say that the 'unbanning of organisations in an atmosphere where there was already a basic commitment to peaceful negotiations was a logical consequence'. [166]

Beginning with the speech of February 1990, De Klerk used a strategy of reform by both stealth and *blitzkrieg*, to invoke the terms injected into

165. Willem de Klerk, *F.W. de Klerk*, p. 54.
166. *The Argus*, 9 September 1990.

South African political discourse by Samuel P. Huntington.[167] Even the NP caucus was given only a broad outline of what the speech was to contain prior to its delivery. De Klerk, however, insists that it was a team effort, involving decisions that were taken 'after widespread consultation, in-depth analysis and careful evaluation of advice from security and other advisers'.[168]

Undoubtedly De Klerk went too fast for many of the more conservative elements in the NP's support base, who defected to the CP. In the 1989 elections the CP won over 30 per cent of the total white vote; by mid-1991 it was widely believed to enjoy the support of perhaps as many as 40 per cent of whites and, possibly, a narrow majority of Afrikaner support. The NP caucus and the cabinet, however, remained firmly behind De Klerk – at the time of writing not one defection has occurred in the three-year period of his presidency. A contributing factor to this apparent solidarity has been the government's declaration that no future general elections will be held under the existing constitution. Backbenchers, in other words, would not face the prospect of exhausting struggles to retain their seats against ferocious CP opposition.

De Klerk initially committed himself to referring the draft of a new constitution to a referendum among voters who elected the existing parliament. He also expressed the view that Africans should simultaneously be given an opportunity to vote on the draft, 'so that we can obtain absolute certainty that every component part of the South African population has expressed its views'.[169]

Political exigencies, however, forced a change of strategy. After a series of by-election losses to the CP, De Klerk opted for the high-risk gamble of asking the white electorate in a referendum whether it wished the process initiated on 2 February 1990 to be continued. On 17 March 1992, after a brief and rancorous campaign, an overwhelming victory laid to rest allegations that De Klerk did not have a mandate for what he had been doing. It was clear that at the grass-roots level most white voters, when confronted with the choice of *'praat of skiet'* ('talk or shoot'), opted for negotiation.

Formally the ANC opposed what was a racially exclusive referendum that, moreover, effectively gave whites a veto power over the continuation of the negotiating process. It was made more uneasy by the tenor of De Klerk's campaign, which stressed that the NP was not about to capitulate to 'simple majority rule', nor acquiesce in a new constitution in which property rights and the job and pension rights of civil servants

167. Samuel P. Huntington, 'Reform and Stability in a Modernizing Multi-Ethnic Society', *Politikon*, vol. 8, no. 2, 1981.
168. *The Argus*, 9 September 1990.
169. NP Information Service, transcript of TV interview, 17 February 1991.

would be vulnerable.[170] In spite of its misgivings the ANC appreciated that the greater danger was De Klerk's defeat, and accordingly it encouraged its white supporters (a miniscule proportion of the electorate) to vote 'Yes'. More importantly, it avoided mass protests or other disruptive tactics that could have alienated whites during the referendum campaign.

The effect of this thumping victory was to restore confidence to an NP that had watched helplessly as its support base seemed visibly to erode. At the multiparty talks, CODESA (the Convention for a Democratic South Africa), that had begun in December 1991, the government negotiators firmed up their stance on 'power-sharing' as a more consensual alternative to the 'majoritarianism' advocated by the ANC, and declined to support the ANC's demand that a new constitution be drafted by an elected constituent assembly that would adopt the constitution by a two-thirds majority. Far from making the government more flexible and ready to make compromises, ANC negotiators believed that the referendum victory had made the government more cocky, even arrogant.

Aside from some oblique references to past injustices, De Klerk initially declined to emulate some of his ministers and apologise for apartheid, as many black organisations demanded. Instead, he continually parried the issue, saying:

Some of our people continue to be obsessed with past grievances. Some insist on apologies to everything that has occured in the past. Many mistakes were made by all sides and parties. If we dwell on the real or imagined sins of the past, we shall never be able to find one another in the present.[171]

In October 1992 De Klerk finally did bring himself to expressing regret, albeit in a seemingly grudging way. He acknowledged that Afrikaners had 'clung on too long to a dream of separate nation-states' when it had already become clear that this vision could not be completely realised. For that, he continued, 'we are sorry.' Like all of the other ethnic communities, Afrikaners had made mistakes, but never had they been 'evil, despicable and malicious'. On the contrary, 'the struggle for justice runs through our history like a golden thread.' It was hard to reconcile this claim with the cruel realities of apartheid. Predictably, his apology was not enough for the ANC, which curtly dismissed it, accusing De Klerk of failing to recognise that apartheid was based upon the concept of racial superiority, which had to be rejected in principle.[172]

170. Cape National Party Information Committee Referendum Pamphlet, *Vote Yes for the Future of SA* (no date).
171. *The Argus*, 27 April 1991.
172. *Die Burger*, 10 October 1992; *Cape Times*, 12 October 1992.

True to his commitment to abolish racial discrimination, De Klerk has moved rapidly on the legislative front. By the end of the 1991 parliamentary session all remaining discriminatory laws, except for the constitution itself, had been repealed. De Klerk initially declined to abolish the racially based own affairs administrations of the tricameral parliament because he considered it 'inappropriate and inadvisable' to tinker with the constitution when the country was on the threshold of negotiations for a new constitution. Moreover, he argued, since the own affairs/general affairs division was a central principle of the constitution, abolishing the own affairs administrations would amount to a fundamental change that, in keeping with the NP's undertaking, would require ratification in a referendum.[173] By late 1992, however, the anomalousness and wastefulness of racially separate administrations had become so glaring that De Klerk decided to initiate enabling legislation that could eliminate it.

Considerations of space preclude a detailed analysis of the course of the negotiating process that was initiated after the unbanning of the ANC and other organisations and the release of Nelson Mandela.[174] It soon became apparent though, that negotiating a democratic constitution for a society as riven by conflict as South Africa was not going to be easy. On many occasions De Klerk has stressed that it is not his policy to surrender power or 'hand this country over to anarchy'. In a tough speech to the Natal NP Congress in September 1992 he explained what he meant by power-sharing:

Domination is rejected by the National Party. Just as the majority rejected subjugation by the minority in the past, so will South Africans reject majority domination and subjugation and abuse of their rights in the future. When we say that we do not ask for continued minority domination or continued privilege for any minority to the extent that . . . a democratic majority properly elected is robbed of the power which being a majority should grant, but we say that a system within which with 51 percent of the vote you have 100 percent of the power, is not the right system for South Africa and that is in essence what power-sharing means.[175]

This was not a view of democracy congenial to the ANC, which construed it as a cunning device to thwart the 'transfer of power to the people'. Ultimately it was these rival conceptions of democracy upon which the negotiating process foundered in May 1992.

The institutional form that power-sharing was to take was spelled out

173. *Debates of Parliament*, 24, 1991, col. 1989.
174. For a fuller account see David Welsh, 'Turning Point', *Towards Democracy* (journal of the Institute of Multi-Party Democracy), 3rd quarter, 1992.
175. F.W. de Klerk, *Verbatim Transcript of Speech at the Congress of the Natal National Party*, 25 September 1992, p. 4.

in a document released by the NP in September 1991.[176] It proposes a *regstaat* (constitutional state) in which the sovereignty of parliament is replaced by the sovereignty of the constitution. The central government is to consist of two houses, the first elected by universal franchise (all races) on the basis of proportional representation, the second elected by regions, each of which will enjoy equality of representation. The second house is to be charged with the duty of representing minority and regional interests. A curious proposal is that each party winning a particular (as yet unspecified) amount of support in elections to regional legislatures is to be entitled to an equal number of the region's seats in the second house, thereby ensuring, it is claimed, that every democratic party enjoying a reasonable measure of support at regional level would enjoy equal representation in the second house.

Even more curious is the proposal for the structure of executive authority in the central government. The NP favours institutionalised coalition government – and De Klerk has often spoken admiringly of the Swiss system of consensus government (though without acknowledging that it rests upon convention and not constitutional prescription). The plan proposes a collective presidency, consisting of the leaders of the three largest parties in the first house; chairmanship of the presidency is to rotate on an annual basis, and the presidency will take decisions by consensus. Similarly, it will appoint a multiparty cabinet by consensus.

A further major principle of the NP's proposals was the maximum devolution of power to regional and local governments. Initially, there was reluctance to use the term 'federal' to describe the proposals, but by the second half of 1992 any such inhibitions had been jettisoned and the NP eagerly began to canvass support for federalism. In De Klerk's view, significant powers and functions should be vested in regional governments, and these would be enumerated and entrenched in the constitution. Regional governments, however, would have to function in accordance with the constitution, including a justiciable bill of rights. As at the level of central government, regional government would also have to embody checks and balances to prevent the abuse of power and majority tyranny.[177]

It will be apparent from even this brief survey of De Klerk's proposals that direct references to race or ethnicity are scrupulously avoided. Whereas P.W. Botha insisted that the building blocks of any future constitution had to be the 'groups' statutorily defined in the Population Registration Act of 1950 (which was repealed in 1991), De Klerk quickly recognised that this principle was a major obstacle to constitu-

---

176. National Party, *Grondwetlike Regering in 'n Deelnemende Demokrasie* (election pamphlet), Arcadia, 1991.
177. F.W. de Klerk, verbatim transcript, p. 5.

tional negotiation, He accepted, instead, that groups (of whatever kind) had to be formed on the basis of voluntary association. Minorities, he stresses, have to be protected against domination by majorities, but the definition of what a minority is varies with the context:

. . . central to the National Party's policy of power-sharing is the protection of minorities in the society. It is our view that if we are talking about minorities in the political arena it is the political party that is the most effective vehicle or channel for the protection of minority interests . . . minorities should be defined differently for different purposes. Minorities in our multi-cultural country refer, for instance, to language groups. Minorities refer, in the religious sense, to church denominations. Minorities in the economic sense refer to professional groupings, to employers on the one hand, to certain types of employees on the other hand, and minorities in the political sense, as well as majorities, *define themselves within political parties*. When we speak about minorities, therefore, we do not speak in the political sense of a basis of ethnicity. That is cultural; that relates to language and culture. Politically, we speak about parties and we say that on the basis of freedom of association parties define themselves. (emphasis added)[178]

Similarly, with respect to federalism, De Klerk has been careful to pre-empt criticism that it was a devious way of retaining a form of apartheid: 'An ethnic basis for the determination of [regional] boundaries will not succeed. Other commonalities such as economic, geographical and topographical factors should rather determine the boundaries of regions.'[179]

Virtually none of these proposals has been acceptable to the ANC, which has repeatedly accused De Klerk of refusing to contemplate losing power or, alternatively, of seeking to place such limits on the power of the majority as to paralyse it. In a bitter statement about the breakdown of constitutional negotations in 1992, Nelson Mandela claimed that the reason for the crisis was that

the ruling National Party keeps looking for ways to exercise power even if it loses a democratic election . . . Their real concern is to protect the power, privileges and greed of the National Party leadership and top-ranking officials in the security forces'.[180]

As has been suggested, it was the power-sharing/majoritarianism conundrum that was the fundamental cause of the failure of CODESA to reach agreement on the composition and decision-making procedure of a constitution-making body. No less serious as a cause of the strained relationship between the NP and the ANC has been the apparently endemic political violence that has claimed the lives of more than

178. *Ibid.*, pp. 9–10.
179. *Ibid.*, p. 5.
180. ANC, *Statement by Nelson Mandela at the Press Conference held on 9 July 1992.*

10,000 people by 1993. The ANC believes that the state has a deliberate strategy of weakening the ANC, and it cites in support of this contention allegations of police partisanship, favouring Inkatha Freedom Party vigilantes who attack ANC supporters, and hit squads that have assassinated ANC activists. Further evidence of state partisanship emerged, much to De Klerk's embarrassment, when it was revealed in mid-1991 that the state treasury had made secret payments to Inkatha, ostensibly to assist with the funding of rallies against sanctions.

In response to the question posed in mid-1991, 'Do you still trust De Klerk?', Mandela replied:

I would like to think there are people undermining him because I think he is too honest to play this kind of game. But my problem is the fact that he has not been able to use his capacity to put an end to the violence so that we can move forward.[181]

A little more than a year later Mandela was asked a similar question and he replied by describing a meeting with De Klerk at CODESA on May 1992 where he complained about inadequate police action against armed Inkatha demonstrators. According to Mandela's account De Klerk replied, 'Mr Mandela, when you join me, you will realise I do not have the power which you think I have.' Mandela went on to say:

If there is anything that has cooled relations between me and Mr De Klerk, it is his paralysis as far as violence is concerned. Because I believe he has got the capacity to put an end to the violence. That is the issue for me, and we need to resolve it.[182]

It is almost certainly not true that De Klerk has in some sinister way orchestrated a campaign of violence against the ANC; but he has had to cope with the consequences of the 'total strategy' launched in the time of Botha. Essentially this strategy declared open season on the ANC in exile and its alleged internal supporters. It meant also that significant elements within the security forces became imbued with an outlook that saw in the ANC and its allies an enemy that was to be eliminated by whatever means. There can be little doubt that De Klerk has been sincere in his efforts to ensure that the security forces behave in a non-partisan way but, as his comment to Mandela implies, stamping out of the activities of rogue elements may be beyond his control.

In response to the ANC's accusations of official complicity in the violence, De Klerk has equally vehemently accused the organisation's tactics of being a material cause of violence. Repeatedly he has demanded of the ANC that it disband its armed wing *Umkhonto we Sizwe* (*MK*) and not merely suspend the operations; repeatedly he has

181. *The Argus*, 18 July 1991.
182. *Ibid.*, 15 September 1992.

condemned the ANC's strategy of 'mass action' and the tendency of some of its leaders to use inflammatory language. In turn, the ANC responds that it has no intention of disbanding *MK* until at least an interim government of national unity is in place and the security forces, including those of the homelands, are firmly under its control. Moreover, it insists, in the absence as yet of an effective franchise, what form of effective leverage does it have other than 'mass action'? The point may be valid but equally valid is the view, expressed by De Klerk, that mass action heightens tension in a volatile atmosphere and aggravates an already seriously ailing economy.

Democratisation of a society with so profoundly undemocratic a tradition as South Africa was never going to be a smooth process. Power-holders do not simply capitulate to their challengers – unless they have been comprehensively defeated, which is far from being the case with South Africa's ruling bloc. The impetus to seek a negotiated settlement came from the mutual recognition by De Klerk and Mandela that the contending forces were deadlocked and that the conflict could be perpetuated only at horrendous cost. In the years since De Klerk's initial liberalisation, neither the government nor the ANC has been able decisively to gain the upper hand. De Klerk remains in control of a formidably strong state; the ANC retains formidable grassroots support. As Ken Owen put it:

As matters stand today, [the NP government] have 100 percent veto power; yet they cannot properly govern the country without the acquiescence of the ANC. They must consult the ANC on budget matters, on housing, on health, on all sorts of questions. If they neglect to do so, they face boycotts, crime, calls for sanctions, mass action and a resumption of the campaign to make the country ungovernable.[183]

Aside from the important differences between the government and the ANC over what kind of democratic institutions are appropriate to South Africa's circumstances, the transition has been made much more complex by the combination of three distinct processes: first, the attempts to achieve a ceasefire and the cessation of violence; secondly, the effort to agree upon a constitution-making process and a constitutional draft itself; and thirdly, the beginning of the campaign for the first democratic elections. Mandela has acknowledged that it has been a mistake to embark on an electioneering campaign while negotiating: 'One party is talking to the other while trying to undermine that party. Now that destroys the whole atmosphere of negotiations'.[184]

A further complicating factor has been the tripolar nature of the conflict. Clearly the major political forces are the NP and the ANC, each

183. *Sunday Times* (Johannesburg), 9 February 1992.
184. *The Argus*, 15 September 1992.

with an array of allies, but any assumption that a settlement involving only these two will suffice is ill founded. The Inkatha Freedom Party, led by Chief Mangosuthu Buthelezi, is scarcely a major force nationally in terms of the percentage of the national vote it is likely to win, but it is a major player regionally in the KwaZulu heartland, even if its ability to win majority support from Zulu-speakers remains to be electorally tested. As it has amply demonstrated in the Transvaal, even decidedly minority support (at least according to poll data) does not preclude Inkatha's playing a significant spoiling role. Any constitutional settlement that is imposed upon Inkatha against its wishes would be resisted.

In September 1992, the government and the ANC, after a four-month breakdown of formal negotiations that had featured angry exchanges of memoranda, agreed to resume the negotiating process. The Record of Understanding signed by De Klerk and Mandela detailed agreement on a complex plan for a democratically elected constitution-making body that would contain deadlock-breaking mechanisms and function within a stipulated time-frame. Further agreements dealt with the sensitive issues of the release of political prisoners, hostels (from which Zulu occupants have launched murderous attacks on several occasions) and the carrying of dangerous weapons in public. Both leaders recommitted themselves to the National Peace Accord of 1991.[185]

Buthelezi immediately rejected the agreement, believing that he had been slighted by exclusion from the meeting, which had dealt with issues close to Inkatha's interests. In an angry statement he accused the government and the ANC of assuming that they could determine the future of the country without regard to Inkatha.[186]

Little purpose would be served by speculating about the future of these tangled and difficult processes. It is by no means assured that the contending forces will ultimately be able to reach a settlement. On the other hand, both De Klerk and Mandela are well aware that they need each other – and Buthelezi – to reach a settlement and that if a settlement eludes them a wasteland stares all South Africans in the face. Low economic growth rates since the 1980s, burgeoning unemployment and the devastating effects of drought have concentrated politicians' minds on the urgent need for a settlement, which appears to be a necessary, though by no means sufficient, condition for even modest economic growth.

Entering his fourth year of the presidency, De Klerk has weathered strain that has visibly aged him. By late 1992, there were murmurings in the NP caucus and at the grassroots level that he and his negotiators had made too many concessions to the ANC, especially with regard to

185. The full text is published in *Die Burger*, 28 September 1992.
186. *Ibid.*

the release of political prisoners. In some ways Mandela faced similar problems from the grassroots of the much more internally diverse ANC.

With the possibility of South Africa's first inclusive election as soon as late 1993, De Klerk has put his party in election mode. In 1991 the NP opened its ranks to all races and since then has been busily recruiting members in the African, coloured and Indian communities. Survey data suggest considerable support for De Klerk (though less for the NP) among coloured and Indian people, but only marginal support among Africans, where the ANC's support is massive. De Klerk has on several occasions expressed the view that the NP could win a democratic election. At a meeting in Oudtshoorn in October 1992 he told the party faithful that 'it was not a dream' that the NP could become the majority party in a new dispensation. He claimed that as many as 30 per cent of the prospective electorate were 'doubtfuls' who could be recruited to the NP banner.[187] Few analysts shared De Klerk's predictions: in an election in which colour is likely to be a major determinant of party preference, the NP's historical baggage of apartheid, even if jettisoned, is likely to inhibit it from gaining anything more than marginal support from Africans.

Even if De Klerk's hopes are not realised, he has carved himself a special niche in South Africa's history, as the man who broke the back of apartheid. His critics accuse him of seeking to preserve a form of neo-apartheid by means of a white veto (which he denies), but in his first three years as President he has surely made it impossible for apartheid to be re-established in its full and cruel rigour. Whatever his political future may be, De Klerk at least opened the Pandora's Box of change – and made sure that its contents could not be put back.

Hopes of an accommodation rest on the mutual recognition that the NP and the ANC have sunk all of their political and moral capital into attaining a political settlement: neither can realistically back out of the process now. Mandela, despite his tense and brittle relationship with him, appears to recognise that De Klerk is the only leader who is capable of leading white South Africa out of the corner into which it had painted itself.

Conclusion

Just as this chapter has avoided being a general account of the evolution of apartheid, so will the conclusion eschew an attempted overview of the causes of its demise. It was virtually inevitable that it would fail: the critics who maintained that it flew in the face of the reality of tightening ties of economic interdependence were ultimately proved right.

187. *Ibid.*

Each post-1948 South African leader was forced to acknowledge this interdependence, and to rationalise it in his own way. Vorster acknowledged reality by, among other things, abandoning 1978 as the magic year that would prove a turning point in South African history; Botha went a good deal further and essentially jettisoned the core of traditional apartheid thinking; and De Klerk embarked upon the process of politically and constitutionally complementing Botha's acceptance of a common citizenship. Only the benefit of historical hindsight, however, enables one to see these developments as stages of a logical progression.

At the same time there are some forces that have been operative throughout the period under consideration but whose significance has varied with time and circumstance. Whatever its critics may aver, the mainstream of Afrikaner nationalism retained a strong sense of morality. Each of the leaders discussed in this chapter claimed (on however dubious grounds) that the NP's vision of apartheid was morally defensible. Gerrit Viljoen, a former chairman of the Broederbond and a key figure in the De Klerk administration, wrote of the Afrikaner *volk* that it had given expression to a unique and unusual form of nationalism, namely a nationalism qualified by Christianity (*'n Christelik gekwalifiseerde nasionalisme*):

Where nationalism as a cultural form of sinful humankind can so easily degenerate into its 'black angel' of chauvinism and imperialism, this coupling of the national and the Christian was and is a touchstone and a pricking of the conscience which, in spite of our mistakes as a *volk*, always required of us serious moral accountability in our *volk's* struggle and life.[188]

These sentiments chimed with a powerful theme in the writing of N.P. van Wyk Louw, the unofficial but undoubted Poet Laureate of Afrikaans literature. In *Lojale Verset* (Loyal Opposition) he deals with *Volkskritiek*, meaning the criticism of a *volk* coming from within its own ranks (the word does not translate smoothly into English):

The major critique arises when the critic places himself not outside but in the midst of the group he is criticising, when he knows that he is indissolubly bound by love and by fate and by debt to the *volk* he dares to censure; when he speaks not of 'them', but of 'us' . . . Criticism is a nation's conscience.[189]

Volkskritiek suffered in the earlier post-1948 period. It was frowned upon by the party leadership because it created the impression of disunity and thereby gave the still-powerful opposition a handy stick

---

188. Gerrit Viljoen, *Ideaal en Werklikheid: Rekenskap deur 'n Afrikaner* (Cape Town: Tafelberg, 1978), pp. 35–6.
189. N.P. van Wyk Louw, *Lojale Verset* (Cape Town: Nasionale Boekhandel, 4th imp. 1970), pp. 107–8.

with which to beat the NP government – and, as has been shown, Verwoerd's intolerant authoritarianism made *volkskritiek* a hazardous business. The impulsion to test policies and practice against moral norms, however, survived; and in the more tolerant Vorster years 'loyal opposition' increased.

Another dialectic was at work that forced critical self-appraisal on key figures, more in Afrikaner civil society than among the politicians. This was the recognition that Afrikaner nationalism itself was an anti-colonialist force. Even that quintessential Briton Harold Macmillan had noted in his 1960 speech that it was the oldest of the African national-isms. How could the Afrikaners' own urge for freedom be reconciled with the racial domination they practised? In a famous essay written in 1963, Piet Cillié, a pillar of the Cape Nationalist establishment, dealt with this painful contradiction:

We rejected domination of ourselves, but we have not found the domination of other peoples by ourselves equally reprehensible [*verwerplik*]. It is not so many years ago that some of our foremost political leaders spoke openly of their policy towards the non-white people as 'mastership' [*'baasskap'*: the reference is to Strijdom] and 'permanent domination'. We acquiesced with little protest, and we still acquiesce in the absorption of masses of black labourers into our industrial economy without the slightest plan to give them expanding political rights that would be commensurate with their expanding economic power. These are colonialist attitudes, and they stand condemned not only in the eyes of a hostile world but also before our own best Afrikaner principles.[190]

Cillié called for a 'return to our belief in freedom' (which was the title of his essay). Earlier, N.P. van Wyk Louw had raised the same issue in another famous essay: 'I would rather go under than continue to exist in injustice.'[191]

Verwoerd sought to address this dilemma: the Afrikaner nationalists would shed colonial rule and themselves become decolonisers, thus remaining in step with the worldwide trend. In an assessment of Verwoerd, Alan Paton wrote that his greatest achievement was to abandon *baasskap* and replace it with separate development:

By doing so he stilled many an uneasy Afrikaner conscience, and won back to his side the troubled Afrikaner intellectuals and churchmen. On the positive side he also gave opportunity to many idealistic Afrikaners to feel that, in directing soil conservation in the Reserves, in planning the new towns and villages, in directing the higher education of Coloured and Indian and African

190. Cillié, *Baanbrekers vir Vryheid*, pp. 3–4.
191. Van Wyk Louw, *Liberale Nasionalisme* (Cape Town: Nasionale Boekhandel, 1958), p. 63.

students, in working in the various departments of Bantu affairs, they were also serving their own country and people.[192]

Paton's comments were shrewd since they suggest that apartheid and its subsequent more 'positive' formulation derived a good deal of its driving force from a unique capacity to yoke together an appeal to the ideological zealots who had no scruples about exploiting racial fears, and the idealists who genuinely believed that apartheid could be an instrument of liberation. In real life, of course, the two categories were not so sharply differentiated and many individuals experienced the tension between racism and idealism within their own minds.

Verwoerd's new vision, however, set up its own contradiction. There was a gap – and it would widen – between the proclaimed and beneficent intentions of what was often called grand apartheid, and reality on the ground. Reality was the tightening coils of restrictive legislation, the entrenchment of migrant labour, deepening poverty in the homelands, forced removals and, all too often, a callous view of people as just so many labour units. The impracticability of the vision would become even more dramatically apparent after Verwoerd, troubling more and more consciences.

Another difficulty was that apartheid had always been defended in quasi-sociological terms as a means of reducing friction. Interracial contact caused friction; therefore reduce friction by reducing contact. Apartheid, however, was more about the reinforcing of inequality than about reducing friction. Far from reducing friction it massively increased it, as increasing black alienation demonstrated. *Volkskritiek* did not miss the point.

In a striking comment on racial ideologies Reinhold Niebuhr said that

most rational and social justifications of unequal privilege are clearly afterthoughts. They are created by the disproportion of power which exists in a given social system. The justifications are usually dictated by the men of power to hide the nakedness of their greed, and by the inclination of society itself to veil the brutal facts of human life from itself.[193]

Reference has been made previously to apartheid's creating its own mechanism of cognitive dissonance, whereby unpalatable evidence was screened out of its perception. The mechanism, however, was not infallible: just as millions of Africans 'illegally' slipped through the influx control net, so uncomfortable facts about the unworkability of apartheid and its devastating impact on people could not be kept from people who were becoming better educated, better off, more sophisti-

---

192. Alan Paton, *The Long View* (London: Pall Mall, 1968), pp. 270–1.
193. Quoted in Paul Baxter and Basil Sansom (eds.), *Race and Social Difference* (Harmondsworth: Penguin, 1972), p. 121.

cated – and more cynical about the humbug dished out by many of their politicians.

As Afrikaners became more middle-class and developed a sizeable business and professional class, the previously inward-looking, even narcissistic nationalism attained a more benign equilibrium. Schalk Pienaar remarked in 1978: 'Much more than in the past there is a readiness to accept them [people of colour] as fellow-human beings and to accommodate them in the South African system.'[194]

There was a shift away from the more parochial norms of a narrower nationalism to the acceptance of more universalistic values. Growing numbers of businesspeople, scholars, writers, journalists, clergy and professionals now exhibited a new emotion: embarrassment, even shame, that they supposedly required discriminatory rules to protect them. Van Wyk Louw's credo struck a resonant chord. In an autobiographical account of his own conversion a leading *verligte* scholar who renounced the NP, Professor Sampie Terreblanche, expresses his shame at not leaving the NP sooner. In the light of hindsight, he writes, the NP from the mid-1970s on was 'like a ship drifting in a stormy sea without a navigator or a compass'.[195] Heightened moral sensibility did not spread evenly within the Afrikaner community: class, regional, age and sectoral differences prevented an even percolation. Space precludes a fuller discussion of this argument, but it is asserted here that in this process lies a major source of the original *verligte/verkrampte* dispute and the subsequent CP breakaway. The concept of Afrikanerdom was always something of a reification; increasingly it became a myth.

Skeuring (the vivid Afrikaans word for split) had at least three indirect effects on how the NP regarded apartheid. It liberated the more *verligte* elements from the paralysis that necessarily followed the effort to keep incompatible elements together; the existence of the HNP and the CP held up a mirror to modern-minded Nationalists to show them what the NP had been like in the not-so-distant past (the image repelled them and hastened the process of dissociation); and it forced the NP, shorn of a sizeable chunk of its traditional support base, to look for new allies.

It has been no part of the argument here to suggest that the reasons for the demise of apartheid are to be found exclusively in changes that have occurred within the ruling bloc. That would be as one-sided an interpretation as that which locates the reasons for change exclusively in the revolutionary struggle waged by the liberation movement, aided by the international sanctions campaign. Clearly, the rise of black militancy, increasing black resources such as trade union and consumer power,

---

194. Pienaar, *10 Jaar Politieke Kommentaar*, p. 70.
195. Sampie Terreblanche, 'My Stellenbosse Sprong na Vryheid', in Bernard Lategan and Hans Müller (eds.), *Afrikaners Tussen die Tye* (Johannesburg: Taurus, 1990), p. 117.

together with the palpable failure of apartheid policies such as influx control, homelands and Bantu education, propelled the state into a crisis of legitimacy. Economic decline, the loss of international financial confidence and the sheer cost of maintaining an increasingly unworkable system deepened the crisis and pushed South Africa into a deadlock, which could have been perpetuated only at horrendous cost.

Neither revolution from above nor revolution from below fully captures the causes and dynamics of the transition. A closer approximation is provided by Timothy Garton Ash's notion of 'refolution', which he uses to describe the changes of 1989 in Poland and Hungary:

> It was in fact, a mixture of reform and revolution . . . There was a strong and essential element of change 'from above', led by an enlightened minority in the still ruling communist parties. But there was also a vital element of popular pressure 'from below' . . . in both countries the story was that of an interaction between the two.[196]

196. Timothy Garton Ash, *We the People* (Cambridge: Granta Books, 1990), p. 14.

6

THE HEAD OF GOVERNMENT AND ORGANISED BUSINESS

Louwrens Pretorius

Relationships between South African heads of government and associations which represent business interests have evolved largely around their common, though often conflicting, concerns with apartheid policies.[1] The relationships have always been somewhat contradictory. While successive heads of government have attempted to bar business associations from politics, they have never denied them the right of articulating their economic interests. The government has, in fact, found it increasingly difficult to contain the entry of business and other interest groups into politics.

The focus of this chapter is on interactions through which government–businesss relationships have been formed and expressed. Specific interests, issues and policies which animated the interactions are mentioned; not because they are the objects of analysis but to contextualise and clarify the actions of the protagonists. The vexatious topic of interest groups' influence on the formulation of public policies recurs throughout the chapter. This is not, however, a systematic analysis of interest-group influence. The discussion can at best reveal some of the conditions which constrained or facilitated the major protagonists' attempts to shape the contents of public policies.

The focus is primarily on the principal manufacturing and commercial interest groups, the Afrikaanse Handelsinstituut (AHI), Association of Chambers of Commerce (Assocom) and the Federated Chambers of Industry (FCI).[2] The South African system of interest-group politics is complex. The evolution of relationships between government and a wide range of interest groups which operate in a socially and politically divided society can be discussed in the available space only at the cost of extreme simplification. Even the present limited focus entails a good deal of risk. It cannot, for example, be assumed that statements about

1. The terms 'business associations' and 'organised business' are used to refer to 'associational interest groups' (see G.A. Almond and G.B. Powell, *Comparative Politics,* Boston, MA: Little, Brown, 1966, p. 78), which represent business interests. The term 'business' is used loosely, but on the whole refers to the private sector at large.
2. Assocom and the FCI amalgamated in January 1990 to form the South African Chamber of Business (SACOB).

these associations also apply unproblematically to their regional affili-
ates or to their corporate members. Neither is it possible to generalise,
with regard to business–government interactions, from one set of
policies (such as those which govern the geographical mobility of
labour) to another (such as those governing money supply).

This consideration points to another qualification: the focus of this
chapter is on interactions with regard to issues and policies which
directly governed the racial ordering of South African society, namely
apartheid policies. The relationships which formed around purely
economic issues and policies are not necessarily similar to those which
form the subject matter of the present discussion. Distinctions between
economic and political policies are, of course, themselves likely to be
indicative of political positions. Government and organised business
have tended to disagree on whether or not interventions with regard to
policies which regulated the supply of labour, for example, constituted
interference in politics. Such disagreements are in themselves important for understanding the evolution of government–business relationships, but they cannot be explored in any detail in this chapter.

The focus on the head of government and three leading business
associations does not restrict the scope of discussion to these two sets
of entities. Owing to the conventions and dynamics of a cabinet-type
executive, it is neither sensible nor possible consistently to maintain an
analytic distinction between the head of government and the government (or cabinet). Hence I often refer simply to the government and also
draw attention to interactions in which individual cabinet ministers
were important actors.

A further expansion of the area of discussion is essential because
business associations interact with government in an environment
which includes other interest groups. It is suggested below that the
relationships between government and organised business have been
affected in important ways by the existence (and demise) of a network
of Afrikaner organisations and by the activities of a variety of African
organisations. With regard to the latter, it is further suggested that the
increasing intrusion of trade unions into the relationship between
organised business and government may result in a corporatist-type
system of interest representation.[3]

The discussion begins with an overview of some general features of
the South African system of interest representation.[4] Attention then
shifts to relationships between organised business and, respectively,
Verwoerd, Vorster, Botha and De Klerk. The discussion of the Verwoerd

3. On corporatism see P.C. Schmitter and G. Lehmbruch (eds.), *Trends Toward
   Corporatist Intermediation* (Beverly Hills, CA: Sage Publications, 1979).
4. See also L. Pretorius, 'Interactions between Interest Groups and Government in
   South Africa', *Politeia Unisa*, vol. 1, no. 1, 1982.

and Botha administrations include relatively extensive sections on the Economic Advisory Council (EAC). This body merits attention by virtue of the official reasons given for its establishment, its composition and its formal task of serving the head of government with policy advice. I also deal – in a separate section – with processes which had their origins during the Vorster administration but which culminated during the Botha administration. The cases illustrate the effective intrusion of business and other interest groups into policy processes, despite the rule against such intrusions.

General Features of the Interest Group System

Interest-group involvement in processes related to the formulation and implementation of apartheid policies has always been circumscribed by rules of interaction laid down by the head of government. Throughout the period under review, the basic rule was one that attempted to bar interest groups from effectively influencing the content of policies which had an obvious bearing on the racial ordering of society. In South African political discourse, as it is employed by both government and business, the rule barred business associations and other interest groups from participation in politics. In terms of this discourse politics is seen as the exclusive domain of political parties, parliament and the government. Thus, 'the business of business is business and not politics.' Until very recently, the rule was intended to apply particularly to groups opposed to government policies.

The successive heads of government have nevertheless not denied business associations the right to articulate their interests. They have in fact created and reaffirmed opportunities for this. In their turn, business associations have regularly – albeit with fluctuating degrees of emphasis and publicity – made their views on apartheid policies known to government. This seeming contradiction makes sense in terms of a number of considerations. Heads of government have not been powerful enough to adhere to their own rules. They and the business associations have chosen definitions of politics and economics which suited their respective policy objectives. They and business associations are also functionally dependent on each other.

Perhaps the most important consideration is that relationships between government and organised business are, to paraphrase Karl Marx somewhat out of context, only rarely made under conditions of the protagonists' own choosing. In South Africa the conditions of interaction have been markedly influenced by Afrikaner and African political movements and organisations which exist outside the formal boundaries of political party and parliamentary politics. At least until the late 1970s the government granted black social, economic and political groups little access or even opportunity for organisation; that is, unless they were willing to participate within the framework of apartheid institutions. Black groups which actively opposed government policies were subjected to systematic persecution. Since the late 1970s the situation has become somewhat more complex. The intrusion of African groups into relationships between government and business associations will be noted in subsequent sections of this chapter. For the present, the discussion is limited to the white, and particularly the Afrikaner, side of the political system.

One of the outstanding features of the South African political system has been the power of the head of government.[5] Members of the cabinet and of the National Party (NP's) parliamentary caucus have been known to disagree with the way a head of government should deal with policy issues. Unlike the system in the United States, where the President leads his party only partially,[6] the South African head of government has always led his party definitively. The style of leadership has varied. One extreme was the autocracy of Dr H.F. Verwoerd. Another was B.J. Vorster's broad tolerance of ministerial autonomy. Such differences have had important consequences for the ways in which cabinets have worked and in which governments and interest groups have interacted with each other. However, even Vorster determined the basic rules for his government's relationships with 'outside bodies'.

In June 1949 Dr D.F. Malan told his party's caucus that while theoretically the cabinet was to govern, 'in reality all final decisions rest with the Prime Minister'.[7] In March 1954 he reaffirmed and elaborated this rule when he criticised the working groups of the caucus for acting like 'little governments'. He insisted that the caucus was not a policy-making body but one which determined the party's parliamentary strategy. He also condemned an alleged tendency among the working groups to receive 'submissions from outside bodies'.[8] Malan's statements referred to National Party organisational units or factions outside the caucus. A similar rule had, however, forcefully and repeatedly been invoked against extra-parliamentary and extra-party interest groups.

---

5. H. Kotze, 'Aspects of the Public Policy Process in South Africa', in A. Venter (ed.), *South African Government and Politics* (Johannesburg: Southern Book Publishers, 1989); R.A. Schrire, 'The Formulation of Public Policy', in A. de Crespigny and R. Schrire (eds.), *The Government and Politics of South Africa* (Cape Town: Juta, 1978). But see also the somewhat different assessment by Seegers in chapter 2 in this volume.

6. M. Shaw, 'The Traditional and Modern Presidencies', in M. Shaw (ed.), *The American Presidency since Roosevelt* (London: Hurst, 1987), p. 249.

7. B.M. Schoeman, *Van Malan tot Verwoerd* (Cape Town: Human and Rousseau, 1973), p. 30.

8. *Ibid.*, p. 65.

This usually took the form of warnings against 'interference in politics'.[9]

In their turn, business associations have been inclined to describe themselves – as Assocom did in 1953 – as non-political bodies which regarded it as their task to 'support the Government's economic policies when they appear calculated to promote the general interest, and to oppose them when they do not'.[10] This stance, however, has always been somewhat ambiguous. As the mouthpiece of organised industry put it in 1951:

This Chamber is . . . a non-political, non-profit service organisation . . . [whose job it is] to give praise where praise is due and to criticise any action which will militate against the interests of industry and the national economy. But, it is not a function of this Chamber to appraise the relative merits or demerits of any democratic political party or ideology.[11]

The rule against the involvement of outside bodies in policy-making has been reiterated by all Malan's successors. They have all criticised the ways in which such bodies, including business associations, have articulated their interests and policy preferences. The essence of the message seems to have been that political opposition and policy prescriptions by interest groups were not regarded as legitimate activities – especially in public. But even Verwoerd's intolerance of political views other than his own did not lead to the exclusion of organised business from access to government. In other words, the rule did not question the business associations' right to pursue their members' economic and business interests. Most narrowly interpreted, the rule reflected Afrikaner nationalists' insistence on political self-determination. In a broader sense, it expressed a commitment to political conventions that recognised parties, elections and parliaments as the appropriate and authoritative instruments of governance.

Although the rule was invoked against even the Afrikaner Broederbond, all interest groups were not equally affected by this ban on political involvement. At least until the advent of P.W. Botha's administration, heads of government acted on and were visibly constrained by the twin convictions that they were the guardians of Afrikaner political self-determination and that they must maintain the support of the Afrikaner majority in the white electorate. This provided Afrikaner associations such as the AHI with privileged personal access to government and, presumably, some leverage in shaping the economic aspects of apartheid policies. For the primarily English associations like Assocom and

9. Cf. note 18 below.
10. *Commercial Opinion*, March 1953, pp. 457, 459.
11. Editorial in *The Manufacturer*, March 1951, p. 5, referring to the United South Africa Trust Fund. See chapter 4 by Giliomee in this volume.

the FCI, the opportunities for access have been mostly routine and official.

The expansion of Afrikaner participation in mining, industry and commerce brought with it an increasing commonality of interests and policy preferences between Afrikaans and English business associations. Especially since the mid-1970s, this has benefited English business by virtue of the AHI's readiness to participate in conveying these shared positions to the government. It has in fact been claimed that the Anglo-American Corporation supported the expansion of Afrikaner entrepreneurship into mining with the specific objective of enhancing 'sympathy for business in government circles'.[12]

During the first three decades of Afrikaner Nationalist government, the system was overwhelmingly biased in favour of Afrikaner associations. Their privileged access to the head of government was not simply a consequence of electoral arithmetic. It was a benefit accorded to the members of a closely knit political family. For most of its history the NP was much more than a party which competed with others for votes. It was also the parliamentary spearhead and protector of a well-organised Afrikaner nationalist movement. Through a process of ethnic mobilisation, Afrikaner interest groups were woven into a remarkably coherent network of economic, cultural, religious and political organisations.[13] Interaction between Afrikaner interest groups and NP governments was greatly facilitated by their interlocking directorates. The network functioned as a vehicle for structuring and maintaining ideological coherence, for canvassing and forming opinions, for cultivating policy consensus (or failing that, limiting public disagreement) among the elite of Afrikaner interest groups, and for mobilising popular support.

Besides the National Party itself, the Afrikaner Broederbond was for long the single most important link in the network. Acting in strict secrecy and through front organisations such as the Federasie van Afrikaanse Kultuurverenigings, the Broederbond played a major role in establishing other Afrikaner organisations and directing and coordinating their activities.[14] It guided the Afrikaner economic movement (*inter alia* through its Economic Institute), aided the creation of the Afrikaanse Handelsinstituut in 1942 and helped to lay the foundations for the

12. M. Lipton, *Capitalism and Apartheid* (Cape Town: David Philip, 1986), p. 310.
13. H. Adam and H. Giliomee, *The Rise and Crisis of Afrikaner Power* (Cape Town: David Philip, 1979); F.v.Z. Slabbert, 'Afrikaner Nationalism, White Politics, and Political Change', in L. Thompson and J. Butler (eds.), *Change in Contemporary South Africa*, (Berkeley, CA: University of California Press, 1975).
14. E.P. du Plessis, *'n Volk Staan Op* (Cape Town: Human and Rousseau, 1964); D. O'Meara, *Volkskapitalisme* (Johannesburg: Ravan Press, 1983); J.H.P. Serfontein, *Brotherhood of Power* (London: Rex Collings, 1979), I. Wilkins and H. Strydom, *The Super Afrikaners* (Johannesburg: Jonathan Ball, 1978).

establishment, in 1960, of the Prime Minister's Economic Advisory Council.[15]

The direction and decisiveness of Broederbond influence on public policies is a much disputed matter.[16] That the Broederbond and the NP government have always been intertwined in a relationship of considerable mutual influence is indisputable. The organisation's participation in policy processes has always been assured, because all the Nationalist heads of government, as well as the vast majority of cabinet members, have been members. The Broederbond's key political resource was the purposefully cultivated distribution of its membership throughout leading positions in all sectors of Afrikaner society. It became an invaluable conduit of organised Afrikaner interests. But this does not necessarily point only to Broederbond influence over government. It also indicates the organisation's potential as a medium for exerting governmental power and influence on other sectors of society. Either way, the existence of the network and the Broederbond's central position in it ensured access to government for Afrikaner business interests despite the public injunctions against the influence of outside bodies.

Since the late 1960s the influence of the Broederbond, either as policy-maker or policy conduit, has steadily declined. This decline was associated with the expansion of Afrikaner economic power and the attendant divergence of socio-economic class and sectoral interests within the ranks of *die volk*. These trends and the associated ideological conflicts were themselves related to the gradual fragmentation of the network. With all of this came the expansion of the range of common interests between Afrikaner and English entrepreneurs and business associations, as well as a gradual increase in government's permeability to non-Afrikaner business interests.[17]

Verwoerd: The Rejection of Business?

The transition from the 1950s to the 1960s was marked by black rebellion in South Africa and by the 'winds of change' in the rest of Africa. The political upheavals were accompanied by dark economic scenarios. These were brought to a climax by tragic events in Sharpeville,

15. The persons most closely associated with the establishment of the AHI, Economic Institute and Reddingsdaadbond included the elite of ascendant Afrikaner business corporations as well as a number of future cabinet ministers. The latter group included A. Hertzog, N. Diederichs, T.E. Dönges, S.P. le Roux, C.R. Swart, A.J.R. van Rhyn and H.F. Verwoerd.
16. See chapter 4 by Giliomee in this book.
17. Lipton, *Capitalism and Apartheid*, pp. 235–6, 281, 306–7. See also chapter 4 by Giliomee in this book.

a black township in the Transvaal. On 21 March 1960 the Pan-Africanist Congress (PAC's) campaign against the pass laws was launched. On the same day police gunfire killed 69 and wounded 180 people at Sharpeville. Later that day two more persons were killed during police action in Langa near Cape Town. At the end of March a state of emergency was declared. In the first week of April the PAC and the African National Congress (ANC) were banned. These events exacerbated an already declining trend in business confidence and performance.

For most of the preceding decade, business associations had cautiously avoided taking public issue with government on its apartheid policies. When they did do so, the government had tended to react by warning them not to 'enter the political arena'.[18] But then, business associations generally describe themselves as non-political bodies whose field of endeavour is 'economic policies'.[19] This did not, of course, mean that organised business had remained literally uninvolved in politics. Low-key approaches to ministers had always been regular practice. According to Posel, however, organised business had been inclined to focus its lobbying activities on the implementation of policy at the departmental level rather than on the formulation of policy at the cabinet level.[20] Although the AHI enjoyed the special privileges of access at the top levels of government, it too observed 'the norm of a non-political public profile'.[21]

A possible switch to a more assertive and public mode of articulating political interest was indicated by the business associations' reaction to 'the crisis' of early 1960. On 12 May 1960 the AHI, Assocom, the FCI, the Steel and Engineering Industries Federation of SA (SEIFSA) and the Transvaal and Orange Free State Chambers of Mines handed a joint statement to Prime Minister Verwoerd. In the statement – the publication of which had been purposely delayed – they called for the abolition of curfew regulations, for amendments to liquor laws and for limited amendments to the system of influx control.[22] This did not constitute a particularly determined attack on apartheid. The associations presented their proposals as ways of 'alleviating genuine grievances'. But they could also be interpreted as having affirmed the associations' preference for the modification of influx controls in a way which would

18. From a quotation attributed to the Minister of Transport, reacting to business objections against the 'job colour bar' during the 1950s, as quoted by Lipton, *Ibid.*, p. 143.
19. Cf. *Commercial Opinion*, March 1953, p. 457.
20. D. Posel, 'Interests, Conflict and Power: The Relationship between the State and Business in South Africa during the 1950s', paper presented to the conference of the Association for Sociology in Southern Africa, July 1985, pp. 21–2.
21. *Ibid.*, p. 22.
22. *Cape Argus*, 3 June 1960; *Commercial Opinion* July 1960, pp. 6–8.

facilitate the establishment of a pool of permanently urbanised and relatively mobile African workers.[23]

Shortly after publication of the joint statement, Assocom released its own statement of policy. It advocated the development of the 'Bantu areas as an integral part of the economy of the Union as a whole' and opposed the Verwoerdian idea of limiting the utilisation of white capital to industries located on the borders between African homelands and white South Africa. It proposed that 'restrictions imposed upon the occupation of property for business or other economic purposes on racial grounds in any area of the Union should be progressively relaxed' and that 'Natives should be permitted to acquire freehold title in urban native townships.' It also called for the repeal of work reservation and expressed support for a gradual development of representative trade unions.[24] Unlike the joint statement, Assocom's policy pointed to a political concern beyond economic interests pure and simple. 'It is essential', the association said, 'to obtain greater co-operation among all people in South Africa, white and non-white. There should be imparted to non-whites a sense of inclusion in the shaping of the Union's future . . .'[25]

Assocom's statement was a frontal attack on key apartheid measures and policies. Verwoerd's annoyance with this was probably intensified because this statement was published at a time when the government had already been in private discussion with other signatories of the joint statement.[26] However, even if all the associations had kept their proposals inside closed meetings, they would not have affected government policy. That much was made clear when the minister of finance said that the government had 'no objection to suggestions being made by employer organisations in this country, provided those suggestions are constructive and free of ulterior motives, and provided they do not conflict with the basic policy of the National Party'.[27] In his statement Verwoerd said:

However well intended, those who have made such proposals often do not have sufficient facts at their disposal by which they can test the effects of their proposals and it therefore remains the task of the Government, with full

23. Lipton, *Capitalism and Apartheid*, pp. 140–65; S.B. Greenberg, *Race and State in Capitalist Development* (Johannesburg: Ravan Press, 1980), pp. 191–5.
24. *Commercial Opinion*, June 1960, pp. 14–17. The statement was adopted by the Assocom executive in May 1960, but it resulted from a decision which preceded Sharpeville.
25. *Ibid.*, p. 14.
26. *Ibid.*, pp. 15, 17; *Hansard*, 20 May 1960, cols 8336–7. He was also in the process of suppressing divisions within his government, party and the Afrikaner churches, as evidenced by events surrounding the Sauer speech and the Cottesloe Conference. See chapters 4 and 5 in this book.
27. *Hansard, ibid.*

knowledge of the position after consideration of all the facts and consequences, and after consultation with its experts to make the necessary decisions.[28]

Before the events of May and June, Verwoerd had accepted an invitation to open the 1960 Assocom congress. The acceptance was retracted in an acerbic letter signed by his assistant private secretary. In it Verwoerd informed Assocom that discussion of its stance on 'this matter of colour policy' would 'serve as little good purpose . . . as to discuss the same points of policy with an opposition party'.[29]

Verwoerd's censure of Assocom indicated his often reported dislike of advice which ran counter to his own convictions. It also reflected Afrikaner nationalists' insistence on political self-determination. Assocom's statement declared that implementation of apartheid would jeopardise the economy. This contradicted Verwoerd's belief that economic growth and apartheid could be advanced simultaneously. However, if that proved to be impossible, then economic development was the lesser priority. In Verwoerd's view, as he expressed it to representatives of Assocom and the FCI in 1951, the 'implementation of the apartheid policies had to take account of economic possibilities . . . [but] the desire for economic gain could not be allowed to take precedence over more urgent considerations . . . [namely] the interests of preserving white civilization'. This goal required the maintenance of white political supremacy and that in turn required strict limitations on the residence of Africans outside the reserves.[30] An editorial in *Die Burger*, a Nationalist mouthpiece, revealed an important reason behind the government's rejection of the business lobby's proposals:

> Those so-called economic proposals are rejected because the political implications thereof are rejected, and it is time that businessmen who want to talk about these things should be asked to consider the political consequences of their economic proposals, like they ask others to consider the economic consequences of their political measures.[31]

The connection between the government's reaction to business interventions and the party's political and constitutional struggles became clear during the republican referendum campaign of 1960. When a number of corporate leaders added their voices to that of organised business, *Die Burger* claimed that 'a clear pattern in the opposition-oriented business world is being discerned in Government circles'. This, it said, seemed to the government to be 'an attempt to mobilise the most influential part of the English business world against

28. *Ibid.*, col. 8337.
29. Quoted in *Business Day*, 21 October 1986.
30. *Commercial Opinion*, September 1951, pp. 178–9.
31. *Die Burger*, 23 June 1960.

the Government'.[32] Deputy minister B.J. Vorster told an AHI meeting that 'businessmen would be well advised to attend to their own affairs and to leave the governing of the country in the hands of the Government.'[33] Verwoerd himself linked 'the campaign conducted against South Africa by certain businessmen' to opposition to the proposed republican constitutional form.[34]

Assocom denied political involvement in the referendum, emphasised that it had been 'obliged by our economic principles to make statements which, on occasion, have run counter to present government policy', and denied that the organisation's policy proposals constituted political policy.[35] The AHI and the other associations had escaped the government's rebukes because they kept a low profile and proceeded through what the government regarded as acceptable channels. The FCI decided to 'work within the compass of what parliament determines' and the AHI opted to 'strive for close feeling and co-operation with the government and its departments in order to watch over the interests of the businessman and to be helpful to the authorities with sober and practical advice'.[36] The AHI also announced that it 'supported the government's policy of separate development in principle but reserved the right to differ about its implementation' and made public a memorandum in which it expressed support for a policy of 'border areas development'.[37]

Twenty-five years later, a *Business Day* columnist claimed that Verwoerd's letter to Assocom introduced a period of 'at least 10 years before government and Assocom made any direct contact'.[38] One major review of P.W. Botha's presidency points to the Carlton (1979) and Good Hope (1982) conferences as 'the first active attempts that any National Prime Minister had made to win the support of business in a Government initiative'.[39] Historian Merle Lipton, citing interviews with Assocom officials, reported that 'for some years, government departments refused to receive, or even reply to correspondence from, Assocom officials.'[40] The reality was somewhat different.

On 1 July 1960 two Assocom delegates took their seats in the Prime Minister's newly established Economic Advisory Council (EAC).

32. *Die Burger*, 6 June 1960.
33. *Cape Argus*, 17 June 1960; *Die Burger*, 18 June 1960.
34. *Die Burger*, 4 July 1960.
35. *Commercial Opinion*, November 1960, p. 12.
36. Quoted in Greenberg, *Race and State in Capitalist Development*, pp. 203–4.
37. *Commercial Opinion*, June 1960, p. 15; *Die Burger*, 7 July 1960. The memorandum was formulated in January 1960.
38. *Business Day*, 21 October 1986.
39. B. Pottinger, *The Imperial Presidency* (Johannesburg: Southern Book Publishers, 1988), p. 117.
40. Lipton, *Capitalism and Apartheid*, p. 151.

Moreover, by late 1960 the president of the Johannesburg Chamber of Commerce perceived that 'the tenor of the Prime Minister's statement, issued after the first meeting of the Economic Advisory Council, appeared to be somewhat more sympathetic than some other pronouncements on the approach that Commerce brings to national questions'.[41] During that EAC meeting Verwoerd said that the Council

... has shown that, notwithstanding differences of opinion on certain subjects, there is ample scope for fruitful co-operation between government and private enterprise, especially as the Government recognises the key role which private enterprise could and should play in the development of our country.'[42]

The 1960 congress of Assocom – where the executive's policy statement had been endorsed – was, moreover, attended by an impressive array of government officials, led by the Minister of the Interior, Tom Naude. Naude stressed the 'high value which the Government attach to the policy advice of chambers of commerce' and emphasised the desirability of regular meetings between Assocom and the government.[43] At the opening of the AHI's 1960 conference the Minister of Finance, Dr T.E. Donges, invited the 'South African entrepreneur . . . to grasp opportunities and to tackle new development . . . not only [to] serve his own interest, but also the interests of the country as a whole'. He told delegates that 'the government believes in private enterprise and respects the profit motive, and it is its policy to stimulate development through the private sector.'[44]

Some of these statements were in all likelihood partly propaganda. But they do indicate that interactions between the government and Assocom were not suspended in 1960. They also point to the reasons why Verwoerd allowed the maintenance of such interactions even while he and his ministers were publicly inveighing against Assocom.

Verwoerd: The Incorporation of Business?

In 1939 the Eerste Ekonomiese Volkskongres (First People's Economic Congress) adopted a resolution which called on government to establish a 'central economic council' with the purpose of 'guiding and co-ordinating all economic activities'.[45] In 1942, following the recommen-

41. *Commercial Opinion*, October 1960, p. 68.
42. *Ibid.*, p. 71.
43. *Commercial Opinion,* November 1960, pp. 5, 17.
44. *Volkshandel*, October 1960, p. 11.
45. This summary of the background to the establishment of the EAC is based on Du Plessis, *'n Volk Staan Op*, pp. 129, 151–3; Pretorius, 'Interactions between Interest Groups and Government', pp. 16–7, O'Meara, *Volkskapitalisme*, pp. 147, 176–8; *Commercial Opinion,* November 1948, p. 232, November 1951, p. 255, June 1951, p. 47, July 1952, p. 112, November 1952, p. 301; *Die Trans-*

dations of an interim report of the Industrial and Agricultural Requirements Commission and lobbying by the Economic Institute and the AHI, the Smuts government established the advisory Social and Economic and Planning Council. However, the Nationalists had in mind a coordinating council with executive, and not only advisory, powers. The 1944 'action programme' of the Cape National Party announced the intention to use the resources of the state to protect the 'legitimate interests of producers, distributors, workers and consumers'. This statement of intent was accompanied by the demand for a central economic council which could advise the government on relevant measures. After the NP victory, the possibility of establishing such a body was repeatedly discussed in parliament and elsewhere. A bill which provided for the establishment of an economic advisory council was tabled in 1952 but allowed to lapse.

The proposals were not well received by Assocom or the opposition parties in parliament. They had expressed concern that the economic council – in conjunction with a proposed labour council – should be an instrument for centralised and directive planning. After the bill of 1952 lapsed, the idea of a central economic council was kept alive by the interlocked executives of the Broederbond, the Economic Institute and the AHI. In August 1958 two veterans of the Eerste Ekonomiese Volkskongres, Verwoerd and Albert Hertzog, discussed the idea while they were laying plans for Verwoerd's succession as Prime Minister.

In December 1959 Verwoerd announced his intention to appoint an economic advisory council, which was formally constituted in July 1960. It was to meet 'the need for economic-scientific advice, but also especially for a forum for discussion and more or less informal consultation and co-ordination between the State on the one side and private enterprise interests on the other'.[46] The task of coordinating the execution of the government's decentralisation policy was allocated to the Permanent Committee for the Location of Industries (PCLI). Whereas the Economic Advisory Council was a representative body of state agencies and business and labour organisations, membership of the PCLI was limited to state agencies.

Public commentary by ministers, officials and newspaper editors highlighted the expectation that the EAC would play some role in formulating the economic components of apartheid policies. The first series of meetings of the EAC did in fact concentrate mainly on issues

---

valer, 15 September 1950; *Hansard*, 17 May 1951, col. 7035–8, 18 May 1951, col. 7050, 22 January 1952, col. 68–9, 23 January 1952, col. 101–2; *Volkshandel*, January 1951, pp. 10--11, February 1951, p. 5; and Schoeman, *Van Malan tot Verwoerd*, p. 134.

46. H.F. Verwoerd, 'Samestelling en Funksies van die Ekonomiese Adviesraad', official statement, 22 March 1960.

related to the development of border industries in particular and to apartheid economics in general. Verwoerd, supported by other ministers, insisted that cooperation between the state and the private sector was necessary and desirable for the effective implementation of economic policies.[47] In fact government support for cooperation had been expressed long before the events of 1960; one early occasion was a 1951 meeting between Verwoerd and representatives of the FCI and Assocom.[48]

On the one hand, Verwoerd's public denunciation of attempts by business to intervene in policy processes served his government's specifically political interest in maintaining Afrikaner self-determination. On the other hand, as the ministerial calls for private sector cooperation in 'development' indicate, he also perceived the benefits of business support in the pursuit of political and economic objectives. Separate development required capital investment. In its turn, business shared government's interest in economic growth and political stability. The creation of the EAC provided for the cultivation of such commonalities. The exclusionary nature of Afrikaner Nationalism precluded public consultations between government and business. The institution of a representative advisory body brought with it the opportunity to cultivate the support of the private sector without doing so in public view.[49] It is also not beyond the realms of possibility that the offering of representation to English business associations may have been considered valuable with the republican referendum in view.

For the business associations, membership of the council was attractive precisely because it had the potential to ensure access to the upper echelons of government. Business leaders expressed satisfaction with the EAC, probably in the hope that it could contribute to alleviating problems which were arising from 'conflicting industrial and labour policies . . . [which] have been aggravated by racial and ideological legislation'.[50]

The government, however, did not intend to allow private sector interest groups to participate effectively in the formulation of government policies. This became clear when the government released the details of its plans for the development of border industries before the first meeting of the EAC. As the *Financial Mail* commented at the time,

47. *Ibid.*; A.J. Norval, 'Co-ordinated Planning', *The Manufacturer*, December 1959, pp. 33–9; M.D.C. de Wet Nel, 'Opening Address...[1959] Convention of the South African Federated Chamber of Industries', *The Manufacturer*, December 1959, pp. 9–19; T.E. Donges, 'Ons Ekonomiese Krag en Ontwikkelings-Moontlikhede', *Volkshandel*, October 1960, pp. 10–13; *Hansard*, 20 May 1960, col. 8343.
48. *Commercial Opinion*, September 1951, pp. 178–81.
49. Pretorius, 'Interactions between Interest Groups and Government', p. 18.
50. *The Star*, 8 December 1959.

government obviously intended that advice from the private sector via the EAC would remain within the limits of 'accepted government policy'.[51] Indeed, Verwoerd himself commented that the 'many constructive thoughts' which had been expressed at the EAC meeting 'should prove very helpful to the Government in the *implementation* of its policies'. [emphasis added][52]

Vorster: 'The Channels are always Open, but . . .'

During his first few years as Prime Minister Vorster was preoccupied with South Africa's relations with African states, sport policy and the *verkramptes* in Nationalist organisations. The government was soon to be confronted, however, by the black consciousness movement and with an increasingly militant black workforce. By 1974, South Africa's regional position moved into a new phase with the independence of Mozambique and Angola. Two years later, on 16 June, students in Soweto rebelled against apartheid education policies. Black rebellion spread around the country and has continued since. The black consciousness movement, the strikes and the rebellion triggered processes which had important consequences for the relationship between the head of government and organised business.

Vorster's leadership style also had an important bearing on that relationship. Following Verwoerd's domineering reign, Vorster 'introduced a more . . . relaxed touch to the premiership'.[53] In the cabinet he became the 'chairman of the board'; in his dealings with business he addressed representatives in their clubs.[54] The relaxed style – which did not extend to the political formations that fell foul of Vorster's definition of subversion – and the measure of ministerial autonomy which accompanied it eased the political atmosphere and encouraged white 'outside bodies' to articulate their disagreements with government somewhat more openly than before. Such disagreements increased as rapid economic growth brought with it the demand for fewer restrictions on the geographic and occupational mobility of labour.[55]

51. *Financial Mail*, 10 June 1960, p. 522.
52. Quoted in *Commercial Opinion*, October 1960, p. 70.
53. L. Gandar, quoted in J. D'Oliveira, *Vorster – the Man* (Johannesburg: Ernest Stanton, 1977), pp. 212–3.
54. H. Giliomee, 'Afrikaner Politics: How the System Works', in Adam and Giliomee, *The Rise and Crisis of Afrikaner Power*, pp. 202, 256; see also chapter 4 in this book. Within the broad framework set by government policies, ministers became their own gatekeepers. That enabled business associations and individual entrepreneurs to seek out sympathetic policy-makers. However, as Giliomee has pointed out, the consequent 'departmentalism' prevented the formulation of clear policies.
55. A. Stadler, *The Political Economy of South Africa* (Cape Town: David Philip, 1987), p. 81; Lipton, *Capitalism and Apartheid*, pp. 138–82.

The entry of Afrikaners into the upper reaches of industry and commerce encouraged this openness.

While access to decision-points became easier for organised business, the government remained averse to public calls for the abolition of apartheid policies. The occasion for reaffirming these conditions for interaction between government and organised business came in October 1976 as a result of the protracted black rebellion following the events in Soweto on 16 June.

In some ways, the 1976 rebellion and the reactions of organised business were replays of those following Sharpeville 16 years earlier. Unrest and the accompanying increased militance of black workers intensified pressure on apartheid labour policies. However, the sense of 'crisis' was, it seems, less acute than in 1960.[56] According to the *Financial Mail*, 'caution' but not 'pessimism' reigned in business circles. This was associated with the perception that adverse foreign reaction was not imminent and 'that Mr Vorster [was] firmly in the saddle'. There was an awareness among businesspeople that the perceptions and reactions of foreign investors and bankers could have a severely detrimental effect on an economy which was already under pressure.[57] This awareness did not, however, encourage a rush to the political hustings which was equal to that of 1960.

In early August 1976, the Transvaal Chamber of Industry (TCI) put a number of policy proposals to the Prime Minister. These dealt with municipal government, housing and public amenities in urban townships and with transport, education, influx control, job reservation and a number of other discriminatory measures.[58] The proposals did not call for fundamental changes in apartheid policies. They did, however, indicate some degree of business concern at a time when commentators marvelled at the lack of action by both business and government.

The silence on the sides of both government and organised business persisted well into October. At that time the government had not even acknowledged receipt of the TCI's memorandum. It was being suggested that organised business was not the appropriate vehicle for representing business interests in the wake of the rebellion.[59] A survey by the *Financial Mail* indicated that the AHI, the FCI, SEIFSA and the Building Industries Federation of South Africa were not about to challenge government policies. When the FCI held its annual congress in October, its director, Dr Hennie Reynders, reaffirmed the organisa-

56. Greenberg, *Race and State in Capitalist Development*, p. 206.
57. *Financial Mail*, 2 July 1976, pp. 13–16, 21–4.
58. *Ibid* 20 August 1976, pp. 633–4.
59. *Ibid.*, 27 August 1976, p. 723; 3 September 1976, pp. 821–3, 826; 8 October 1976, pp. 132, 134; 22 October 1976, pp. 302–3.

tion's traditional inclination against public intervention in political issues.

The recommendations which emanated from the FCI's 1976 congress did not go much beyond favouring the phasing out of job reservation. However, in 1975 the FCI had recommended cautious moves towards the restructuring of the system of labour relations and had implored government not to impede the development of black unions.[60] It may well be that the FCI stance was intended to safeguard efforts at 'quiet lobbying' in the field of industrial relations policy.

Around mid-October there were reports that branches of Assocom and the FCI were planning to approach the government with strong calls for policy change.[61] These plans were probably prompted by an upward trend in worker stay-aways. The government was not impressed with the comments it did hear. But unlike Verwoerd, Vorster tended to affect a grudging tolerance for opposition. Consequently he did not decline the opportunity to open Assocom's congress. He used it to state the terms on which business associations could deal with the government. He affirmed the right of business associations to disagree with him about public policy, but insisted that the formulation of policy was a matter for his government, which 'derived its legitimacy from a mandate given by the electorate'. But he also claimed that

> over the years the government has gone to great lengths to meet the legitimate difficulties of the business sector with regard to the utilisation of labour . . . The channels for conveying such suggestions are always open, either by approaching individual government departments and/or their ministers directly, or through forums such as the Economic Advisory Council and others.[62]

Vorster's statement implied a continuation of Verwoerd's Janus-faced approach to organised business. On the one side Vorster maintained the Nationalists' somewhat perverted constitutionalist approach to policy debates. On the other, he pointed to the government's awareness that the success of political policies required economic productivity.[63]

Assocom delegates reportedly reacted with indignation to Vorster's

---

60. *Rand Daily Mail*, 7 October 1976; *The Star*, 18 June and 9 December 1975. The appointment of Reynders as director of the FCI signalled the increasing prominence of Afrikaners in industry. It also indicated the ascendancy to influential positions in labour relations of relatively *verligte* Afrikaners such as Reynders and Anglo American's Chris du Toit. Reynders later became the chairman of the National Manpower Commission.
61. *Rand Daily Mail*, 15 October 1976.
62. Quoted in *Hansard*, 4 February 1977, cols 783–5.
63. Labour questions had received the attention of the EAC ever since its inception. Pretorius, 'Interactions between Interest Groups and Government', p. 20.

speech and gave overwhelming support to a motion calling on the government to remove the racial barriers impeding the socio-economic advancement of the country's black community.[64] But in the midst of serious unrest in Soweto and elsewhere, Assocom's reaction remained weak in comparison to that of 1960.[65] As if to confirm doubts which had previously been expressed about organised business' ability to intervene effectively in 'the crisis', the corporate elite set the scene for the most notable business response to the black rebellion of 1976.

The November 1976 Businessmen's Conference on the Quality of Life of Urban Communities was sponsored by prominent Afrikaans and English entrepreneurs. It resulted in the creation of the Urban Foundation (UF). The UF was charged with the task of 'tackling a fundamental cause of black frustration and anger: the poor quality of life in urban townships.'[66] This meant, in effect, that the UF was established to implement the emerging business strategy of de-racialising the economy and creating a black middle class as a buffer against black revolution. A primary means to that end was the provision of housing for blacks in urban areas, as well as the general upgrading of black townships.

The UF had been conceived as a development agency rather than a pressure group. But it could not pursue its mission while government policy restricted housing supply and prevented individual security of residence and tenancy in black townships. After an initial period of 'timorous and wary avoidance of political questions',[67] the UF consequently began to take on the role of a pressure group. In this capacity it became involved in alliances with a wide range of interest groups which were entering the political arena despite the government's censure of such activities.

From Vorster to Botha: The Intrusion of Interest Groups into Politics

Vorster insisted that the formulation of political policy was the task of the government and the governing party. The processes which led to and followed the report of the Wiehahn Commission of Inquiry into Labour Legislation nevertheless proved that the government could not remain impervious to the influence of outside bodies. The Commission, appointed during Vorster's administration, played an important role in policy changes, for which organised business could claim at least some

---

64. *Rand Daily Mail*, 21 October 1976.
65. J. Kane-Berman, *Soweto: Black Revolt, White Reaction* (Johannesburg: Ravan Press, 1978), pp. 161–2.
66. *Financial Mail*, 19 November 1976, p. 697.
67. Kane-Berman, *Soweto*.

of the credit. These changes in turn facilitated the development of African trade unions and so introduced an increasingly significant third party into the interactions between government and organised business.

By the end of the 1960s African trade unions were not particularly significant political or even industrial actors. Attempts at unionising African workers were actively discouraged by employers, and trade unionists were often persecuted by the state. In any case, they were excluded from the state-sanctioned machinery for collective bargaining until 1979. But African worker activism rose sharply after the beginning of the 1970s and their potential power was displayed in the Durban strikes of 1973 and the stay-aways of 1976. On the other side of the political spectrum, white workers were losing influence.[68]

The early 1970s saw the dilution of job colour bars as a result of business pressures – which included the efforts of Afrikaner entrepreneurs in both private and public corporations to ease the increasing shortages of skilled labour. With this came a growing realisation among some influential employers and government officials that the accommodation of African workers within the official labour relations system could not be indefinitely postponed.[69] This realisation was encouraged by the increasing worker activism and the expansion of an independent (mainly African) trade union movement. Initially, the government responded to the calls for consultation between employers and workers with variations on the so-called committee system. But worker activism and pressure by foreign governments and unions created a momentum for change.[70] The changes were formalised in the Wiehahn Commission's report and in the acceptance of its key recommendations by the government.

S.P. Botha became Minister of Labour in Vorster's cabinet in mid-1976. Against the background of increasingly strained industrial relations and the Soweto rebellion, he appointed Professor N.E. Wiehahn as his labour advisor and as chairman of the Commission of Enquiry into Labour Legislation. The membership included representatives of trade unions and trade union federations and of Assocom, the FCI, SEIFSA and the government Department of Labour. Except for representation through the Trade Union Council of South Africa, which could have been regarded as speaking for 'mixed' unions, African workers were not represented. The primary purpose of the Commission seems to have been to cultivate the agreement of important interest groups – including

68. H. Adam, 'Interests Behind Afrikaner Power' in Adam and Giliomee, *The Rise and Crisis of Afrikaner Power*.

69. This and the following paragraph is based largely on S. Friedman, 'How to Assist Change', unpubl. research report, South African Institute of Race Relations, 1986, 'Case A: Labour Relations', pp. 1–4.

70. *Ibid.*, p. 4.

conservative white unions – to the introduction of a state-sanctioned system for collective bargaining which would incorporate African unions.[71]

The commission achieved a remarkable degree of consensus among its members – thus limiting, but not preventing, opposition from conservative white trade unions. As part of an attempt to institutionalise the Commission's preference for a tripartite mode of consensus building on issues concerning industrial relations, a permanent consultative and advisory forum, the National Manpower Commission (NMC), was established. As in the case of the EAC and of the Wiehahn Commission itself, the NMC's membership included representatives of state agencies, trade unions and organised business.[72]

Contrary to the hopes of its designers, the new industrial relations system did not succeed in controlling the emergent African unions, or even in drawing them into the net of registered unions. The unions avoided the NMC. Instead, they used the opportunities created by the reforms to advance their own power by embarking on a wave of strikes and intensive membership drives.[73] These virtually compelled a small but influential group of employers to deal with the unions outside of the official bargaining system. The FCI in particular worked behind the scenes to lobby the department of manpower to relax controls on unions.[74]

Especially after the mid-1980s, the independent unions were increasingly, though eventually unsuccessfully, persecuted by the government. The instruments used for this ranged from legislation initiated by the department of labour to police harassment.[75] The post-Wiehahn reforms were nevertheless significant because they marked the decline of government's ability to keep non-Afrikaner nationalist interest groups out of policy formulation – even in public. The corollary of this was the effective intrusion of organised black groups into the relationship between organised business and government.

The reforms also illustrated the double-edged nature of government–interest group relationships. Group pressures, such as those exerted through African worker strikes and the FCI's 'quiet lobbying', encour-

71. *Ibid.*, p. 5.
72. Pretorius, 'Interactions between Interest Groups and Government'.
73. With reference to the possible effects which omissions, or commissions by heads of government, may have had on the conditions which facilitated union growth, note Welsh's comments on Vorster and Botha in chapter 5 of this volume.
74. Friedman, 'How to Assist Change', p. 7.
75. In July 1991 it was revealed that government activity in this arena included the provision of funds to the Inkatha-related union, UWUSA. UWUSA was launched in 1986 as a counter to the trade union federation COSATU (established in late 1985).

aged policy reforms. But government also used a commission of inquiry consisting of interest-group representatives to involve business associations and trade unions in the legitimation of such reforms. This was an instance of what was becoming a more generally employed 'practice of assembling the leaders in a particular field . . . in confidential meetings where [ministers] argue the case for reform. After consensus has been established, everyone is bound to these decisions'.[76] The process can be described as proto-corporatist: it involved members of the government and the leaders of interest groups in policy bargaining outside those 'political processes provided for in [the] Constitution' on which Vorster had placed so much emphasis in his address to Assocom.

The indications that policy-making was increasingly permeable to interest groups were reinforced by processes which closely involved the activities of the Urban Foundation. The establishment of the UF introduced the role of a 'specialist change agency' into the relationship between organised business and government.[77] It was noted above that, given the generalised restrictions which government policies placed on the pursuit of the UF's mission, it had to complement its activities as a development agency with those of a pressure group. Its early lobbying efforts, which spanned the period from roughly 1977 to 1985, were targeted at restrictions on the movement and settlement of African persons in urban areas.

Two such campaigns set the scene for the UF's participation in a process which eventually resulted in the abolition of influx control and a new government urbanisation policy. They concerned leasehold rights for African urban residents and the coloured labour preference policy (which inhibited the employment and settlement of Africans in the Western Cape), respectively. The actors in the campaigns comprised a divergent array of black and white interest groups, government officials and members of parliament, as well as the relevant ministers and the head of government. The Urban Foundation's role was essentially that of an alliance-builder. In the Western Cape case, for example, it conducted a sustained campaign to bring the widest possible range of pressures to bear against government policies. At the same time it acted to establish and maintain links between the relevant cabinet minister and the black community formations.

Friedman's analysis of the campaigns suggests a number of generalisations about the role of interest groups in policy processes during the

76. Giliomee, 'Afrikaner Politics', p. 210.
77. From March 1987 to January 1989 the author held the position of senior research officer in the Urban Foundation. The following interpretation of the Urban Foundation's role is based on knowledge gained during that period and on Friedman, 'How to Assist Change – Case B: Bars on African Permanence in the Western Cape'.

first five years of P.W. Botha's administration. One is that the policy changes were the consequences of complex interactions between a range of actors. Although the UF played an important role in creating and maintaining reform alliances, the participating black formations (such as the squatter movement in the Western Cape) and the government agencies were effectively the agents of power. Another general truth is that the mediating role of a change agency such as the UF was sustainable only to the extent that it remained useful to the major protagonists. Its usefulness in turn depended largely on its capacity to mobilise expertise and to network with other interest groups and with government. Finally, the roles played by ministers and government officials were profoundly influenced by their perceptions of President Botha's preferences and, ultimately, by his decisions.[78] Lawrence Schlemmer's comments on business influence on public policy convey a similar conclusion:

The pattern of events which led to the repeal of the influx control laws would suggest that the government can be responsive to private sector influence, but only where such influence is in agreement with expert opinion, where there is substantial acceptance of the reform measure within government's own support groups, and after its own enquiries have provided evidence and a rationale for the reform.[79]

Conclusions about the effective intrusion of interest groups into politics during Botha's period of office should nevertheless be qualified. From around 1985, the reform processes which characterised Botha's first years as head of government lost momentum. With this came an apparent increase in public disagreements between the head of government and segments of English – and some Afrikaans – business.

Botha: 'The End of a Perfect Day'

P.W. Botha has been credited with having used 'the skills and expertise of businessmen and academics on an unequalled scale, as evidenced by their participation in commissions and consultations and even their appointment to senior Government positions'.[80] Botha himself participated in communicating that impression.[81] It is not altogether clear how one should evaluate such claims. Verwoerd and Vorster also had recourse to the advice of business people and academics, albeit within the limits of ideological frameworks which were more rigid than those

78. *Ibid.*
79. L. Schlemmer, 'South Africa's National Party Government', in P.L. Berger and B. Godsell (eds.), *A Future South Africa* (Cape Town: Human and Rousseau, 1988), p. 22.
80. *Pretoria News*, 12 January 1981.
81. *Hansard*, 6 February 1980, cols 211, 234.

which marked the Botha administration. Even so, it may well be true that Botha was, at least during the first five years of his administration, more inclined than his predecessors to call on and listen to non-government advisors.

One of Botha's early initiatives entailed the appointment of three corporate executives to the Public Service Commission to advise on the rationalisation of the civil service. At the inception of that process, the administrative head of the Department of the Prime Minister, J.E. du Plessis, told the press that the working groups of the various cabinet committees would consult with experts from the private sector.[82] Inputs from the private sector were also brought to bear on the management of the quasi-state Armaments Development and Manufacturing Corporation and, some years later, on the processes of privatisation and deregulation.[83] This opening to the private sector was not an altogether novel trend. Some of Botha's most influential business advisors – such as W.J. de Villiers, F.J. du Plessis and C.J. Human – had long held prominent positions in the network of Afrikaner organisations and in consultative forums such as the EAC and Botha's Defence Advisory Council. It should also be noted that the ostensible opening to capital involved an approach to corporate elites rather than to the business associations.

At the 1979 Carlton summit between Botha and the country's corporate elite, his closing words were that those present had 'come to the end of a perfect day'. The sentiment was returned by many. Business people believed that, unlike his predecessors, Botha was 'at least prepared to listen to them' and that they were having some influence on policy.[84] Historian Merle Lipton and other important commentators of the time came to similar conclusions.

Lipton claimed: 'Unlike previous Nationalist leaders, Botha courted capitalists.' Citing his speeches at the Carlton conference, in parliament in 1980 and at the Good Hope conference in 1981, she further claimed that Botha 'urged [capitalists] to participate in politics, and [that] he appointed them to government commissions and committees'.[85] The critical question is: what did Botha say to the capitalists? In February 1980 he told parliament that the Carlton conference dealt with 'joint action by the State and the private sector in order to achieve certain objectives' with regard to the economic development of a Southern African 'constellation of states'.[86] At the Carlton conference itself he

82. *Financial Mail*, 19 October 1979.
83. *Hansard*, 6 February 1980, col. 234; 21 April 1986, col. 3817; *Financial Mail*, 22 June 1979; *Sunday Times* (Johannesburg), 14 October 1979.
84. *Financial Mail*, 19 October 1979; 23 November 1984.
85. Lipton, *Capitalism and Apartheid*, p. 322.
86. *Hansard*, 6 February 1980, cols 211, 248–9.

had demarcated the respective roles that government and the private
sector had to play in the regional order which he wanted to create. In his
view, 'the basic responsibility of government is to establish, maintain,
and protect the national and international order within which private
enterprise can fulfil its functions of producing goods and services.'
Botha emphasised the private sector's production functions and talked
about the economic strategy which was under consideration by the EAC
and other state agencies.[87]

How did this differ from Verwoerd's invitations to private enterprise?
The Carlton and Good Hope conferences signalled adjustments in
economic decentralisation policy. Botha was beginning to draw economic rather than political boundaries. These cut across the political
demarcations between South Africa's officially designated white and
black territories. Seemingly unlike Verwoerd, Botha also insisted: 'No
government can successfully prescribe what to produce, how to produce, for whom to produce and where to invest'.[88] Furthermore, Botha's
relationships with English business were forged at a time when Afrikaans–
English relationships had begun to heal. This was far from the deep
mutual distrust and prejudice which marked white society at the time of
Verwoerd's cynical combination of appeals for Afrikaans–English
reconciliation and 'warning[s] about the dangers of the *Engelse geldmag*
(English money power)'.[89] Even under these different sets of circumstances, Botha's words must not be misconstrued as an open invitation
to business 'into politics'.

By 1981 some observers were becoming sceptical of the rapprochement. As one commentator put it: 'In the two years since the cementing
of the alliance between Government and big business [at Carlton] the
partnership has withered'.[90] In early 1985, at the time when relationships between Botha and segments of business were becoming visibly
strained, a cautious assessment of Botha's 'courtship of capital' was
offered by the executive director of Assocom. He noted that although
the Carlton and Good Hope summits

served to create a far better relationship between the South African government
and the business sector, it would be wrong to see it as partnership. In the final
analysis, business and government have separate tasks to do – each remains
free to criticize, complain or appeal to public opinion. But it did provide
stronger grounds for mutual confidence, and for the reform programme which
Prime Minister Botha was preparing to initiate.[91]

87. P.W. Botha, Address at the Carlton Conference, transcript in *The Star*, 22
    November 1979.
88. *Ibid*.
89. See chapter 4 in this volume.
90. *Rand Daily Mail*, 10 September 1981.
91. R.W.K. Parsons, 'Business and Reform in South Africa: History, Strategy and

Perhaps the assessment reflected Assocom's hard-earned under-standing of the limits on the business sector's influence in changing apartheid policies. The mutual confidence of which he spoke was in any case on the wane by 1985. That year saw the beginning of an intense period of public political campaigning by organised business – in particular by Assocom and the FCI – and by some individual corporate leaders.[92] The activity may have been triggered by Botha's ostensible 'invitation to politics'[93] and encouraged by the increasingly public stand that corporate notables took on political issues during the constitutional referendum campaign of 1983. But the underlying forces driving the campaigning came from elsewhere.

After the Soweto rebellion in 1976 black townships simmered con-tinuously. The early 1980s were a period of sustained activism, fuelled by attempts to introduce new forms of influx control, the exclusion of Africans from the tricameral parliament, dissatisfaction with a new system of black local authorities, and protests against local authority rent and service charges. The activism was driven by the increasingly powerful African trade unions and a wide range of community, profes-sional and student associations. At the national level they were being drawn into loose federations such as the United Democratic Front and the National Forum.[94] Meanwhile the ANC was also reasserting itself as a major force in South African politics.

The South African government's repressive reaction to the escalating unrest encouraged calls for disinvestment and other forms of foreign economic pressure against its policies. As the political and economic conditions in the country deteriorated, the pressure on business to make hard political choices, and to do so in public, increased.

Organised business fired its first salvo of 1985 when, in January, the AHI, Assocom, the Chamber of Mines, SEIFSA and the National African Chambers of Commerce (NAFCOC) presented visiting US Senator Edward Kennedy with a memorandum which outlined their collective views on a number of issues, including support for 'meaning-ful political participation for blacks' and the cessation of forced removals.[95] While Kennedy was the recipient of this document, the

Tactics' (address to the US Council for International Business, New York, May 1985), *Industrial Relations Journal of South Africa*, vol. 6, no. 1 (1986), p. 62.

92. For the latter, the year culminated in September, when a group of businessmen met members of the ANC leadership in Zambia.
93. *Financial Mail*, 23 November 1983; *Finansies & Tegniek*, 15 May 1987.
94. H. Barell, 'The United Democratic Front and the National Forum', in SARS (ed.), *South African Review 2* (Johannesburg: Ravan Press, 1984); M. Swilling, 'Stayaways, Urban Protest and the State', in SARS (ed.), *South African Review 3* (Johannesburg: Ravan Press, 1986).
95. Memorandum signed for the AHI, Assocom, Chamber of Mines of SA, NAFCOC and SEIFSA, Johannesburg, 7 January 1985. Access to government for NAFCOC

South African government and an increasingly hostile anti-apartheid
and pro-disinvestment lobby in the USA were its intended audience.
The *Financial Mail* sketched a somewhat exaggerated picture of
unprecedented business unity in 'condemnation of government and its
social and economic policies' – a unity which included 'the grassroots
businessmen of the Afrikaans community from the AHI'. The columnist
concluded that organised business had Botha's 'back . . . against the
mast'.[96] In fact, the President survived until he was felled by illness and
a party rebellion some four years later.

At least part of the impetus behind the business lobby came from black
consumer boycotts organised by community organisations. These affected the Eastern Cape in particular, but other parts of the country too.
Motivation for the boycotts varied from local socio-economic grievances to general political demands.[97] Whatever the mix was in particular
regions of the country, the boycotts, together with a marked increase in
strike activity, encouraged organised business to maintain a political
profile. But while Assocom and the FCI tended to keep up the pressure
with a series of public statements, the AHI was retreating from the
frontlines. The AHI's president expressed the view that there was 'no
substantial impatience' with the government in business circles. This
was in direct contradiction to the FCI's executive director, who said that
'businessmen are getting very impatient with government.' But the
director also kept to the FCI's traditional approach. He advised against
a public confrontation and in favour of a low key approach: 'This
government does not like to be addressed through the media – and they
make the rules in this game'.[98]

The AHI's solidarity with its English counterparts seemed especially
fragile when, in early 1986, it declined to react to the FCI's strongly
reformist and widely publicised business charter and action programme. The publication of the charter indicated an end to the FCI's
low-key approach, a shift to definite opposition to government policies
and a claim to the right to express itself on manifestly political issues.
The charter called, among other things, for the abolition of all statutory
discrimination. It also advocated equal rights of political participation
for all South Africans.[99] In June 1985 Assocom had released its own

was one of the outcomes of the Soweto rebellion. See Pretorius, 'Interactions
between Interest Groups and Government'; and P. Hudson and M. Sarakinsky,
'Class Interests and Politics: The Case of the Urban African Bourgeoisie' in SARS
(ed.), *South African Review 3*.

96. *Financial Mail*, 18 January 1985.
97. K. Helliker, A. Roux, and R. White, '"Asithengi!" Recent Consumer Boycotts',
in SARS (ed.), *South African Review 4* (Johannesburg: Ravan Press, 1987).
98. *Financial Mail*, 18 January 1985.
99. The FCI released three documents on 21 January 1986: 'A Positive and
Constructive Role for Business in the Reform Process in South Africa', 'South

Lombard Report, with which it too had entered the constitutional debate. Assocom and NAFCOC expressed support for the FCI.[100] The AHI vice-president thought that 'manifestos by organised commerce and industry are in order as long as they keep in a disciplined way to those economic parameters about which they are able to render authoritative commentary'.[101]

Earlier, in July 1985, the government had acted on the rising tide of black rebellion and the attendant violence by imposing a state of emergency. This was lifted in March 1986, only to be replaced by a second state of emergency some three months later. By then the country's economy was in a severe downturn, exacerbated by international reaction to Botha's Rubicon speech of August 1985. Assocom and FCI responded to the first state of emergency by calling for substantial political reform as well as the restoration of law and order. In July 1986 the two organisations, joined by a trade union federation, the Council of Unions of South Africa (CUSA), issued a similar call. An attempt to involve the more powerful Confederation of South African Trade Unions (COSATU) in a joint union-employer delegation to the government failed.[102] These events, however, indicated the beginnings of joint business–labour interactions with government.

In response to the FCI's efforts, Botha wrote to its president that 'instead of criticising the government in the most irresponsible fashion, you should be helping it'.[103] Scepticism regarding the usefulness of further government–business meetings undermined confidence in the 1986 Bryntirion conference, the follow-up to the Carlton and Good Hope meetings. It has, however, also been established that some business people did find considerable symbolic value in the conference.[104] Botha himself made it clear that the conference was not an occasion for the formulation of public policy: 'During this year I have already on different occasions explained the government's policy and received my party's support for the policy.'[105] At the 1987 AHI

African Business Charter of Social, Economic and Political Rights', and 'Action Programme of South African Business'.

100. The formal title of the document is 'Removal of Discrimination against Blacks in the Political Economy of the Republic of South Africa'.
101. *Volkshandel*, March 1986, p. 15.
102. South African Institute of Race Relations (SAIRR), *Race Relations Survey 1985* (Johannesburg: SAIRR, 1986), p. 563; SAIRR, *Survey 1986 Part 1* (1987), pp. 250–1; SAIRR, *Survey 1986 Part 2* (1988), p. 560.
103. Quoted in *Financial Mail*, 18 July, 1986.
104. *Financial Mail*, 31 November 1986. A.Y. Sadie, 'Regerings- en Sake-elite se Persepsies oor die Invloed van die Suid-Afrikaans Sakesektor op Openbare Beleidsformulering', unpubl. Ph.D. thesis, University of Cape Town, 1990, pp. 236–9.
105. P.W. Botha, 'Toespraak by Geleentheid van die Opening van die Sakeberaad met die Privaatsektor', Pretoria, 7 November 1986, photocopy, pp. 2–3, 6–7.

congress, Botha again repeated the well-known injunction: 'Let each of us – the government and the private sector – carry out the responsibilities entrusted to us in our own terrain.' Even so, the delegates were unusually outspoken 'on matters where politics and economics were inseparable', although they stayed clear of forbidden issues such as the Group Areas Act.[106]

But the levels of business activism remained uneven. For example, while it seemed that the AHI was becoming slightly more daring than usual in challenging government policies, there were signs that the FCI was retreating to its former less public mode of activity. This followed an investigation which had shown that the organisation's finances were in a bad state and that the FCI management had lost touch with the members. The consequent changes in the FCI's top management and a decision 'to spend less time on political questions and more on bread and butter issues' also reflected 'the shift in the business mood' about political involvement.[107]

Thus the 'perfect day' came to an end – at least in public. As with Verwoerd and Vorster, the public clashes between organised business and government were not accompanied by the suspension of relationships. Delegations still met the President and his ministers, but the level of publicity was toned down. When a group of senior Assocom, FCI, South African Agricultural Union (SAAU) and AHI members met Botha in August 1986, for example, it was said that they did so on a 'personal basis and not as official delegations of these bodies'. It was also announced that the issues discussed would not be made public.[108]

However, in mid-1988 a package of proposed legislative amendments regarding informal settlements and group areas precipitated a renewed wave of activity by organised business. The positions taken by different business associations varied according to the particular bills concerned, but the general thrust was in opposition to the government. One of the first associations which entered the field in outright opposition was the FCI. It argued, *inter alia*, that the bills would have a severely detrimental effect on some 500,000 employees of FCI members.[109] The Urban Foundation campaigned intensively against all the bills, but concentrated on the proposed squatting legislation. It used elements of the strategy forged almost a decade earlier in the Cape, namely mobilising a wide spectrum of interest groups against specific government measures. The effort included a joint approach to government by the UF and seven other business and professional associations, as well as submis-

106. *Citizen*, 22 May 1987; *Sunday Times/Business Times* (Johannesburg), 24 May 1987.
107. *Business Day*, 15 May 1987; 18 May 1987.
108. *Citizen*, 19 August 1986.
109. *Business Day*, 29 July 1988.

sions by the UF to the relevant parliamentary standing committees and the President's Council. These submissions had the backing of all the leading business associations.

Although the UF's efforts added valuable impetus to the eventually successful stream of opposition to the legislation, its activity was neither decisive nor central to the process. Its influence in fact declined during the late 1980s,[110] chiefly because of a decline in mutual political trust between the UF on the one hand and the State President and some of his ministers on the other. At the time this distrust characterised government–business relationships in general.

Another reason for the decline of UF influence was that alliance-building and the development of expertise had become virtual ends in themselves. The efforts to construct an alliance across a wide spectrum of policy issues, ranging from local government to rural development, lessened the organisation's research and political capacities. The UF attempted to institutionalise its strategy of alliance-building and exper-tise-mobilisation through the formation in 1985 of the Private Sector Council on Urbanisation (PSC), whose membership roll has usually included representatives of the AHI, Assocom, the FCI, SEIFSA, the SAAU and perhaps NAFCOC. Through its secretariat – in effect the Urbanisation Unit of the Urban Foundation – the PSC worked assidu-ously to construct a 'private sector view on urbanisation policy'. But the PSC membership has tended to be somewhat unstable. This fact, and the consequent wide and variable range of corporate, associational and personal interests and preferences involved, did not help progress towards coherent positions on a wide range of policy issues. Such factors, combined with the head of government's increasing intolerance of business intervention in politics, weakened both the UF and the PSC.

One of the better opportunities for action by the PSC was missed when it did not react to the 1988 squatter and group areas bills as a unified body. Instead, many PSC associational members were involved in the campaign against the bills on their own account (though they did express support for UF representations to government). The PSC's major policy project – formulating a comprehensive private sector consensus on urban policy – came to fruition only in 1990.[111] By then the PSC's efforts had been overtaken by the advent of negotiation politics and the attendant likelihood of a fundamental transformation of the political system.

110. Sadie's research indicated that only some 9 per cent of the 'governmental elite' spontaneously rated the UF as having a great deal of 'influence on the government'. The comparable percentages for the AHI, Assocom and FCI were 41 per cent, 27 per cent and 17 per cent respectively. Sadie, 'Regerings- en Sake-elite', pp. 210–11.

111. See the series *Urban Debate 2010. Policies for a New Urban Future* (Johannesburg: Urban Foundation, 1990).

The Economic Advisory Council: A Satisfactory Relationship?

The Economic Advisory Council existed as a representative consultative forum for 25 years. In April 1985 the State President announced that
the composition of the Council would be changed. That, he said, would
be another step in his continuing attempts 'to establish satisfactorily the
relationship between the Government and private sectors'. According
to Botha, doubts expressed about the effectiveness of the EAC contributed to the decision to change the Council's composition. The dissatisfaction was related to the fact that the public sector's representatives on
the EAC outnumbered those of the private sector by a considerable
margin. Consequently Botha reconstituted the body by appointing
business people from different economic sectors on the basis of proportional sectoral contribution to gross domestic product.[112] The effect was
that the representatives of organised business and trade unions (as well
as individual academic experts) were replaced by corporate notables
who were selected by the head of government himself.

The business associations were not pleased by their exclusion from
the EAC. Assocom objected that organised business would not have
sufficient participation in policy decisions. An unidentified 'business
leader' invoked the Council's legitimating role when he said that the
change implied 'that there is no obligation on our part to support these
policies'.[113] If the old EAC did in fact generate dissatisfaction in the
ranks of organised business, the complaints had an ironic outcome. As
one commentator put it:

Verwoerd, who faced harsh criticism by organised business in his day,
nevertheless gave the major employer organisations two seats each on the
EAC, while P W Botha, who has enjoyed much business support with only
occasional criticism, has now taken these seats away.[114]

The restructuring of the EAC was, in effect, a formalisation of Botha's
Carlton and Good Hope approaches to the corporate elite.[115] But why
was this done at the cost of organised business? The journal *Finansies
& Tegniek* suggested, somewhat disingenuously, that the old EAC did
not inspire confidence in the State President and that quibbles about its
form were thus irrelevant.[116] A senior official in the Office of the State
President believed that the corporate notables 'would probably be
representative also of the workers and production and would create a

112. *Hansard*, 18 April 1985, cols 3786–7; Sadie, 'Regerings- en Sake-elite', pp.
    265–6.
113. *Financial Mail*, 5 July 1985.
114. Quoted in *ibid*.
115. Botha himself associated the restructuring of the EAC with the Carlton and Good
    Hope conferences.
116. *Finansies & Tegniek*, 5 July 1985.

direct link to the market'. Moreover, he thought that 'organisations such as Assocom do not always have sufficient communication with their members.'[117]

Botha's announcement to parliament on 18 April 1985 suggests the most obvious reason for – and implication of – the restructuring of the EAC. His courtship of the corporate elite had, from the outset, very little to do with the representation of business associations in policy formulation. Botha went directly to corporate leaders because he wanted to cultivate the productive capacity of business rather than its representative skills. Botha's restructuring of the EAC might well have decreased its value as an instrument for policy legitimation. But then he apparently had little use for interest associations and other popular organisations. That much was illustrated by his public and quite explicit subjection of the National Party to his will on the occasion of its 1979 Natal congress.[118] Botha equally explicitly barred the EAC from dealing with issues which he regarded as political.[119] Hence the new Council concerned itself primarily with general economic policies, such as a national economic strategy, the shaping of fiscal and monetary policy and the refinement of priority guidelines to reduce government expenditure as laid down by the President's National Priorities Committee.[120]

Whatever the precise reasons for the change may have been, the new form soon invited criticisms of ineffectiveness. A financial weekly, for example, speculated that the new EAC was being inhibited by diversification of opinions: unlike business associations, the corporate individuals 'speak only for themselves'. Inputs into the policy process were also subject to a measure of confusion because government still dealt with organised business at other levels and the latter's message 'was often different from that of the individuals in the EAC.'[121] According to another source, the EAC suffered because 'there was no formal structure for gathering consensus within the sectors . . . the council needed bodies such as Assocom, FCI and AHI which are skilled in reaching consensus among businessmen'.[122] Sadie's research, in contrast, has uncovered considerable satisfaction with the post-1985 EAC.[123]

117. *Ibid.*
118. Pottinger, *The Imperial Presidency*, pp. 49–62; L. Pretorius, 'The National Party: Organisation, Decision, Cohesion, Negotiation', paper presented to the Workshop on Political Conceptions of Negotiations in South Africa, University of South Africa, July 1987.
119. Sadie, 'Regerings- en Sake-elite', pp. 268, 276.
120. *Hansard*, 25 January 1985, col. 11; 11 July 1984, cols 11,275, 11,282; 19 April 1985, col. 3862; 21 April 1986, cols 3817–18. The chairman of the EAC is a coopted member of the NPC, which itself consists of cabinet ministers.
121. *Finansies & Tegniek*, 15 May 1987.
122. *Business Day*, 25 April 1986.
123. Sadie, 'Regerings- en Sake-elite', p. 269.

De Klerk, Employers and Unions: Towards Corporatism?

F.W. de Klerk's accession to the presidency and his rapid moves towards a 'politics of negotiation' brought with it an increasing incidence of interest-group visits to the office of the head of government. An apparent intensification of business involvement with politics was encouraged, it seems, by a widely held view that the political environment had become favourable for – and indeed demanded – such a role for business. It must be noted, however, that the indicators of business views on its involvement in politics have been mixed.

Lee and his associates reported: 'Almost unanimously the [50 interviewees in top positions with business corporations and associations] believed the role of business in influencing public policy has been legitimised by the new government.'[124] With regard to preferred strategies for interaction with government, on the other hand, they found a preference for low-key approaches by alliances of business associations and, it seems, a tendency to underplay politics in favour of technical issues.[125] By mid-1991 the hopes for closer government–business cooperation persisted. These gained strength with the appointment of a senior corporate executive as part-time special advisor to the Minister of Economic Coordination and Public Enterprises. There were also reports of growing cooperation between the SA Chamber of Business (SACOB) and the Department of Trade, Industry and Tourism over the drafting of the national economic development programme.[126] SACOB has also repeatedly stated its intention to play a significant role in constitutional processes.

The experiences of the preceding 30 years suggest that an enthusiastic reception of business into politics should be interpreted with caution. De Klerk told business people: 'In collaboration with the private sector, we intend to put our country on the road to economic growth and prosperity.'[127] The content of this message is not necessarily different from similar statements by Botha or, for that matter, Verwoerd: they suggest interactions with regard to economic rather than political policy.

The context within which the relationships between business and the head of government should be interpreted has of course changed radically since the end of the Botha administration. But in 1987 De Klerk had given notice that he would prefer to maintain the traditional

124. R. Lee, M. Sutherland, M. Philips and A. McLennan, 'Speaking or Listening: Observers or Agents of Change? Business and Public Policy: 1989/1990', in L. Schlemmer and R. Lee (eds.), *Transition to Democracy* (Cape Town: Oxford University Press, 1991), p. 109.
125. *Ibid.*, pp. 110–16.
126. *Sunday Times/Business Times* (Johannesburg), 2 June 1991.
127. Lee *et al.*, 'Speaking or Listening?', p. 103.

norms for interaction between government and business. Commenting on the role businesspeople 'should play in the reform process', he said:

My philosophy is sovereignty within one's own sphere. Whenever a government interferes in business it is a mistake and there is an outcry from the business community. The opposite is also true; whenever business becomes too directly involved in politics, it is not good for business and it's not good for the country. I believe the various disciplines, in this case government and organised business, must respect each other's autonomy. Government is doing so. Its policy of deregulation and privatisation and its efforts to promote the concept of a free economy is proof of this. Business would be making a mistake to interfere directly in politics.

I believe the emphasis on reform through business must be in the business field itself. Obviously business and government can't be divorced from each other. There is an interrelationship and communication channels must be kept open – but within the framework of respecting each other's autonomy.[128]

As we have seen, the Nationalist heads of government have generally attempted to shape the political opportunities of business and other interest groups. But heads of government are also subject to shifting configurations of power. De Klerk's philosophy of 'sovereignty within one's own sphere' may have to accommodate strengthening currents of power which emanate primarily from black formations. In fact, his views may well be compatible with some form of corporatism and hence with a current tendency in relationships between government, business and trade unions.

The increasingly politicised stance of organised business and individual corporate leaders during the latter half of the 1980s was a reaction to both international economic sanctions and domestic trade union pressure.[129] This did not necessarily entail an anti-government alliance of capital and labour. The joint protest by Assocom, FCI and CUSA against the 1986 emergency, for example, was probably expedient. But the publication of a draft Labour Relations Amendment Bill (LRA) in December 1986 set in motion a series of events which, in 1990, culminated in a path-breaking tripartite agreement on draft legislation. The parties to the agreement were two trade union federations (COSATU and the National Council of Trade Unions, NACTU), the employer federation South African Consultative Committee on Labour Affairs (SACCOLA), and the government.

The agreement was not easily achieved. At some points in 1989, for example, it seemed as if the employers and the unions were about to become an anti-government alliance which could effectively nullify the

128. *Financial Mail*, 25 September 1987.
129. P. Frankel, 'Business and Politics: Towards a Strategy', in R. Schrire (ed.), *Critical Choices for South Africa* (Cape Town: Oxford University Press, 1990).

labour relations legislation that had been unilaterally enacted by government. At other times the relationships between SACCOLA and the unions seemed to be irretrievably damaged.[130] However, the State President's announcements of 2 February 1990 encouraged a rapid move towards agreement between the unions and SACCOLA. This accord undermined the government's proposed amendments to the LRA. When an attempt to have the accord enacted was blocked in the cabinet, the unions met with De Klerk. He appointed a tripartite working party to deal with the matter. The working party's efforts resulted in the September 1990 Laboria Minute, which embodied an agreement on the amended labour relations legislation. COSATU subsequently announced that it would, under certain conditions, join the National Manpower Commission. In October 1990 COSATU, NACTU and SACCOLA made joint representations on the LRA to a standing committee of parliament.

The outcome of the process, the Labour Relations Amendment Act of 1991,[131] thus formalised an agreement which came about by way of a typically corporatist mode of interest intermediation. That corporatist trends may well become stronger was further suggested by the launching, in October 1992, of a national economic forum consisting of representatives of organised business, labour and government.[132] There are also indications that variations of this form of government–interest-group interaction may emerge in other policy arenas – notably in education and with regard to the provision of certain public services (such as roads, sewerage and electricity) to black communities.

Concluding comments

Up to the late 1980s, Nationalist heads of government maintained that the prescription of political policy was not legitimate terrain for business and other interest groups. The general, albeit uneven, trend has, however, been one of increasing interest-group involvement in politics. In the case of organised business, involvement grew as apartheid policies increasingly clashed with economic performance and as the growing political power of African formations forced greater public opposition to apartheid from business associations. The political commitment of people such as the FCI leadership of the mid-1980s and

130. See South African Institute for Race Relations, *Race Relations Survey 1987/88, 1988/89* and *1989/90* (Johannesburg: SAIRR, 1988, 1989 and 1990); A. Fine and E. Webster, 'Transcending Traditions: Trade Unions and Political Unity', in SARS (ed.), *South African Review 5* (Johannesburg: Ravan Press, 1989).
131. *Weekly Mail*, 20 December 1990 to 10 January 1991; *South African Labour Bulletin*, vol. 14, no. 8 (May 1990), p. 7; *The Star*, 15 February 1991.
132. *Business Day*, 30 October 1992.

certain corporate leaders may also have had an impact. Yet with the exception of FCI's Business Charter and Assocom's Lombard Report, organised business has on the whole tended to articulate its political preferences in economic terms.

Successive heads of government reacted to business pressure by invoking the long-standing rule against the involvement of outside bodies in politics. The rule did not imply an absolute prohibition on interest-group access to government. Rather, it was an expression of the government's determination to maintain what it regarded as its electoral mandate to govern. At least until the advent of the Botha administration it also reflected Afrikaner nationalist insistence on self-determination. Despite the rule, Afrikaner interest groups such as the AHI have always enjoyed privileged access to government. This was a consequence of the close organisational and ideological links which existed between government and such groups.

For all the leading business associations, the opportunities for access had been institutionalised in bodies such as the EAC and the NMC. For the primarily English associations such as Assocom and the FCI, opportunities for access expanded as Afrikaner involvement in the economy increased. Despite Verwoerd's, Vorster's and Botha's often harsh condemnation of business interference in politics, the opportunities were maintained because the Nationalist government – like all governments – had an interest in cultivating the support of interest groups for its policies, in enlarging the productive capacity of business and in harnessing that capacity for its own political purposes.[133]

Over time the combined effect of black industrial and political activity, foreign pressures, local economic conditions, the divisions within the Afrikaner nationalist network – in short, the increasingly complex dynamics of the political system as a whole – has been to diminish the head of government's ability to contain interest-group intrusions into politics. Perhaps the most significant manifestation of this was the Labour Relations Amendment Act of 1991. The process that led to its enactment, and its subsequent outcomes, point towards the possible evolution of a corporatist system of interest-group intermediation with regard to labour policy. In other words, the trend may be in the direction of a system which is marked by the effective 'opening of the institutional areas of the state to the representation of organised interests of civil society'[134] and by the participants' acceptance of joint respon-

133. Cf. D. Yudelman, *The Emergence of Modern South Africa* (Cape Town: David Philip, 1984).
134. G.A. O'Donnell, 'Corporatism and the Question of the State' in J.M. Malloy (ed.), *Authoritarianism and Corporatism in Latin America*, (University of Pittsburgh Press, 1977), p. 48.

sibility for the implementation of the agreed policies. It remains to be seen whether such a trend will persist in areas of policy which are of common concern to government, organised business and the trade unions. As regards the present, it is clear that trade unions have become the significant other in relationships between organised business and the government.

7

THE HEAD OF GOVERNMENT AND SOUTH AFRICA'S FOREIGN RELATIONS

Deon Geldenhuys

Introduction

For more than 40 years after the end of the Second World War the story of South Africa's foreign relations was one of growing international adversity and isolation. Its domestic racial policies and control over South West Africa/Namibia placed South Africa at odds with the world community. South African leaders, from Jan Smuts to P.W. Botha, found themselves trapped between the solid, self-made rock of white domination and the hard place of international hostility. They had few real options in the realm of foreign policy, other than to counter foreign antagonism and safeguard the domestic political order as best they could.

In 1990 the international tide began turning for South Africa as the country began turning its back on its offensive racial policies. The Republic's international rehabilitation was assisted by the granting of independence to Namibia. These developments were in turn materially influenced by a sea-change in global politics and by the ascendance of President F.W. de Klerk.

The discussion of South Africa's foreign relations from Malan to De Klerk will be arranged chronologically according to the various leaders' periods of tenure. Within each of these periods, the close interplay between South Africa's domestic politics and foreign relations will be highlighted. How did successive heads of government handle the constraints that apartheid imposed on the country's international relations? More specifically, how did they respond to external adversity? Attention will also be given to the major foreign policy issues that each leader had to face, and to the structures and processes of foreign policy-making employed by each. By focusing on these aspects, several continuities and changes in South Africa's foreign relations can be identified.

Although the National Party's assumption of power in 1948 heralded a major break with the outgoing Smuts government's domestic policies, there were remarkable continuities in the realm of South Africa's foreign relations. As suggested, these refer particularly to growing international hostility on the one hand and typical South African responses on the other. They need to be recorded briefly so that we are better equipped to understand South Africa's post-1948 foreign relations.

The Legacy of the Final Smuts Years, 1945–1948

In the interwar years, South Africa was a respected member of the family of nations. Its racial policies were entirely consistent with colonial policies that enabled white minorities to rule in autocratic fashion over black majorities all over Africa; white supremacy seemed part of the natural order of things. Largely because of the international standing of Smuts, the Union enjoyed a role and influence in world affairs quite out of proportion to its relative power.

South Africa's reputation was further enhanced in 1939 when Smuts led the country into the Second World War. South Africans made a valiant contribution to the Allied war effort and their leaders looked forward to a just reward for the country's services once the war was won.

But it was not to be. Instead of bouquets, South Africa received some unexpected political brickbats. At the very first session of the UN General Assembly in 1946, Smuts found himself in the dock facing charges of unfair treatment of the Union's Indian population and a rejection of his request that the mandated territory of South West Africa be incorporated into South Africa. The great Smuts's international stature could not prevent what were two major diplomatic setbacks for South Africa.[1]

These events reveal a fundamental parting of the ways between South Africa and the international community as represented by the UN. The Union was out of step with the new post-war international morality with its emphasis on 'the enthronement of the rights of man', to quote Winston Churchill.[2] Although Smuts gave expression to this value system in drafting the preamble of the UN Charter, he showed no intention of applying it in his own country. Indeed, in 1946 he declared that 'we in South Africa did not recognise equal rights . . . and had never recognised it [equality] and would never recognise it.'[3] As if to remove any lingering doubts about his position, Smuts stated in 1948: 'Equal rights has never been our policy . . . Our policy has been European paramountcy in this country'.[4] But Smuts realised the contradiction

---

1. J. Barber and J. Barratt, *South Africa's Foreign Policy: The Search for Status and Security 1945–1988* (Johannesburg: Southern Book Publishers, 1990), pp. 16–25.
2. Quoted by D. Geldenhuys, *The Diplomacy of Isolation: South African Foreign Policy Making* (Johannesburg: Macmillan, 1984), p. 50.
3. Quoted by Barber and Barratt, *South Africa's Foreign Policy*, p. 26.
4. Quoted by D. Geldenhuys, 'The Effects of South Africa's Racial Policy on Anglo-South African Relations, 1945–61', unpubl. Ph.D. thesis, Cambridge University, 1977, p. 109.

between his actions on the domestic and international stages. 'On one side I am a human and a humanist, and the author of the preamble to the [UN] Charter', he wrote in March 1947.

On the other hand I am a South African European, proud of our heritage and proud of the clean European society we have built up in South Africa, and which I am determined not to see lost in the black pool of Africa'.[5]

On another occasion in 1947 he lamented: 'The world does not know or understand us, and we feel this deeply, even when we are conscious that we are much to blame in it all'.[6]

While Smuts was quick to brand the UN 'a cockpit of emotion, passion and ignorance',[7] he was realistic enough to admit that 'public feeling [at the UN] is strongly against our colour bar policy in South Africa'.[8] UN interference, he said in 1947, had left South Africa 'in a delicate and even dangerous situation', adding the far-sighted warning that the possibility of UN sanctions against the Union should be taken 'very seriously'.[9]

Smuts was no less resentful than his successors of a new phenomenon created by the UN. 'Countries who cannot govern themselves now sit in judgment on others who have done their job fairly well in spite of all sorts of difficulties', he complained. Because this interference had a 'profoundly disturbing and upsetting' influence on South Africa,[10] Smuts was determined to resist it. He was indeed the creator of what became a standard South African response when under attack at the UN, namely to seek refuge in the UN Charter's so-called domestic jurisdiction clause.

Alarmed at the way in which the new UN went about its business, Smuts at an early stage called for a revised world body that would be more modest 'but more real and effective than this general Areopagus or talking shop in which incompetents and misfits rule by counting of heads'.[11]

The adversity that Smuts and his successors encountered at the UN was in no small measure the result of the exertions of local black political organisations. Continuing a practice established even before the birth of the Union of South Africa, representatives of the unenfranchised black majority mobilised international support in their struggle for political rights at home. The UN became the focal point of

5. Quoted *ibid.*, p. 49.
6. Quoted *ibid.*, p. 36.
7. Quoted by Barber and Barratt, *South Africa's Foreign Policy*, p. 21.
8. Quoted by Geldenhuys, 'Effects of South Africa's Racial Policy', p. 48.
9. Quoted by Barber and Barratt, *South Africa's Foreign Policy*, p. 27.
10. Quoted by P. Beukes, *The Holistic Smuts: A Study in Personality* (Cape Town: Human and Rousseau, 1990), pp. 181, 182.
11. Quoted *ibid.*, p. 182.

this campaign in the post-war world. In 1946, the African National Congress petitioned the UN Secretary-General that the Union's racial policies required special attention and also despatched its leader, Dr A.B. Xuma, to the world body to lobby delegates.[12] In later years, black South Africans' struggle against apartheid would increasingly be played out on the international stage.

Smuts' unhappy experiences at the UN only enhanced the importance he attached to the Commonwealth. Long a fervent champion of the Commonwealth, Smuts regarded it as a 'happy group of communities working together harmoniously in peace as in war'.[13] It was not only South Africa's principal forum for participating in world politics, but also a safe haven where it could be shielded from the critical attention it drew at the UN. The problem with this view was that it portrayed the Commonwealth largely in terms of the old closely knit all-white club. The emergence of a multiracial Commonwealth upon the granting of independence to India, Pakistan and Ceylon (Sri Lanka) shattered Smuts' hopes at an early stage.

Closer home, there was no evidence that Britain intended abandoning its colonies in Southern Africa. But this created a problem for South Africa's expansionist ambitions. Like his predecessors, Smuts wanted Britain to transfer the High Commission Territories of Bechuanaland (Botswana), Basutoland (Lesotho) and Swaziland to South Africa. He envisaged that they would then, together with South Africa and other territories in the region, be drawn together in an organisation for regional cooperation along the lines of the Pan-American Union.[14]

A final relevant feature of Smuts' conduct of foreign relations is that effectively he was in sole command of South Africa's foreign policy formulation. This was not surprising, considering that he was a states-man of world repute and vastly experienced in international affairs. Supremely confident in handling South Africa's foreign relations, Smuts continued the practice, followed since 1910 and even after the establishment of the Department of External (later Foreign) Affairs in 1927, of the Prime Minister acting as his own Foreign Minister. It should be added that Smuts's pre-eminence in foreign affairs was merely an extension of his domination of the cabinet in domestic policy matters. His was, in short, a highly personalised way of conducting foreign relations. Elements of this style would later be displayed by some of Smuts' Nationalist successors.

What this brief survey of the final Smuts years points to above all is

12. Geldenhuys, 'Effects of South Africa's Racial Policy', p. 54.
13. Quoted *ibid.*, p. 119.
14. D. Geldenhuys, 'South Africa's Regional Policy', in M. Clough (ed.), *Changing Realities in Southern Africa* (Berkeley, CA: University of California Press for Institute of International Studies, 1982), p. 126.

that South Africa's racial policies were already 'becoming the stuff and substance of her foreign policies', as Hancock put it.[15] Smuts encountered an inhospitable international climate that left South Africa with very limited options in its foreign relations. This, then, was the situation the Nationalists inherited.

D.F. Malan, 1948–1954: Further Out of Step with the Time

There was no international applause when 74-year-old Dr D.F. Malan led a coalition of his Herenigde Nasionale Party and the Afrikaner Party to victory in the general election of May 1948. The world was apprehensive, if not downright suspicious, of a leader who had vehemently opposed South Africa's participation in the Second World War, whose followers had flirted with National Socialist ideas and whose policy of apartheid was the very antithesis of the post-war preoccupation with human rights. In Britain, South Africa's principal ally, there was the additional concern that the Nationalists' republican sympathies and their antipathy towards the Crown would spell the end of South Africa's Commonwealth membership.[16]

Malan was painfully aware of the international misgivings about his new government. Within weeks of assuming office he appointed a retired diplomat, Charles te Water, as roving ambassador to counter what Malan described as the 'campaign of hostility and unfairness' being waged against South Africa abroad. Malan believed that this adversity was but a passing phenomenon and within ten months of Te Water's appointment he confidently asserted that the ambassador had done 'excellent work' to 'put matters in the right light'.[17] But the new government was not taking any chances and also decided that the State Information Office would henceforth concentrate on 'combating the hostile propaganda against South Africa abroad'.[18] Malan, as indeed also his successors, would discover that no amount of official information from Pretoria could easily set matters straight in an international climate that was singularly hostile to the Nationalists' racial policies.

The widening gulf between South Africa and the new international morality was vividly illustrated in December 1948 when the UN General Assembly adopted the Universal Declaration of Human Rights. South Africa was one of only eight countries to abstain from the vote. If anything, this challenge to world opinion spurred the UN into even greater efforts to make South Africa conform to the new international

15. W.K. Hancock, *Smuts: The Fields of Force, 1919–1950* (Cambridge University Press, 1968), p. 473.
16. Geldenhuys, 'Effects of South Africa's Racial Policy', pp. 111–16.
17. Quoted by Geldenhuys, *Diplomacy of Isolation*, p. 10.
18. Quoted *ibid.*, p. 16.

value system. At the seventh session of the General Assembly in 1952, the broader question of race conflict arising from apartheid joined the issue of South Africa's treatment of its Indian population on the agenda. The status of South West Africa was the third issue over which South Africa was arraigned before the Assembly during Malan's premiership. On all these issues, a gradual hardening of positions on both sides became evident. For its part, South Africa continued Smuts' practice of digging in behind article 2 (7) of the Charter when its domestic policies were under assault and adopting a similar legalistic position with regard to South West Africa.

Like Smuts, Malan too had serious reservations about the UN. Echoes of Smuts are detectable in Malan's remark in September 1948 that the UN 'incited the feelings of the natives in our country against us' and generally bedevilled race relations in the Union and South West Africa.[19] Malan associated world opinion with the UN and he had no doubt what was demanded: 'They want all colour bars to disappear from South Africa. They will not be satisfied until there is absolute equality between European and non-European in South Africa', he told parliament in August 1948. Behind these demands he saw a diabolical objective: 'By concession after concession they want to force us in their own direction; they wish to drive us to suicide as a white race in our country . . . we as a white race are not prepared to commit suicide.'[20]

The latter assertion was essentially a reformulation, in more forthright language, of Smuts' earlier insistence that he would not allow South Africa's 'clean European society' to be 'lost in the black pool of Africa'. But unlike Smuts, Malan and his successors elevated the equation of world opinion with white suicide to a key component of their world view. Resolute defiance of international demands accordingly became an article of faith for Nationalist leaders.

The threat that the UN, as the principal articulator of world opinion, allegedly posed to the existence of white South Africans was also reflected in Malan's denunciation of the UN as a 'danger' to Africa. The organisation fomented unrest by persuading the 'immature and in many cases barbaric races of Africa' that they were oppressed and had to obtain freedom by all means, he said.[21]

It comes as no surprise that Malan's government gave notice early on that it would reconsider South Africa's membership of the meddlesome world body. In 1951 it temporarily withdrew the Union's mission from the UN.[22] Yet Malan acknowledged in 1953 that under the prevailing conditions the world could not manage without an international organi-

---

19. *Hansard*, vol. 64, 1 September 1948, col. 1371.
20. *Ibid.*, 31 August 1948, col. 1291.
21. *Ibid.*, vol. 85, 4 May 1954, col. 4493.
22. Geldenhuys, *Diplomacy of Isolation*, p. 12.

sation. He was not against the existence of the UN *per se*, Malan repeatedly told parliament, but he believed the organisation should be reformed – obviously to make it more acceptable to South Africa.[23] In this regard too, Malan followed Smuts.

Growing international adversity again enhanced the value of Commonwealth membership for South Africa. Fears expressed in Britain and South Africa that Malan would break with the Commonwealth were soon dispelled. In his very first broadcast after assuming office, Malan readily acknowledged 'the uniquely friendly relations existing between our country and the United Kingdom and other members of the British Commonwealth of Nations'.[24] In London to attend the 1949 Commonwealth Conference, Malan spoke in similar vein of the Commonwealth as 'an inner circle with whom we have special ties'.[25]

Malan recognised the benefits that the Commomwealth link held for the Union. South Africa was, for instance, well placed 'to be *au fait* with world conditions and to receive information', particularly from the British government, Malan explained in 1953. He in fact made a strong case for the retention of Commonwealth membership, arguing that there were no grounds for withdrawing for the sake of greater freedom: 'the Commonwealth permits us the greatest freedom that I can imagine', Malan said.[26] The latter was a reference to the Commonwealth's landmark decision of 1949 that a country could retain membership after declaring itself a republic and severing its constitutional links with the British Crown. South Africa could therefore follow the precedent created by India by opting for republican status – and thereby realise a long-cherished goal of Afrikaner Nationalists – without having to leave the Commonwealth.

The Commonwealth was also a cause for concern, however. Malan warned that the admission of new Asian states to full Commonwealth membership showed that 'the danger of interference [in member countries' internal affairs] cannot be regarded as imaginary'.[27] He also feared that if other Commonwealth members interfered in South Africa's affairs via the UN, it 'will break down the Commonwealth'. He therefore appealed to Commonwealth countries to help confine the UN 'to what its constitution intended for it' – above all to respect the domestic jurisdiction of states.[28]

23. G.C. Olivier, *Suid-Afrika se Buitelandse Beleid* (Pretoria: Academica, 1977), p. 81.
24, Quoted Geldenhuys, 'Effects of South Africa's Racial Policy', p. 116.
25. Quoted *ibid.*, p. 190.
26. Quoted *ibid.*, p. 160.
27. Quoted *ibid.*, p. 117.
28. *Hansard*, vol. 82, 7 July 1953, col. 57.

Another foreign policy issue on which the Nationalists' pre- and post-1948 positions differed markedly was alignment with foreign powers. Having strongly opposed South Africa's participation in the Second World War, the Nationalists in 1946 declared themselves in favour of a policy of neutrality. By rejecting commitments to participate in war, the party wanted to avoid a recurrence of South Africa being dragged into other people's – particularly Britain's – wars, as they saw it.

On the eve of the 1948 election, the Nationalists abandoned their advocacy of neutrality in favour of a commitment to support the West in the event of any major East–West war. Communism, Malan's party maintained, posed a mortal threat to South Africa and the West at large. What is more, the Nationalists identified the 'Red Menace' with that most potent of bogeys, the 'Black Peril': communists and blacks were allegedly making common cause against whites in Africa.[29]

With white civilisation in South Africa perceived as under dire threat, Malan's government quickly made the search for alliances a top foreign policy priority. Shortly after taking office Malan told parliament that South Africa was 'waiting for an invitation' to join NATO,[30] evidently believing that the Western alliance needed South Africa's contribution in resisting communist expansionism. The invitation never came. South Africa was equally unsuccessful in its efforts to draw the European colonial powers, the Commonwealth and the United States into an African defence organisation. One reason why South Africa failed in this quest is that it refused to support any defence scheme that would involve arming blacks, whether in South Africa or outside.[31] This is a clear illustration of the constraints that Malan's domestic policies of white supremacy and black subservience imposed on South Africa's foreign relations.

The linkage between domestic and foreign policies was unambiguously articulated in Malan's so-called Africa Charter, in terms of which South Africa wanted to play a part in shaping the future of Africa in a way compatible with its own perceived interests. The first declared aim of the Charter was to ensure that Africa developed along the lines of 'Western European Christian civilisation'. Secondly, Africa should be reserved for the black and white population of the continent and protected from Asian penetration. Thirdly, the militarisation of the 'native of Africa' should be prevented, since it could endanger 'our white civilization': 'One does not hand a rifle to a child', Malan cautioned. Fourthly, Africa should be kept free of communism. Since

29. See K. A. Heard, *General Elections in South Africa 1943–1970* (Oxford University Press, 1974), pp. 30–46; N.M. Stultz, *The Nationalists in Opposition 1934–1948* (Cape Town: Human and Rousseau, 1974), pp. 131–59.
30. Quoted by Geldenhuys, 'Effects of South Africa's Racial Policy', p. 241.
31. *Ibid.*, pp. 241–4.

the realisation of the Charter's aims depended on the cooperation of the colonial powers, Malan sought an understanding through consultations with them, Britain in particular.[32] However, nothing came of this endeavour and Malan's anachronistic Africa Charter proved a futile attempt to stem the tide of decolonisation.

Malan never made any secret of his reservations about the liquidation of European colonial empires in Africa. He never understood the indigenous forces at work within the colonies or the motivations of the former imperial powers. Instead, he saw decolonisation as the result of a conspiracy orchestrated by communists, India and the UN. Malan also questioned the colonial peoples' readiness for governmental responsibilities. 'It will take years and generations before the Natives will be able to stand on their own feet so that they will no longer require the leadership and control of the white man', he said in 1951.[33] Where Britain had precipitately granted 'equal rights for all and equal franchise for all', as in Nigeria and the Gold Coast (Ghana), it had produced a strong 'anti-white' agitation. This led Malan to conclude that if the same rights were to be conceded in other colonial territories, 'it means nothing less than driving the white man out of practically all that lies between us and the Sahara'.[34] South Africa would then be reduced to a white island in a black sea, one whose shores would be battered by the tide of black liberation. The Union's black population, Malan knew, could not be insulated from events elsewhere on the continent. For Malan, therefore, the perpetuation of the colonial order was a precondition for the maintenance of white rule in South Africa.

Coupled with his anxiety about developments in colonial Africa was Malan's concern that the interests of whites in Africa were being sacrificed on the altar of expediency. 'We consider the black man so much', he complained to parliament in 1954:

Has it not become time for us to think a little also of the position of the white man in the world? One finds in the world today, and especially in England, that there is a sickly sentimentality in regard to the black man'.[35]

Malan here introduced a theme that was to be repeated for years to come: the world was afflicted by some mental illness that impaired its judgment on matters affecting white South Africa. But perhaps the notion was not all that novel: recall Smuts' lament that 'the world does not know or understand us'.

Malan was determined that South Africa would not leave whites elsewhere in Africa in the lurch. He claimed a leadership role for South

32. Quoted by Barber and Barratt, *South Africa's Foreign Policy*, pp. 36, 37.
33. *Hansard*, vol. 75, 16 May 1951, col. 6819.
34. Quoted by Geldenhuys, 'Effects of South Africa's Racial Policy', p. 262.
35. *Hansard*, vol. 85, 4 May 1954, cols 4495, 4496.

Africa – as an independent state ruled by whites and with the largest white population on the continent – in matters of race relations in the rest of Africa. His belief was that apartheid provided a formula – indeed, the sole role model – for ordering race relations wherever whites found themselves in Africa.[36]

In its immediate environment South Africa was not content to merely 'act as advisor' to the local inhabitants, as Malan put it,[37] but insisted on gaining control of the three British High Commission Territories to which each of his predecessors had also laid claim. Apart from historic considerations and no doubt a strong dose of national pride, Malan had other compelling reasons for demanding the transfer of Bechuanaland, Basutoland and Swaziland. South Africa could not 'permit Negro states, Bantu states, to arise within our borders – states which are free and independent and which can lay down their own policies in every respect', he declared.[38] Malan was restating the old concern that liberal racial policies in neighbouring territories could have an unsettling effect on black South Africans. But he added another dimension: Pretoria was worried that the High Commission Territories could become 'centres of subversion for black nationalists', as Barber and Barratt put it.[39] The latter concern was a forerunner of what subsequently became a central preoccupation in South Africa's regional relations.

Prime Minister Malan lost no time in conveying to London South Africa's claims to the British territories and he made it clear that Pretoria's patience was wearing thin. But it was a case of fools rushing in where angels feared to tread. If Smuts, the idol of the British, had failed in his quest for transfer under far more favourable international conditions (for South Africa), there was no chance that an Afrikaner Nationalist Prime Minister, who moreover preached and practised apartheid, would succeed.

The expansionist impulse was even more pronounced with regard to South West Africa. In 1947, in opposition, Malan responded to Smuts' setbacks at the UN by proposing that the world body's trusteeship recommendation for South West Africa should be rejected and the territory summarily incorporated into the Union.[40] Once in power, Malan said his government was not set upon full incorporation but closer integration between South Africa and South West Africa, adding that there would be 'practically no difference between the two'.[41] By making it plain to the world that South Africa had not the slightest

36. *Ibid.*, vol. 64, 1 September 1948, col. 1324.
37. *Ibid.*
38. *Hansard*, vol. 82, 11 August 1953, col. 1328.
39. Barber and Barratt, *South Africa's Foreign Policy*, p. 42.
40. Geldenhuys, 'Effects of South Africa's Racial Policy', p. 84.
41. *Hansard*, vol. 64, 31 August 1948, col. 1288.

intention of relinquishing its control over South West Africa, Malan ensured that the Union's conflict with the UN continued and indeed intensified during his tenure.

Malan's approach to relations with Africa also contained a strong functionalist element. It was inevitable that South Africa would through trade and attempts to control disease become integrated with dependent territories elsewhere in Africa, he said shortly after taking office.[42] Pretoria gave tangible effect to this functionalist approach by participating in the Commission for Technical Cooperation in Africa South of the Sahara (CCTA) and the Commission for Scientific Cooperation in Africa South of the Sahara (CSA), both established in the early 1950s. Absent were the grand visions of regional associations held out by Smuts and indeed also by Malan's Nationalist successors.

Malan's ill-considered reopening of the issue of the High Commission Territories is, finally, revealing for another reason: it is an example of the Prime Minister's poor understanding of the ways of the world. It is commonly held that Malan lacked the interest, knowledge, experience and skills necessary in foreign affairs – qualities with which Smuts had been so richly endowed. Malan had no pretensions to be a world statesman; in fact, he wanted to show the voters that he would not neglect his principal domestic duties for the sake of personal prestige abroad, something the Nationalists had accused Smuts of doing. This is one reason why Malan did not undertake nearly as many foreign visits as the peripatetic Smuts. Nonetheless, Malan upheld convention by assuming responsibility for the External Affairs portfolio. But unlike Smuts, Malan did not monopolise foreign policy-making. His domestic preoccupations, coupled with his known inadequacies in international affairs, caused Malan to rely quite extensively on the expertise of a number of cabinet ministers – notably N.C. Havenga, Minister of Finance, and Eric Louw, Minister of Economic Affairs and Mining – in making and managing foreign policy.

J.G. Strijdom, 1954–1958: Cautious Adaptation to African Trends

Prime Minister J.G. Strijdom, who assumed office in December 1954, was an unlikely man to begin adapting South African foreign policy to changing circumstances in Africa. His political credentials suggested everything but flexibility. Known as the 'lion of the north' for his fearless, combative style, Strijdom was a hardliner in both domestic and foreign policy matters. The two blended neatly in his fierce republicanism and antipathy to the Crown and Commonwealth. Yet the exigencies

42. Quoted by Barber and Barratt, *South Africa's Foreign Policy*, p. 35.

of office had a moderating effect on Strijdom, causing him to handle foreign relations with a measure of caution that few would have expected of him. Domestically, however, he preached and practised apartheid with undiminished vigour – and so neutralised any gains he might otherwise have made in the realm of foreign policy.

Strijdom bluntly acknowledged that 'the ideological policy to which the outside world objects is . . . that we will not allow political equality between white and non-white'.[43] But he saw nothing inherently wrong with this policy and was adamant that it would not be changed to suit either domestic or foreign critics. In London to attend the 1956 Commonwealth Conference, Strijdom said he was 'well aware of the fact that from time to time unfriendly criticism' was levelled against his government, but he immediately attributed this to 'biased and ill-informed people' who created a 'false and distorted picture' of the Union's racial policy. In defending apartheid before the British, Strijdom even reminded his audience that it was the traditional policy of South Africa, to which the esteemed Smuts had also basically subscribed.[44]

Like Malan, Strijdom seemed concerned about the rising tide of international adversity. His break with tradition by appointing a Minister of External Affairs in January 1955, in the person of Eric Louw, may have been influenced in part by a need to counter foreign hostility more effectively. The State Information Office underwent one of its periodic reorganisations to make it more effective in fulfilling its principal task, the dissemination of information abroad.[45] Reference can also be made to Pretoria's recalling its mission from the tenth session of the UN General Assembly in 1955, its withdrawal from UNESCO the same year and its decision to maintain only token representation at the UN until 1958. All this was carried out in protest against UN interference in South Africa's domestic affairs.[46]

What these various moves have in common is that they merely addressed the symptoms of South Africa's growing alienation from the world community. The Strijdom government realised that apartheid was the root cause of this alienation, but since the policy was considered vital to white survival in South Africa there was no way in which Strijdom was going to restructure the domestic base to meet the exigencies of foreign relations.

Apartheid was not merely a means of safeguarding the future of whites in South Africa. Strijdom believed, like Malan, that apartheid was an appropriate – indeed indispensable – formula for white survival elsewhere in Africa too. Within days of becoming Prime Minister,

43. *Hansard*, vol. 94, 7 May 1957, col. 5563.
44. Quoted Geldenhuys, 'Effects of South Africa's Racial Policy', pp. 228, 229.
45. Geldenhuys, *Diplomacy of Isolation*, p. 17.
46. *Ibid.*, p. 12.

he said that it might be necessary to extend apartheid beyond South Africa's borders, which would require a sustained effort to convert whites and non-whites to the north to the virtues of apartheid.[47] Strijdom rejected the policy of racial partnership pursued in the Federation of Rhodesia and Nyasaland (Malawi) on the grounds that the numerically superior black group would, once it became sufficiently developed, wrest the political initiative from whites.[48] White survival on the continent – a key concern of Strijdom's Africa policy – could be ensured only by the greatest degree of understanding and cooperation, notably with regard to race relations, among various white communities in Africa, the Prime Minister maintained. South Africa, he said, could never hope to maintain 'White civilisation' if it were 'alone and isolated'.[49]

But Strijdom's entire Africa policy was not geared to preserving white rule. The familiar *status quo* elements were accompanied by clear signs that South Africa was beginning to prepare itself for the post-colonial era to its north. Whereas Malan never reconciled himself to the idea of independent black states emerging out of the European colonies, Strijdom realised that it would be futile to continue resisting the inevitable. Far from regarding emerging black states as enemies, Strijdom said he was 'extending the hand of friendship' and recognising their right of existence. He expected them to acknowledge in turn that there was a place for both black and white states in Africa. He also saw a need for them to cooperate, particularly in view of the existence of a common enemy – the Soviet Union.[50] This justification for cooperation with independent black states would be heard frequently in the years to come.

To demonstrate South Africa's *bona fides*, Strijdom despatched a delegation to attend Ghana's independence celebrations and congratulated Sudan on reaching statehood.[51] But Strijdom was not prepared to accommodate another consequence of independence, the establishment of diplomatic ties with the new black states. True, he conceded in 1957 that such links would in due course have to follow, but insisted that the Union's white population would slowly have to be prepared for this novel idea.[52]

Strijdom's acceptance of independence by no means extended to the three British High Commission Territories. While he shared all his

47. Geldenhuys, 'Effects of South Africa's Racial Policy', p. 269.
48. Olivier, *Suid-Afrika se Buitelandse Beleid*, p. 130.
49. *Hansard*, vol. 88, 18 April 1955, col. 4025.
50. Quoted by Barber and Barratt, *South Africa's Foreign Policy*, p. 38; Olivier, *Suid-Afrika se Buitelandse Beleid*, p. 131.
51. Olivier, *Suid-Afrika se Buitelandse Beleid*, p. 131.
52. *Ibid*.

predecessors' conviction that South Africa had an historical and constitutional right to incorporate the territories, he did not give the matter the
same prominence as Malan had; moreover he approached it in a
remarkably conciliatory fashion. The Prime Minister raised the transfer
issue with the British government when he visited London in 1956 but
failed to make any headway. Expressing 'deep disappointment' that the
matter had been dragging on for over 40 years, Strijdom added the
familiar argument that the longer transfer was delayed, the greater the
danger of a racial policy being followed in the territories that would
conflict with South Africa's.[53]

Another familiar danger that Strijdom saw in Africa was, of course,
communism. His government continued earlier attempts to draw the
Western powers into a defence organisation for Africa south of the
Sahara. The purpose of such an organisation would be to counter
communist penetration of Africa – and in so doing help to safeguard the
political *status quo* in the Union. In this scheme of things, South Africa
reserved a key role for itself on the basis of its claimed strategic
importance to the West in resisting communist machinations.[54] Strijdom's
view of the world was, like Malan's, based on the notion of a global
power struggle between East and West in which South Africa was called
upon to join forces with the latter. For the Union there was also a
communist danger from within, in the shape of its black population's
supposed susceptability to this alien ideology. One way in which the
Strijdom government tried to counter the domestic threat was to request
the Soviet government to close its consulate in the Union in 1956.
Among other things, the Soviet mission was suspected of subversive
activities.[55]

Like its predecessor, the Strijdom government failed in its ambitious
endeavour to set up a continental defence pact. There was, however, a
good deal of compensation in South Africa's conclusion of the Simonstown Agreement with Britain in 1955. Although it fell well short of the
alliance coveted by the Nationalists since 1948, the agreement provided
for extensive military ties between the Union and a major Western
power. This was indeed the high point of South Africa's post-war
military cooperation with foreign powers.

The Commonwealth continued to provide South Africa with another
valuable link with Britain and a few other Western nations. While Prime
Minister Strijdom repeatedly stated his party's intention of establishing
a republic, once a sufficiently large majority of white voters favoured
such a step, he took particular care to stress that such a change would

53. Geldenhuys, 'Effects of South Africa's Racial Policy', p. 292.
54. Olivier, *Suid-Afrika se Buitelandse Beleid*, p. 132.
55. G.C. Olivier, 'South Africa's Relations with Africa', in R. Schrire (ed.), *South Africa: Public Policy Perspectives* (Cape Town: Juta, 1982), p. 273.

in no way affect South Africa's policy of cooperation with Britain and other Commonwealth countries.[56] This implied that Strijdom had no intention of severing the Commonwealth connection. But, like Malan, he too was apprehensive about the extension of Commonwealth membership to newly independent black states. Strijdom feared that this would further weaken the cohesion of the association and moreover expose South Africa to greater interference in its internal affairs. Even so, South Africa did not oppose Ghana's admission to the Commonwealth on that country's achieving independence.[57]

A final feature of Strijdom's handling of foreign affairs that bears emphasis is that he engaged in very little personal diplomacy. His sole foreign visit while in office was to Britain in 1956 to attend the Commonwealth summit. It was no secret that Strijdom, like Malan, did not relish attending Commonwealth meetings. Strijdom's preoccupation with domestic matters and his inexperience in foreign affairs probably also played a role here. Both these considerations must have influenced Strijdom in appointing Louw in 1955 as the Union's first Minister of External Affairs. From then on Louw carried the major burden in managing South Africa's international relations and he was also one of the principal architects of its foreign policy.

Strijdom's relatively brief tenure as Prime Minister was not a distinguished one. The fiery regional politician turned out to be a fairly weak national leader who is not remembered for any major innovations on either the domestic or the international front.

Dr H.F. Verwoerd, 1958–1966: The International Politics of Domestic Decolonisation

Hendrik Verwoerd's distinctive imprint is to be found in South African politics to this day. His domestic political course had a profound effect on the country's foreign relations too. In both areas the Verwoerd premiership represented watersheds.

A key to understanding Verwoerd's political legacy is the nature of his leadership. Here was a man with a superb intellect, a tremendous capacity for work, a fierce determination and single-minded dedication to his cause. His formidable powers of intellectual persuasion overawed ministers and helped to establish Verwoerd's unchallenged supremacy in the cabinet. Another factor was his popular standing: Verwoerd, despite his lack of flamboyance, quickly achieved a following in Afrikanerdom that no Nationalist leader before or after him has equalled. To his followers, Verwoerd was a charismatic, visionary leader.

56. Geldenhuys, 'Effects of South Africa's Racial Policy', pp. 233, 234.
57. Olivier, *Suid-Afrika se Buitelandse Beleid*, p. 131; *Hansard*, vol. 94, 2 May 1957, cols 5212, 5213.

It is not surprising that Verwoerd soon established himself as the dominant figure in the formulation of South African foreign policy (as indeed in other fields too). And as his self-assurance in international relations grew, Verwoerd felt less and less need for the advice of Eric Louw or of his successor as Foreign Minister in 1964, Hilgard Muller. The analogies with Smuts are only too obvious.

Verwoerd's premiership was marked by a deepening confrontation between South Africa and the international community over Pretoria's racial policies. Yet, paradoxically, the 'architect of apartheid' (as Verwoerd was commonly known) believed that the policy he enunciated would defuse this very conflict. In expounding his so-called new vision for South Africa's black population in 1959, Verwoerd was mindful of foreign opinion. 'We must ensure that the outside world realises, and that the Bantu realises, that a new period is dawning', he said. It would be a period in which the white man 'will move away from discrimination against the Bantu as far as his own areas [i.e. the reserves or homelands] are concerned', and lead the black 'through the first stage towards full development'. Should blacks prove themselves capable, Verwoerd added, this process could eventually lead the black territories to 'full independence', upon which they would opt out of the South African state.[58]

In April 1961, Verwoerd offered parliament a telling explanation for this radical departure in policy:

The Bantu will be able to develop into separate Bantu states. It is a form of fragmentation which we would not have liked if we were able to avoid it. In the light of the pressure being exerted on South Africa there is however no doubt that eventually this will have to be done, thereby buying for the white man his freedom and the right to retain domination in what is his country, settled for him by his forefathers.[59]

A year later Verwoerd also conceded that the government had not in the early 1950s – when he was Minister of Native Affairs – foreseen that the situation in Africa and indeed within South Africa would in under ten years necessitate the granting of self-government to the black areas.[60]

Clearly, then, Verwoerd hoped that separate development, which he said was consistent with the growing trend towards self-government in colonial territories, would bring South Africa into step with the time and thus neutralise foreign criticism. He miscalculated badly, however.

58. *Hansard*, vol. 99, 27 January 1959, cols 60–5; A.N. Pelzer, *Verwoerd Speaks: Speeches 1948–1966* (Johannesburg: Afrikaanse Pers, 1966), p. 278.
59. *Hansard*, vol. 107, 10 April 1961, col. 4191.
60. G.D. Scholtz, *Dr Hendrik Frensch Verwoerd, 1901–1966*, vol. 2 (Johannesburg: Perskor, 1974), p. 134.

International opinion demanded self-determination for blacks in the country as a whole, and not merely in a fraction thereof. Major black South African political organisations likewise rejected a policy that denied them any political rights in the bulk of the country, which Verwoerd claimed as the exclusive preserve of whites. Far from granting South Africa peace with itself and with the world community, Verwoerd's separate development exacerbated conflict on both fronts.

The year 1960 provided dramatic evidence of South Africa's domestic combustibility and the ever widening gulf between Pretoria and the world. In February, British Prime Minister Harold Macmillan delivered his celebrated 'wind of change' speech in parliament in Cape Town. As a fellow member of the Commonwealth, it was Britain's 'earnest desire to give South Africa our support and encouragement', Macmillan said. But then he added a frank qualification:

. . . there are some aspects of your policies which make it impossible for us to do this without being false to our own deep convictions about the political destinies of free men to which in our territories we are trying to give effect.

The British leader was in effect serving public notice to South Africa that because of this fundamental conflict in political values, Britain could no longer be relied upon to remain South Africa's close associate and benefactor. Macmillan's address is of course best remembered for the catch-phrase 'wind of change' which, he said, 'is blowing through this continent . . . this growth of national consciousness is a political fact and our national policies must take account of it'.[61]

Verwoerd, his radical views on decolonising South Africa notwithstanding, had serious reservations about the way in which the colonial powers tried to handle this national consciousness, misgivings that he voiced in no uncertain terms in replying to Macmillan's address. The South African Prime Minister's impromptu response to his counterpart's speech – contrary to convention and common courtesy he had not been given a copy of Macmillan's address in advance – was an impressive and skilful performance that won him his spurs in the field of international politics and further enhanced his domestic standing.[62]

The dust had hardly settled on Macmillan's visit when South Africa was jolted by another event that thrust it more sharply into international contention than ever before. The Sharpeville shootings on 21 March plunged South Africa into a crisis in domestic politics and foreign relations alike. The local business community and foreign investors panicked, triggering a massive outflow of capital and a sharp decline on

61. The full text of the speech is appended to H. Macmillan, *Pointing the Way, 1959–1961* (London: Macmillan, 1967), pp. 473–82.
62. See the text of Verwoerd's reply in Pelzer, *Verwoerd Speaks*, pp. 337, 338.

the local stock market.[63] South Africa was showered with a veritable torrent of international condemnation over the police action at Sharpeville. The UN Security Council, in its first direct involvement with the South African issue, resolved that the situation in the Union had led to international friction and could, if continued, endanger world peace and security. The Council called on the South African government to abandon apartheid.

For Verwoerd there was no question of reconsidering his government's racial policies. He claimed that there was a deeper reason behind Sharpeville and accompanying disturbances, 'which has nothing to do with apartheid'. Unrest was a worldwide phenomenon that occurred in cycles, he said, and was particularly evident in African territories gaining independence.[64] Predictably, Verwoerd also saw a familiar conspiracy behind the events: communist agitators had had a hand in the disturbances which, he insisted, had been timed to coincide with the Commonwealth summit scheduled for May.[65]

When the clamour for political reform failed to subside, Verwoerd responded with what became something of a slogan: the government 'will have to stand like walls of granite because the survival of a nation is at stake'.[66] The equation of demands for the abolition or even melioration of apartheid with national (white) suicide was of course already embedded in the Nationalist mindset. And the image of granite walls was indeed the popular portrayal of Verwoerd's leadership style: an unbending man of burning conviction. It may be that Verwoerd invoked the granite simile to signal to the outside world that there was no point in exerting pressure on his government since it would not submit. As Verwoerd put it, 'The greater the pressure on us to make concessions, the more emphatic we must be in refusing to do so.'[67]

The Commonwealth Conference of May 1960 provided further evidence of South Africa's rapidly deteriorating foreign relations. Because of Sharpeville, the apartheid issue overshadowed the conference and Macmillan recorded that the feeling against South Africa was 'swelling to really dangerous proportions'.[68] The South African delegation, led by Louw, left the conference under no illusion that the country's continued membership as a republic would not be treated as a mere formality by other members, and that its racial policies might well be the deciding factor.

63. Barber and Barratt, *South Africa's Foreign Policy*, p. 97.
64. *Hansard*, vol. 104, 22 March 1960, cols 3877, 3878.
65. *Ibid.*, vol. 106, 9 February 1961, col. 1042.
66. Quoted by Geldenhuys, 'Effects of South Africa's Racial Policy', p. 334.
67. Quoted by Geldenhuys, *Diplomacy of Isolation*, p. 23. Also see Barber and Barratt, *South Africa's Foreign Policy*, p. 65.
68. Macmillan, *Pointing the Way*, pp. 171, 172.

Verwoerd adopted a pragmatic stance on Commonwealth membership. Both before and after the referendum on a republic held in October 1960 he repeatedly expressed his preference for continued membership after South Africa became a republic. Verwoerd interpreted the outcome of the referendum – a narrow victory for a republic – as a vote for retaining Commonwealth membership. Yet Verwoerd at the same time made it plain that South Africa's position might become untenable if apartheid was elevated to a major issue in the association.[69] The Prime Minister was adamant that 'we shall certainly not go and plead for our membership of the Commonwealth by going to other member states and delivering pleas to them in support of our policy'. By doing so, he said, South Africa would admit that 'they are allowed to interfere' in its domestic affairs.[70]

Predictably, Verwoerd's 'accept-us-as-we-are' approach ran into opposition at the Commonwealth Conference of March 1961, where he applied for continued membership after South Africa's scheduled declaration of a republic on 31 May 1961. Far from being treated as a mere formality, Verwoerd's request became embroiled in the whole question of apartheid. To avoid what he considered the possible humiliation of having his application rejected in a vote, or having conditions imposed in return for retaining membership, Verwoerd withdrew his request.[71] South Africa was in effect forced out of the Commonwealth; apartheid had claimed another victim in the country's foreign relations.

Verwoerd took the decision to end South Africa's Commonwealth membership without consulting his cabinet, not to mention parliament. That he could act unilaterally on a matter of such consequence attests to his status and self-assurance in foreign policy matters.

For Verwoerd, exclusion from the Commonwealth was a price well worth paying. By leaving 'we have freed ourselves from the pressure of the Afro-Asian nations who were busy invading the Commonwealth', he proclaimed. South Africa was not prepared to allow these countries 'to dictate what our future should be'.[72] By the same token, he ruled out a return to the Commonwealth because that 'must entail giving up the struggle of the white man to maintain himself in this country'.[73] Foreign interference was thus again defined in terms of the fight for continued existence.

The Prime Minister's hopes that departure from the Commonwealth would free South Africa from pressure for political change from this

69. Geldenhuys, 'Effects of South Africa's Racial Policy', pp. 313–18.
70. *Hansard*, vol. 106, 23 January 1961, cols 25, 26.
71. Geldenhuys, 'Effects of South Africa's Racial Policy', pp. 399–410.
72. Quoted by Pelzer, *Verwoerd Speaks*, p. 506.
73. *Hansard*, vol. 107, 28 March 1961, col. 3845.

quarter were in vain. The Commonwealth mirrored the growing universal preoccupation with apartheid. As before, the UN was the focal point of the international offensive against South Africa. In 1962 the General Assembly passed its first sanctions resolution against South Africa, requesting member states to sever diplomatic links with the Republic and restrict economic ties. The following year the Security Council called for a voluntary arms embargo against South Africa.

South Africa also experienced setbacks in other UN organs. In 1963 it was excluded from the Economic Commission for Africa and the following year the Republic withdrew under duress from the International Labour Organisation, the Food and Agriculture Organisation and the World Health Organisation.[74] Not surprisingly, Verwoerd's cabinet seriously considered the question of continued UN membership, but decided against leaving the world body.[75]

South Africa was from the outset excluded from the Organisation of African Unity (OAU), founded in 1963. Like the UN General Assembly, the OAU also attempted to extend South Africa's diplomatic isolation by calling on member states not to set up diplomatic relations with the Republic. Initially, however, some of the new states seemed interested in establishing diplomatic links with Pretoria, but they were rebuffed by Verwoerd. When the matter was raised at the 1961 Commonwealth summit, Verwoerd maintained that a little more progress should be made with apartheid to avoid the establishment of black diplomatic missions causing confusion and incidents in South Africa. He also insisted that an exchange of missions was always based on existing friendships, a condition that would have disqualified many of the newly independent states given their open antagonism towards the Republic.[76] Verwoerd nonetheless favoured a form of *ad hoc* diplomatic exchange that could overcome many of the obstacles mentioned.[77]

During the Verwoerd years Africa became a matter of high priority in South Africa's foreign relations, as the establishment of a separate Africa division in the Department of External Affairs in 1959 indicates. There was, however, little evidence of a coherent Africa policy in step with the time. For Verwoerd the problem was not the granting of independence to 'wholly black man's countries', of which Ghana and Nigeria were examples; this was in any case the course that South Africa wished to follow with regard to its own homelands, he said in 1961.[78]

74. D. Geldenhuys, *Isolated States: A Comparative Analysis* (Cambridge University Press, 1990), p. 182.
75. Geldenhuys, *Diplomacy of Isolation*, p. 12.
76. *Hansard*, vol. 107, 23 March 1961, cols 3493, 3494.
77. Olivier, *Suid-Afrika se Buitelandse Beleid*, p. 138.
78. *Hansard*, vol. 107, 23 March 1961, cols 3506, 3507.

Verwoerd's main concern was the 'so-called multi-racial or non-racial policy' that Britain pursued in Kenya and the Central African Federation. Not only would such a policy lead to black domination, it would also pose a dire threat to the preservation of white South Africa itself. In true Nationalist fashion, Verwoerd found the answer to Africa's racial problems in his party's own policies. Accordingly, he prescribed that there should be neither human nor political intermingling between black and white, but a permanent coexistence. Wherever possible a white state, such as South Africa, should be created to serve as guardian over neighbouring black territories to 'make the masses ripe for their participation in government', thereby ensuring true independence at the end of the day.[79]

This plea for gradualism based on racial separation was clearly a forlorn one: it was made in the very year that 17 African colonies gained their independence. Disillusioned, Verwoerd rounded on the Western powers for abdicating their responsibilities and abandoning the white people in Africa. On both counts Western powers were inspired by a desire to appease the non-aligned countries, he alleged. This state of affairs was also symptomatic of what Verwoerd termed a psychosis that emphasised the rights and freedoms only of blacks in Africa.[80] On another occasion Verwoerd, following Malan, offered the diagnosis that 'the world is sick' because of its preoccupation with the lot of blacks and its unceasing criticism of South Africa, and he warned South Africans against being carried along in that 'sick-bed'.[81]

Verwoerd's appeal to whites in other parts of Africa to fight for their rights[82] and his open identification with their cause was put to the test when Rhodesia's white rulers declared unilateral independence in 1965. The Prime Minister made it plain from the outset that South Africa would not support UN-imposed sanctions against Rhodesia. To do so, he maintained, would mean sacrificing the Republic's adherence to the principles of non-interference and non-aggression. But apart from this moral issue, pragmatic considerations weighed heavily with Verwoerd. If South Africa were to enforce sanctions against Rhodesia, the country would seal its own doom, he warned. Clearly, South Africa could not support international sanctions against a fellow white-ruled country that was being punished for an offence comparable to the Republic's denial of political rights to the black majority. Verwoerd furthermore explained that in view of the poor track record of African countries under black rule, 'realism demands that South Africa must avoid becoming

79. *Ibid.*, vol. 104, 9 March 1961, cols 3018, 3019.
80. *Ibid.*, vol. 104, 9 March 1961, cols 3013–18.
81. Olivier, *Suid-Afrika se Buitelandse Beleid*, p. 171.
82. *Hansard*, vol. 104, 9 March 1961, col. 3020.

co-responsible for such a possible real danger' occurring in Rhodesia too.[83]

Another regional issue bound up with domestic policies was the future of the High Commission Territories. Verwoerd abandoned South Africa's long-standing quest for the incorporation of the three British dependencies, but he wanted to draw them into the Bantu homelands scheme. If South Africa were to become the guardian of the territories, he suggested in 1963, 'we could lead them far better and more quickly to independence and economic prosperity than Great Britain can do.'[84] South Africa would ensure that they became black democratic states, but they would be steered away from multiracialism, the Prime Minister said,[85] confirming that a primary consideration was to prevent policies being pursued in these neighbouring territories that would conflict with South Africa's domestic course. With the High Commission Territories accommodated in the separate development grand design, Verwoerd envisaged a common market together with a consultative political body of free black and white states in Southern Africa.[86] Britain predictably rejected his guardianship proposal and led the territories to independence in its own way. Verwoerd's blueprint for regional relations – a common market in the economic realm and a Commonwealth-type arrangement in the political sphere, drawing together South Africa, its (independent) homeland states and adjacent countries – formed the basis of the Republic's regional policy in subsequent years.

A further feature of Verwoerd's approach to Africa was its assumption of the primacy of economic over political considerations in South Africa's relations with black states. The notion that divisive political factors would in the end submit to powerful economic forces of cohesion in fact became another basic tenet of the Republic's Africa policy. Verwoerd was relying not only on normal trade relations as an instrument of foreign policy but, like his predecessors, he emphasised Pretoria's willingness to provide direct, bilateral aid to black countries. Aid was regarded as a means of contact, but Verwoerd made it conditional upon the black African states muting their hostility towards South Africa.[87]

The status of South West Africa was another regional and indeed international issue that exercised Verwoerd's mind. South Africa continued to treat the territory as a *de facto* fifth province, to the extent of allowing white voters in South West Africa to participate in the South African referendum on a republic in October 1960. The report of the

83. Quoted in Geldenhuys, *Diplomacy of Isolation*, p. 25.
84. Quoted in *ibid*.
85. Quoted by Barber and Barratt, *South Africa's Foreign Policy*, p. 95.
86. Quoted by Geldenhuys, *Diplomacy of Isolation*, p. 25.
87. Geldenhuys, 'South Africa's Regional Policy', pp. 131, 132.

Odendaal Commission of Inquiry into political, economic and social conditions in the territory, released in 1964, provided for further integration by recommending that Pretoria's policy of ethnic fragmentation be extended to South West Africa.[88] While Verwoerd was no doubt pleased about this supposedly expert endorsement of the applicability of grand apartheid beyond South Africa's borders, he had to move with caution in giving effect to the proposals. The disputed legal status of South West Africa was the subject of a hearing by the International Court of Justice, proceedings having been instituted by Ethiopia and Liberia in 1960. To have introduced drastic political changes in the territory while the status issue was *sub judice* could have produced serious international repercussions. In 1966 the court eventually produced a controversial non-finding, namely that Ethiopia and Liberia had no legal rights or interests in the matter before the court. Verwoerd hailed the outcome as a major victory, but South Africa's opponents were outraged. Having failed to eject South Africa from South West Africa through legal means, they returned to the political arena: a General Assembly resolution of October 1966 terminated the mandate over South West Africa.[89]

The South West Africa issue provided an interesting case study of Verwoerd's dealings with the UN. While he was no more enamoured of the world body than any of his predecessors, Verwoerd nonetheless displayed a conciliatory attitude to the UN by permitting a fact-finding visit to the territory by the UN Special Committee for South West Africa in 1962.[90] The Carpio-De Alva mission ended in a cocktail of farce and fiasco, with the UN very much the embarrassed party.

The previous year Verwoerd had demonstrated an even more surprising degree of flexibility when he agreed to receive the UN Secretary-General in South Africa. Dag Hammarskjöld's visit was in pursuance of the Security Council resolution adopted in the wake of the Sharpeville incident. Despite his extreme sensitivity about foreign interference, Verwoerd held extensive talks with the UN envoy on South Africa's domestic policies.[91]

These instances of international contact could not mask South Africa's growing alienation from the world community. One indication of this is that Verwoerd paid only one official visit abroad (to attend the 1961 Commonwealth summit) during his tenure. Just how unwelcome a guest the South African leader was, is revealed in Washington's

88. A. du Pisani, *SWA/Namibia: The Politics of Continuity and Change* (Johannesburg: Jonathan Ball, 1985), pp. 161–6.
89. Barber and Barratt, *South Africa's Foreign Policy*, p. 88.
90. *Ibid.*, pp. 86, 87.
91. Geldenhuys, *Diplomacy of Isolation*, p. 24.

turning down Verwoerd's proposal to visit President John F. Kennedy.[92] South Africa also began experiencing the material effects of enforced isolation in the military sphere. Verwoerd's assertion in 1962 that South Africa was 'by nature a safe and sure and permanent friend [of the West] . . . in this strategic position' at the southern tip of Africa could not prevent two of its major arms suppliers, Britain and the United States, heeding the UN Security Council's calls in 1963 and 1964 for a voluntary arms embargo against the Republic.[93] Verwoerd subsequently acknowledged the obvious when he said that there was no longer any prospect of the West admitting South Africa into a military alliance. These considerations no doubt influenced the Verwoerd government's decision to embark on a massive rearmament programme and to build up a local arms industry.[94]

For all his intransigence and defiance, Verwoerd was not oblivious to the damage that apartheid was causing South Africa's foreign relations. In 1962 he conceded that the Republic had differences of opinion with many if not most other nations about its colour policies. Since he regarded foreign demands as completely unreasonable, Verwoerd proclaimed: 'In isolation in the area of colour policy lies our strength!' If South Africans submitted to external demands because they feared isolation, he said, they would go under.[95] 'Without any hesitation', Verwoerd declared, 'my choice is to have fewer friends and ensure the survival of my nation.'[96] But he was at pains to state that isolation in this one area did not mean general isolation. In most fields, he maintained, South Africa remained a popular friend and partner in the community of nations.[97] By the end of Verwoerd's tenure in 1966, fewer and fewer countries would endorse such a view.

B.J. Vorster, 1966–1978: From Outward Movement to Inward Retreat

John Vorster took over the reins of power at a time when white South Africans were riding the crest of a wave of prosperity and confidence. The turmoil and uncertainties of the early 1960s seemed a distant memory, and whites appeared oblivious to their country's low international standing. With the domestic base secure, the Republic could face the world with renewed confidence. And Africa could be approached

92. *Ibid.*, p. 18.
93. Quoted by D. Geldenhuys, 'South Africa and the West', in Schrire (ed.), *South Africa*, p. 321.
94. *Ibid.*, pp. 306, 307.
95. Quoted by D. Geldenhuys, *Internasionale Isolasie: Suid-Afrika in Vergelykende Perspektief* (Johannesburg: Rand Afrikaans University, 1985), p. 65.
96. Quoted by Geldenhuys, *Diplomacy of Isolation*, p. 24.
97. Quoted by Geldenhuys, *Internasionale Isolasie*, p. 65.

from a position of strength: South Africa, Vorster asserted, was not just another African country but a leader in every sphere.[98] He clearly articulated this new mood of self-assurance when he declared in 1968 that it had been a mere seven years since people had wondered what the future of the Republic would be. Now, however, 'South Africans have the answers to most – if not all – of their questions. Doubts have gone and fears have vanished'.[99]

Developments in the region were also favourable for a new approach to South Africa's foreign relations. The independence of Botswana and Lesotho in 1966 and Swaziland two years later, all under conservative pro-Western governments, seemed to offer Pretoria the ideal opportunity for giving effect to the Verwoerdian design for a Commonwealth-cum-common-market arrangement in Southern Africa. At the same time, South Africa realised that the tide of national liberation had reached its shores and that it had to be handled cautiously lest it jeopardise the Republic's domestic political order.

However, there were also some more ominous developments in South Africa's immediate region. The guerrilla wars being waged against the Portuguese colonial governments in Angola and Mozambique, albeit at a low level, showed no signs of abating. Rhodesia was facing the increasing wrath of the international community because of its rebellion against Britain, and the Smith government's black nationalist opponents embarked on an armed offensive. In Namibia, as the UN General Assembly renamed South West Africa in 1968, the South West Africa People's Organisation (SWAPO) launched a war of liberation in 1966. Security considerations therefore became prominent in South Africa's dealings with the region, with a 'white security group' emerging in the sub-continent.[100] Apart from Namibia, South Africa's only direct involvement in actual combat was in Rhodesia, to which Vorster in 1967 despatched a paramilitary police force. In Vorster's view, this was an investment in the Republic's own security because 'I know of no terrorism in Southern Africa which, in the final analysis, is not directed against South Africa . . . The ultimate aim of all terrorists is to take South Africa away from us.'[101]

Confidence in South Africa's strength and concern over its regional security were joined in Prime Minister Vorster's first major foreign policy initiative, of which he was the principal architect. In 1967 he embarked on the so-called outward movement. Its major thrust was directed at Africa, as Vorster believed that a rapprochement with black Africa was the key to an improvement in South Africa's foreign

99. Quoted by J. Barber, *South Africa's Foreign Policy 1945–1970* (Oxford University Press, 1973), p. 213.
100. Barber and Barratt, *South Africas Foreign Policy*, p. 138.
101. Quoted *ibid.*, p. 139.

relations over a wider front. In the final analysis, Vorster of course wanted to see an external environment compatible with the Republic's domestic political order.

The new prime minister painstakingly prepared his followers to accept one of the prices of such a *rapprochement*: the installing of black diplomats in white South Africa. In the end, this was much ado about very little: only Malawi, in 1967, chose to exchange diplomats with the Republic. This was nonetheless one of the most tangible achievements of the outward movement. Another modest success was the acceptance by a number of black states of South Africa's offers of aid.[102] Vorster had no success in drawing black states into non-aggression pacts with South Africa, however. This offer, which he made in 1970, reflected the importance of the Republic's security concerns: by entering into such agreements black states would have undertaken not to provide support for insurgents wishing to operate against South Africa.

The idea of non-aggression treaties can also be seen in the context of Vorster's repeated warnings against the 'Red Menace', vowing that 'we shall rise against it and oppose it with all the means at our disposal.'[103] South Africa, he said in 1970, would not tolerate terrorism or communist domination (the former being seen as an instrument of the latter) in Southern Africa, and was determined to fight the danger even beyond the country's borders.[104]

While he was ever ready to fight the communists, Vorster wanted to 'enter into amicable relations with African states' and 'to do our duty towards Africa', as he put it in 1969. This duty flowed from South Africa's position as a white state on the continent, one that understood 'the soul of Africa' better than any other.[105] And so the dialogue initiative of the late 1960s and early 1970s was launched. This more narrowly focused outgrowth of the outward movement produced some initial results when several African states indicated a willingness to enter into a dialogue with South Africa. Vorster, in turn, declared himself willing to discuss apartheid with his interlocutors. The initiative soon petered out because of the fierce resistance of most African states. Another reason was a conflict in objectives: whereas the black states saw dialogue as a means of persuading Pretoria to abolish apartheid, Vorster saw the exchanges as an opportunity 'to discuss my policy with and explain it to each and everybody, because . . . more nonsense has been written about separate development than about any other subject

---

102. For details of South African aid, see Olivier, 'South Africa's Relations with Africa', p. 291.
103. Quoted by Barber and Barratt, *South Africa's Foreign Policy*, p. 112.
104. Quoted by Geldenhuys, 'South Africa's Regional Policy', p. 135.
105. Quoted by Olivier, 'South Africa's Relations with Africa', p. 280.

I know.'[106] He clearly intended persuading other African leaders that separate development was the only reasonable and viable policy for South Africa.

Despite the setbacks Vorster did not give up hope of improving South Africa's position in Africa. In 1974 he met with President Felix Houphouet-Boigny of the Ivory Coast and Senegal's President Leopold Senghor, and early the following year he held talks with President William Tolbert in Liberia. These diplomatic breakthroughs failed to produce any substantive and lasting political benefits for South Africa.

Meanwhile, a new foreign policy initiative was emerging. Vorster set his sights lower than previously, concentrating on consolidating South Africa's position in the region. Dramatic, unforseen developments for the first time seemed to place the *cordon sanitaire* around South Africa under immediate serious threat. Not only were wars raging in Rhodesia and Namibia, but Portugal's African empire was about to collapse following the Lisbon *coup d'état* of April 1974. Vorster sensed a greater urgency than ever before to find peaceful settlements to the conflicts on South Africa's borders, lest they spill over into the Republic.

The new phase in South Africa's foreign policy began with a series of meetings with Zambian officials early in October 1974, in a joint endeavour to break the international deadlock over Rhodesia. A few weeks later Vorster followed with one of his most celebrated speeches. Southern Africa, he said, had come to the crossroads and had to choose between peace and escalating conflict.[107] The next month Vorster appealed to the world to give South Africa a six months' chance, adding that others would thereafter 'be surprised where we will stand'[108] – a reference to its international position. All these moves were designed to set the scene for the new *detente* initiative.

Detente reached its culmination in the historic Victoria Falls conference in August 1975, attended by Vorster, Zambian President Kenneth Kaunda and members of the Rhodesian government and their black nationalist opponents. The resolution of the Rhodesian conflict was the principal purpose of the summit the South African leader had done so much to convene. This was probably Vorster's finest diplomatic hour.

The following month, *detente*'s influence could also be seen in Namibia, when the Turnhalle constitutional conference, initiated by Pretoria, got under way. The continuing impasse between South Africa and the international community over the future of Namibia was, after all, a major obstacle to an improvement in the Republic's foreign relations, particularly with African countries. The dramatic changes in

---

106. Quoted by Olivier, *Suid-Afrika se Buitelandse Beleid*, p. 144.
107. Quoted by Geldenhuys, 'South Africa's Regional Policy', p. 136.
108. Du Pisani, *SWA/Namibia*, p. 280.

the regional political landscape in the mid-1970s added urgency to the search for a settlement in Namibia. With Angola, ruled by the Popular Movement for the Liberation of Angola (MPLA), as sanctuary, SWAPO was set to intensify its armed struggle to eject South Africa from the territory. Yet Vorster made it plain that he would not accede to UN demands 'that South West Africa be handed over to Swapo and Sam Nujoma'; he was not even willing to talk to Nujoma, whom he labelled an adventurer.[109] The Turnhalle conference, Vorster hoped, would produce an internal settlement on the independence of Namibia (or its separate ethnic groups) and thus preserve the country as a vital link in the Republic's *cordon sanitaire* that shielded it against subversive forces from the north.[110]

The era of *detente* was short-lived, its demise caused primarily by the collapse of the Vorster–Kaunda settlement effort for Rhodesia and South Africa's intervention in the Angolan war. For Vorster, the failure of *detente* was a severe setback, as he had entertained high hopes for the initiative – hopes that went well beyond a Rhodesian or a Namibian settlement. In his 'crossroads' speech, Vorster had expressed the wish to build a United Nations of Southern African states. He had hoped that South Africa, Rhodesia, Namibia, Botswana, Lesotho, Swaziland, Angola, Mozambique and Zambia would join forces for the sake of peace, progress and development.[111] He had also variously envisaged an economic power bloc and a constellation of politically completely independent states with close economic ties emerging in the region; as the most developed country in Africa, Vorster added, South Africa intended taking the lead in bringing about such arrangements.[112] In addition, Vorster was not oblivious to the wider foreign policy benefits that might flow from a diplomatic breakthrough in Southern Africa. Progress in the region, so the familiar argument went, would improve South Africa's foreign relations in the rest of Africa and beyond.

It is an irony that South Africa's intervention in the Angolan war in October 1975 helped to scuttle *detente*, because Pretoria had hoped that its involvement would actually promote the initiative. The belief was that by intervening on the side of the pro-Western National Union for the Total Independence of Angola (Unita) and National Front for the Liberation of Angola (FNLA) movements against the Marxist MPLA, South Africa would prove itself as a reliable ally of black states opposed to communist intervention. Soviet involvement in Angola, Vorster

109. Quoted *ibid.*, p. 316.
110. *Ibid.*, pp. 272–316.
111. Quoted *ibid.*, p. 278.
112. Quoted by D. Geldenhuys and D. Venter, 'Regional Cooperation in Southern Africa: A Constellation of States?', *International Affairs Bulletin*, vol. 3 (3), December 1979, p. 49.

contended, was aimed at creating 'a string of Marxist states across Africa from Angola to Tanzania'.[113] However, the fact that most African states decided to recognise the MPLA as the legal government of Angola and the OAU's near unanimous condemnation of South Africa's intervention weighed heavily with Pretoria in its decision to withdraw its forces in March 1976. Another major consideration was that US military support on which South Africa had relied, failed to materialise.[114]

Vorster made no secret of his bitterness at being left in the lurch by the Americans in the Angolan war. The experience had confirmed a lesson South Africa had previously learned, he said in January 1976: 'When it comes to the worst, South Africa stands alone.'[115] But despite his deep disenchantment with the USA, Vorster agreed to cooperate with a new American-led search for peace in Southern Africa in 1976, focusing on Rhodesia. Vorster met US Secretary of State Henry Kissinger in June and September in West Germany and Switzerland respectively. The upshot of the initiative was the abortive Geneva Conference (October–November) of all parties involved in the Rhodesian conflict.

Kissinger knew that Vorster's cooperation was vital to produce a Rhodesian settlement, for the embattled colony depended for its very survival on South Africa. It was only in this narrow context that South Africa participated from a position of relative strength in the American-directed peace initiative. For the rest, Vorster had a decidedly weak hand to play. South Africa's regional security had deteriorated quite sharply after Angola and Mozambique had become independent in 1975 under avowedly Marxist governments that were openly antagonistic towards Pretoria and supportive of the liberation movements in Namibia, Rhodesia and South Africa itself. There was moreover a heavy communist military presence in Angola in particular.

What weakened Vorster's position even more was that his domestic base appeared insecure too. In June 1976 massive unrest and violence erupted in black townships across the country, with Soweto the focal point. Like Verwoerd at the time of Sharpeville, Vorster read all manner of evil motives into the 1976 riots, including the charge that it was part of a communist-inspired revolution.[116]

South Africa was again experiencing a crisis in both domestic politics and foreign relations. It displayed many of the features of the Sharpeville

113. *Hansard*, vol. 60, 30 January 1976, col. 366.
114. See A. du Preez, *Avontuur in Angola: Die Verhaal van Suid-Afrika se Soldate in Angola 1975–1976* (Pretoria: J.L. van Schaik, 1989); P.L. Moorcraft, *African Nemesis: War and Revolution in Southern Africa 1945–2010* (London: Brassey's, 1990), pp. 76–89.
115. *Hansard*, vol. 64, 30 January 1976, col. 375.
116. Barber and Barratt, *South Africa's Foreign Policy*, p. 206.

crisis of 1976, only in more acute form: a flight of capital and people as investors and ordinary citizens lost confidence in South Africa's future, with the tide of international condemnation and indeed isolation rising to dangerous new heights. South Africa's foreign relations took a further hammering in 1977. In September, black activist Steve Biko died in police custody and the following month the government resorted to a massive internal security clampdown. International reaction was swift and severe: the UN Security Council imposed a mandatory arms embargo against South Africa in November.

Under these dire conditions Vorster no longer preached dialogue and *detente* but instead warned that South Africans were on their own in a hostile world.[117] He was particularly scathing about the West, which, he said, had 'lost its will to take a firm stand against the increasing [communist] menace'. In the event of a communist onslaught, the Republic 'will have to face it alone, and certain countries which profess to be anti-communist will even refuse to sell [us] arms'.[118] Perceived Western unreliability and indifference also helped to inform sporadic official suggestions that South Africa should become neutral in the East–West conflict or side with the so-called Fifth World of fellow outcast countries. Moreover, Pretoria toyed with the idea of a South Atlantic Treaty Organisation as an alternative to NATO; America's refusal to support South Africa in Angola and also Britain's decision in 1975 to terminate the Simonstown Agreement had made it abundantly clear to the Vorster government – if further clarity was needed – that the Western alliance had no intention of siding with South Africa or getting it on the West's side in the Cold War. Vorster's visits to Uruguay and Paraguay in 1975 and to Israel the following year, together with the subsequent expansion of ties between South Africa and Israel, suggest that these were not simply emotional responses to Western inaction, but a form of reinsurance against continued Western aloofness.[119]

Not surprisingly, the concept of a total national strategy had by 1977 found its way into the South African military vocabulary. It was only under Vorster's successor, though, that this notion became the dominant paradigm in which government operated. Meanwhile, Vorster's South Africa began to resemble a garrison state.[120]

It was under these inauspicious conditions of mounting internal and external threats that a (white) general election was held in November

117. *Ibid.*, p. 227.
118. Quoted *ibid.*, p. 227.
119. J.E. Spence, *The Strategic Significance of South Africa* (London: RUSI, 1970), pp. 28–30.
120. See P.L. Moorcraft, 'Towards the Garrison State', in F. McA. Clifford-Vaughan, *International Pressures and Political Change in South Africa* (Cape Town: Oxford University Press, 1978), pp. 86–105.

1977. This was an exceptional election in that foreign rather than domestic policy issues dominated the campaign. In fact, Vorster said he had called the election to allow voters to express themselves *inter alia* on external interference in South Africa's affairs. The ruling National Party fought the election principally against the Carter administration, rather than against its domestic opponents. Just how charged the atmosphere was is captured in Vorster's oft-quoted remark that the end result of American pressure on South Africa 'would be exactly the same as if it were subverted by the Marxists': whereas the latter used brute force to destroy the Republic, the American way was strangulation with finesse.[121] In this furious bout of America-bashing, Vorster had no stauncher disciple than the highly visible and voluble 'Pik' Botha, who had succeeded the unpretentious Hilgard Muller as Foreign Minister in April 1977. Vorster had read the popular white mood well: the National Party scored its greatest electoral victory ever.[122]

The 1977 election represented a low point in South Africa's increasingly troubled relations with the West, the United States in particular. Under Vorster's predecessors the relationship had already acquired a dualistic love-hate character, but the dissociative features became more pronounced than ever in Vorster's final years. Yet South Africa could never afford to turn its back completely on the West. Thus Vorster in September 1976 in a remarkably submissive utterance acknowledged that 'America is the leader of the free world, and I am part and parcel of the free world, and therefore America is my leader.'[123] Two years later he appealed to the West to 'make sure that South Africa does not fall prey to the Marxist onslaught' – in the West's own interests.[124]

Just how important the West remained to South Africa, particularly in view of its decline in regional power ratings, was evidenced in Vorster's new moves on Namibia in 1977–8. The external track of South Africa's established two-track policy on Namibia was gaining precedence over the internal track. Realising that the Turnhalle conference – the domestic track to a settlement – would not attract any international support because of its ethnic composition and SWAPO's refusal to participate, Vorster agreed to terminate the conference in October 1977. The international track was followed through South Africa's cooperation with the so-called Western contact group formed late in 1976 to act as intermediaries between Pretoria, SWAPO and the UN (using Security Council resolution 385 of January 1976 as the basis for their endeavour). Vorster had clearly lost whatever initiative he may have had on Namibia. In April 1978 Pretoria accepted the Western

121. *The Star*, 30 August 1977.
122. Geldenhuys, *Diplomacy of Isolation*, p. 36.
123. Quoted by Barber and Barratt, *South Africa's Foreign Policy*, p. 217.
124. Quoted by Geldenhuys, 'South Africa and the West', p. 310.

nations' settlement package for Namibia.[125] It would, however, take several more years before that country became independent and South Africa finally extricated itself from the Angolan imbroglio.

Vorster's handling of the Angolan issue in 1975–6 is of relevance here too because it provides an instructive case study of his government's foreign policy-making. Another revealing case study concerns the foreign activities of the Department of Information between 1973 and 1977. These two cases had several features in common: an obsession with secrecy on the part of the policy-makers; the confinement of decision-making to very few people; a lack of inputs from various interested parties in government, notably Foreign Affairs; and a lack of firm direction and control by the Prime Minister.[126] This rather pitiful final picture of Vorster's leadership stands in sharp contrast to the reputation he had established early in his premiership as a particularly skilful chairman of the cabinet who emphasised the team concept of government, as opposed to Verwoerd's more presidential style that had put him above and apart from his cabinet colleagues.

A further irony is that Vorster, who at the start of his premiership promised that the improvement of South Africa's international position would be a matter of high priority,[127] left office with the Republic's foreign relations in dire straits. A period begun on such a high note of confidence ended in despair.

P.W. Botha, 1978–1989: The Era of Coercive Diplomacy

Compared with his Nationalist predecessors, P.W. Botha could boast a wealth of experience in foreign affairs when he became Prime Minister. Prior to his election as head of government in September 1978, Botha had served as Minister of Defence for fully 12 years. In this capacity he regularly pronounced on aspects of South Africa's foreign relations and on world politics in general. He did so in the forthright fashion of a Cold War warrior who would brook no compromise with the forces of communism that were bent on subjugating the entire world to their evil designs. More than any of his predecessors, Botha had developed 'a clear-cut, almost dogmatic, view of the world in military-strategic and geo-political terms'.[128] These were the beliefs that Prime Minister (later State President) Botha brought to bear in the conduct of South Africa's foreign relations.

125. Du Pisani, *SWA/Namibia*, pp. 319–92; Barber and Barratt, *South Africa's Foreign Policy*, p. 203.
126. Decision-making in the Angolan and Information debacles is discussed in detail in Geldenhuys, *Diplomacy of Isolation*, pp. 75–89.
127. *Ibid.*, p. 72.
128. Barber and Barratt, *South Africa's Foreign Policy*, p. 248.

The new Prime Minister had reason to see the world as decidedly inhospitable. He entered office with the sword of Western sanctions dangling over South Africa because of its insistence on holding elections in Namibia in the face of Western opposition and SWAPO's refusal to participate. Long known for his hawkish views on Namibia, Botha appeared determined not to abandon the internal settlement track in favour of the international route to an accord. The latter track was further endorsed by the UN Security Council when it passed resolution 435, embodying the Western settlement plan, the very day after Botha took over the reins of power.[129] While the diplomatic tussle over the future of Namibia continued, with Botha seemingly pursuing the diplomacy of brinkmanship that Vorster had introduced in dealing with the Western powers on Namibia, the war between South Africa and SWAPO raged on relentlessly. Botha found no cause for cheer in Rhodesia either, where the internal settlement of March 1978 and a general election the following year failed to resolve the conflict.

If Western actions or inactions gave Botha cause for concern, he was positively alarmed about Soviet machinations in Southern Africa. In expounding a local version of the domino theory in October 1978, the Prime Minister warned the West that if the Soviet Union gained a foothold in Namibia through its 'pawn' SWAPO – in addition to the Soviet presence in Angola – Moscow would control a solid bloc of states along the west coast of Southern Africa. Zaïre would be the next to succumb to Cuban pressure, thus creating a string of Marxist-oriented states from coast to coast, cutting Africa in two and leaving the (white) south isolated and exposed.[130]

Faced with such a hostile external environment, coupled with the familiar concerns about communist subversion within South Africa, it is not surprising that the new Prime Minister gave renewed prominence to the notion of a total onslaught against South Africa. The onslaught in turn defines the context of Botha's total national strategy, the blueprint for both domestic and foreign policies. These concepts of course reveal the influence of military thinking on Botha's government.

South Africa, Botha said in 1980, 'is subjected to a communist-inspired onslaught [aimed at] the overthrow of the present constitutional order and its replacement by a subject communist-oriented black government'. This was part and parcel of a communist onslaught 'directed against the whole free Western world', to which South Africa belonged. Because a conventional war against South Africa would be too expensive, Botha reasoned, 'an indirect strategy is being pursued with every possible means', such as sanctions and propaganda.[131] The

129. *Ibid.*, p. 264; Du Pisani, *SWA/Namibia*, pp. 407 ff.
130. Quoted by Geldenhuys, 'South Africa and the West', p. 319.
131. Quoted by D. Geldenhuys, *Some Foreign Policy Implications of South Africa's*

onslaught was considered 'total' in terms of both the measures used and the targets selected: political, economic, military, social and cultural elements were involved on both fronts. But while the onslaught itself was orchestrated by communist forces, Pretoria saw the political and ideological aspirations of the West, the UN, the OAU and a host of other groupings represented in the offensive against South Africa. Predictably, the Southern African terrorist threat, as Botha depicted it, also featured in the onslaught;[132] this meant that the ANC and SWAPO, among others, were considered mere agents of a communist conspiracy.

Botha insisted that '[t]here is only one way to withstand this onslaught, and that is to establish a total national strategy'.[133] This essentially meant the management of South Africa's so-called power bases – the political, economic, social and security – as an integrated whole. The mechanism used was the national security management system. The specific policies that the government hoped to implement through its total national strategy were spelled out in Botha's 12-point plan, first enunciated in August 1979.[134] Both the security system and the policy document are of direct relevance to Botha's handling of South Africa's foreign relations.

The national security management system consisted of a network of bodies designed to give effect to the total national strategy. At its apex stood the State Security Council (SSC), one of a number of cabinet committees. Chaired by the State President, the SSC consisted also of the ministers of Defence, Foreign Affairs, Justice and of Law and Order as standing members, together with five top officials. Other ministers and senior officials could be coopted. The Council's statutory function was to advise the government on the formulation and implementation of 'national policy and strategy in relation to the security of the Republic'. It was a brief wide enough to embrace virtually every area of government action both at home and abroad. Under Botha the Council indeed became a major forum for the actual formulation of foreign policy – notably towards Southern Africa – thus reducing the full cabinet to a subordinate role. The elevation of the SSC into a principal policy-making body reflected important features of Botha's leadership style: following the Angolan debacle in 1975–6 he wanted to formalise and regularise top-level decision-making; he placed a high premium on expert advice (thus the involvement of top bureaucrats), and he was familiar and comfortable with a forum that bore a distinct military imprint.

"Total National Strategy" (Johannesburg: SAIIA, 1981), pp. 3, 4.
132. Quoted *ibid.*, p. 5.
133. Quoted *ibid.*, p. 8.
134. For details, see *ibid.*, pp. 60–2.

To be fair, the SSC was established under a law of 1972, but Vorster rather neglected the Council. Its rejuvenation under Botha was part of a thorough-going reorganisation of top-level decision-making and of the public service generally; Botha was a true organisation man committed to what his 12-point plan called effective decision-making by the state, orderly government and efficient, clean administration.[135]

This same grand plan also laid down foreign policy guidelines. Point 8 provided for the creation of 'a peaceful constellation of Southern African states with respect for each other's cultures, traditions and ideals'.[136] Although the idea of closer regional cooperation was a very old one and Vorster had, moreover, introduced the concept of a constellation, Botha promoted the formation of such a regional associa-tion to a major foreign policy priority. Its importance was related to the security situation in the region; the constellation design was essentially a defensive strategy, circumstances forcing the Republic to retreat behind the perimeters of Southern Africa.

Botha's constellation plans rested on a number of assumptions. The first was that the so-called moderate countries in the region all faced a common Marxist threat and had to join forces to combat the danger; they could not rely on Western support. He also assumed that security, economic and political considerations too were inexorably steering the countries in the region towards ever closer and more formal links. A further assumption was that regional solutions should be found for such regional problems as Rhodesia and Namibia, since foreign mediators could not be relied upon. A final critical assumption was that a constellation would be built on the existing regional order, which for South Africa included independent homeland states. Pretoria hoped that between seven and ten countries would join South Africa in the proposed constellation.[137]

These assumptions were ill founded. Instead of entering South Africa's proposed constellation, neighbouring black states joined forces in what Pretoria regarded as a counter-constellation, the Southern African Development Coordination Conference (SADCC). In the end, Botha's constellation was scaled down to a confederal arrangement of sorts involving South Africa and its former black homelands.

The ninth of Botha's 12 points declared 'South Africa's firm deter-mination to defend itself against interference from outside in every possible way'. Botha boasted that 'we are better able . . . to defend South Africa militarily than ever before in the country's history.'[138] The main military danger facing the country was that of unconventional

---

135. Quoted *ibid.*, p. 37.
136. Quoted *ibid.*, p. 18.
137. Geldenhuys and Venter, *Regional Cooperation*, pp. 50–68.
138. Quoted by Geldenhuys, *Some Foreign Policy Implications*, p. 22.

warfare or, in official parlance, Marxist terrorism. Pretoria repeatedly warned neighbouring states of severe retaliation if they allowed their territories to be used as springboards for terrorist attacks in South Africa.[139]

The last foreign policy guideline contained in Botha's 12-point plan committed South Africa to follow, 'as far as possible, a policy of neutrality in the conflict between the super powers, with priority given to Southern African interests'. Neutrality and a preoccupation with regional relations (i.e. the constellation idea), Botha explained, were two of five strategic options open to South Africa in its foreign relations.[140]

The first of these options, the traditional one of unreserved alignment with the West, Botha argued in 1979, should be reviewed because of the lack of reciprocity on the part of Western powers. Disenchantment with the West was not a novel sentiment in Pretoria, least of all for Botha who as Defence Minister had repeatedly chided Western nations about their attitudes to South Africa and who in 1976 had already raised the possibility of the Republic adopting a neutral position between East and West.[141] As head of government Botha continued on the same track, early on accusing the West of, among other things, breaking promises made to South Africa (an apparent reference to the 1975–6 Angolan war), pursuing a disastrous policy in Africa and Southern Africa, preventing South Africa from bringing salvation to economically ruined black states, denying the truth about the Republic's strategic significance, and contributing, in blissful ignorance or out of stupidity, to the incitement of terrorism against South Africa.[142] These were the symptoms of what Botha in 1980 diagnosed, in by now all too familiar terms, as a 'paralysis in the mind of the West to acknowledge the importance of South Africa'. He would, however, concede two healthy exceptions to this general state of Western affliction: Prime Minister Margaret Thatcher and President Ronald Reagan.[143] These were the two Western leaders who maintained the most conciliatory approach to South Africa during the Botha years. For his part, Botha realised that the United States and Britain were vital diplomatic shields against the growing international clamour for comprehensive and mandatory economic sanctions against South Africa. And South Africa also needed the services of the United States in particular to resolve the Namibia conflict. Botha's idea of neutrality, therefore, did not mean that the Republic could simply turn its back on the West. He was essentially

139. *Ibid.*, pp. 22, 23.
140. Ibid., p. 25.
141. Ibid., p. 27.
142. Quoted *ibid.*, p. 6.
143. Quoted *ibid.*

continuing South Africa's old love-hate relationship with the West.

An entirely different strategic option mentioned by Botha was an alliance with the communist bloc, but this was obviously more rhetoric than reality.

The remaining option called for an alliance with other so-called outcast countries, such as Israel and Taiwan. Botha's tenure was marked by an expansion in relations between South Africa and these two countries; he visited Taiwan in 1980 to reciprocate a visit to South Africa by his Taiwanese counterpart earlier that year. Botha was nonetheless realistic enough to acknowledge that 'the shifting fortunes and instability' – pariahhood is not a permanent condition – made an alliance with such states 'a hazardous enterprise'.[144]

Although the 12-point plan's references to foreign policy contained little that was new, it was nonetheless one of the most comprehensive and coherent statements of official thinking on South Africa's international relations since Malan's Africa Charter. Some of these views continued to inform South Africa's conduct in the region – its principal foreign policy arena – long after the notion of a 12-point plan had disappeared from the official political vocabulary. The total national strategy, of which the plan had been part and parcel, proved a far more enduring concept and guide to action. It is, then, in the context of an overall strategy to combat a total onslaught that South Africa's regional policy under Botha should be assessed.

Regional politics entered a new and particularly ominous era in 1980. In June the ANC staged spectacular acts of sabotage against SASOL plants, followed by equally devastating raids on other strategic targets over the next two years. Pretoria perceived a direct link between these attacks and the ANC's presence in neighbouring states. Botha reasoned that the only way to remove the ANC threat was to have the organisation's armed wing ejected from its sanctuaries in surrounding states. In due course this rather limited objective seems to have been overtaken by more ambitious goals, such as replacing hostile neighbouring governments by ones favourably disposed to South Africa. The means used ranged from direct military attacks on ANC targets in neighbouring states, through the manipulation of economic links and the sabotage of infrastructure, to military support for rebel movements. These actions have commonly been branded destabilisation, with Angola the principal target and Zimbabwe, Mozambique, Botswana, Lesotho and Zambia also on the list of aggrieved states. This was the era of a militant regional policy, which many observers took as evidence of the decisive influence of the military establishment in Botha's decision-making structures. There can be little doubt that the offensive regional strategy

144. Quoted *ibid.*, pp. 33, 34.

was fully consistent with Botha's own convictions and flowed logically from his earlier warnings mentioned above.[145]

The strategy of coercing neighbours into compliance paid handsome diplomatic dividends for South Africa when Angola in February 1984 signed a ceasefire agreement with the Republic, followed by the Nkomati Accord between South Africa and Mozambique the next month. (It was subsequently revealed that South Africa had secretly concluded a similar non-aggression agreement with Swaziland in 1982.) Fortunately for Botha, the Nkomati Accord came shortly after the white referendum that overwhelmingly approved the introduction of the new Tricameral Constitution. So by a happy coincidence of events, Botha could project himself abroad as a regional peacemaker and domestic reformer. A number of West European governments rewarded Botha for his dual initiatives by officially receiving him in mid-1984. This was his finest diplomatic hour.

The international acclaim and Botha's renewed confidence in South Africa's future[146] were both short-lived. The ceasefire agreement with Angola failed to hold and South Africa was drawn ever deeper into the Angolan war.[147] The Nkomati Accord likewise failed to meet the high hopes of the two signatories, who blamed each other for violating the agreement. With Botha's image as a regional peacemaker in tatters an even worse blow fell: the introduction of the new constitution in 1984 sparked off massive protest actions across the country. The foreign accolades Botha had received for his constitutional reforms were soon drowned by a new wave of international condemnation of Pretoria's suppression of the popular uprising. Such was the extent of the challenge to its authority that the government in July 1985 declared a partial state of emergency, followed by a countrywide emergency the following year. The unrest, as the official euphemism put it, caused death and destruction on a scale not previously witnessed in South Africa.

Thus South Africa was plunged into its third major domestic crisis, which displayed several features of the earlier Sharpeville and Soweto crises. Again the Republic's foreign relations were thrown into turmoil, but this time the consequences were more serious than ever before.

145. See Moorcraft, *African Nemesis*, pp. 161 ff. For a rather different but challenging interpretation of Botha's regional strategy, see J.M. Roherty, *State Security in South Africa: Civil-Military Relations under P.W. Botha* (Armonk, NY: M.E. Sharpe, 1992).

146. Barber and Barratt, *South Africa's Foreign Policy*, p. 299.

147. On South Africa's post-1976 military involvement in Angola, see Moorcraft, *African Nemesis*, pp. 183–249.; W. Steenkamp, *Borderstrike! South Africa into Angola* (Durban: Butterworths, 1983); W. Steenkamp, *South Africa's Border War 1966–1989* (Gibraltar: Ashanti, 1989); H.-R. Heitman, *War in Angola: The Final South African Phase* (Gibraltar: Ashanti, 1990); F. Bridgland, *The War for Africa* (Gibraltar: Ashanti, 1990).

Apart from voluntary withdrawals from South Africa by nervous foreign investors, governments and international organisations imposed a vast range of economic sanctions against the Republic. For South Africa the most damaging economic restrictions were those implemented by the European Community in 1985–6 and by the United States under its Comprehensive Anti-Apartheid Act of 1986, while the so-called bankers' sanctions of 1985 subjected the Republic to a global credit freeze.[148]

Early in this new crisis Botha had a highly publicised opportunity to defuse the situation. His address to a National Party meeting in Durban in August 1985 was widely expected to reveal bold new reform initiatives. Pretoria had indeed sent such signals to foreign capitals. In the event, Botha's speech failed to meet expectations; instead of being conciliatory, he was at his intransigent, bellicose worst, throwing down the gauntlet to both his domestic opponents and his foreign critics. This act of bad faith on Botha's part – as many foreign governments saw it – provided grist to the mill of the international sanctions lobby.

If Botha ever needed confirmation for his claims of a total onslaught, circumstances seemed to provide it in the second half of the 1980s. South Africa's enforced international isolation reached unprecedented heights. Its relations with most neighbouring states were severely strained, mainly over their support for the liberation movements or for sanctions against the Republic. Pretoria resumed its destabilising activities with a vengeance. In Namibia a final settlement still eluded the parties and the war dragged on. The same applied to Angola. Domestically, the revolutionary climate reached a new intensity after 1984. For Botha, events at home and abroad vindicated his insistence on the need for a total national strategy to ensure South Africa's survival.

Although by the end of 1985 enforced isolation had become the world community's most favoured means of promoting political change in South Africa, international mediation was not written off. In the first half of 1986 the Commonwealth's Eminent Persons Group (EPG) met Botha and several other South African leaders to help pave the way to all-party constitutional negotiations. There seemed to be cautious optimism all round that the EPG mediation could break the domestic political logjam. Yet Pretoria torpedoed the entire initiative when the South African Defence Force carried out simultaneous raids on Gaborone, Harare and Lusaka – three Commonwealth capitals – on the very day the mission was due to meet members of the cabinet. Having failed in their attempt to mediate, the Commonwealth nations decided on a further tightening of sanctions against South Africa.

148. For details, see Geldenhuys, *Isolated States*, pp. 333 ff.

A year later, South Africa's international prospects suddenly began to brighten because of moves initiated in a rather unlikely quarter. The Soviet Union, under President Mikhail Gorbachev, indicated its willingness to join with the United States in finding peaceful settlements to regional conflicts in the Third World.[149] For both South Africa and Angola, war-weary after years of fighting without victory in sight for any party, the new superpower accord provided a welcome prospect of ending the horrendously costly wars in Angola and Namibia. After several rounds of talks between South Africa, Angola and Cuba, with the United States acting as mediator, the three parties to the conflict signed a final peace agreement in New York in December 1988. It provided for the independence of Namibia under Security Council resolution 435, for the withdrawal of South African forces from the territory and from Angola, and for the departure of Cuban soldiers from Angola.

Botha, who had long adopted his own granite stance on Namibia and Angola, surprised friend and foe alike by agreeing to relinquish South African control and release Namibia into the uncertainties of independence under what seemed likely to be SWAPO rule. The new state of superpower relations evidently persuaded Botha that the Soviet Union was not bent on keeping Angola in the Marxist camp, let alone extending the Soviet sphere of influence to Namibia and ultimately South Africa. Botha was also aware of the tremendous financial burden that the war imposed on South Africa, particularly during a period of economic hardship at home. And there were growing signs of war fatigue among white South Africans, who witnessed an endless stream of casualties returning from a distant conflict.

By signing the Namibia peace accord South Africa took a giant step towards removing a major source of conflict with the international community, black African states in particular. But the ultimate proof of South Africa's *bona fides* on Namibia would be its final withdrawal from the territory upon the latter's achievement of independence. While Botha paved the way, it would be left to his successor to see the process of decolonisation through to the end. Yet the Namibia settlement could not reverse South Africa's international fortunes as long as apartheid remained. Despite Botha's political reforms, the white power structure remained solidly intact; South Africa's international isolation consequently showed no significant signs of being relaxed. When Botha left office in August 1989 South Africa could still be ranked as one of the most isolated countries in the world.[150]

149. See P. Nel, 'Old and New Thinking on the Banks of the Moskva and the Apies: Perceptions, Images and Ego Defences in Soviet–South African Relations', *International Affairs Bulletin*, vol. 15, no. 3, 1991, pp. 48–86.
150. For details, see Geldenhuys, *Isolated States*, pp. 91 ff.

F.W. de Klerk (1989–): The Ending of South Africa's Ostracism

F.W. de Klerk's presidency, which began in September 1989, has already earned its place in the history books as one that marked profound changes in both South Africa's domestic politics and foreign relations.

A vast improvement in the Republic's international position has been the direct consequence of major political reform on the home front. By abandoning apartheid and committing himself to the establishment of a non-racial democracy, De Klerk jettisoned the overriding aim of all previous South African governments' foreign policy, namely the preservation of a white-controlled state.[151] By so doing he has begun to remove the main factor that has bedevilled South Africa's foreign relations since 1945. The international community has, in turn, rewarded De Klerk's domestic initiatives by abolishing ostracising measures. As De Klerk put it, 'the normalisation of our foreign relations has proceeded as rapidly as normalisation inside South Africa.'[152]

De Klerk's first major step on the road to a post-apartheid and post-isolation South Africa was taken in February 1990 in his celebrated opening speech to parliament. He announced the lifting of the banning orders against the ANC, Pan-Africanist Congress (PAC) and South African Communist Party (SACP), and the freeing of their imprisoned leaders.[153] These decisions were designed to remove obstacles to negotiations on a new political order. The following year major pieces of apartheid legislation, such as the Land Acts of 1913 and 1936 and the Group Areas Act, were abolished.[154]

Through negotiation, De Klerk told parliament, his aim was to create a totally new and just constitutional dispensation for South Africa.[155] A new South African nation, he reasoned, should be built on the basic values and ideals of the world's successful democracies and economies, which he defined as justice, peace, prosperity, progress and participation.[156] To this end De Klerk in February 1991 unveiled his manifesto for the new South Africa. Two features of these statements bear emphasis. The first is the repeated reference to new, so as to underline the fundamental break De Klerk was trying to make with the old apartheid South Africa. Secondly, the President explained his domestic

151. See Barber and Barratt, *South Africa's Foreign Policy*, p. 1.
152. 'Statement by State President F.W. de Klerk to the World Economic Forum, Davos, Switzerland, 2 February 1992', p. 2. Copy by courtesy of the Department of Foreign Affairs, Pretoria.
153. *Hansard*, vol. 16, 2 February 1990, cols 12–16.
154. *Ibid.*, vol. 23, 1 February 1991, cols 8–13.
155. *Ibid.*, vol. 16, 2 February 1990, col. 2.
156. *Ibid.*, vol. 23, 1 February 1991, cols 4, 5.

policies in terms of universally accepted political norms, at last bringing South Africa into step with the spirit of the time.

In his major pronouncements on political reform, De Klerk paid a good deal of attention to South Africa's foreign relations, thereby acknowledging the relevance of the former to the latter. On assuming office in 1989, he asserted that the time had arrived for South Africa 'to restore its pride and to lift itself out of the doldrums of growing isolation, economic decline and increasing polarisation'.[157] In subsequent speeches, De Klerk expressed satisfaction 'that we have succeeded in breaking out of the dead end of isolation'[158] and that South Africa was returning to the international fold 'after almost forty years in the political wilderness.'[159] South Africa could look forward to 'resuming our rightful position in the wider comity of nations and restoring the many ties which were severed over the years'. He confidently predicted that if a new South African nation were built on the values and ideals mentioned in the manifesto for the new South Africa, 'we shall become part of the international community – finally, fully and with honour and dignity – and play a full role in the rest of Africa and the world.'[160]

South Africa's relations with other African states have been placed on a new footing by De Klerk's domestic reforms. In his February 1990 speech, the President declared that Southern Africa had an historical opportunity to set aside its conflicts and ideological differences and draw up a joint programme of reconstruction. He proclaimed that 'the season of violence is over' in the region and that the time for reconciliation had arrived – an obvious allusion to peace moves in Namibia, Angola and Mozambique, as well as to South Africa's internal peace process. Already at that early stage De Klerk noted 'unusually positive results' in South Africa's relations with other African states; in the preceding months, he had been received by the presidents of Mozambique, Zaïre, the Ivory Coast and Zambia.[161] The fact that De Klerk was a guest of honour at Namibia's independence celebrations in March 1990 is further evidence of South Africa's political rehabilitation in Africa.

These developments have for the first time placed South Africa within reach of meaningfully strengthening ties with fellow African countries. De Klerk's views on the road ahead are a mixture of old and new thinking, of modest and grandiose ideas. He has proposed regional talks 'to foster confidence, economic growth and security' along the lines of

157. Quoted in *ibid.*, vol. 17, 2 April 1990, col. 5384.
158. *Ibid.*, vol. 23, 1 February 1991, col. 21.
159. 'Statement by State President F.W. de Klerk to the World Economic Forum', p. 2.
160. *Hansard*, vol. 23, 1 February 1991, cols 5, 21.
161. *Ibid.*, vol. 16, 2 February 1990, col. 4.

the Conference on Security and Cooperation in Europe.[162] More substantially, the President envisages a Southern African economic association or community in which South Africa will play a constructuve role.[163] While De Klerk has said that South Africa, as the regional power, does not wish to dominate others in Southern Africa,[164] he shares the old vision of South Africa 'becoming an international role player because of the leadership role which history has carved out for us on a continent facing many problems'.[165] A related idea is that South Africa is the undisputed economic engine of Southern Africa, as De Klerk has put it, and could also act as the gateway for foreign interests wishing to tap trade and investment opportunities in the region.[166] This leads to what is probably the most ambitious idea that De Klerk has canvassed in the foreign policy realm: the division of Africa into four regional groupings, each formed around an engine of growth, to help pull the continent out of its economic woes. The regions are Southern Africa (with South Africa as its core), West Africa (Nigeria), East Africa (Kenya) and North Africa (Egypt). It can be no coincidence that De Klerk's foreign visits have taken him to Kenya and Nigeria and that South Africa has lately been cultivating links with Egypt.[167]

De Klerk's decision to unshackle the political process and to break with apartheid and white minority rule was materially influenced by events in world politics. The collapse of the Soviet empire removed the threat of communism, which had for so long dominated Pretoria's perceptual map of the world and served as a pretext for all kinds of excesses in both domestic politics and foreign relations. With the demise of communism in Eastern Europe and the Soviet Union there was no longer any credible communist threat against South Africa's external or internal security. This made it much easier – and less risky – for De Klerk to unban the ANC and its SACP ally: their perceived patron state, the Soviet Union, was no longer in the business of exporting revolution to distant regions.[168]

Another external factor that evidently weighed with De Klerk in embarking on a new domestic course was sanctions. He clearly regarded

162. 'Statement by State President F.W. de Klerk to the South African Institute of International Affairs, Johannesburg, 19 November 1991', p. 5. Copy by courtesy of the Department of Foreign Affairs, Pretoria.
163. *Ibid.*, p. 4.
164. *Beeld*, 29 April 1992.
165. Interview with F.W. de Klerk in *Leadership South Africa*, vol. 9, no. 6, 1990, p. 38.
166. F.W. de Klerk, *Partnership* (A Leadership SA publication), September 1992, p. 12.
167. See *The Star*, 9 April 1992; *Sunday Times* (Johannesburg), 12 April 1992.
168. See F.W. de Klerk in *Hansard*, vol. 23, 1 February 1991, cols 20, 21; vol. 16, 2 February 1990, col. 3.

the ending of South Africa's ostracism as a major achievement, by implication conceding that international sanctions had been a matter of much concern to Pretoria. The ruling National Party for the first time openly acknowledged the severe damage that sanctions had caused the South African economy when the party campaigned for a 'yes' vote in the March 1992 referendum on constitutional negotiations. Party propaganda warned *ad nauseam* that a 'no' vote would bring back sanctions, with terrible and unaffordable consequences for South Africa.[169] It therefore seems reasonable to conclude that the material deprivations of sanctions contributed to De Klerk's decision to abandon apartheid and thereby restore the Republic's sorely needed foreign economic relations.

South Africa's gradual return to the international fold since De Klerk's watershed announcements of February 1990 can readily be charted. One indicator is the expansion of the country's official representation abroad. In 1989 the Republic had full diplomatic relations with only 25 states; at the time of writing the figure is 35. The additions include Morocco, Hungary, Japan, Russia and Denmark, while lesser forms of South African representation have recently been established in Angola, Kenya, Madagascar, Zambia, Mauritius, Togo, Turkey and Bulgaria, among others. In all, South Africa is officially represented in 51 states (homeland states excluded). And then there are De Klerk's visits abroad, which already far exceed those undertaken by all his predecessors since 1948. Included in his destinations have been Namibia, Morocco, Qatar, Singapore, Japan, Russia, the United States and a host of European countries. In the economic sphere, reference can be made to the lifting of EC sanctions in 1990–91 and the repeal of the US Comprehensive Anti-Apartheid Act in 1991, examples followed by numerous other important trading partners of South Africa. Foreign restrictions on socio-cultural interaction with South Africa have likewise been dropped, notably the international sports boycott, bans on visits by artists and entertainers to and from the Republic, and prohibitions on air links.[170]

Given this vastly improved international climate, South Africa has for the first time since 1948 begun to dispose of its deeply ingrained suspicions of the outside world. The old enemy images (attached not only to communists but also to the West, the UN, the OAU and the Commonwealth, among others) are giving way to notions that the world community is on the side of Pretoria. This refers specifically to support for the De Klerk government's commitment to negotiate a new consti-

169. See, for example, NP referendum advertisements in *Sunday Times* (Johannesburg), 1 March 1992; *The Star*, 4 March 1992; *Beeld*, 16 March 1992.
170. D. Geldenhuys, 'South Africa: From Isolation to Reintegration', *Strategic Review for Southern Africa*, vol. 13, no. 1, May 1991, pp. 62–95.

tutional arrangement based on Western values. Only under such conditions could the De Klerk government have welcomed the despatch to South Africa of scores of foreign missions – including the Vance mission sent by the UN Security Council in July 1992 – to monitor the political violence in South Africa. But the most dramatic manifestation of Pretoria's new views of the world is to be found in the government's appeal, in September 1992, to the UN Secretary-General to intervene to get the stalled negotiation process back on track.[171] Previous international attempts to mediate in the South African conflict were imposed from outside and not particularly welcomed by South African governments, which have always jealously protected national sovereignty and guarded against external interference in the country's domestic affairs. Clearly, De Klerk has made a major concession on these hallowed principles of South African foreign policy.

A final feature of De Klerk's handling of foreign relations that calls for attention is the decision-making bodies he uses. Shortly after taking office De Klerk began restructuring Botha's vast national security management system. Although the SSC has been retained with its statutory function and composition, it has lost the pre-eminence it enjoyed under Botha. The political office-bearers on the Council now form a separate Cabinet Committee for Security Affairs and only this committee – not the full SSC, which also includes top officials – may take actual decisions. Like the other three cabinet committees, that for security affairs must as a rule submit its decisions to cabinet for final approval. The full cabinet has thus been restored to the highest policy-making and coordinating body in government.[172] And since the Republic no longer faces anything approximating a total onslaught from abroad, the security imprint on its foreign policy has disappeared. South African foreign policy is no longer part and parcel of a total national strategy, a notion that has itself vanished from the official vocabulary. Foreign Minister Pik Botha's status as the President's principal advisor on foreign affairs and that of the diplomatic corps as the main instrument of South African foreign policy have been restored. Yet Botha (whose instinct for political survival makes him the world's longest-serving foreign minister, in office since 1977) finds his role circumscribed by De Klerk's frequent engagement in personal diplomacy.

171. *Beeld*, 11 September 1992.
172. H. Kotzé and D. Geldenhuys, 'Damascus Road', *Leadership South Africa*, vol. 9, no. 6, 1990, pp. 23, 24.

Tomorrow's Leaders – Yesterday's Issues?

South Africa's foreign relations came full circle between 1945 and 1992.

The parting of the ways between South Africa and the international community, which began with the establishment of the UN, was accentuated under Smuts' Nationalist successors. Their systematic application of apartheid was variously regarded as an affront to human dignity and a crime against humanity. From early on the community of nations resolved to punish South Africa for these transgressions by forcing it into isolation. But for South African leaders, from Malan to Botha, this very internal order that offended and outraged the world was considered a *sine qua non* for white survival at home. South African foreign policy was inevitably geared to the preservation of the domestic value system. Any kind of compromise between South Africa and the outside world on apartheid was effectively impossible.

Under F.W. de Klerk all that has changed. His domestic reforms have liberated the political process and have freed South African foreign policy of the need to defend the indefensible. The ending of apartheid has meant the end of decades of rising isolation and the beginning of South Africa's journey back to international respectability and participation. De Klerk is in a way returning South Africa to where it stood at the end of the Second World War, before the advent of a new international morality began alienating the country from the rest of the world.

While De Klerk has brought the old order to an end, he is unlikely to lead the new post-apartheid and post-isolation South Africa. That will be left to South Africa's first black president. In that sense De Klerk's tenure – probably the last by a white incumbent – represents more of a transitional phase than a new beginning on both the domestic and foreign policy fronts. His successors are bound to pursue domestic and foreign policies that are intended to emphasise the break with the past.

Like earlier Nationalist leaders, a new South Africa's rulers will experience severe constraints in translating their aspirational interests into operational ones; the king invariably encounters a more complex world than that envisaged by the crown prince. In the realm of foreign relations, tomorrow's leaders may have to contend with a new kind of isolation: not the ostracism of the apartheid era, but isolation caused by South Africa's international insignificance and major powers' indifference to the plight of yet another black African state. Whereas successive Nationalist leaders from Malan to Botha desired to be left alone by the outside world, a new government's leaders may instead deplore being disregarded by the powers of consequence. If South Africa's future lot should indeed be benign neglect from abroad instead of coercive interference, its rulers may still learn from the Nationalists how a small state can contend with international adversity.

8

THE FUTURE OF THE PRESIDENCY

Robert Schrire and David Welsh

During the first decade of the twentieth century, when whites in South Africa were deciding the constitutional framework for the emerging state, constitutional theorising was not particularly sophisticated. The choice at that time was viewed as one between federalism with a weak central government or a Westminster-type centralised system with a powerful sovereign parliament and cabinet. It was that which was chosen – in part at least because whites believed that a strong central government would be most effective in handling the 'native problem'. Some nodding obeisance to federalism was included in the constitution, in the form of provincial councils, but these were unable to conceal the essentially unitary character of the state.[1]

That choice produced the current political system which, until recently, served white political interests well. Political power was used to create a European fragment in an African context. Whites received the benefits of a strong government devoted to securing their economic, cultural and political interests. Governments sought to secure white interests long before the apartheid slogan was coined, and white leaders continue to seek to preserve the interests of their racial constituency now that apartheid is no longer formally in force. Since 1948, six middle-aged white male Afrikaner leaders have controlled the state, despite the reality that fewer than 5 per cent of the total population is from that segment of society.

However, now that it is widely accepted that black participation in the government and politics of South Africa is inevitable, many whites are fearful that the centralised state that served their interests so well for so long may in fact constitute a major threat to their vital interests. Elements such as parliamentary sovereignty, a first-past-the-post electoral system and centralised administration, which enabled whites to create an imperial presidency and to build up the repressive capability of the state, based upon unrestricted power and concealed by a web of statutory secrecy, could be used against them if a new government comes under the control of hostile groups. The ruling National Party

---

1. David Welsh, 'Federalism and the Problem of South Africa', in Murray Forsyth (ed.), *Federalism and Nationalism* (Leicester University Press, 1989), pp. 252–60.

(NP) now advocates maximum devolution of power in a federal system and a 'collective presidency' in which the major parties will be represented.

Black South Africans, for so long excluded from the political kingdom, initially sought to participate in the polity on the same basis as whites and demanded full equality within the existing state structures. It was perfectly reasonable that blacks, as the victims of the South African state, should demand their turn as the new beneficiaries. Thus after 1960, when black politics was largely prevented from operating legally in South Africa, political formations such as the African National Congress (ANC) and later the United Democratic Front tended to demand full participation in a unitary Westminster-type polity.

During most of the period covered by this book, racial issues dominated the political agenda. Politics revolved around black demands for political power and white responses of repression and cooption. Most observers confidently anticipated an intensification of this process, with an ultimate black victory at the cost of the remaining democratic elements of the polity. Indeed, whites themselves contributed to the erosion of many democratic principles and practices as an inevitable cost of the battle to protect white domination.

The rise to power of F.W. de Klerk in 1989 and his dramatic and unexpected reversal of policy may have changed this gloomy scenario. Since 1990, De Klerk has dedicated his government to the search for a negotiated constitutional settlement based upon 'power sharing'. Whether this process is successful or not, there can be no doubt that the nature of the South African presidency will change dramatically and irrevocably.

During early 1992, negotiations took place between the NP-controlled government, the ANC and 17 other political groupings to resolve the obstacles to a new constitution. Although these negotiations, known as the Convention for a Democratic South Africa (CODESA) broke down later that year, the recognition that none of the political forces in South Africa is powerful enough to impose a settlement unilaterally is perhaps the only guarantee that the process will continue as long as the prospect for a successful conclusion exists. Since the process of negotiation is not that between a defeated regime and a victorious challenger, a settlement will almost certainly have to rest upon a series of compromises.

What type of constitution is likely to emerge and what will the presidency look like? Much will depend upon the nature of a compromise devised by the two most important groups at the negotiations, i.e. the NP and the ANC.

In the analysis below, we have focused on the broad principles of the major players while recognising that the details and, indeed, even some of the principles may be changed in the course of the negotiating process.

The National Party

The NP has undergone a veritable paradigmatic revolution since 1989. It accepts that South Africa is one nation and has thereby repudiated its former policy of ethnic partition. It also accepts that the new polity must be non-racial, democratic and constitutional.

At the same time it interprets these concepts in ways which favour its interests. It continues to define the South African 'nation' as one made up of ethnic minorities, but it no longer insists that these minorities are to be statutorily defined, or that they should be the building blocks of a new constitution. Accordingly, the NP now favours a non-majoritarian form of government. 'Power-sharing', as defined by the government, will essentially ensure that all the major political factions with 'substantial' support should form part of both the legislature and the executive.

This can be achieved through the adoption of the principle of proportionality, both in the election of the legislature and in the composition of the executive. The legislature would be bicameral, with a lower house elected by all the voters on the basis of proportional representation, and the upper house based upon some form of regional representation. This system would not necessarily be out of step with existing systems of representation, such as those of the United States, Germany or Switzerland.

The NP's proposals for the restructuring of the executive are more controversial. The national cabinet would be based upon an enforced or statutory coalition between the largest parties represented in the legislature, even if one party had a solid majority of legislative supporters there. This would thus entail an over-representation of minority parties and an under-representation of a possible majority group.

In addition, executive power would be limited. The present powerful presidency would be replaced by a more constrained and diffused executive structure. It would operate on the principle of consensus within the governing group. One institutional possibility that embodies this principle would be the Swiss model, where the executive is collegial, with a rotating presidency. Swiss political institutions that operate on the principle of 'amicable agreement' rather than majority rule have been an important element in fostering the stability of a democratic polity in spite of potentially disruptive linguistic and religious cleavages. The system is much admired by De Klerk and his advisors. Another possibility would be to elect the President from the lower house and a Premier from the upper house with the condition that both offices may not be filled by candidates from the same political party.

Two additional controls over central executive power are proposed by the NP. First is the insistence on a rigid constitution containing such checks and balances as a bill of rights covering key interests such as property rights, cultural interests and civil liberties enforceable by the supreme court, based possibly upon the German Constitutional Court model. Judicial review would thus be a central characteristic of the legislative process.

Secondly, the system proposed by the NP would be founded squarely upon federal principles. Power would be devolved to regional and local government authorities and this would be enshrined in the constitution. The boundaries of these geographical units, their powers, and their ability to raise their own financial resources and extract resources would be entrenched.

Thus the thrust of the NP proposals is towards more limited government. It is no coincidence that the creators of the executive state are now the strongest advocates of its dissolution; or that a party which achieved power on the basis of ethnic exclusivity is now the strongest advocate of power sharing and multiracial coalition government. Power is to be separated, shared and controlled.

The ANC

The ANC, like the NP, does not have a fully detailed constitutional blueprint, but it has produced several constitutional documents outlining its basic principles, from which it is possible to discern its fundamental position on most key issues. Nelson Mandela, the ANC's leader, has repeatedly said that he favours 'an ordinary democracy' and has been at pains to draw a distinction between 'majority rule', which he demands, and 'black majority rule', which he rejects. In general, ANC thinking tends to favour a traditional Western-style majoritarian democratic model. It supports a South Africa which includes the homelands and is centralised in structure, though with 'strong and effective' local and regional government. Although these local authorities will have important functions to perform, they will remain subordinate to the central government and will exercise only delegated powers. The state, in other words, will be unitary, though with federal characteristics.

Parliament will be elected on the basis of universal adult franchise and proportional representation. A National Assembly will serve as the lower house and will be elected on a straightforward proportional representation basis. It will be charged with the task of drawing up legislation. The upper house, to be called the Senate, will be elected on a basis which gives smaller regions over-representation. It will be of lesser importance than the National Assembly, but will have the power to delay the adoption of legislation and will also act as guardian of the constitution. The implicit model of these legislative proposals appears to be a hybrid of the British Westminster system and the American Senate, with the innovation of proportional representation.

The proposals are, perhaps deliberately, somewhat vague about the nature of a future executive authority. The ANC supports the presidential form of government with a Prime Minister and cabinet, perhaps inspired by the French model. In terms of recent refinements to policy the ANC has opted to have the President elected by parliament. It also advocates a justiciable bill of rights, an independent judiciary and an ombudsman.

The Politics of Constitution-Making

As recently as early 1990, most observers would have questioned even the possibility of an agreement on a new constitution between the ANC and the NP. The NP seemed to be wedded to some form of group rights with an ethnic/colour component and a 'power-sharing' arrangement, which in practice entailed a white veto. The ANC seemed wedded to a simple majoritarian system based largely upon Western models of democracy.

The dynamics of change unleashed by De Klerk in February 1990 have produced frequent changes in the 'bottom line' of most of the key political groupings. Both the ANC and the NP now agree that the electoral system must be based upon a national legislature elected on a colour-blind common voters' roll.

The dynamics of the negotiations which have already taken place have made it possible to visualise agreement on the following important issues:[2]

– a bicameral legislature with a lower chamber elected through proportional representation and an upper chamber elected on some form of regional basis;
– the president to be chosen by the legislature, not elected directly;
– the executive cabinet, at least for an interim period, to be constituted on a proportional basis so that all the major parties in the legislature will have a voice in national government;
– decentralisation of government in order to give significant powers to the regions;
– an independent judiciary and an entrenched bill of rights that will protect individual rights – and thereby many 'group rights' such as language and culture; and
– all of the homelands reincorporated as regions of South Africa.

The contentious issue of strong versus weak government is directly related to the issue of majoritarian versus power-sharing government. The ANC, as the presumed voice of the African majority, believes that

2. R. Schrire, *Adapt or Die: The End of White Politics in South Africa* (New York and London: Ford Foundation, 1992).

it would be a major beneficiary of a majoritarian system. It therefore advocates such a system in a modified form. The NP, as the historical home of only white and especially Afrikaner voters, is less confident of its ability to remain a key player in a majoritarian polity. It therefore demands a guarantee that the rules of the game will give it political influence which the outcome of majoritarian democracy might not. Consistently the NP has sought to reassure its constituency that it will not capitulate. Equally consistently it has demanded a constitution that will make it impossible for minorities to be marginalised and, hence, vulnerable to domination by the majority.

Both the ANC and the NP, in formulating their constitutional proposals, are greatly influenced by their presumed interests. Although both appeal to universal normative values – the ANC to non-racialism and democratic values, the NP to the rights of minorities – both are largely motivated by calculations of the impact of various constitutional models on their power positions.

Donald Horowitz, a noted political theorist, captures the larger issues involved as follows:

> . . . the need for institutions that will disperse power so as to avoid destructive conflict at the center or . . . the need for institutions that will concentrate power sufficiently to cope with the country's urgent problems of inequality. Is it possible to have both – to have enough dispersion to avoid mutually exclusive outcomes and enough concentration to devise and implement effective policies to ameliorate discontent?[3]

The already substantial narrowing of the gap between the ANC and the NP on these issues, while encouraging, does not as yet constitute a political consensus. Indeed, thus far the negotiating dynamic at CODESA, and elsewhere, has tended to seek areas of agreement rather than to grapple directly with tough issues of principle. A considerable gap still exists between the majoritarian/centralist position of the ANC and the power-sharing federalist position of the NP.

In May 1992 the CODESA process stalled and, amidst mounting violence between rival black organisations, hostility between the government and the ANC increased, and for nearly five months the formal negotiating process was broken off. Working Group Two of CODESA had failed to reach 'sufficient consensus' on the composition and procedures of a constitution-making body. Ostensibly the disagreement centred on a dispute between the government and the ANC over what percentage votes a constitution-making body should require for the adoption of clauses in the draft constitution. In reality the dispute

---

3. Donald L. Horowitz, *A Democratic South Africa?* (Cape Town: Oxford University Press, 1991).

stemmed from the fundamental disagreement over the majoritarian/ power-sharing positions mentioned above.

The ANC believed that the NP government, loth to lose power, was intent on inserting veto devices into the constitution-making body and the final constitution so that a new and popularly elected government, based upon a majority vote, would be thwarted in its attempt to govern effectively. The government, on the other hand, accused the ANC of wanting total power in a strongly centralised state, so that minority parties would be shut out of power more or less permanently.[4]

In its deliberations on general constitutional principles, Working Group Two did not get around to discussing the nature of a future presidency. Indeed, the ANC, which regarded CODESA purely as a preliminary clearing house, firmly declined to debate institutional details of a future constitution, insisting that these could be discussed only by an elected constituent assembly whose task it would be to draft the new constitution. There were, however, vigorous debates about the NP government's proposal for an 'enforced coalition', whose components have been mentioned above. The ANC and its allies pointed out, legitimately, that the track record of such coalitions was exceedingly poor; no less legitimately the government's negotiators pointed out that while democratic institutions were difficult to sustain in deeply divided societies, in those cases where they had survived a key, if not *the* key, instrument had been the broad-based coalition which ensured that no minority party was permanently marginalised – as happened to Catholic parties in the extreme case of the Northern Ireland parliament.

Resolution of this issue is fundamental to South Africa reaching a democratic settlement. As we have noted in this chapter, and as the contents of this book confirm, the NP itself has been the architect and builder of an all-powerful centralised state. Its record hardly provides a credible moral base for its proposals to disperse power and protect minorities. Nevertheless it would be an error to suppose that the NP's concerns derive entirely from the malign residue of apartheid or that, more generally, minorities do not have legitimate fears of an overbearing and potentially oppressive majority.

Apart from any concern to ensure that a future South African democracy is not subverted by the tyranny of the majority, there are compelling reasons why the likely future majority party, the ANC, should wish neither to harass nor to persecute its erstwhile oppressors. Thanks in no small part to its having jealously preserved a substantial monopoly of managerial, technological and professional skills, the relative security and contentment of the white minority will be an

4. David Welsh, 'Turning Point', *Towards Democracy* (journal of the Institute for Multi-Party Democracy), vol. 1, 3rd quarter, 1992.

indispensable requirement for a growing economy in the 'New South Africa'. The ANC recognises this constraint, not least because of its awareness that it may shortly have an impatient and expectant constituency to satisfy. Generous treatment of minorities, including encouraging parties rooted in minority segments to become part of a coalition 'government of national unity', is an approach favoured by Nelson Mandela, if only as an interim measure (or so-called sunset clause). It is very likely that a settlement will be based on this principle.

By early 1993 the negotiating process appeared to be on track once again, and hopes were being entertained that an interim power-sharing government could be installed during the ensuing year. One may speculate that the ANC's implacable opposition to constitutionally required coalition in general, and to the N.P.'s proposed 'collective presidency' in particular, will be maintained. The NP, however, is likely to prove no less intransigent in refusing to back away from at least some form of power-sharing. Recent indications have suggested that it is increasingly pinning its hopes of minority protection on federalism.

Perhaps the most optimistic prediction, as far as the majoritarian/power-sharing issue is concerned, is the possibility of a pact providing for a period (ten, 15 years?) of coalition rule by the principal parties. Such a pact would obviously not be part of the constitution, so that the likelihood of its acceptance by the parties will be dependent on building up some minimal degree of trust – which in early 1993 looked like a tall order.

As we have indicated, the institutional details of a future presidency remain shrouded in uncertainty. Our speculation, however, is that ultimately the presidency is more likely to revert to the ceremonial role that it possessed before 1983 than to be a powerful executive resembling that of the United States, or to be part of a system of *cohabitation* as in France. Whatever the presidency's lack of power may be, however, it is likely to be a symbolically important office, which in turn makes adoption of the relatively anonymous (and colourless) Swiss presidency improbable.

In a spirited scholarly exchange Juan J. Linz and Donald Horowitz have debated the rival merits of parliamentary and presidential systems[5]. Linz's arguments for favouring parliamentary systems rest upon the proposition that they are more conducive to stability because they cope with and absorb political crises more easily. Other scholars favour parliamentary systems for deeply divided societies because they lend themselves more easily to power-sharing, collegial executive govern-

5. Juan J. Linz, 'The Perils of Presidentialism', *Journal of Democracy*, no. 1, 1990; Donald L. Horowitz, 'Comparing Democratic Systems', *Journal of Democracy*, no. 4, 1990.

ment, whereas presidentialism is inherently a zero-sum institution since only a single person can be the incumbent.

Horowitz challenges these views, disputing in particular the belief that the zero-sum, winner-take-all characteristic imputed to it is a structural feature of presidentialism. He reinforces his argument by referring to the Nigerian (Second Republic) and Sri Lankan presidencies, where special rules were adopted to ensure that the winner of presidential elections would require a broad base of support across ethnic lines. In Nigeria, for example, the winning candidate needed at least 25 per cent of the votes in two-thirds of the 19 states. The successful candidate, in other words, could not win by garnering support from just one large ethnic group.

In his prescriptions for South Africa Horowitz advocates a similar system, parallel with his proposals for 'vote-pooling' as a means of mitigating severe inter-ethnic hostility. Regarding a possible South African presidency, he writes:

There is no reason to doubt that a South African president, elected directly by the people on the basis of a vote-pooling formula, would become a barrier to racial or ethnic exclusivity and that the office would become a focal point for intergroup conciliation and compromise. Members of all groups would have reason to claim a piece of the presidency if they helped elect the president.[6]

For all the undoubted attractions of Horowitz's proposals, the weight of the empirical evidence nevertheless supports the contention that parliamentary systems are more conducive to stability than presidential systems. Moreover, South Africa's tradition, in spite of the changes introduced in 1983, remains a parliamentary one, and none of the major political actors seems inclined to dispense with the principle of an executive that is responsible to parliament.

One final conclusion can be reached with confidence. Whatever the precise nature of South Africa's future constitutional system, it will not be a continuation of the past pattern of minority control and centralised power. Tragically, however, that legacy will weigh heavily upon the future and will influence, for better and worse, the exercise of executive power.

6. Horowitz, *A Democratic South Africa?*, p. 210.

A CHRONOLOGY OF HISTORICAL
DEVELOPMENTS UNDER SOUTH AFRICA'S
PRIME MINISTERS/PRESIDENTS SINCE 1948

Daniel François Malan (1948-1954)

Rising to the premiership with the National Party's unexpected victory in 1948, D.F. Malan began immediately to codify and extend South Africa's traditional racial segregation. During Malan's tenure, parliament passed the Prohibition of Mixed Marriages Act (1949), the Population Registration Act (1950), the Group Areas Act (1950), the Bantu Authorities Act (1951) and the Separate Amenities Act (1953) – the latter overriding judicial precedent which called for 'separate but equal' facilities for all race groups. Catholic and Protestant mission schools were brought under government control in order to enforce segregation further. Malan's government reacted to early opponents of apartheid with the Suppression of Communism Act of 1950 and the Public Safety Act of 1953. During the popular defiance campaign of 1952, organised by the ANC and allied groups, the state imprisoned 8,500 protestors. Through these arrests and other repressive measures, Malan's government effectively undermined calls from the ANC and others for non-violent, passive resistance. He retired from his office and politics in 1954 at the age of 80.

Johannes Gerhardus Strijdom (1954–1958)

Strijdom, selected by his party colleagues as the successor to Malan, held office during a period of increasing mobilisation among anti-apartheid groups. In 1955 the ANC rejected the government's policy of separate education through a widespread school boycott and in 1956, with its allies, endorsed the Freedom Charter. In the same year the South African Congress of Trade Unions was born, linking the African and multiracial trade unions to the ANC. Several white women protesting against the government's attempts to strike coloureds from the common voters' roll – especially because of the violation of constitutionalism this move represented – began silent demonstrations outside parliament and formed the Black Sash, so named for the garment they wore to mark the death of the constitution. However, in 1956 the Nationalists succeeded in putting coloureds on a separate voters' roll to elect four white 'representatives' to parliament; they extended the pass laws to include African women (against which 20,000 women of all races protested in a Pretoria march); and they outlawed multiracial trade unions, forcing those in existence to separate along racial lines. To increase state control, the government passed the Riotous Assemblies Act, which stipulated that a permit was required for meetings of more than 12 persons. Protests continued, notably a bus boycott in Johannesburg, which lasted three months and succeeded in the rescinding of a fare increase, and marches in Cape Town protesting at a bill barring blacks from attending white church services. Strijdom's tenure ended with his death, caused by a blood disease, in 1958.

Dr Hendrik Frensch Verwoerd (1958–1966)

Moving into leadership from his position as Minister of Native Affairs, Verwoerd was already deeply involved in apartheid legislation. In 1959, he established a further major pillar of the policy – the African homelands – through the Promotion of Bantu Self-Government Act, which removed all representation of blacks (even through white representatives) from parliament and prepared the way for Verwoerd's vision of a 'commonwealth' of Southern Africa, with independent black states which would be politically separate but economically entwined with a purely white South Africa. Segregation was extended to higher education. A rift in the ANC led to the formation of the Pan-Africanist Congress (PAC), which stressed 'Africanism'. Verwoerd banned both organisations in the aftermath of mass demonstrations against the pass laws at Sharpeville on 21 March 1960, during which police shot and killed 69 blacks. Later that year, in a surprise move, Verwoerd called and won a white referendum on the republican issue. In 1961 South Africa became a republic and withdrew, under pressure, from the British Commonwealth. The next three years saw increased tension: the ANC abandoned its policy of non-violence and began a campaign of sabotage through its military wing, *Umkhonto we Sizwe* (Spear of the Nation); the Sabotage Act of 1962, in reaction to increased violence, made provision for long detentions without trial; the '90-Day Act' suspended much of the legal right to *habeas corpus*; and in 1964 eight *Umkhonto we Sizwe* members, including Nelson Mandela, Walter Sisulu, and Govan Mbeki, were arrested and sentenced to life imprisonment. In September 1966, Verwoerd was assassinated by a deranged messenger on the floor of parliament.

Balthazar John Vorster (1966–1978)

B.J. Vorster moved into Verwoerd's place from his post as Minister of Justice. Unrest and the communist threat were high on his agenda and in 1967 his government enacted the Terrorism Act, extending the definition of communism to cover any act or process which worked against the state and providing for indefinite detention without trial. Multiracial political parties were outlawed in 1968, and white parliamentary representation of coloureds ended. Black consciousness leader Steve Biko formed the South African Students' Organisation in the same year. In 1973, while trade union membership was growing through a series of strikes by black labour, Steve Biko and seven other black consciousness leaders were banned. Biko died in detention in 1977. Vorster received several setbacks in the interim: a *coup* in Portugal in 1974 opened the way for Marxist–Leninist regimes in Angola and Mozambique; the United Nations formally suspended the credentials of the South African delegation in 1974 (eight years after its ineffective termination of South Africa's mandate to administer South West Africa/Namibia) and invited the ANC and the PAC to sit in the UN as observers. Police firing into a mass student protest in Soweto against inferior education on 16 June 1976 led to nationwide protests and an estimated 1,000 killed. Vorster clamped down quickly through the broadened governmental powers of the Internal Security Act of 1976. The homelands policy remained on track, however, and Transkei gained independence in 1976 (followed by Bophuthatswana, Venda and Ciskei in 1977, 1979 and 1981, respectively). Vorster was forced to resign in the wake of the Information Scandal of 1978 which involved gross misappropriation of government funds.

Pieter Willem Botha (1978–1989)

Botha, in his capacity as Minister of Defence, was relatively untouched by the Information Scandal and took advantage of party turmoil to gain the premiership. Immediately he was faced with UN resolution 435 calling for UN-supervised democratic elections to bring independent government to Namibia. In South Africa, 1979 saw the passage of the Industrial Relations Act, officially recognising African trade unions and paving the way for their substantive progress, and the formation of AZAPO (the Azanian People's Organisation), a new black consciousness organisation. In 1980 students began their prolonged and widely supported school boycott. In the same year, Zimbabwe gained independence, the ANC and KwaZulu chief minister Gatsha Buthelezi split publicly, and nationwide protests over poor economic conditions and inferior education for blacks fomented white fears of unrest. A group of MPs led by NP member Andries Treunicht split in 1982 to form the

Conservative Party (CP). Meanwhile the ANC had renewed its sabotage campaign with bomb attacks against a SASOL plant (1980) and the Koeberg nuclear power plant (1982); it also planted a car bomb in Pretoria in 1983 which killed 19 passers by. The government retaliated with South African Defence Force (SADF) air attacks on alleged ANC installations in Mozambique. Also in 1983, a whites' only referendum approved a new constitution proposing a racially delineated tricameral parliament, which led to even greater and widespread unrest throughout the country.

In 1984, South Africa and Mozambique signed the Nkomati Accord to end Pretoria's funding for rebel forces in Mozambique (though funding apparently continued for some time). In 1985 police arrested several leaders of the United Democratic Front (UDF), which had been lauched in 1983 and was widely perceived as a front for the ANC. Six of these people were charged with treason. By 20 July of that year, the President (as he was now termed under the new constitution) declared a selective state of emergency (SOE) over areas of unrest in the wake of 19 deaths by police fire at a funeral in Langa, and in August Botha rejected calls for fundamental change from home and abroad in his 'Rubicon speech'. International creditors subsequently refused to rene-gotiate overdue loans and South Africa plunged into financial crisis. White business and media representatives flew from South Africa to meet with members of the ANC in Zambia for the first time shortly thereafter.

The year 1985 also saw African trade unionists join together to form the Congress of South African Trade Unions (COSATU) and govern-ment media restrictions imposed in SOE areas. Tensions continued to mount in the following year: The leader of the Progressive Federal Party (PFP), Frederick van Zyl Slabbert, resigned from white politics; the SADF attacked alleged ANC bases in Botswana, Zambia and Zim-babwe, which proved the final straw for the Commonwealth's Eminent Persons Group which subsequently washed its hands of the South African government; the SOE, which had been lifted in March, was reimposed nationwide in June; and in October the United States Congress passed the Comprehensive Anti-Apartheid Act (including far-reaching sanctions) over a presidential veto. In December Botha imposed near total censorship over any reporting of political protest. In 1987, as the CP took over from the PFP as the official opposition in parliament, Van Zyl Slabbert organised a delegation of 60 white South Africans to meet ANC representatives in Dakar; the National Union of Mineworkers held a three-week strike to underline black economic power; and violence in Natal began to escalate dramatically as the Zulu cultural/political organisation Inkatha (which had launched a rival trade union to COSATU) gained influence. In the 'independent' homeland of

Transkei, Major General Bantu Holomisa led a successful coup to oust the Prime Minister and named himself as the successor.

In 1988, Botha clamped down even further against anti-apartheid organisations, whose leaders had largely been removed from the scene through detentions under the SOE. He in effect banned 17 such groups, including the UDF, and restricted COSATU to non-political activity. From Lusaka, the ANC issued widely publicised constitutional guidelines for a democratic South Africa. Negotiations over the future of Namibia, mediated by the United States and involving Angola, Cuba and South Africa (with the Soviet Union in observance), began in earnest, culminating in an accord providing for the withdrawal of all Cuban troops from Angola and for the implementation of UN resolution 435 for Namibia's independence. Early in 1989, Botha was forced to resign the NP leadership after suffering a stroke. Six months later he resigned the presidency when it became clear he had lost the support of the party to its new leader, F.W. de Klerk.

Frederick Willem de Klerk (1989–)

President De Klerk began careful experiments in liberalisation soon after taking office. With the blessing of the Organisation for African Unity given to ANC/South African government negotiations in the Harare Declaration shortly after his tenure began, he allowed mass anti-apartheid demonstrations in several cities around the country, which were carried out peacefully with little police interference. He released Walter Sisulu and seven other long-term political prisoners, and desegregated all public beaches. Accelerating the process dramatically with his first address to open parliament on 2 February 1990, De Klerk proceeded to unban the ANC, the South African Communist Party and the PAC; to lift restrictions on the UDF and COSATU as well as 31 other organisations; and to promise to release political prisoners and suspend the death penalty. On 11 February he released Nelson Mandela after 27 years in prison, which paved the way for the first set of formal talks between the ANC (of which Mandela became the effective leader in South Africa) and the government. The Groote Schuur Minute calling for negotiations towards a peaceful settlement resulted, signed by both Mandela and De Klerk. After Mandela's extensive international tour, a second formal meeting between the ANC and government produced the Pretoria Minute, in which the ANC agreed to cease its armed struggle against the state and the government agreed to release remaining political prisoners and make provision for the safe return of South African exiles. In the interim there had been successful military *coups* in both 'independent' Ciskei and Venda, and Namibia had gained independence and voted SWAPO into power. By October, the SOE was lifted nationwide and the NP opened its membership to all races.

In his second address opening parliament, on 1 February 1991, De Klerk announced the government's intention to remove all remaining apartheid laws. By mid-year, the Native Land and Trust Act of 1936, the Group Areas Act and the Population Registration Act were repealed. Soon afterwards the ANC held its first legal national conference in South Africa since 1960, and the United States lifted its economic sanctions. In December 1991 a forum for negotiation was established – the Convention for a Democratic South Africa (CODESA) – and 19 political groups representing all races sat down together to hammer out a mutually acceptable form of transition and government for the 'New South Africa'.

Despite considerable progress on several key issues, the process stalled in May 1992 amidst renewed hostility between the government and the ANC. Negotiations were broken off for several months, but towards the end of 1992 bilateral negotiations took place between the ANC and the Government and a Memorandum of Understanding was signed.

The first five months of 1993 were particularly eventful. Formal multilateral negotiations resumed, after a break of almost a year, under great pressure to move rapidly to a transitional authority and non-racial elections. The pressures increased as a result of the dramatic changes in leadership caused by the assassination of South African Communist Party leader Chris Hani and the deaths of former ANC President Oliver Tambo and Conservative Party leader Andries Treurnicht. These developments took place within the context of continuing high levels of political violence.

INDEX

administration, 15, 17, 51–65, 67–79, 164;
  see also bureaucracy; executive; Public Service; state
administrative policy, 52
administrative power 14, 18–19
affirmative action 75; Afrikaner, 108
Africa Charter, 252–3
African defence pact, 252, 258
African National Congress, *see* ANC
African nationalism, 169–70
African population, 3, 111, 114–20, 126–9,
  135–208, 217, 226; urban 139, 141, 142,
  147, 158, 159, 160–61, 168, 169–70, 175,
  176, 182, 186, 226; *see also* ANC; apartheid; homelands; reserves *and under the
  names of heads of government*
African states, 166, 252–4, 255, 256–7, 264–
  73, 279, 286–7 281
Afrikaans language 97, 110, 172
Afrikaanse Handelsinstituut, *see* AHI
Afrikaner nationalism, 83, 87–8, 97, 103–14,
  138, 140, 167, 205, 214
Afrikaner Party, 82, 104
Afrikaner–English relations, 85, 111, 123
Afrikaners, 3, 47, 48, 52, 54, 70, 71, 74, 87,
  103–5, 107, 108, 114, 136–7, 165–8, 175,
  176, 177, 207, 215; *see also* 'verligte–
  verkrampte' dispute
AHI, 213, 214, 216, 219, 221, 233–4, 235–6
alignment with West, 252, 280
ANC, 58, 98–9, 117, 122, 161–2, 184, 191–
  7 *passim*, 199, 200–201, 203, 248, 281,
  294–5, 297–8, 301–5 *passim*; demands,
  116, 177; dialogue with, 192, 303, 304; De
  Klerk and 191–7 *passim*, 191–202 *passim*;
  see also negotiations *and under the names of
  heads of government*
Anglo American Corporation, 112, 122, 214
Angola 126, 269, 272–3, 276, 281–2, 284
anti-apartheid mobilisation, 247–8, 300, 304;
  see also political organisations, black
anti-semitism, 110
apartheid, 19, 28, 48, 53, 73–4, 78, 83, 86–
  7, 102, 105–6, 108, 115–16, 119–20, 129–
  32, 137–96, 200–201, 203–8, 216–18, 246–
  7, 250, 254, 256–7, 290; laws, 125, 132,
  148, 162, 305; reforms 56–7, 58, 78, 164;
  see also African population; coloureds; homelands; reserves
apartheid (term), 116, 179
appeal court, 14, 32
armed struggle, 194
arms embargo, 264, 268, 274
ARMSCOR, 67, 231
Assocom, 112, 213–14, 216–20, 221, 225,
  227, 233, 234–5, 238, 239

AZAPO, 302

Bantu Administration Boards, 54
Bantu Authorities Act, 300
Bantu Homelands Citizenship Act, 127
Bantu Self-Government Act, 301
Basson, Japie, 152
beaches, desegregation of, 304
Biko, Steve, 129, 174, 274, 302
bill of rights, 9, 36, 133, 176, 198, 293, 295
bills, passing of, 25, 31
Black Administration Boards, 46
black consciousness, 170, 171, 174, 223
Black Sash, 300
blacks, 3, 32, 34, 41–4, 47, 48, 50, 65–6, 99,
  114–20, 126–9, 207; *see also* African population; coloureds; Indians
border areas development, 219, 221–2, 222–3
Botha, M.C., 131, 152, 164, 177
Botha, P.W., 58–9, 61–5, 84, 178–90, 230–
  39, 302–4; and the African population 178–
  90; and the ANC, 184–5, 189, 278; and
  apartheid, 179, 181, 189; black citizenry
  under, 130–32; and business 230–39; and
  the cabinet, 60–65; and the citizenry, 123–
  32, 133; and the constitution, 17, 27; developments under, 302–4; the executive under,
  60–65, 67–71; and foreign relations, 276–
  84; leadership, 4, 17–18, 28, 59, 60, 90, 96,
  126, 189; and National Party, 90–91, 95–6
Botha, R.F. 'Pik', 90, 176, 177, 289
Botha, S.P., 182, 227
Britain, 248, 249, 258, 261, 266, 280
Broederbond, 87, 105–6, 108, 111, 123, 124,
  213, 214–15, 221
Bureau for Information, 63, 174–5
bureaucracy, 17, 18, 28, 29, 37, 39, 45–8,
  50–54, 60–65, 76, 78, 79, 126, 164; *see also*
  administration; state
bureaucratic ideology, 70–71
Die Burger, 92, 93, 106
business, 122–3; Afrikaner, 109, 213–15;
  black, 175, 217; English, 112–13, 121,
  213–15
business, corporate, 218, 231, 238–9, 241
business, organised, 95, 112–14, 122–3, 209–
  44, 303; summits 122–3, 219, 231–2, 235;
  *see also under the names of heads of govern-
  ment*
business community, 110
bus boycott, 301
Buthulezi, Mangosuthu, 133, 170, 184, 187,
  202

cabinet, 4, 8–9, 10, 13–24, 26–7, 28, 31, 34,
  50–56, 60–65, 69, 72–3, 78, 89–90, 92,

198, 212; post-apartheid 289, 293, 295; republican (first) 16–19
Cabinet Committee for Security Affairs, 72, 289
capital: flight of, 274
capitalism, 103, 231
Carlton meeting, 122–3, 219, 231–2
caucus, 8, 9, 80–81, 84, 88–9, 100, 212
censorship, 14, 29, 303
centralised future state, 291, 294, 297
centralisation, 67
Chambers of Commerce, 220
Chambers of Industry, 224
Chamber of Mines, 216
chronology, 300–305
church apartheid, 149
churches, 108, 124–5
Ciskei, 304
citizenry 102–34, 169, 185–6, 187; in the new South Africa, 132–4
civil servants, 48–50
civil war, threat of, 193
coalition, enforced, 198, 293, 297, 298
CODESA, 74, 98, 196, 292, 296–7, 305
coercive power, 73
collective bargaining, 28–9, 228
collegial government, 23, 293, 298
colonialist aspects of apartheid, 205
coloured labour preference, 180, 229
coloured people, 13, 14, 54, 57, 83, 97, 110–11, 115, 116, 117–18, 128, 129, 130–31, 148, 162, 170, 181, 302; and the tricameral system, 27, 61, 30–31, 130–31, 182, 183
Coloured Persons Representative Council, 118, 130
Commission for Administration, 69–70, 76
commissions/committees of inquiry 51–2
common market, African, 266
Commonwealth, 110, 111, 113, 248, 251, 255, 258, 262–4, 283
Commonwealth Eminent Persons Group, 188–9, 283, 300
communist agitators, 262
communist bloc alliance, 281
communist onslaught, 58, 252, 258, 274, 283; *see also* SA Communist Party
community councils, 46
community life rights, 133
confederation, 181
consensus government, 198
Conservative Party, 77, 87, 93, 95–6, 125, 193, 195
constellation of S A states, 279
constitution(s), 6–36, 57, 99, 183, 185, 198; future 34–5, 99, 195, 197–9, 288–9, 291–9; *see also* negotiations
constitution-making body, 296–7
constitutional review, 32, 33
constitutionalism, 8, 35–6
consumer boycotts, 234

control boards, 43, 46
conventions of government, 16, 25–6
Cooperation and Development portfolio, 178
corporatism, 242–3
corruption, 73
COSATU, 77, 235, 241, 303, 304
Cottesloe Conference, 108, 152
counter-revolutionary thesis, 57, 58
courts, 14–15, 18, 21, 24, 32, 36
credit freeze, 283, 303
crime, 99
Cuba, 277, 284
cultural associations, Afrikaans, 87, 104
CUSA, 235

death penalty, 304
decolonisation, 155, 205, 253, 257, 265; domestic, *see also* TBVC states
defence force, *see* SADF
defence pact, 252, 258
defiance campaign, 145, 146, 300
De Klerk, F.W., 190–203, 304; address, first parliamentary, 194–5, 304; and the African population, 190–203; and the ANC, 191, 194; apology for apartheid, 196; and business, 240–42; and the caucus, 100; the citizenry under, 132–4; conversion, 193; criticism of, 202–3; developments under, 304–5; dual agenda, 74; executive under, 71–7; and foreign relations, 285–9; leadership, 4, 35, 100, 132, 203; mandate, 194; Mandela's relationship with, 200, 203; and the NP, 97–8, 99–100; negotiation views, 197; and organised business, 240–42; personal qualities, 191; solidarity under, 195; strategy of reform, 194–5; support, 203; and violence, 194; visits abroad, 288
Democratic Party, 122
Department of Constitutional Development and Planning, 68
Department of Defence, 63
Department of Foreign Affairs, 59–60
Department of Information, 276
Department of Planning, 53
deregulation, 28, 231
detente initiative, 271
detention, 29, 161, 272, 301, 302
devolution of power, 198, 292, 295
De Wet Nel, M.D.C., 152, 156
dialogue initiative, 270–71
diplomatic relations, 98, 166, 257, 264, 270, 288, 289
discrimination, 175, 176, 177, 181
discriminatory laws, 197
disinvestment, 233
Dönges, Eben 159, 160, 163, 220
Du Plessis, Barend, 190, 193
Dutch Reformed Church, 108, 124–5, 139, 152

Economic Advisory Council, 211, 215, 219–20, 221–2, 238–9
Economic Commission for Africa, 264
economic development programme, 240
Economic Institute, 221
economic interdependence, 155–6, 204
economic policy, 4, 131, 177, 211–12, 221–2, 214–15, 231–2, 287, 288; *see also* business
economic reform, 30
economic relations, 287, 288
economic sanctions, 280, 283, 305
economic strategy, 131, 232
economy, 99, 113, 161, 193, 201, 202, 208, 218, 233, 235
education, 28, 76, 109, 114, 118, 124–5, 133, 143, 148, 149, 171, 172, 300, 301, 302
Eerste Ekonomiese Volkskongres, 220, 221
Eiselen, W.W.M., 136, 153, 154
electioneering, 99
elections, 82, 113
electoral college, 26, 27, 60
electoral system, 13, 99
electoral threat, 81–3, 99
English-speakers, 74, 103–4, 105, 109–14, 121–3, 125, 162; relations of Afrikaners and, 85, 111, 123
Eskom, 46
ethnic division, white, 103–14, 136
ethnic hostilities, African, 98
European Community, 283
executive, 2, 8–17, 18–27, 29, 30, 33–4, 35, 37–79, 135–208, 293–4, 295, 298–9; under De Klerk, 71–7; future, 198, 293–4, 295; *see also* administration; cabinet; public service
Executive Council, 10, 16
exiles, return of, 304
expenditure on blacks, 119–-20
expertise, development of, 237

Fagan Commission 142–3
FAK, 214
farm labour, 139, 141, 155
farmers, protection of, 108–9
FCI, 214, 216, 219, 224–5, 228, 233, 234, 235, 236–7
federalism, 177, 181, 198, 199, 292, 298
Federated Chambers of Industry, *see* FCI
fifth world, 274
foreign relations, 245–90
franchise, 9, 13, 14, 54, 83, 110–11, 137, 138, 294
free enterprise, 30
free-market system, 133
Freedom Charter, 300
freehold, African, 112, 148, 182, 217
frontline states, 58
Fusion government, 82

gender bias of state, 69, 74, 75
general affairs departments, 68, 181
Ghana, 257, 259
Goldstone Commission, 98
Good Hope Conference, 219, 232
Gorbachev, Mikhail, 284
government, 7–8, 16, 18, 25–6, 198, 211, 212, 224–6, 240–41, 292, 295; *see also* cabinet; executive; judiciary; legislative; parliament; regional government; state
governors-general, 9, 10, 11, 15
Groote Schuur Minute, 304
group areas legislation, 236, 237, 285
group rights, 33, 295

Harare Declaration, 304
Havenga, N.C., 83
head(s) of government: and the executive 37–9; future, 291–9; *see also* Prime Minister(s); President(s); executive
Hendrickse, Allan, 26, 27, 96, 124
Herenigde Nasionale Party, 82, 167
Herstigte Nasionale Party, 85, 87, 93, 125, 166
Hertzog, Albert, 85, 87, 107, 124, 125, 152, 211
Hertzog, J.B.M., 55
Heunis, Chris, 183
High Commission Territories, 156–7, 248, 254, 255, 257–8, 266
hit squads, 200
Hofmeyr, J.H., 55, 139
homelands, 13, 73, 127, 132, 151, 152, 154–7, 159, 160, 168–9, 175, 176, 179–80, 181, 186, 217, 260, 266; employment by, 43, 47, 48, 49–50, 66; independence, 127, 154, 157, 168–9, 181; reincorporation 294, 295; *see also* Tomlinson Commission
hostels, 202
House of Assembly, 31, 60
House of Delegates, 31
House of Representatives, 31
housing, 28, 175
human rights, 33, 133; *see also* group rights

ideology, 86–7, 95, 99, 206
immigration policy, 166
imperial presidency, 30–32, 35, 96, 120
Indians, 30–31, 181, 183, 246
Industrial and Agricultural Requirements Commission, 221
industrial conciliation, 171
industrial relations, 182, 225, 228
Industrial Relations Act, 302
industrial rights, 127
influx control, 57, 119, 127, 182, 188, 216–17, 230
informal settlements, 236
information, 28, 38, 59, 174–5
Information Scandal, 16, 19, 58, 126, 174

Inkatha Freedom Party, 133–4, 200, 202, 303
integration, economic, 155
intelligence service, 63
interdepartmental committees, 62
interest groups, 210, 211–15, 226–30, 233, 236–7, 241–2; *see also* business, organised
interim government, 201, 298
Internal Security Act (1982), 29, 302
international climate, 288
international involvement in SA, 98, 289
international isolation, 3, 268, 274, 283
international mediation, 282–3
Iscor, 46
Israel, 274, 281

Jansen, E.G., 142–3
job reservation, 181–2, 217, 225, 227
Joint Management Centres, 30, 62–3
judicial review, 9, 12, 15, 17, 32–3, 294
judiciary, 11, 32–3, 295, 295

Kaunda, Kenneth, 271
Kennedy, Edward, 233
Kennedy, John F., 268
Kissinger, Henry, 273
Koornhof, Piet, 175, 176, 177
Kruger, Jimmy, 174
KwaZulu, 186–7

labour, 126–7, 137, 155, 180, 223, 224, 225, 227, 228, 229; legislation, 171, 226, 241–2
Labour Party, 130
labour relations, 225, 227, 241–2
land, 114, 168, 179
Land Acts, 285
land affairs, 31
Landman, Willem, 154, 157
language, 97, 110, 172
leadership: definition of, 185
leadership qualities, personal, 93–6
leasehold rights, 229
legal equality and citizenship, 102–3
legislative authority, 15, 18, 23–4
legislative process, 20, 30–31
legislative reform, 197
legislative supremacy, 14
legislature, 8–9, 12–16, 18–24, 234; proposals for future, 293, 294, 295; *see also* parliament
legitimacy crisis, 187, 193, 208
Le Roux, Frank, 174
liberalisation, 304
local authorities, 12, 28, 43, 45–6, 66, 67, 68, 69, 187, 233; future, 294
local initiatives, 68
Louw, Eric, 256, 259, 260
Lutuli, Chief Albert, 151

Macmillan, Harold, 94, 155, 205, 261

majority rule, 122, 133, 195, 199, 294, 295–6, 297–8
Malan, D.F., 89, 137–46, 249–55, 300; and the Africans, 115, 137–46; and the ANC, 145–6; and apartheid, 114–15, 139, 142, 254; and business, 212–13; the citizenry under, 104–5, 106, 114–15, 119; developments under, 300; and foreign relations, 249–55; leadership, 84, 85, 93–4, 142, 144; and the NP, 83, 85, 91, 93; racial views, 114–15, 117, 138–9, speeches 107
Malan, Magnus, 100
Malawi, 270
Mandela, Nelson, 75, 117, 190, 192, 194, 203, 301, 304; commitment to peace, 194; constitutional proposals 294; relationship with De Klerk, 200, 203; and negotiation crisis, 199; support, 203
Marais, Jaap, 85, 165
Maree, W.A., 152
mass action, 201; *see also* protest
Matanzima, Kaiser, 170
Mbeki, Govan, 301
media, 28, 88, 96, 97–8, 123–4, 126, 234, 303; *see also* press; television
Memorandum of Understanding, 305
Meyer, Piet, 111–12, 121
Meyer, Roelf, 100
migrant labour, 127, 155, 156, 162
military influence, 60, 63, 64, 72, 78
military service, 113, 122
ministerial responsibility, 17, 18, 26; collective 26, 27
ministers 14, 26, 27, 34, 61; *see also* cabinet
Ministers' Councils, 23, 24, 25, 61
minorities, 178, 181, 186, 199
minority interests, 13–4, 199, 296, 297–8; *see also* power-sharing
minority parties in cabinet, 26, 27, 61
mixed gatherings, 175
mixed marriages, 125, 148, 162, 300
MK, *see* Umkhonto we Sizwe
moral stances, 83, 108, 115, 125, 140, 196, 204–6
Mozambique, 269, 273, 282
MPLA, 272–3
Mulder, C.P. 'Connie', 19, 84, 127, 167
Muller, Hilgard, 260
multinationalism, 175, 178

NACTU, 241–2
Namibia 193, 245, 246, 250, 254–5, 266–7, 269, 271–2, 273, 277, 280, 284, 286
Nasionale Pers, 84, 93, 106–7
Natal support of National Party, 111
National Assembly, 294
National Co-ordinating Mechanism, 71–2
National Forum, 233
National Manpower Commission, 228
National Party, 13–16, 27, 52–3, 80–116

passim, 121–5, 136, 144, 151, 160, 165–7, 175–7, 185, 193, 200–207, 293–4, 305; constitutional proposals, 197, 293–4; in the De Klerk era, 97–100; moral stances, 83, 108, 115, 125, 140, 196, 204–6; support, 3, 95–6, 97, 109–11, 113, 125, 162; *see also* Afrikaner nationalism; apartheid; negotiations
National Peace Accord, 98, 202
National Security Management System, 62–5, 73, 289
national symbols, 99, 109
National Union of Mineworkers, 303
Native Administration Act (1927), 15
Native Affairs ministry, 136
Native Land and Trust Act, 305
Natives' Representative Council, 158
NATO, 252
negotiations, 35, 98–9, 187, 189, 193–202, 291–8, 305; *see also* CODESA
neighbouring states 281–2, 283
Nigeria, 299
non-aggression treaties, 270
Nujoma, Sam, 170, 272
Nuwe Orde, 104

Odendaal Commission, 267
Office of the State President, 61–2
ombudsman, 295
Oppenheimer, Harry, 110, 112, 113
opposition, role of, 13, 81–3
Organisation of African Unity, 264, 273
Ossewabrandwag, 104, 163
outward movement, 269–74
own affairs, 31, 61, 68, 181, 197

PAC, 161–2, 170, 185, 193, 285, 301, 302
Pact government, 82
Pan-Africanist Congress, *see* PAC
parastatal organisations, 46, 108
parliament, 8, 11, 12–16, 18, 20–27, 30–32, 57, 126, 293–5; republican (first), 18, 57; tricameral, 22–4, 25–6, 27, 30–32; *see also* legislature
parliamentarism, 9, 298, 299
partisanship, 200
party (ies), political, 8–9, 34, 80–101, 126, 301; *see also* caucus; National Party; opposition
pass laws, 119, 158, 159, 161, 182
passive resistance, 300
paternalism, 115, 116, 119
patronage, 51, 91, 97
personality of leader, 93–6
Planning and Development portfolio, 28
Plural Relations portfolio, 173, 178
pluralism, 178
police, 24, 33, 46, 63, 72–4, 74–5, 200
policy-making, 20
political interests of state 56–60, 74

political organisations, black, 161–2, 174, 185, 193, 247–8, 261, 304
political prisoners, 202–3, 304
population development, 164
Population Registration Act, 46, 300, 305
post office, 46
power-sharing, 23, 99, 125, 133, 197–8, 199, 292, 293, 295–6, 298
presidency, 2, 3, 4, 16, 22, 23–5, 26–7, 28, 29–32, 34–5, 60, 125–6, 293, 295, 298; the future of the, 198, 291–9; imperial, 3, 4, 29–30, 126
President(s), executive, 2, 4, 22–33, 60–65, 303–5; *see also* executive
President(s), titular, 9–12, 16, 23–5
President's Council, 20, 23, 24, 31, 34, 57
presidentialism, 9, 298–9
press, 84, 92–3, 106–7, 121, 123–4
Pretoria Minute, 304
Prime Minister(s), 8, 10, 16, 17, 18, 33–4, 51–6, 212, 293, 300–303; post-apartheid, 33–4, 293; *see also* executive
private sector, 222, 231, 240; *see also* business
Private Sector Council on Urbanisation 237
privatisation, 28, 67, 69, 76, 231
proclamation, 15, 28
Progressive Federal Party, 122, 303
propaganda, 29, 277
property rights, 133, 143
proportional representation, 293, 294, 295
protest, 161, 170, 171, 192, 193, 300; *see also* unrest
provincial system, 12–13, 28, 37, 42, 47, 50, 66, 67–8; employment, 42, 47, 50, 66
provincialism, 84, 91, 106–7, 144
public corporations, 44, 45, 46
public funds, control of, 15–16
Public Safety Act, 300
Public Servants Association, 77
Public Service, 18, 28, 29, 37–54, 65–7, 69, 70, 71, 74–5, 76–7, 78, 79, 108, 231; *see also* sub-entries *under* state
Public Service Act (1957), 48, 49, 50, 61
Public Service Commission, 37, 48–9, 51, 52, 54, 231
Public Service League, 77

racial bias of state, 44, 48, 50, 51, 69, 70, 74–5, 79
racial legislation, 108
racial policies: implementation, 13, 18, 19
racial superiority thesis, 196, 246–7
railways and harbours, 46
rationalisation, 18, 29, 69, 76–7, 231
Reagan, Ronald, 280
reform by executive, 30
reform referendum, 4, 194, 195
regional boundaries, 199
regional government 12, 198, 294, 295, 298

regional relations, African, 280, 281–2
Regional Services Councils, 28, 68
regionalisation trend, 73–4
religious bias of state, 74
rent protest, 233
republic referendum, 109, 110, 117–18, 162, 218–19
Republican Constitution: first, 16–22, 57; second, 22–34
reserves, 137, 141, 151, 154, 154; *see also* homelands
revolutionary onslaught, 58
Rhodesia, *see* Zimbabwe
right wing, 95–6, 107, 152, 166, 180, 185
Riotous Assemblies Act, 301
Roos, Tielman, 55
Roux, Jannie, 60, 62
Royal Styles and Title Act, (1952), 9, 152

SA Broadcasting Corporation, 107
SA Chamber of Business, 240
SA Communist Party, 99, 188, 192
SA Congress of Trade Unions, 300
SA Defence Force, 46, 29, 63, 72, 113
SA Foundation, 112
SA Students' Organisation, 302
SA Transport Services employment, 41, 50
Sabotage Act, 301
SABRA, 152, 154
SACCOLA, 241–2
sanctions, 98, 193, 194, 207, 241, 264, 277, 280, 283, 287
Sauer, Paul, 159–60
Sauer Commission, 105, 140, 143, 150
Schlebusch Commission, 57
Schoeman, Ben, 104–5, 144–5, 149, 159, 160, 162, 163
school feeding, 139, 143
schools, 170, 171, 172–3, 300, 302
security, 14, 18, 161, 274
security establishment, 29, 33, 59, 62–5, 77, 78, 189, 200, 289; *see also* state security council; SADF; police
security police, 161
segregation, 115, 137–8, 139
SEIFSA, 216, 224, 227
self-determination concept, 181, 222
semi-state, 45, 46, 47, 50, 53, 66, 76
senate, 20, 57, 91, 294
Separate Amenities Act, 181, 300
separation of powers doctrine, 15, 32
sex laws, 125, 132, 148, 162
Sharpeville, 108, 113, 158, 159, 160, 161, 261–2
Simonstown Agreement, 258, 274
Sisulu, Walter, 301, 304
Slabbert, Frederick van Zyl, 303
Smuts, J.C., 110, 114, 138, 246–9, 256
Sobukwe, Robert Mangaliso, 170
Social and Economic Planning Council, 221

socio-economic factors, 119–20
South Africa Act (1909), 8
South African, *see* SA
South West Africa, *see* Namibia
Soviet Union, 58, 192, 257, 258, 277, 284, 287
Soweto unrest, 171, 172–3, 224, 225, 273
sport, 124, 125, 166, 175, 288
squatter movements, 230
squatting legislation, 236, 237
state, 2–3, 18, 28, 29, 37–79, 108; in the transitional era, 71–7; *see also* bureaucracy; executive; Public Service; semi-state
State Information Office, 249, 256
State Security Council, 18, 29–30, 59, 62, 65, 72, 278–9
states of emergency, 29, 161, 189, 235, 282, 304
statutory bodies, 44, 46
stay-aways, 225, 227
strategic importance of SA, 280
strikes, 170, 223, 227, 228, 234
Strijdom, J.G., 91, 105–6, 147–52; and Africans, 114, 139, 147–9; and the ANC, 151; and apartheid, 108, 147–52, 256–7; the citizenry under, 105, 114; developments under, 300–301; and foreign relations, 255–9; leadership, 85, 93–4, 150, 259; NP under, 83, 85, 91, 93–4, 106–7, 144; racial views, 108, 114, 139, 147
supreme court, 18, 29, 32, 294
Suppression of Communism Act (1950), 300
SWAPO, 269, 272, 277, 278, 284
Swiss system of government, 198, 293, 298

Taiwan, 281
TBVC states, 76, 127, 168–9, 186, 304; *see also* Ciskei, Venda
television, 4, 107, 126
Terreblanche, Sampie, 207
terrorism, 280
Terrorism Act, 302
Te Water, Charles, 249
Thatcher, Margaret, 280
Theron Commission of Inquiry, 57
Tomlinson Commission, 143, 150–51, 179
total onslaught, 58, 124, 192, 277–8, 281, 289
total strategy, 200, 274, 278, 281–2, 289
townships, 226, 233, 273
Trade Union Council of South Africa 227
trade union federations 227
trade unions, 170, 171, 182, 217, 227, 233, 241, 244, 300, 302
transitional era, the state in, 71–7
Treurnicht, A.P., 87, 93, 166, 171, 172–3, 177, 185
tribal leaders, 158, 184
Tricameral System, 22–34, 117, 130–31, 182–4, 233, 282
Turnhalle, 271, 272

Tutu, Bishop, 184

Umkhonto we Sizwe, 200, 201, 301
underground movements, 161
unemployment, 202
UNESCO, 256
Union constitution, 6–16
Union Constitution Act, 10
United Democratic Front, 233, 303, 304
United Nations, 193, 246–8, 249, 250, 251, 256, 262, 264, 265, 267, 268, 277
United Party, 82, 87, 104, 110, 114, 122, 137, 155
United South Africa Trust Fund, 110
United States, 268, 275, 276, 280, 283, 284, 289, 303, 305
Universal Declaration of Human Rights, 249
universities, 170, 171
unrest, 223, 224, 233, 262, 273, 282; *see also* protest; Sharpeville; violence
urban Africans, *see under* Africans
Urban Foundation, 226, 229, 230, 236
urbanisation, 114, 139, 229, 237

Van den Bergh, Hendrik, 170
Van der Merwe, Stoffel, 183
Van der Ross, Richard, 116, 117–18
Van der Walt, Tjaart, 124
verkrampte–verligte dispute, 165–7, 175, 177, 207
Venda, 304
Verwoerd, H.F., 86, 143–6, 149–63, 205; and activists, 158; and the African population, 143–6, 149–63; and the ANC, 145–6; and apartheid, 121, 144–5, 149–63, 260–61; black citizenry under, 128–9, 131; and the Broederbond, 106; and business 112, 212, 215–23; citizenry under, 106–120, 121, 127–9; and the coloured people, 118; and the constitution, 17; developments under, 301; and foreign relations, 259–68; leadership, 17, 94, 152–3, 158–9, 160, 162–3, 164, 259; meetings with Africans, 158; moral stance, 108; and the party 94, 160; and the press, 92, 107; racist views, 129; speeches 157, 158

vested interest, 73
veto, 295, 297
vice-presidency, 33
Viljoen, Gerrit, 124, 133, 204
violence, 72, 78, 98, 99, 183, 189, 193, 194, 200, 271, 289, 296
Vlok, Adrian, 100
voluntary association, 199
Vorster, B.J.: and African leaders, 170; and the African population, 163–78; and apartheid, 121, 163–78; black citizenry under, 127–31; and business, 219, 223–7; and the church, 124–5; citizenry under, 120–31; and coloured people, 128; developments under, 302; and foreign relations, 268–76; and information affair, 19–20; as Justice Minister, 161, 162–3; leadership, 17–19, 85, 94–5, 126, 163–4, 166–7, 177, 221, 276; and the media, 107, 123; moral stance, 108, 165; NP and, 85, 94–5, 165–7; and organised business, 223–9; pragmatism, 165, 167; and unrest, 173–4; views, 165, 167–70, 174, 177
vote, 13, 14, 54, 83, 110–11
vote of no confidence, 26

wages and salaries, 49, 50, 76, 159, 171
welfare, 28
Western powers, 275–6, 279, 280, 281
Westminster system, 8–13, 72, 103
white citizenship, 103–14, 120–26
white population, 3, 99, 103–14, 120–26, 166, 291, 295, 297–8; *see also* Afrikaners; English-speakers
Wiehahn Commission, 171, 226, 227–8
women in state employment, 69, 74, 75
workers, Afrikaner, 108–9
World Council of Churches, 108, 125, 152

Xuma, A.B., 248

youth unrest, 170

Zambia, 271
Zimbabwe, 60, 265, 269, 271, 273, 277